GLOBAL CHALLENGE

A2 level Geography for Edexcel B

Authors:
Alistair McNaught
Michael Witherick

Series editors: Sue Warn and Michael Naish

Edinburgh Gate
Harlow, Essex

Pearson Education Limited
Edinburgh Gate
Harlow
Essex
CM20 2JE
England

ISBN 0582 42980 3

First published 2001
Printed in Great Britain by Scotprint, Haddington
Designed by Amanda Easter
Illustrated by Oxford Design and Illustrators
Picture research by Sandie Huskinson-Rolfe

The Publisher's policy is to use paper manufactured from sustainable forests.

Contents

Unit 1 Weather, climate and ecosystems

Unit 2 Population and economy

Acknowledgements
We are grateful to the following for permission to reproduce copyright photographs:

Adams Picture Library/Robert Bloomfield: p. 4 *t*; Chris Coe/Axiom Photographic Agency: p. 122; Camera Press Limited: p. 143; John Farmer/Sylvia Cordaiy Photo Library: p. 65 *t*; James Davis Worldwide Travel Library: p. 192; Ecoscene/Lorenzo Lees: p. 206 *l*; Ethical Consumer Magazine/Environmental Images: p. 206 *l* (Vanessa Miles) and p. 206 *r* (John Arnould); Julia Waterlow/Eye Ubiquitous: p. 128, Paul Thompson/Eye Ubiquitous: p. 190 *l*; Garden and Wildlife Matters: p. 81; Robert Harding Picture Library: pp. 26 *r*, 126 *b*, 170; Bernard Gerard/The Hutchison Picture Library: p. 4 *b*, Dirk R. Frans/Hutchison: pp. 89 and 90-91 *background*, Igor Gavrilov/Hutchison: p. 119 *l*; Data courtesy of USGS Limited/Images processed by Infoterra Limited: p. 38; Nicola Sutton/Life File: p. 146 *l*; Alistair McNaught: pp. 49, 50 *r*, 51; James Hawkins/Oxfam: p. 201 *l*; John Buckingham/Natural History Photographic Agency: p. 51, Daryl Balfour/NHPA: p. 65 *b*; Paul Franklin/Oxford Scientific Films: p. 26 *l*; Fred Hoogervorst/Panos Pictures: pp. 97, 133, Irene Slegt/Panos: p. 153 *r*; PA Photos/EPA: p. 123; Popperfoto: p. 132, Reuters/Popperfoto: pp. 145, 147, 162, Dave Joyner/Popperfoto: p. 146 *r*; Courtesy of www.reefball.com: p. 78; Science Photo Library: p. 13, NASA/SPL: pp. 1, 23, 27, PLI/SPL: p. 21, NRSC Limited/SPL: p. 50 *l*; NOAA/Skyscan Photography: p. 9; Muriel Nicoletti/Still Pictures: p. 65 *tm*, Adrian Arbib/Still Pictures: p. 65 *bm*, Alan Watson/Still Pictures: p. 71; Hjalte Tin/Still Pictures: p. 81 *l*, Mark Edwards/Still Pictures: pp. 91 *b*, 11, 115, 119 *r*, 125, Hartmut Schwarzbach/Still Pictures: p. 113, Chris Caldicott/Still Pictures: p. 129, Jonathan Kaplan/Still Pictures: p. 164, Ron Giling/Still Pictures: p. 190 *r*, Mike Kolloffel/Still Pictures: p. 201 *r*; Benn Gurr/The Times: p. 161; Topham Picturepoint: p. 126 *t*; TRIP/Eric Smith: p. 115 *l*, TRIP/Spencer Grant: p. 153 *l*, TRIP/E. James: p. 153 *m*; Janine Wiedel Photo Library: p. 81 *m*.

We are grateful to the following for permission to reproduce copyright material:

Guardian News Services for redrawn diagrams 'The welfare burden', *The Guardian* 23 April 1991, 'Millions on the move to Europe', *The Guardian* 14 June 1991, 'The UK's trade loans', *The Guardian* 12 May 1998; Nelson Thornes Ltd for redrawn maps and diagrams 'The global distribution of fertility' and 'The global distribution of death' from Ross et al., *Essential* AS *Geography* (2000), 'A topological map of global population' from Witherick, *Environment and People* (1995), 'The development cable' and 'Factors energising development' from Witherick, *Development, Disparity and Dependence* (1998); News International Syndication for redrawn diagram 'How the NHS relies on overseas doctors' p. 161 © Times Newspaper Limited, 8 November 1999 and cartoon p. 151 © Pugh/Times Newspaper Limited, 20 April 2000; Sage Publication Ltd (Paul Chapman Publishing) for redrawn maps and diagrams 'The global distribution of manufacturing, 1994', 'The global distribution of motor vehicle production, 1995', 'Sequential development of a TNC', 'Different modes of TNC operation', 'The Nike network', 'International and TNC-government relationships', 'Unemployment rates in the EU, UK, USA and Japan 1960-96', 'Europe's major growth axis', 'The emerging urban corridors of Asia Pacific' from Dicken, *Global Shift* (1999).

UNIT ONE Weather, climate and ecosystems

Chapter One: Weather and climate

1 The global challenge of weather and climate

The **weather** is the state of the atmosphere at any given time and place.

Climate is the average weather conditions at a specific place over a time period of 30+ years.

Weather and people

Weather has profound effects on people, societies and ecosystems. In a direct way, health is affected by the weather. Mortality rates amongst the elderly rise in cold periods and heat waves; Seasonal Affective Disorder (SAD) causes depression-like symptoms over the winter months as a result of lack of sunlight. There is some evidence that the spread of influenza epidemics may be related to global wind patterns, shifting the virus to distant, unaffected localities. The indirect impacts of the weather are much more far reaching. Weather influences our leisure pursuits (beach or cinema?), our eating habits (barbecue or roast?) and our clothing purchases (umbrella or sun hat?). Less obviously it might influence the cost of our purchases (was the harvest good or bad?), the balance of trade (is foreign fruit cheaper?) and the state of regional economies (shall we go to Devon or Majorca?).

There are a variety of views on the role of weather and climate in society and these are shown in Figure 1.1. Even the poorest communities can exercise their own control over the weather and climate. As long ago as 500 BC ancient pre-Inca civilisations were designing intricate irrigation systems in drought-prone Peru. At the other extreme, the most sophisticated of societies can do nothing in the face of flash flooding or severe storms.

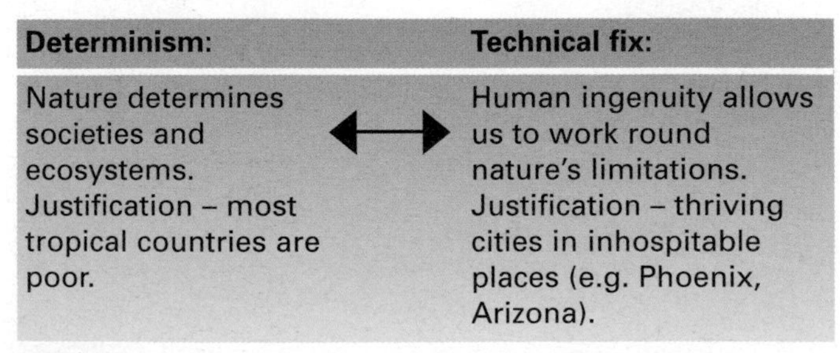

Figure 1.1 *The spectrum of weather influences*

At a small scale, the fortunes of a farmer may be influenced by weather conditions – a wet harvest or dry growing season reducing profits. The farmer's profit will also be influenced by the demand for the crop, costs of imports, exchange rate and the strength of the currency, any government subsidies and alternative 'substitute' commodities. Weather is only one factor among many, but it is one of the least predictable. There is still much to unravel about the relationship between weather and people, but intriguing relationships have emerged. In 1983 Birmingham's main hospital had a tenfold increase in asthma admissions after a thunderstorm had triggered the wide-scale release of irritating fungal spores. Road traffic accident research in Munich related weather conditions to a significant proportion of traffic accidents but – strangely – the worst rise in accident figures coincided with steeply dropping atmospheric pressure.

Exploring weather sensitivity

Not all activities are equally weather sensitive, nor are all elements of weather equally significant in their impacts. Figure 1.2 shows how weather sensitivity is related to 'how different' the weather is from the expected conditions. As the weather departs from the norm, societies and ecosystems experience stress.

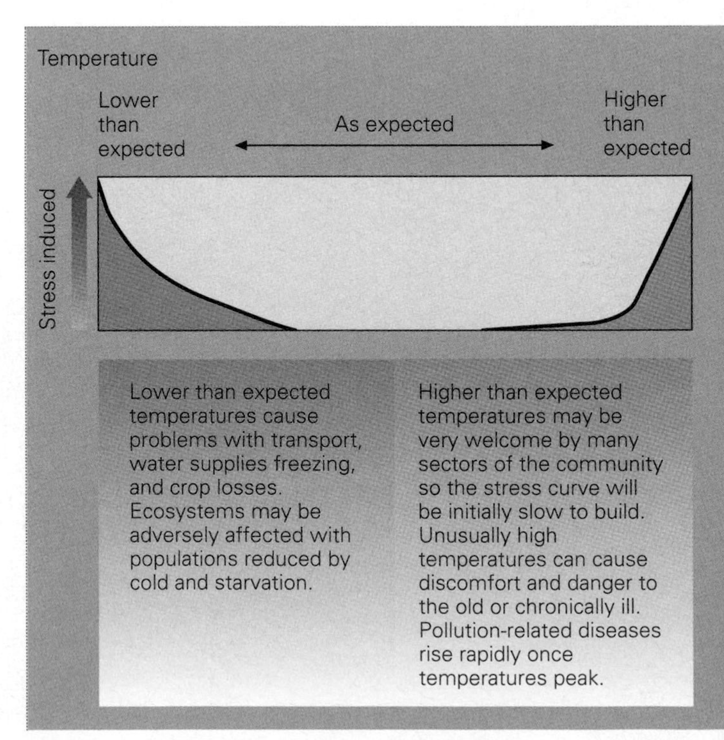

Figure 1.2 *Graphing weather sensitivity*

Impacts of weather and climate on economic activities

Agriculture

Too much rain: Harvest difficulties, risk of crops rotting, damage to standing crops, flood risk for livestock.

Too little rain: Irrigation needed, livestock may lack grazing.

Construction

Severe weather: Very good for business, high demand for repair work.

Dry weather: Good for business, allows contracts to go ahead faster than planned.

Wet weather: Problems and delays with outdoor jobs, poor site conditions.

Cold weather: Possibility of frost damage to setting concrete and mortar.

Energy

Winter weather: Large increase in demand for heating, increased demand for lighting and clothes drying, possible disruption of supplies due to line damage.

Summer weather: Demand for cooking fuels declines.

Insurance

Severe weather: Damage claims may be widespread.

Cold weather: Problems of broken limbs and motor accidents.

Too much rain: Subsidence claims for housing on clay soils, flooding problems and related claims.

Retailing

Wet weather: Sales of waterproofs and umbrellas boom, excellent trading conditions for winter goods, excellent trading for DIY and home repair products.

Tourism and recreation

Wet weather: Increase in foreign holidays to follow the sun.

Heat wave: Surge in demand for outdoor recreation and home-based holidays.

Transport

Too much rain: Road and rail disruption to low lying routes.

High winds: Disruption to road and rail, snow and ice: disruption to road and rail, problems for aircraft and ferries.

Snow and ice: Disruption to road and rail

As a result of the weather sensitivity of so many activities, accurate forecasts are essential.

ACTIVITIES

1 Using Figure 1.2 as a guide, sketch and annotate models of the summer weather sensitivity of:
   a a theme park
   b a large arable farm.

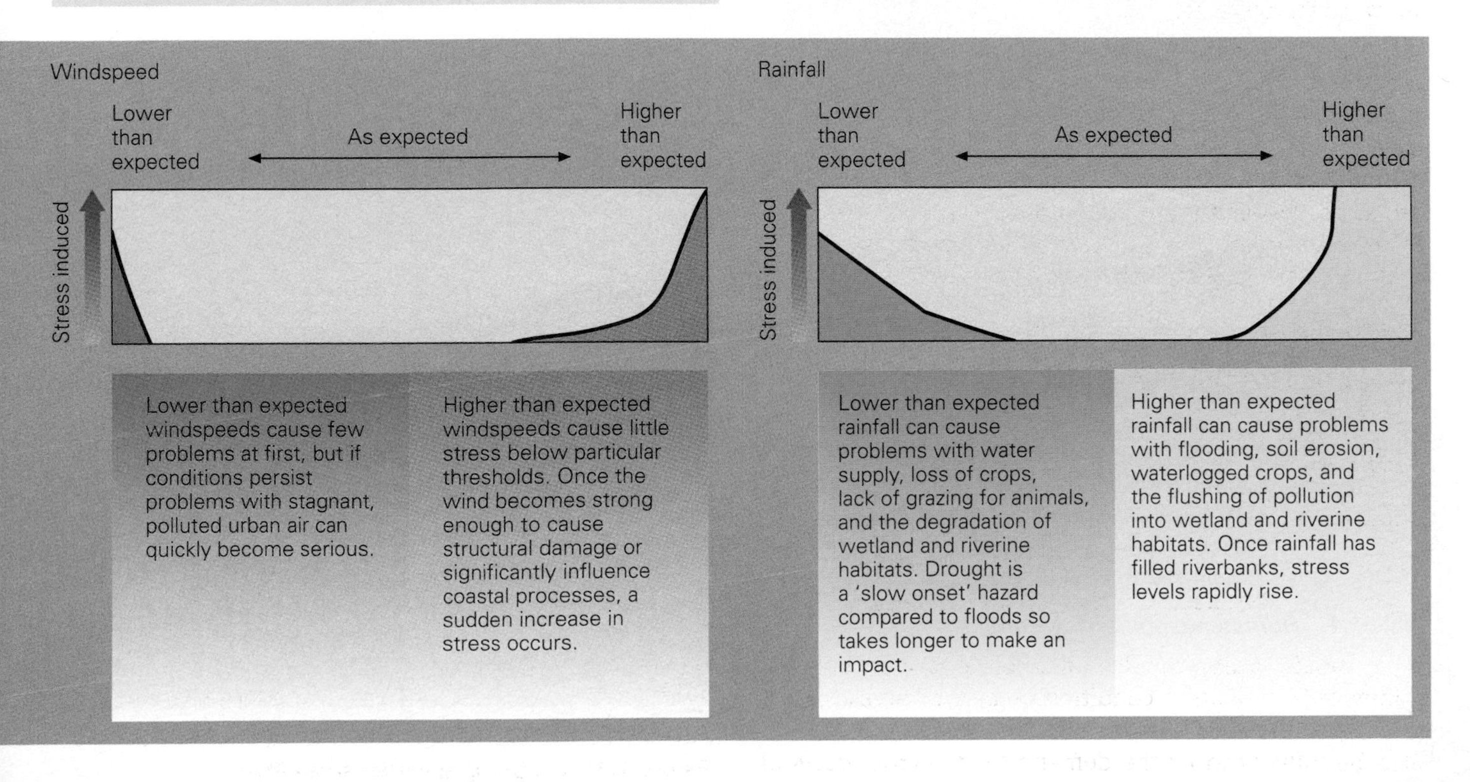

Managing the challenges of weather and climate

Human society has created a wide range of ways of dealing with the challenges of climate and weather. The basic human needs are food, clothing, shelter and community. Extremes of climate pose challenges if they threaten any of the above needs. A range of traditional adaptations to climate extremes is shown in Table 1.1.

Climatic challenge	Examples of adaptation	Named location
Too dry	• Irrigation systems 1) irrigation channels and aqueducts 2) underground irrigation tunnels 3) distribution of water from arterial river • Pastoral nomadism • Strong hospitality codes • Bush skills (sipping tubes, plant sources)	• Inca civilisations, Cuzco, Peru • Qanat systems, Khuzestan, Iran • Egyptian Nile • Fulani tribes, West Africa • Bedouin, Sahara • Bushmen of the Kalahari
Too wet	• Adapted housing – houses raised off floodable land with stilts • Adapted agriculture – rice growing and aquaculture	• Varzea region of the Amazon • Mekong Delta, Vietnam
Too cold	• Adapted clothing – skins and fur • High energy food sources – meat-rich diet • Strong hospitality codes • Adapted transport – dog sled	• Inuit tribes, Greenland • Lapps, northern Finland • Inuit tribes, Greenland
Too hot	• Adapted housing – thick walled, whitewashed • Adapted activities – siesta period early afternoon	• Southern Italy • Managua Nicaragua
Too windy	• Adapted housing – single story, low angled roofs anchored to wall fixings	• Isle of Lewis, Scotland

Table 1.1 *Human adaptations to climate*

ACTIVITIES

1 'Traditional' adaptations (Table 1.1) involve low impact methods using local resources. How do modern cities in extreme locations adapt to the five climatic extremes listed in the table?

Figure 1.3 *Typical wind-resistant design of highland croft – lo roof, thick walls and sheltered site*

Figure 1.4 *Nomadic tribes – strong hospitality codes and high mobility ensure survival in arid climate*

2 Weather forecasting

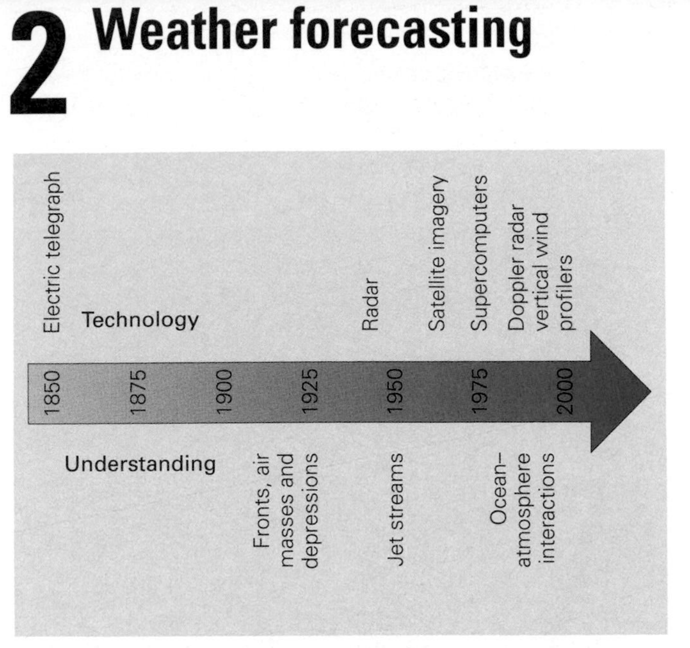

Figure 1.5 *The development of weather forecasting*

The evolution of weather forecasting has been influenced by parallel improvements in our understanding of the weather and in technology (Figure 1.5). Of the technological advances, the advent of supercomputers is probably the most significant as it allowed the development of **Numerical Weather Prediction** (NWP). This involves weather forecasting by looking at current conditions, then solving thousands of calculations to estimate future atmospheric conditions. By 1965 the UK Meteorological Office had fully introduced numerical methods. Now supercomputers are used widely for the analysis of weather data and the preparation of forecasts.

From a conceptual point of view, the discovery of jet streams – fast-flowing rivers of air meandering about 8 km above the Earth – was very significant for short-term forecasting of storm movements. Recent (and ongoing) discoveries concerning the relationship between oceans and the atmosphere may improve our longer-term forecasts.

Future advances in weather forecasting are likely to be based around the following maturing technologies:

- New generation satellites providing higher-resolution images and improved estimates of temperature and humidity.
- Doppler radars that define the location, type, and intensity of precipitation as well as air motion.
- Wind profilers – upward-pointing Doppler radars that provide nearly continuous wind profiles from the ground to the top of the troposphere. All known weather systems and jet streams exist within this layer of atmosphere, averaging 12 km thick.

Types of forecast

The type of forecast depends on the length of time required, the type of data used and the accuracy needed (Table 1.2). There are four different types:

Timescale of forecast	Type of data needed	Scale of data	Accuracy of forecast
Hour	Detailed analysis for all current measurements and trends	Local and regional	High
Day Week	Broad analysis of selected measurements and trends	Regional and global	Medium
Month Season	Analogue analysis comparing current trends with archived records to find similarities	Local and regional	Low
Year	Sea surface temperature anomalies studied to pick up long term climatic triggers	Regional and global	Low for specific time or place

Table 1.2 *Timescales for forecasts*

Nowcasts shortest range (minutes to hours ahead) based on extrapolating from current observations. Nowcasts can be very accurate for small-scale weather features, e.g. the movement of thunderstorm cells across a county.

Short range forecasts (Friday night predictions for the weekend) accuracy declines with increasing prediction length. The forecasts are based on numerical weather predictions whose accuracy tails off rapidly after 48 hours.

Medium range forecasts (from 4–10 days) at the limit of numerical weather predictions as so many cumulative errors have entered the calculations. A useful technique known as 'ensemble forecasting' has improved the accuracy of some of these longer forecasts. By running successive versions of the weather prediction with slightly different starting conditions a group (or ensemble) of forecasts is produced. If these are all very similar in outcome they will reflect inherent stability in the atmosphere and have a high likelihood of being right. If they give divergent answers the weather conditions are more unstable and a forecast will need to be worded to reflect its lower chance of accuracy.

Long range forecasts (up to one month ahead) cannot reliably depend on current weather conditions. Instead they take account of broad patterns in the weather. These include sea surface temperature anomalies and Rossby wave patterns. A method known as 'analogue forecasts' can be used in long-range seasonal predictions by examining the data archives for similarities (analogues) of current conditions.

The costs and benefits of weather forecasting can be difficult to gauge accurately. The most obvious benefits come from the forecasting of severe weather. On 24 August 1992, Hurricane Andrew came ashore in Florida with winds exceeding 160 miles per hour. The US National Weather Service had tracked Andrew for many days. Weather satellites, reconnaissance aircraft, high-speed computers, and sophisticated forecast models enabled accurate predictions of hurricane motion. Andrew caused more than US$20 billion of damage in Florida, leaving more than 30 people dead and 250,000 homeless. In 1900, a similar hurricane struck the unprepared Galveston area, Texas, and killed more than 6,000 people. Table 1.3 shows how both the lead time (advance warning given) and accuracy have been changing for three common weather hazards in the US.

	Flash flood warnings		**Tornado warnings**		**Hurricane warnings**
	Lead time (Min.)	Accuracy (%)	Lead time (Min.)	Accuracy (%)	Accuracy of predicted landfall (km) with 24-hour lead time
1995	17	58	9	59	134
1996	21	75	10	60	130
1997	27	76	11	64	145
1998	30	78	12	68	140

Table 1.3 *Changes in forecast accuracy and lead times for US National Weather Service*

It is not just the prediction of weather disasters that is required. Different user groups need different elements of weather predicted at different timescales (Table 1.4).

ACTIVITIES

1. Analyse the changing lead times and accuracies for flash floods and tornadoes (Table 1.3). How do you explain the differences between the figures for the two hazards?
2. Using a copy of Table 1.4:
   - **a** Consider a six-hour forecast and tick the weather elements which will be relevant to the different user groups. Annotate the cells you tick to show the reasons for your choice.
   - **b** Repeat the exercise for a long-term six-week forecast. How have your choices changed and why?

Weather element	**Activity**			
	Arable farming	Air traffic control	Construction	Coastal fishing fleet
Temperature (maximum)				
Temperature (minimum)				
Windspeed				
Visibility				
Pressure				
Precipitation (amount)				
Precipitation (intensity)				

Table 1.4 *Elements of weather prediction*

Figure 1.6 is a model of the weather forecasting process. It is clear that weather forecasting is more than collecting data and running it through computers. The value of a forecast can be measured by its success in allowing appropriate decisions to be taken.

Forecasting – notable failures and successes

Effective forecasting depends on:

- correctly predicting the type, timing and magnitude of an event
- influencing decision makers to make an appropriate response.

Cost benefits of forecasting in a weather-sensitive industry

A report from the US Air Transport Association (ATA) states that the direct annual cost to sixteen member airlines from diverting and cancelling scheduled flights is US$47 million and US$222 million respectively. Delay cost varies depending on the type of aircraft and the affected airport, but is not insignificant. Annual insurance payout for encounters with turbulence amounts to millions of dollars, while time loss due to the injury of flight attendants is similarly high. Airlines have a need for highly accurate forecasts with sufficient lead time. For example, information about the arrival of thunderstorms at a given hub airport, especially those with damaging wind or hail, is required at least four hours ahead of time to allow airline planners to reschedule flights.

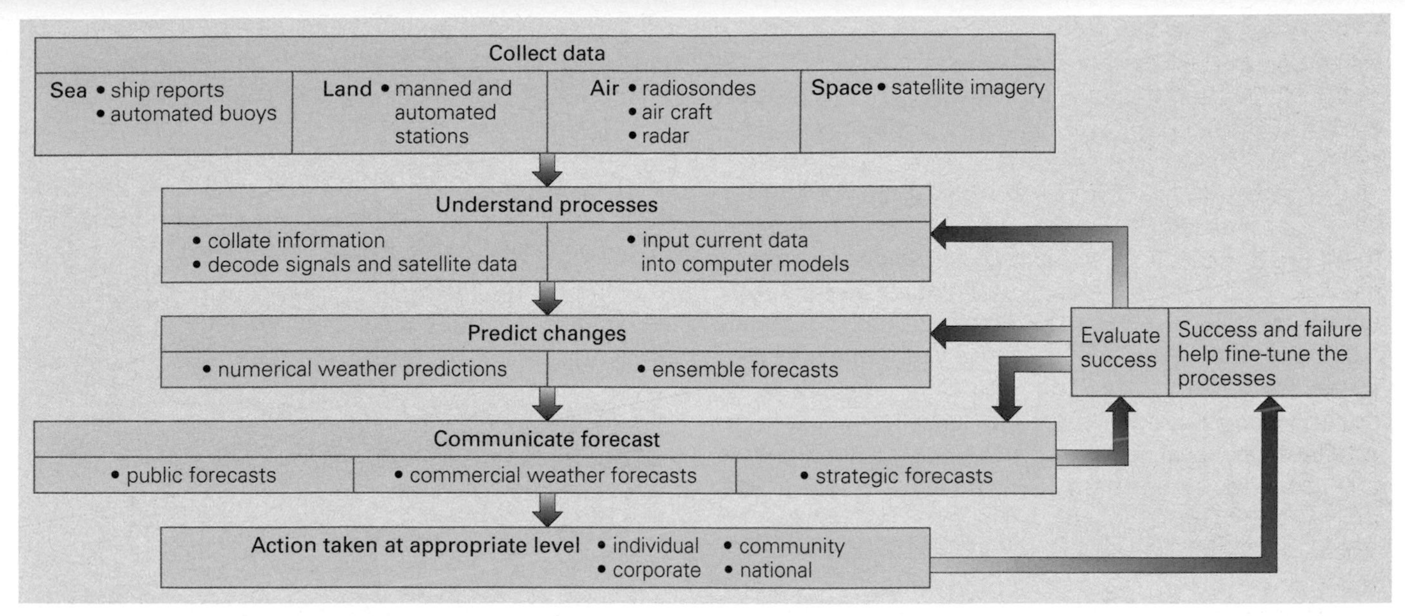

Figure 1.6 *A model of forecast preparation*

Forecast failures

Forecasts can fail for four main reasons, as shown in Table 1.5.

Reason	Example	Solution
Lack of data	Galveston Hurricane, September 1900. 6,000–8,000 deaths from surprise hurricane landfall.	Improve data monitoring network. Develop better monitoring technology (60 years later satellite imagery solved the problem of monitoring oceanic areas).
Lack of understanding of the data	October 1987 storm. A mid-latitude depression intensified explosively (and unexpectedly) over the Bay of Biscay producing winds well over 100 mph across the SE part of England. A total of 18 people died, with considerable damage to property, vehicles etc., and the loss of 15 million mature trees.	Improve modelling of the data.
System develops faster than can accurately be predicted	Munich hailstorm 1984. A stable layer of moist air under a temperature inversion warmed under strong July sunshine. A sudden overturning of the atmospheric layering took place late in the afternoon due to events 300 miles away across the Alps. This created explosive thundercloud development and hailstones up to 9.5 cm in diameter. Total insured losses were more than $500 million.	Model similar weather conditions under which the same conditions might develop and give warnings as appropriate.
Forecast worked but communication failed	31 July 1998, Mt Chiri, North Korea. Dozens of holiday makers died camping in this national park. A combination of inaccurate results from an automated rain gauge and a failure of the authorities to warn campers of flash-flood dangers created the tragedy.	Improve warning procedures, educate decision-makers, improve monitoring network.

Table 1.5 *Forecast failures*

Forecast successes

1) Oklahoma tornadoes, 3 May 1999

Tornadoes are notoriously difficult to predict. The basic cause, a clash between warm moist tropical air and cold dry polar air, has been known for over fifty years (Figure 1.7). These conditions give rise to intense thunderstorms (**supercell storms**). Not all supercell storms spawn tornadoes, and those that do may spawn small tornadoes, large tornadoes or (in the case of the May 1999 storms) multiple tornadoes. In recent years warnings have become much better due to technological advances in radar. These include:

- Vertical wind profilers – upward pointing Doppler radar systems. These bounce radar beams off different layers in the atmosphere. By examining the change in frequency of the returning radar beams (caused by the Doppler effect), the wind speed can be continuously monitored from ground level to the top of the tropopause.
- Truck-mounted Doppler radars (called DOWs – 'Dopplers on wheels'). These can spot tornadoes from up to 8 km distance (whatever the ground visibility) and give detailed feedback on windspeed, direction and possible short-term behaviour.

The conditions required to create tornadoes are:

- two different air masses with contrasting temperatures
- vertical wind shear (upper and lower winds blowing in different directions)
- strong heating of the ground, to generate thunderstorm activity.

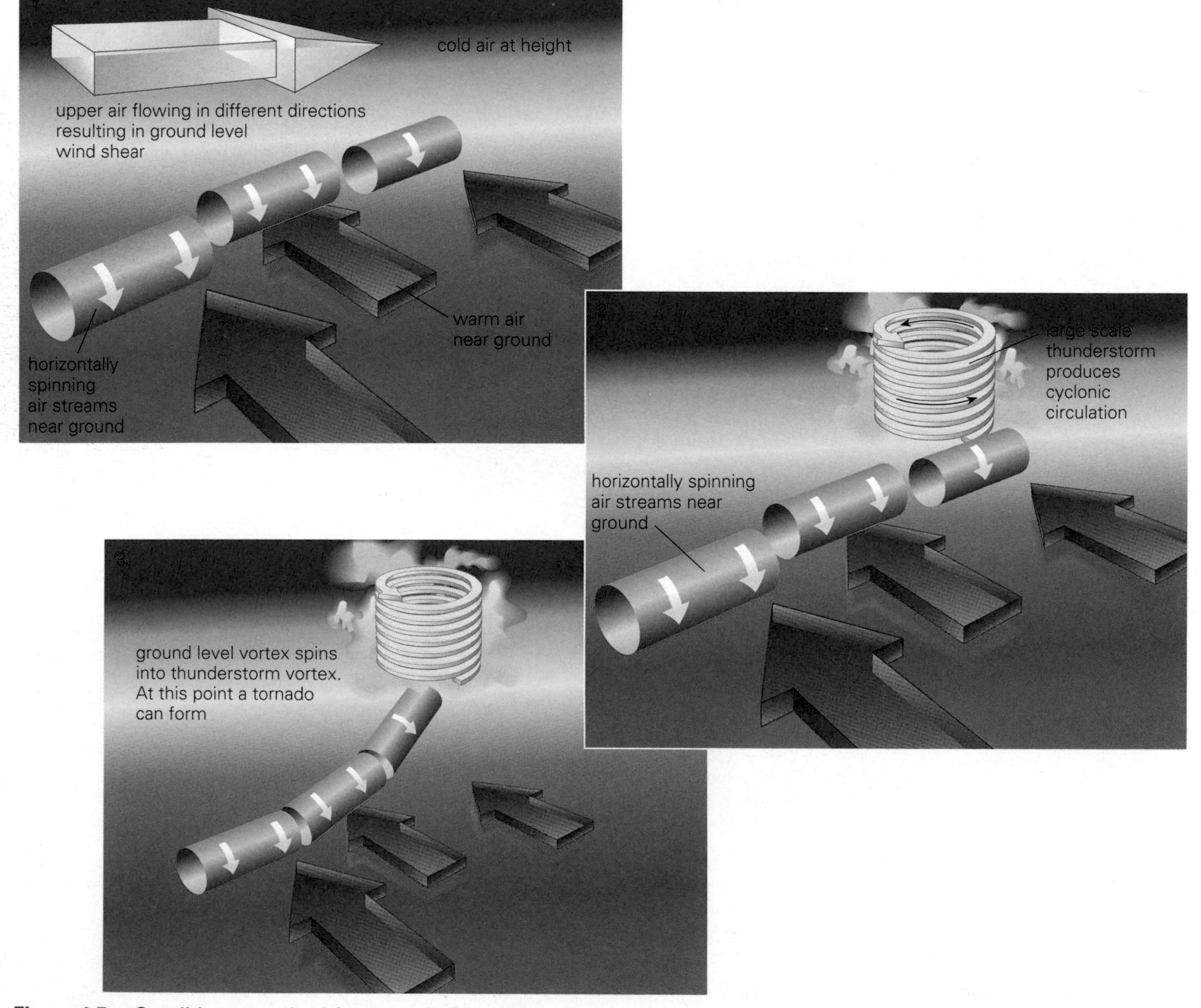

Figure 1.7 *Conditions required for tornado formation*

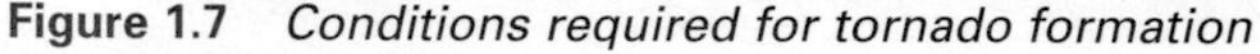

Table 1.6 shows how a 'safe' day rapidly turned into an unsafe one.

Time	Observations	Comment
7.00 am	• weather balloons show minimal wind shear • wide sheets of cirrus cloud	• cirrus cloud reduce daytime heating • low windshear prevents tornadoes forming. LOW RISK
12.00 noon	• vertical wind profilers spot a narrow jet stream snaking over Oklahoma • the cirrus cloud has cleared	• the jet stream is too narrow for the widely-spaced weather balloons to spot. It will produce high windshear along its path • the absence of cloud allows maximum heating in the afternoon. RISK RAPIDLY INCREASING
3.49 pm	• storm prediction centre issues a 'red flag' warning • intensive monitoring takes place to find the supercell thunderstorms which could spawn tornadoes	• whole area now on general alert • multiple supercell thunderstorms forming south west of Oklahoma and Chickasha (Figure 1.6)
5–8 pm	• 65 tornadoes of varying sizes and intensity batter the region • speed gusts up to 300 mph caught on the DOW units • one of the tornadoes was 2 km wide	• 47 people died • 742 people injured

Table 1.6 *Oklahoma Tornado development, 3 May,1999*

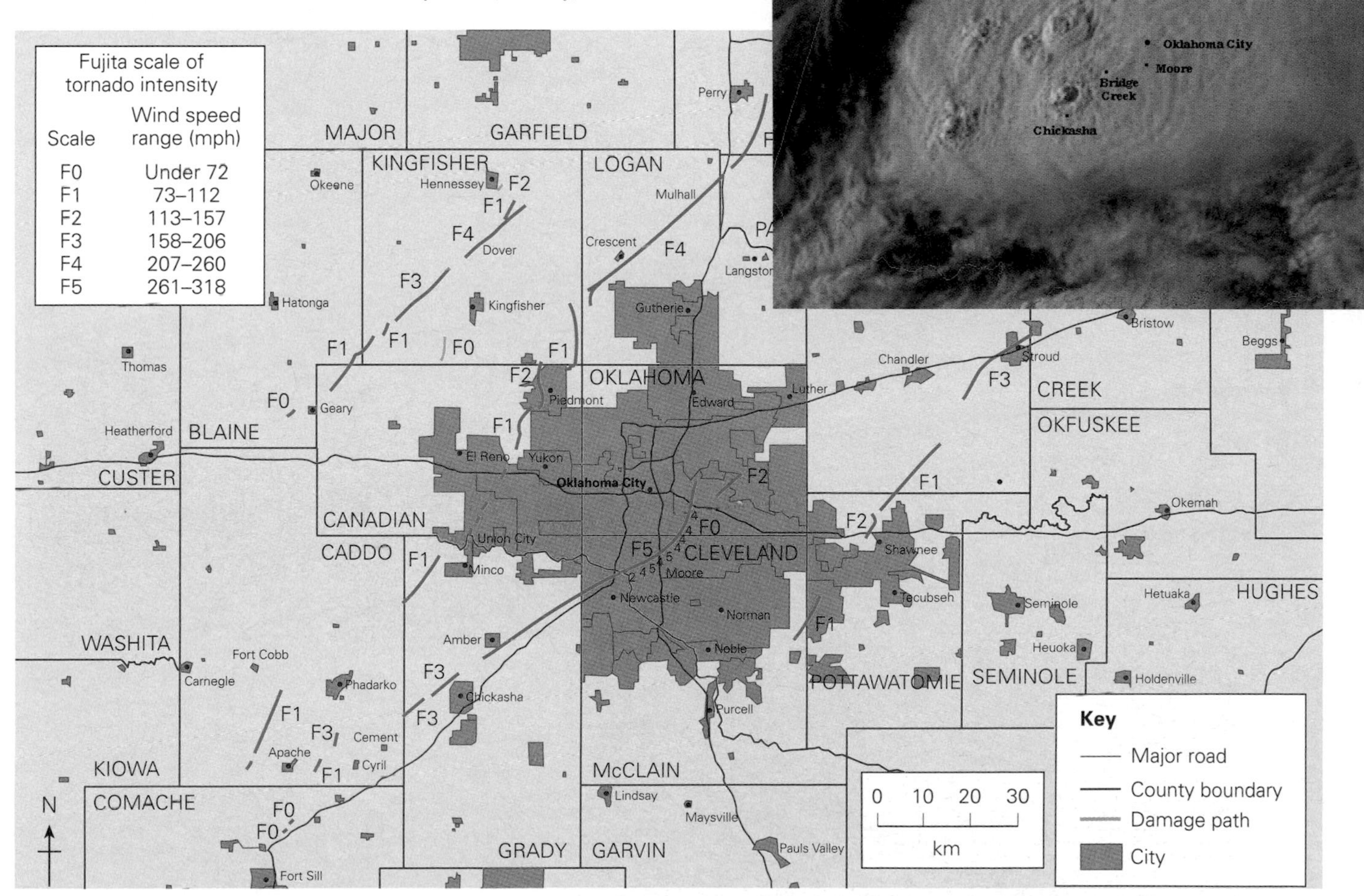

Figure 1.8 *Multiple supercell storms and tornado tracks Oklahoma, 3 May 1999. Each 'blister' shape on the photograph is a supercell thunderstorm.* Source: *NOAA*

Despite the outbreak of powerful tornadoes hitting a large city during a weekday rush hour, the death toll was less than 50 people. Three factors help explain this success:

- Technological – warnings from the National Weather Service gave an average lead time of 32 minutes in the Oklahoma City area (compared to the national average of 11 minutes), giving plenty of time for residents to prepare.
- Educational – nobody in the 4–24 age range died. Statistically the odds against this are more than 4000 to 1, suggesting that intensive tornado education programmes combined with accurate forecasts are highly effective at reducing deaths.
- Logistical – the Warning Decision Support System (WDSS) provides improved computer software to automatically rank storms according to their severe weather threats. This increased the National Weather Service's confidence to issue strongly worded warnings for storms.

2) Mozambique floods, 2000

In contrast to the Oklahoma disaster, a successful flood forecast in Mozambique did not succeed in reducing deaths. In January, a global climate summary prepared by the US National Oceanic and Atmospheric Administration (NOAA) predicted that southern Africa would have higher than average rainfalls between January and March. The floods started on 9 February with heavy rainfall across southern Africa. In Maputo, Mozambique's capital, tens of thousands of people were forced to flee their homes. United Nations officials estimated 150,000 people were at risk of death from lack of food and disease. On 11 February, the Limpopo River burst its banks, worsening the danger. On 22 February, tropical cyclone Eline hit the Mozambique coast, just north of the already flooded areas (Figure 1.9). Flash floods inundated farmlands around Chokwe and Xai-Xai five days later and rivers continued to rise more than four metres above normal levels. An estimated one million people were driven from their homes, and diseases spread rapidly because polluted, infected floodwater was the only water available for drinking.

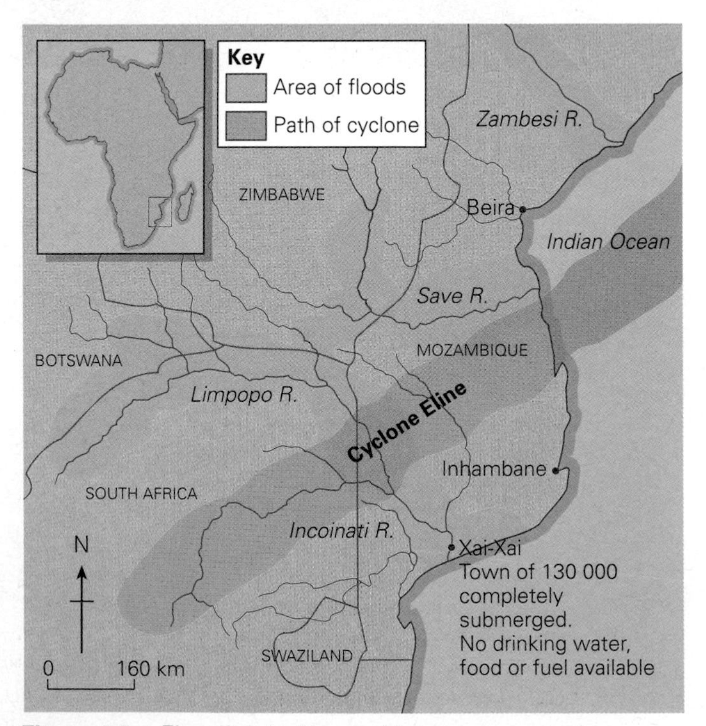

Figure 1.9 *Flooding in Mozambique*

In Mozambique accurate weather forecasts were available, but the flood forecasting was much less effective. Social and economic changes in the region had reduced the capacity of the environment to absorb flood water. These changes included:

- 50% of wetland in southern Africa drained for agriculture therefore less water storage potential
- overgrazing in the river catchments reducing soil and vegetation storage
- urbanisation of some subcatchments increased flood runoff
- dams built on the river systems were designed for water storage, not flood control, therefore were designed to be kept at a high level, offering little relief storage in a flood. When dams threatened to overflow, their sluices were opened, worsening the already swollen rivers
- the **antecedent conditions** (pre-existing water levels in the catchment areas) encouraged rapid runoff from the rainfall.

3 The weather and climate machinery

Temperature, pressure and humidity combine together to produce all weather phenomena from heatwaves to windstorms.

Temperature

The temperature of the air influences its:

- weight (i.e. pressure). Warm air is lighter (low pressure) and cold air is heavier (high pressure)
- wetness, i.e. ability to hold water. Warm air encourages evaporation of water, cold air encourages condensation
- stability. Air that is warmed at ground level becomes more unstable, while air cooling near ground level becomes stable.

Air is heated indirectly by the Sun. The Sun heats the Earth's surface which then heats the atmosphere by contact from below.

Pressure

As already noted, the temperature of the air will influence its weight and therefore the pressure which it exerts on the ground. Differences in pressure create winds, flowing from high to low pressure. Some regions of the world experience higher pressure than expected due to the **global circulation** (see page 12). Areas over the tropics are hot, therefore low pressure might be expected, but these regions lie underneath a descending flow of air from the upper part of the troposphere which creates a high pressure belt.

Humidity

The moisture content of the air influences precipitation types and amounts. Less obvious is the effect of moisture content on temperature. When moisture in the air evaporates, heat is taken from the surroundings. Conversely, condensation results in the release of energy back into the atmosphere. This changing state of water in the atmosphere helps to moderate global temperatures and move vast quantities of heat from the equator (where evaporation takes heat from the environment) towards the poles (where heat is released again during condensation). Wet air is also less stable than dry air, so moist air is more likely to create thunderstorms.

Air at different temperatures can hold different amounts of water. This creates a situation where warm air may feel dry but actually contain more water than 'damp air' at a lower temperature. We therefore need to define the concepts of relative and absolute humidity.

- **Absolute humidity** is the amount of water vapour physically present in the atmosphere measured as gm/m^3.
- **Relative humidity** is the relationship between the actual amount of water vapour present and the total that could be carried at a given temperature. This is normally expressed as a percentage.

Figure 1.10 shows a graph of the relationship between temperature and humidity. On this graph four weather conditions (a1–a4) are plotted. In each one the air has an absolute humidity of 10 gm/m^3. The relative humidity is much more variable, depending on temperature, ranging from 30 % to 100 %. The temperature at which the air becomes saturated and the water vapour condenses is known as the **dew point**.

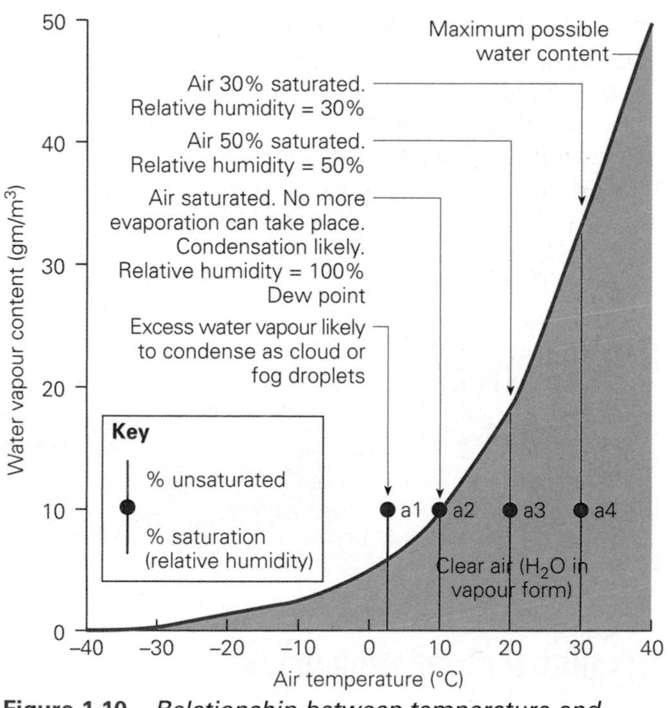

Figure 1.10 *Relationship between temperature and humidity*

The interaction of these three weather variables (temperature, pressure and humidity) can account for almost every weather system. The complexity of climate is found in the varied ways these ingredients interact and influence one another.

ACTIVITIES

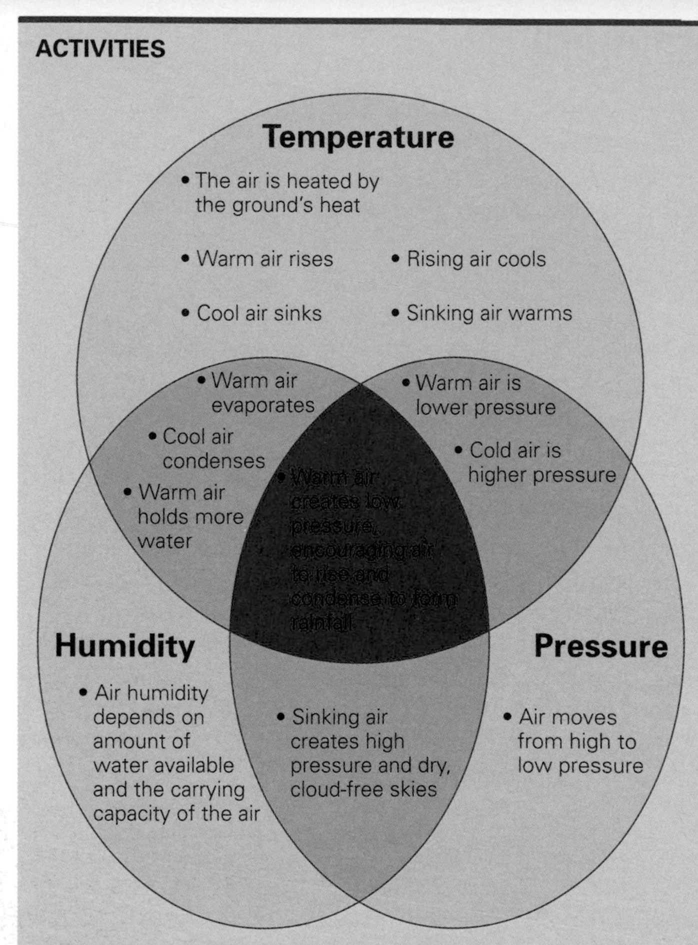

Figure 1.11 *Everyday weather processes*

Place	Latitude	Longitude	Altitude (m)	Mean annual temperature (°C)	Temperature range
Kirkwall	59.1	–2.0	26	7.7	8.9
Stornoway	58.3	–6.5	15	8.1	8.7
Dyce	57.3	–2.0	65	7.9	11.1
Durham	54.7	–1.5	102	8.6	11.8
Santon Downham	52.5	0.7	24	8.9	12.6
Elmdon	52.5	–2.0	96	9.1	12.7
Oxford	51.8	–1.2	63	10.1	13.0
Shawbury	52.8	–2.7	72	9.0	12.2
Gatwick	51.2	–0.2	59	9.6	12.9
Eskdalemuir	55.3	–3.2	242	7.1	11.4
Long Ashton	51.4	–2.7	51	10.0	12.0
Plymouth	50.3	–4.1	50	10.6	10.4
Cork	51.8	–8.3	154	9.4	9.7
Ringway	53.4	–2.2	75	9.5	11.9
Clones	54.2	–7.3	89	8.8	10.5

Correlation coefficients:	Latitude	Longitude	Altitude (raw data)	Altitude (with northerly and southerly stations removed)
Mean annual temperature	–0.85	+0.7	–0.3	–0.7

Spearman 'r' value (+ or –): 1.0, 0.8, 0.6, 0.4, 0.2
Significance level: 1%, 5%
Not significant
Degrees of freedom (Number of pairs – 2): 2, 4, 6, 8, 10, 20, 40

Figure 1.12 *Climate data from the UK*

1 Figure 1.11 shows a simple model of the three weather variables and some of their influences on one another. Use the information in the model to explain the following everyday weather observations:

a Why does the mirror on the bathroom wall steam up?
b Why are hilltops cooler than valley bottoms?
c Why are draughts always cold?
d Why does the car windscreen steam up on the inside?
e Why does washing dry best on a sunny day?
f Why does dew occur in the morning?
g Why is fog more likely to lie in valleys?

2 Figure 1.12 contains statistical climate details for a range of UK stations.

a For each of the four correlations justify why you might expect to find a relationship between the two variables.
b Use the significance graph to assess the correlation (if the significance level is ≤ 5% the relationship is significant).
c Explain why each relationship is significant (or not). What other factors may also influence the relationship?

The global circulation model

Figure 1.13 shows the global circulation model. This model helps explain the broad arrangement of climate on the Earth's surface. The vertical movement of air in the atmosphere creates areas of high and low pressure. Low pressure creates wet conditions because the air is rising, cooling and encouraging condensation, e.g. at the Intertropical convergence zone (ITCZ). High pressure creates dry conditions because the air is sinking, warming and encouraging evaporation, e.g. at the tropics and at the poles. Regional wind systems blow between the high and low pressure zones.

The global circulation helps define major air mass regions of the world, equatorial air, tropical air and polar air (Figure 1.14). It also leads to one of the most significant findings of the last hundred years in terms of understanding weather, the concept of jet streams along major air mass boundaries.

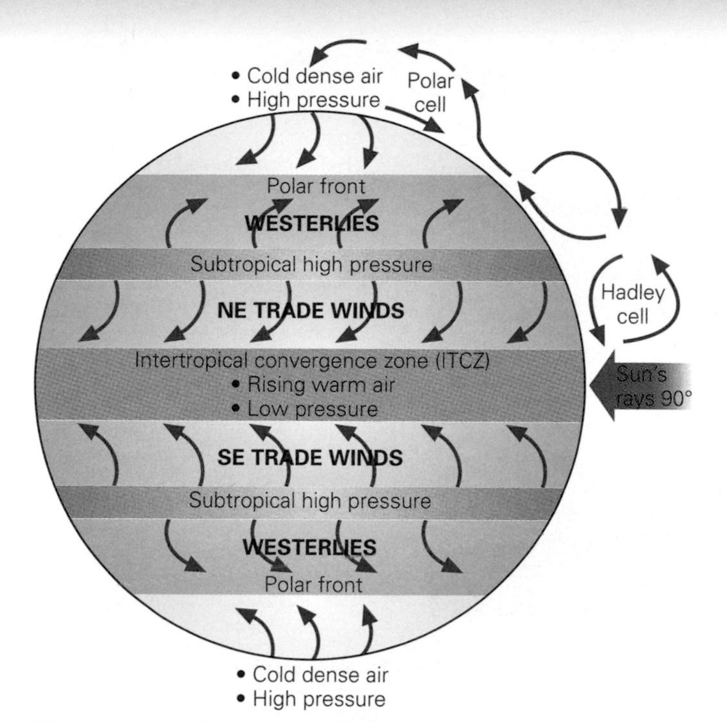

Figure 1.13 *The global circulation model*

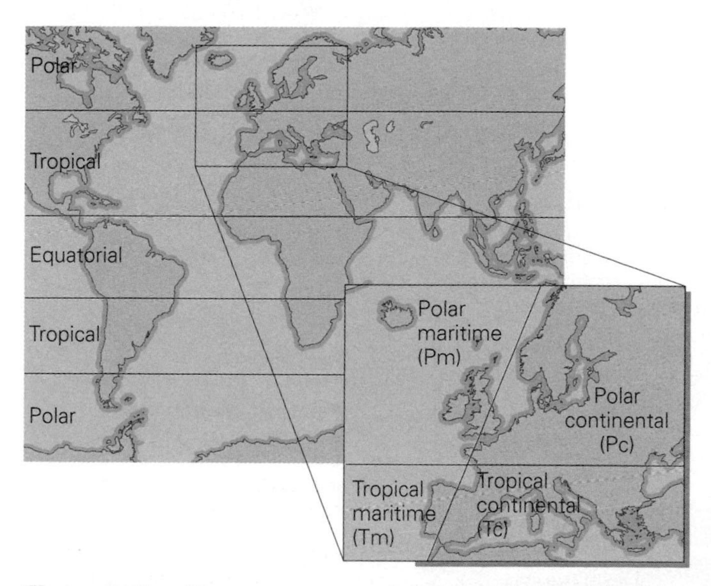

Figure 1.14 *Air masses on a global and regional scale*

The air mass concept

An air mass is a body of air with a uniform nature over a large area. For example, a body of air over an ocean will acquire heat and moisture from the ocean. Conversely, a body of air in the centre of a continent will be dry and hot in the summer and dry and cold in the winter. In their source regions, air masses tend to be very uniform in both temperature and moisture. As the air masses move away from their source regions they may change their character by:

- passing over warmer or colder surfaces
- picking up moisture when crossing water surfaces.

The study of air masses is useful for understanding broad patterns of weather, i.e. when we are under the influence of certain air masses we experience certain types of weather. Figure 1.14 shows how the temperature and moisture characteristics of the air create broad differences in the air masses of Europe. The main air masses influencing the UK are shown in Figure 1.16.

The Coriolis effect

It is evident from the study of wind patterns and current flows that all large scale movements of fluids on the Earth's surface are deflected into spinning vortices. Figure 1.15 shows the effect is very slight near the equator but very pronounced closer to the poles. This is known as the **Coriolis effect** and is due to the fact that the Earth is a spinning sphere. In the northern hemisphere the spin is anticlockwise (looking down on the pole) and the spinning motion deflects winds to the right as they travel. In the southern hemisphere the spin is clockwise and winds are deflected to the left.

Figure 1.15 *The Coriolis effect*

Summer

Arctic maritime (Am)
Very rare in summer. Its arrival would produce cold weather, thunderstorm activity and flash floods.

Polar maritime (Pm)
A source region over the N. Atlantic means that this air is damp and cool, averaging 10°C at sea level. As it moves southerly towards the UK, it begins to warm at its base. Unstable pockets of rising air cause cumulus and cumulonimbus clouds. This air mass is associated with cool, showery weather (in localised thunderstorms) with bright, clear conditions between showers.

Polar continental (Pc)
A source region over continental Europe gives this air mass a high summer temperature, averaging 20°C. It brings dry, warm, sunny weather. As the air passes over the North Sea, it may pick up moisture in its lower layers and experience cooling. This often results in hazy, overcast conditions in eastern England with skies rapidly clearing inland. High pollution levels are associated with this air mass because it is becoming more stable as it moves over maritime areas (trapping pollutants near the ground).

Tropical maritime (Tm)
Forming under the semi-permanent Azores High Pressure region, Tm air is both warm (22°C) and moist. As it moves towards the UK, it travels over increasingly cool, northerly latitudes. If it cools below its dew point temperature, the moisture condenses out as cloud. Owing to the stability of the air, the clouds that form are layer clouds (stratus clouds) that produce dull, drizzly, overcast weather in the summer. The cloudiness reduces the temperatures at this time of year. Away from the coast, air passes over hotter land surfaces and clouds may clear.

Tropical continental (Tc)
This air mass has its source region in North Africa and, although relatively uncommon, it produces very hot (30°C), dry conditions in the UK. There may be coastal fog on the south coast where the air has picked up moisture in its lower layers as it passes over the English Channel.

Winter

Arctic maritime (Am)
This air has its source in the icy seas north of Scandinavia. It is extremely cold and therefore carries little moisture at its source area. As it moves southwards towards the UK, it warms at its base becoming much more unstable and picking up water as it moves over the North Atlantic. This highly unstable moist air can produce ferocious storms in northern Scotland with heavy falls of snow.

Polar maritime (Pm)
In winter, this air cools less quickly than the continental air because ocean areas cool slowly. It still brings cool (5°C) and showery conditions to the UK, but in the sunny spells between the showers it can become quite warm, especially further inland and to the east where the convectional showers are more likely to have died out.

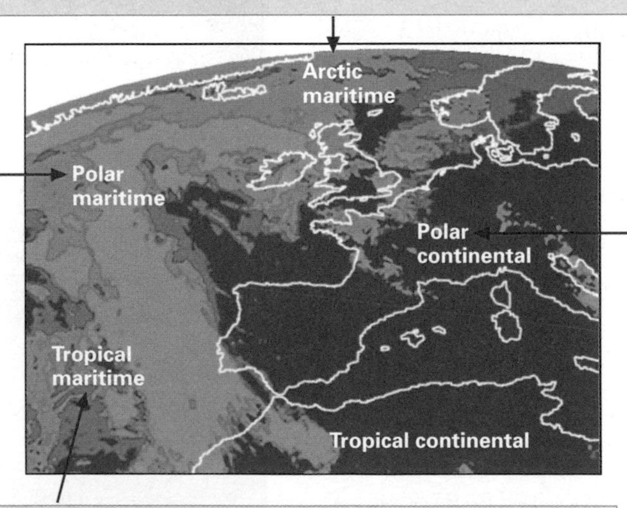

Polar continental (Pc)
The rapid cooling of the continental land surface in winter leads to the build up of cold (–10°C), dense air over Central and Eastern Europe. This brings some of our coldest winter weather. Although the air is dry, it can absorb high levels of water from the relatively warm North Sea and English Channel as it moves towards the UK. This moisture is rapidly converted to snow. The country is likely to experience cold, crisp, bright, but frosty, weather.

Tropical maritime (Tm)
This air mass brings mild and damp conditions in winter. With its source area at temperatures of around 18°C, the air is still relatively warm by the time it reaches the UK. Being damp, it produces stratus cloud and low-level hill fog.

Figure 1.16 *Air masses affecting the UK*

The air masses change as they move towards the UK, largely as a result of advection (Figure 1.16 and Table 1.7). This is the process by which air changes temperature as the air mass moves sideways over a surface that is hotter or cooler than the original air.

Direction of movement	Changes to temperature and stability	Impacts on weather
Southward moving air masses (Pm, Am and Pc)	Advectional warming results in a warm layer at the bottom of the air mass with cooler air on top. This creates great instability.	Pm and Am air masses produce cumulus and cumulonimbus cloud with showery conditions. Pc air is too dry to produce much cloud.
Northward moving air masses (Tm and Tc)	Advectional cooling results in very stable air.	Cooling of moist Tm air can lead to fog. If windy, the fog will lift to form low stratus clouds.

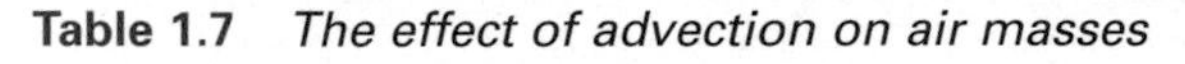

Table 1.7 *The effect of advection on air masses*

Spotting air mass types from a satellite image

In order, the easiest air masses to spot from space are Pm, Tm, Pc and Tc air.

- **Pm air** Instability triggers convection as warm air rises up through cold air. Pockets of rising air create cumulus and cumulonimbus clouds. These are visible as a mottled 'scrambled egg' texture.
- **Tm air** Advectional cooling of an extensive stable air mass creates a uniform mass of undistinguished, untextured cloud. On an infrared image these clouds will tend to be grey in colour, being low down and therefore relatively warm.
- **Pc and Tc air** are notable for their absence of clouds. The time of year will determine whether Pc or Tc is the most likely, but make sure you are not simply looking at an anticyclone (which also consists of a large cloud free area).

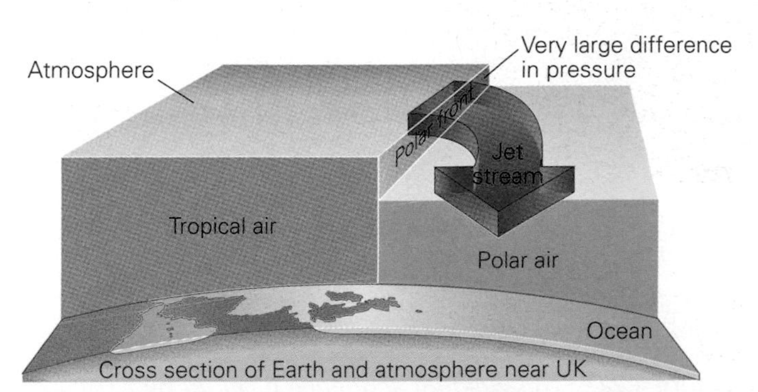

Figure 1.17 *Formation of jet streams along the polar front*

Jet streams

At the polar front, warm tropical air meets cold polar air and a significant pressure difference is created (Figure 1.17). This difference drives a high level wind system around the temperate regions. These winds are known as **jet streams** and flow at speeds varying between a mean of 110 km/hr (70 mph) in summer and 184 km/hr (115 mph) in winter. In extreme cases, speeds of over 370 km/hr (230 mph) have been recorded. The Coriolis effect spins the jet stream round the globe in loops of fast flowing upper air called **Rossby waves**. Figure 1.18 shows a jet stream over the North Atlantic with a pronounced Rossby wave curling south towards Scotland.

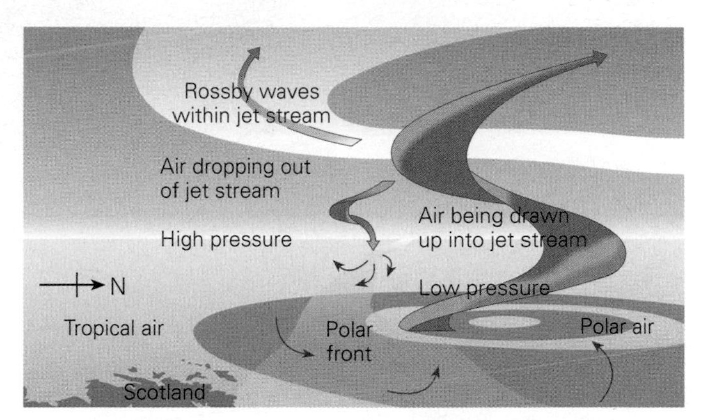

Figure 1.18 *Jet stream, Rossby waves and surface pressure*

Air travels through the Rossby wave at varying speeds, going slower as it turns away from the pole and faster as it bends back towards it. When the jet stream slows down, excess air piles up and descends to the ground. When the jet stream speeds up, air is sucked from ground level to fill the gap (see Fig 1.18 above). Rossby waves therefore create alternate areas of high and low pressure. Areas of high pressure (anticyclones) are characterised by dry, clear conditions due to air warming as it descends. Areas of low pressure (depressions) are characterised by cloudy, wet conditions due to rising air. The winds blow away from areas of high pressure (anticyclones) towards areas of low pressure (depressions). The Coriolis effect deflects the winds blowing into lows and out of highs, spinning them as shown in Figure 1.19.

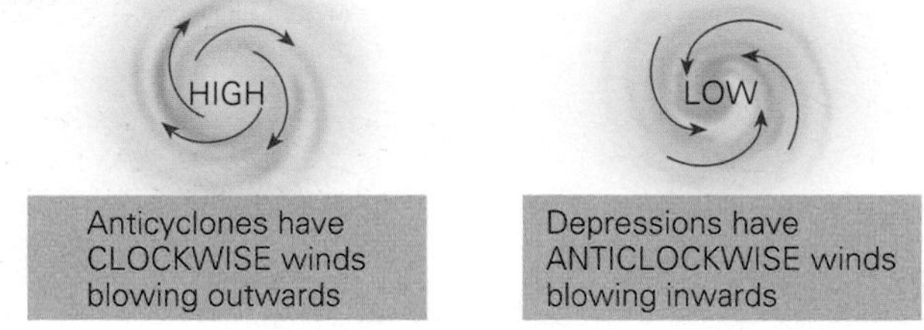

Figure 1.19 *The Coriolis effect on pressure systems*

Interaction of air masses – the formation of depressions

Depressions form when a tropical air mass meets a polar air mass. The boundary, where two different air masses meet, is called a front. Where warm, light, tropical air rises over cold, polar air, a **warm front** is created (Figure 1.20). Where cold, dense, polar air moves towards warm air, it undercuts the warm air forcing it up along a **cold front**. The entire system (low pressure centre and two fronts) moves from west to east, following the jet stream.

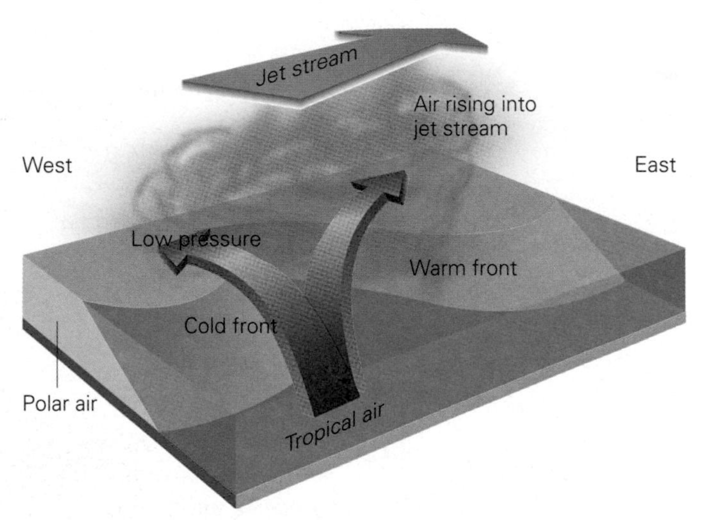

Figure 1.20 *The formation of a depression*

The warm front, with tropical air rising over polar air, tends to have a low gradient (about 1:100) and the shallow angle spreads the influence of the front over a wide area (Figure 1.21). Warm fronts bring rain for many hours. By contrast, the cold front is steeper as the polar air behind undercuts the warm sector and its associated weather forms a narrow band which passes over an observer more quickly. The cold front moves faster than the warm front, and when it catches up an **occluded front** is formed.

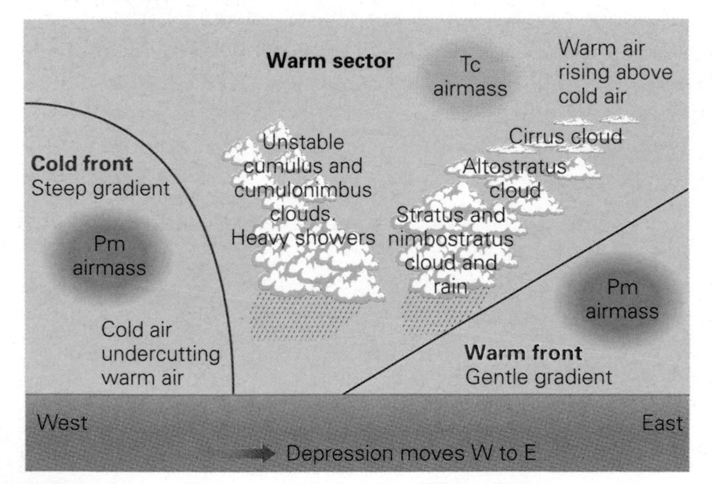

Figure 1.21 *The ingredients of a depression*

A depression brings a distinctive sequence of weather conditions, and this is summarised in Figure 1.22.

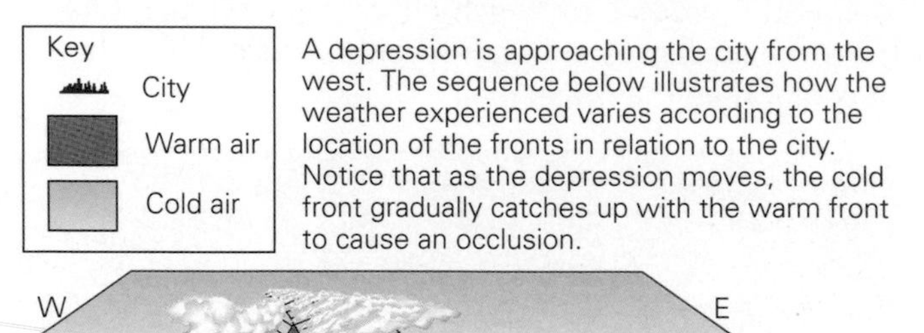

A depression is approaching the city from the west. The sequence below illustrates how the weather experienced varies according to the location of the fronts in relation to the city. Notice that as the depression moves, the cold front gradually catches up with the warm front to cause an occlusion.

Pressure	Steadily falling as warmer (lighter) air approaches	Warm front approaches
Wind	Increasing as strong gradients at front approach	
Temperature	Slow rise	
Cloud	Cirrus, cirrostratus, altostratus, stratus and nimbostratus	
Weather	Cloudy at first, then rain or drizzle likely	
Visibility	Fair at first but deteriorating as front comes closer	

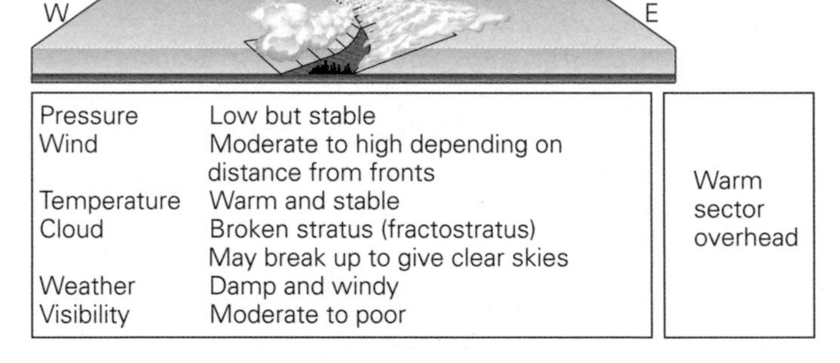

Pressure	Low but stable	Warm sector overhead
Wind	Moderate to high depending on distance from fronts	
Temperature	Warm and stable	
Cloud	Broken stratus (fractostratus) May break up to give clear skies	
Weather	Damp and windy	
Visibility	Moderate to poor	

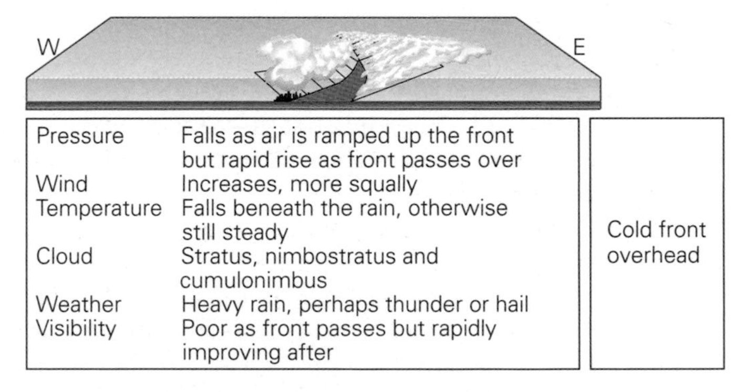

Pressure	Falls as air is ramped up the front but rapid rise as front passes over	Cold front overhead
Wind	Increases, more squally	
Temperature	Falls beneath the rain, otherwise still steady	
Cloud	Stratus, nimbostratus and cumulonimbus	
Weather	Heavy rain, perhaps thunder or hail	
Visibility	Poor as front passes but rapidly improving after	

Pressure	Steady and high	Behind the cold front
Wind	Veering towards north west Steady but squalls near showers	
Temperature	Low and steady	
Cloud	Stratus dispersed. Clear skies with cumulus or some cumulonimbus	
Weather	Sunny with showers	
Visibility	Very good	

Figure 1.22 *The weather sequence brought by a depression*

Depressions and human activity

Table 1.8 indicates some of the main weather hazards associated with the warm, cold and occluded fronts of a depression.

ACTIVITIES

1. Study Table 1.8 and Figure 1.23 which show a fast-moving depression crossing the UK at 30 mph (48 km/hr).
   - **a** When will driving conditions on the M25 first become hazardous?
   - **b** When will flash floods on the M25 be a potential hazard?
   - **c** When will strong winds cause hazards on the Severn Bridge (Bristol)?
   - **d** For how many hours will Reading experience dry, cloudy conditions?
   - **e** When will Swindon experience scattered showers with sunny intervals?
   - **f** When will aircraft at Heathrow need to rely on instruments for landing?

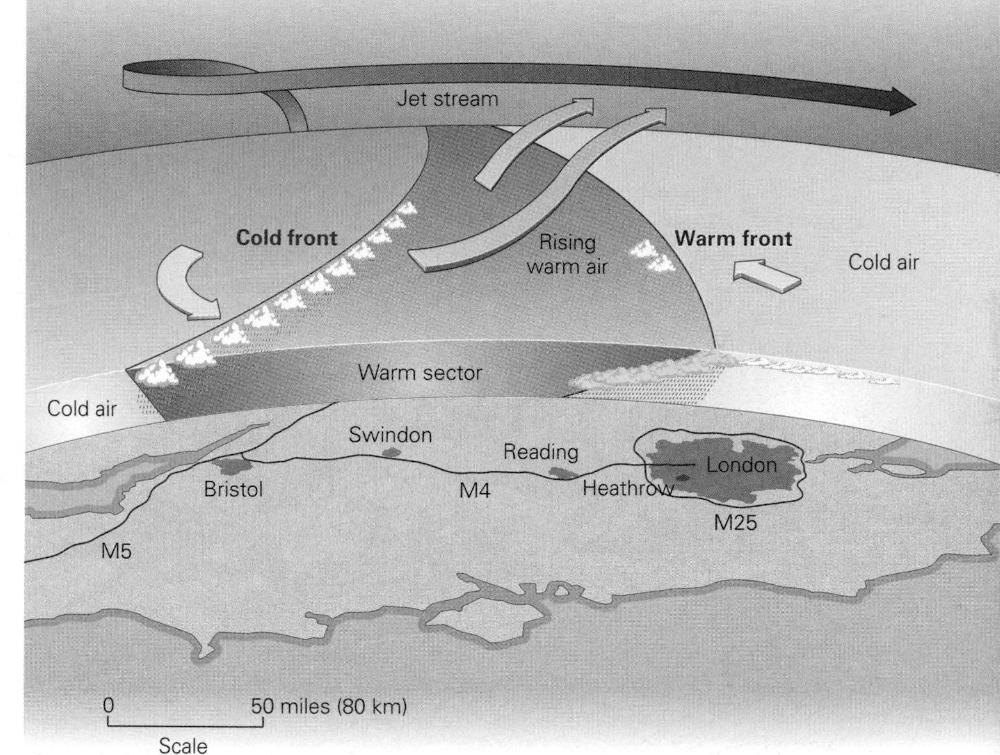

Figure 1.23 *Cross-section of a UK depression – synoptic situation at 9 a.m.*

Type of front	Associated weather elements	Summer impacts	Winter impacts
Warm	• low cloud • poor visibility	• potential impacts on most forms of transport	
	• continuous light to moderate precipitation	• good for plant growth but poor for crop harvests • good for water supplies but poor for recreation and tourism	• possibility of snow/freezing fog and transport disruption • good for recharging water supplies but may cause floods if ground already wet
	• strong winds	• potential impacts on most forms of transport • possibility of structural damage in extreme cases	
Occluded	• prolonged, possibly heavy precipitation	• potential disruption for agriculture, transport and tourism • flood potential	• as for summer with added possibility of widespread snow if conditions are cold enough
Cold	• heavy showers with hail	• poor visibility disrupting transport • flash flooding • leisure/tourism disruption	• as for summer with possibility of heavy localised snow if cold enough
	• strong winds	• potential impacts on most forms of transport • possibility of structural damage in extreme cases	
	• lightning	• disruption of electrical supplies	

Table 1.8 *Impacts of a depression on people*

Anticyclones

In many respects anticyclones are the opposite of depressions as Table 1.9 shows:

	Depressions	Anticyclones
System size	typically about 500 miles (800 km) across	range from 500–2000 miles (800–3200 km) in diameter
System stability	unstable system moving rapidly across an area in 24 hours system lifespan is 2–5 days	stable and slow moving may last from days to weeks depending on type some anticyclones are semi-permanent
Pressure	low typically 970–995 mb	high typically 1025–1040 mb
Temperature	mild in winter cool in summer, due to cloud over maritime air masses	hot in summer cold in winter due to absence of cloud cover
Humidity and precipitation	very humid, rain all seasons possible snow further north in winter	dry but may be associated with fog, especially in autumn and winter
Windspeed	high; often linked with gale warnings	low; often calm near centre

Table 1.9 *Contrasts between anticyclones and depressions*

As well as high pressure regions created by the Rossby waves, anticyclones form in two other ways:

1) In winter, cooling of continental areas results in very cold air at ground level. The higher density of this cold air results in a locally persistent high pressure area. This is common over Siberia and Scandinavia in winter.
2) Even more persistent than the winter 'highs' are the semi-permanent high pressure regions near the tropics. These are created by the descending flow in the Hadley Cell (Figure 1.13). The clear, cloudless skies associated with the anticyclonic conditions results in the extreme aridity of these areas, e.g. Sahara.

Anticyclone weather

Anticyclones produce distinctive weather conditions, summarised below. Anticyclonic weather is governed by three related factors:

- Air is sinking from the upper parts of the troposphere. Sinking air is stable and so conditions do not change rapidly.
- Air is warming. Air nearer to the ground is compressed by the sinking air above it. As air compresses, it warms up. This is known as **adiabatic heating** and creates a 'temperature inversion' with a layer of warmer air above ground level (Figure 1.24).
- Moisture in the air is evaporating as the air warms, so clear, cloudless skies can develop. This has a different effect on weather depending on the season.

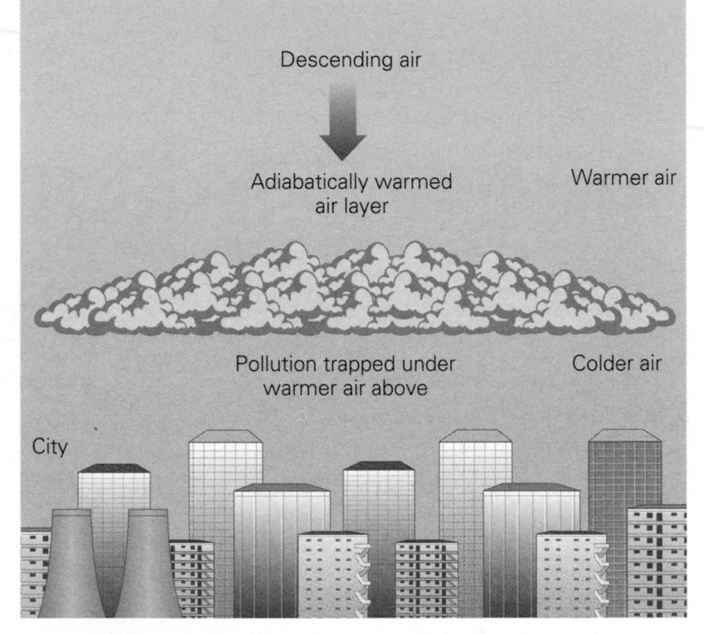

Figure 1.24 *A temperature inversion caused by an anticyclone*

Summer and winter anticyclones

Summer	Winter
Clear skies lead to	
• cool clear nights, possibly misty mornings • high temperatures in the day	• very cold nights, frost, fog and freezing fog • cold, bright, crisp days if air is dry enough to avoid fog formation • gloomy, cold, damp, foggy conditions if air is wet
Absence of precipitation leads to	
• drought hazard	• future drought hazard if groundwater supplies are not replenished
Absence of wind leads to	
• hazy conditions with low visibility	• difficulty in dispersing early morning mist and fog. • cold damp sunless days alternate with foggy cold nights, a condition known as 'anticyclonic gloom'

ACTIVITIES

1 Correlations between air pressure and other weather elements are shown below. Study the data and complete the question.

Daily weather data for London and Plymouth reveal the following correlations:

	Plymouth	London
Pressure v. Wind	-0.45	-0.38
Pressure v. Rain	-0.48	-0.41
Pressure v. Maximum temperature	0.02	0.03

Why does high pressure have such a poor correlation with maximum temperature when anticyclones often bring summer heatwaves?

2 What other influences might affect London's correlations?

Hint: although the correlations are not strong (e.g. -0.41) they are still significant if they are greater than +/-0.15, because the sample size is so large (900). Even a weak relationship can be a significant underlying trend if demonstrated on many data samples.

Health threats from anticyclones

Anticyclonic weather is generally welcomed for its bright, sunny weather, but these weather systems pose many threats to human health as Table 1.10 demonstrates.

Such health risks can be managed in the following ways:

- The Sun Index – forecasting services have developed a standardised Sun Index which assesses risk from sunburn according to predicted UV levels and skin type. The main categories are shown in Table 1.11.
- Air quality forecast – issued on a daily basis. This can be picked up from the UK National Air Quality Information Archive on the web at: www.aeat.co.uk/netcen/airqual/welcome.html. The forecast takes into consideration both the prevailing weather conditions and the wind direction, to account for long range pollutants entering the UK from abroad.

Summer anticyclone	Winter anticyclone
• Summer smog – photochemical reactions with pollutants from vehicle exhausts create low level **ozone**. This causes breathing problems, particularly for asthmatics. Descending air traps pollutants near the ground.	• Descending air traps pollutants near the ground. **Nitrogen oxides** are the main pollutants of winter smogs.
• High levels of pollen and **fungal spores** get trapped near the ground in anticyclonic conditions. These trigger asthma and hay fever in susceptible people.	
• Heatwaves cause **dehydration** in the very young and very old. Even in MEDCs, a heat wave can trigger hundreds of deaths among the elderly.	• **Hypothermia** kills a significant number of old people in poorly heated homes during anticyclonic cold snaps. • Hospital casualty departments experience an increase in **broken bones** and muscle strains from slips on icy surfaces.
• High ultraviolet radiation (UV) can cause sunburn and **skin cancer**. Skin cancer is the most common cancer in the UK. It kills more than 2000 people a year.	

Table 1.10 *Health problems caused by anticyclones*

Table 1.11 *The Sun Index*

	Vulnerability (depends on skin type)			
Sun index	White skin that burns easily and tends not to tan	White skin that tans easily	Brown skin	Black skin
1,2	Low risk	Low risk	Low risk	Low risk
3,4	Medium risk	Low risk	Low risk	Low risk
5	High risk	Medium risk	Low risk	Low risk
6	High risk	Medium risk	Medium risk	Low risk
7,8,9	Very high risk	High risk	Medium risk	Medium risk
10 (highest likely in UK)	Very high risk	High risk	High risk	Medium risk

- Low risk – the sun will not harm you
- Medium risk – avoid being in direct sunlight for more than 1 to 2 hours
- High risk – you could burn in 30 minutes. Avoid direct sunlight, cover up or wear a sunscreen lotion SPF15+
- Very high risk – you could burn severely in 20 to 30 minutes. Stay out of direct sunlight, cover up and use a sunscreen lotion SPF15+

While forecasts help manage health risks associated with anticyclonic conditions, they do not offer long term solutions. Studies indicate that a 1% reduction in the ozone layer increases skin cancer rates by about 5%. Current predictions suggest that ozone will continue to decline because there is a lag of several decades between pollutants entering the atmosphere and the atmospheric systems adjusting to the damage. The pleasure of a bright, sunny day may be increasingly marred by problems of cancer and respiratory distress.

ACTIVITIES

1. Australia has the highest asthma rates in the world, and up to 40% of the population suffer from hay fever. Use an atlas to examine summer and winter pressure patterns over Australia. Suggest climate related reasons for the unusually high incidence of asthma and hay fever.
2. Examine the graphs in Figure 1.25. Suggest which pollutants are most likely to concentrate in:
   a summer anticyclone conditions
   b winter anticyclone conditions.
3. Suggest reasons (both human and physical) for the very different pollution levels recorded in Figure 1.25.

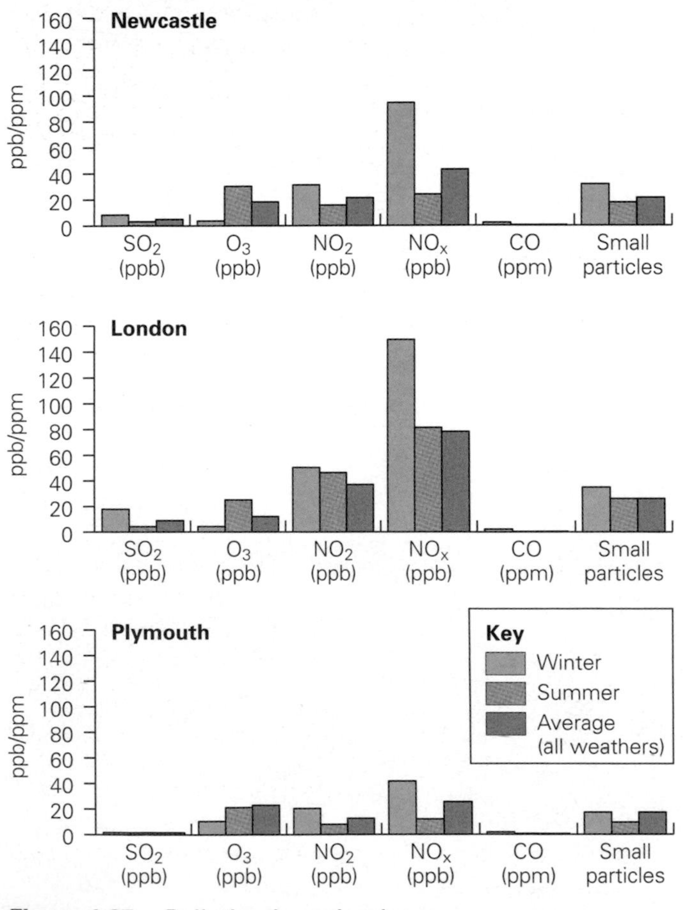

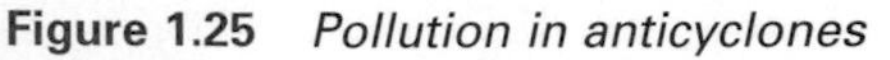

Figure 1.25 *Pollution in anticyclones*

Blocking anticyclones

Figure 1.26 *A blocking anticyclone diverting depression tracks*

Since anticyclones can be stable and persistent features, they sometimes dominate the atmosphere in a region, creating what is known as a **blocking anticyclone**. Blocking anticyclones occur when the Rossby wave pattern produces exaggerated meanders that cut across the polar and temperate zones (Figure 1.26). In these circumstances, the jet stream may split and flow either side of the blocking anticyclone. This gives rise to two weather extremes, the places where the depressions are being steered towards receive much higher rainfall than normal. The places where they are steered from receive much lower rainfall amounts. During the UK drought of 1976, blocking anticyclonic conditions over England and Wales meant depressions were forced north over Scotland or south over the Mediterranean. Scotland and the Mediterranean consequently had wetter than normal conditions, while England and Wales were drier than normal. From situations like this we can begin to appreciate that extreme weather in one part of the world is often connected to extreme weather in another. This is the concept of **teleconnections**. The most far reaching teleconnections are caused not by anticyclones but by the workings of ocean currents, notably the infamous El Niño (discussed in the next section).

Interpreting synoptic charts

Principles

- Air circulates clockwise round high pressure systems (anticyclones) and anticlockwise round depressions.
- Winds flow almost parallel to the isobars (lines joining places of equal pressure). They cross the isobars at a shallow angle, flowing from higher to lower pressure.
- By following the isobars back along the wind direction and you can tell which air mass the wind is blowing from. This gives you a clue about weather conditions.
- Fronts represent the junction between different air masses. Cold fronts normally have polar air behind and therefore bring colder weather. Warm fronts usually have tropical air behind them and bring warmer weather.
- Clouds and rain are found in three main locations:
  1) at or near fronts
  2) near high land
  3) where air has moved over the sea.
- Clear skies and extremes of temperature are found under anticyclones.

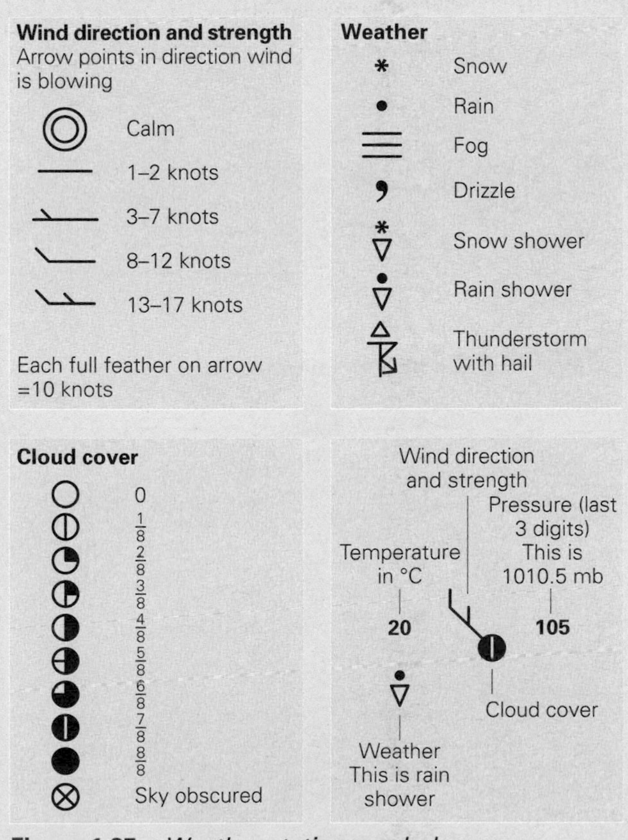

Figure 1.27 *Weather station symbols*

Interpreting satellite images

Figure 1.28 *Interpreting satellite images*
Source: *Meteosat*

Depressions will be anticlockwise swirls of cloud, often shaped like a comma or an inverted 'y'. They are normally easy to spot – the northern end of any long cloud band is usually the centre of a depression.

Anticyclones are even easier to spot – large cloud-free areas are signs of high pressure.

Once the depressions and anticyclones have been spotted, the air masses involved can be determined. Remember that the air flows clockwise round anticyclones and anticlockwise round depressions. The air masses can often be spotted by the cloud type. Mottled cumulonimbus is a sign of unstable (usually south flowing) air. Featureless stratus is a sign of stable (usually northflowing) air. Fronts can be spotted by the tell-tale long line of cloud stretching for hundreds of miles. Weather cannot be determined directly from a satellite image, but it is usually wet under fronts and dry under anticyclones. The temperature will depend on time of day, time of year, distance from the sea and amount of cloud.

4 Global weather and climate

For centuries it has been noted how 'weather catastrophes' periodically form in places far apart, at the same time. In 1982, droughts and fires in Australia coincided with flooding in the arid areas of Peru and Ecuador; wildlife populations plummeted in the Galapagos Islands while beaches in California were reshaped by altered wave conditions. These weather conditions were linked, and the cause was **El Niño**.

El Niño

El Niño (meaning 'the Christ Child') is a warm, southward current that occurs in the Pacific off the coast of Peru in December. The intensity and persistence of this current vary. A large El Niño will cause global scale weather disruption as described above. With a periodicity of 3–7 years El Niño is not uncommon, but the extent to which it causes havoc with the world's normal weather systems is more unpredictable.

Normal conditions

In a normal year, the SE trade winds arising from the global circulation (Figure 1.13) blow from east to west creating the following conditions:

- warm surface waters of the Pacific are blown westwards pooling very warm water near Australasia (Figure 1.29)
- the warm water heats the air in the western Pacific, creating intense convection and thunderstorm activity
- in the eastern Pacific, the removal of warm surface water (blown westward) allows cool, deeper water to rise
- cool upwelling water near Peru creates higher air pressures on the coast of Peru, helping to reinforce the trade wind circulation. Upwelling water is also rich in nutrients, helping to boost the fishing industry.

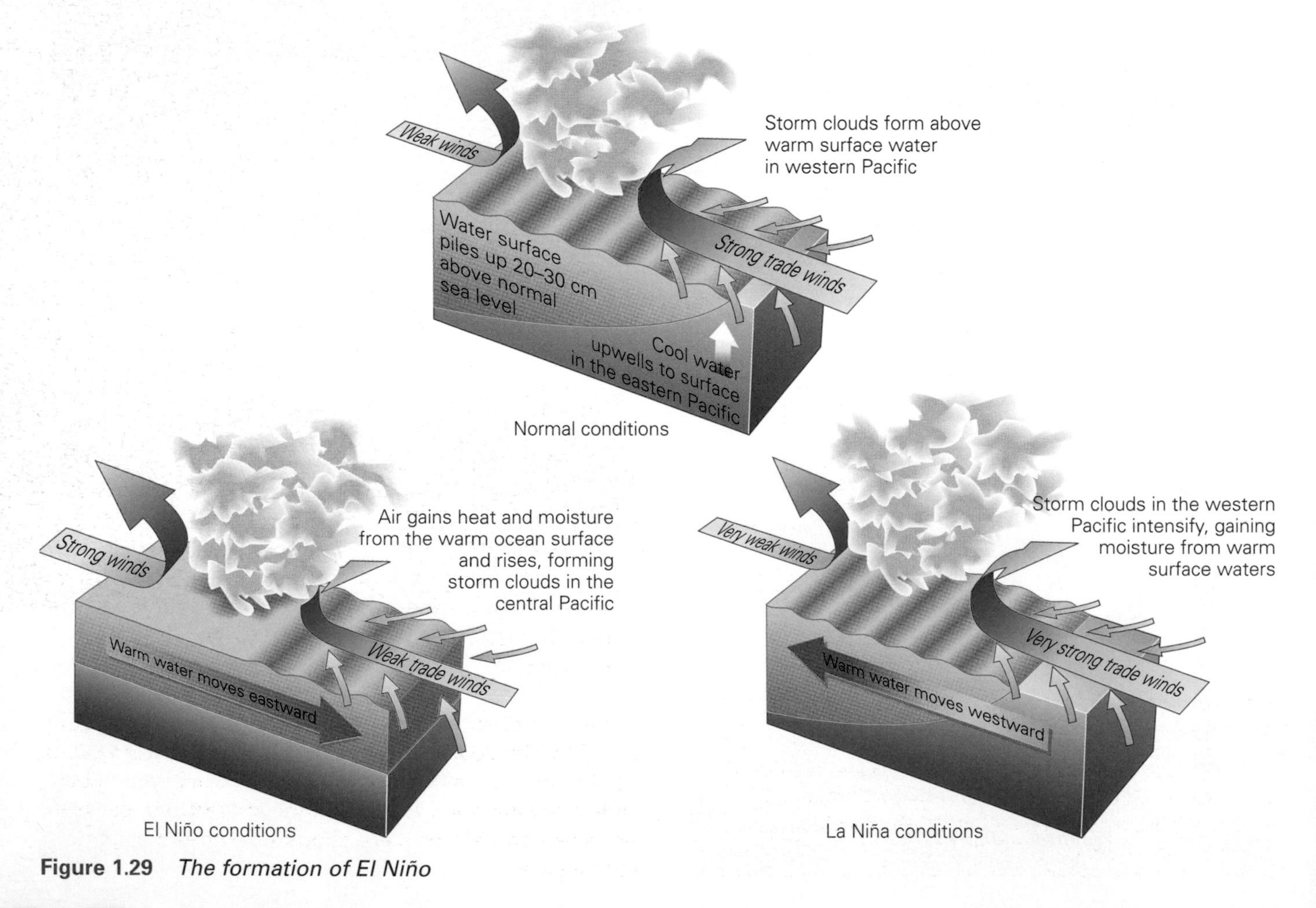

Figure 1.29 *The formation of El Niño*

El Niño and La Niña conditions

If the SE trade winds weaken, a chain of events takes place to create a new condition in the Pacific:

- the warm water piled up in the western Pacific by the trade winds slides back eastwards across the ocean
- the arrival of this warm water at the coast of Peru (El Niño) results in convectional rainfall
- the low pressure resulting from this warm water causes winds to switch direction and blow from west to east, reinforcing the El Niño effect
- the lack of upwelling water offshore Peru causes fish stocks to decline as nutrients are used up
- air descends in the western Pacific to compensate for rising convectional air near Peru
- high pressure develops near Australasia, rainfall ceases and drought develops.

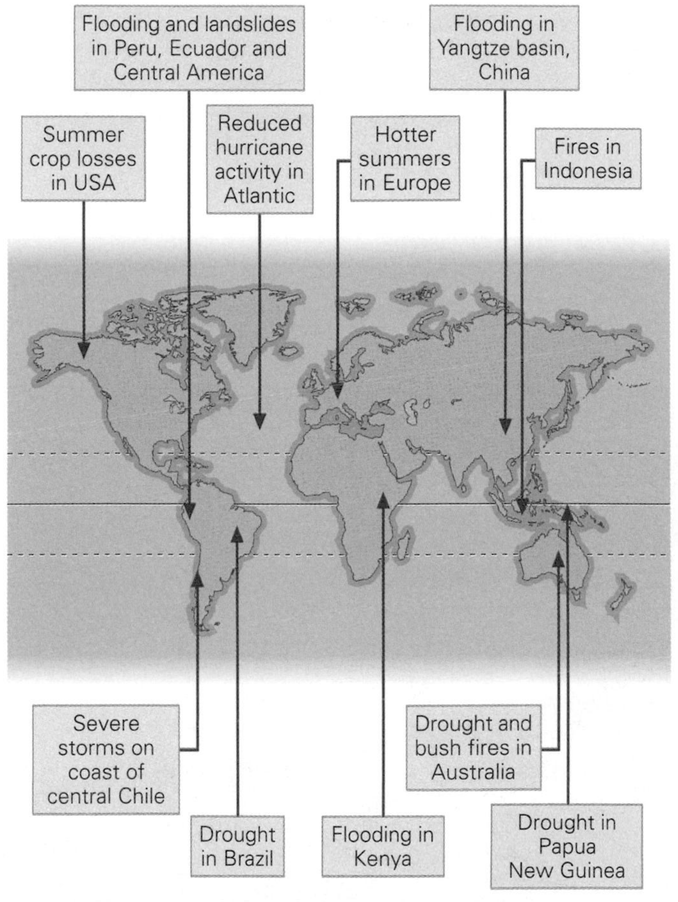

Figure 1.30 *Global impacts of El Niño*

ACTIVITY

Use the USGS El Niño page (walrus.wr.usgs.gov/elnino/) to create an annotated map of North America showing the impact of El Niño / La Niña on ecosystems, landform processes and people.

Figure 1.30 highlights some of the global impacts of an El Niño event. Occasionally, as an El Niño dies out and conditions return to normal, a third weather condition arises – La Niña. This is an exaggerated version of the normal condition where so much warm water has shifted westwards that intensive rainfall creates flooding in Australasia, while intensive droughts grip Peru and other parts of South America. In April and May 2000, the desert around Lake Eyre in Australia flooded during La Niña conditions, creating an inland sea. The desert experienced extraordinary vegetation growth and colonisation by seabirds from up to 1000 km away.

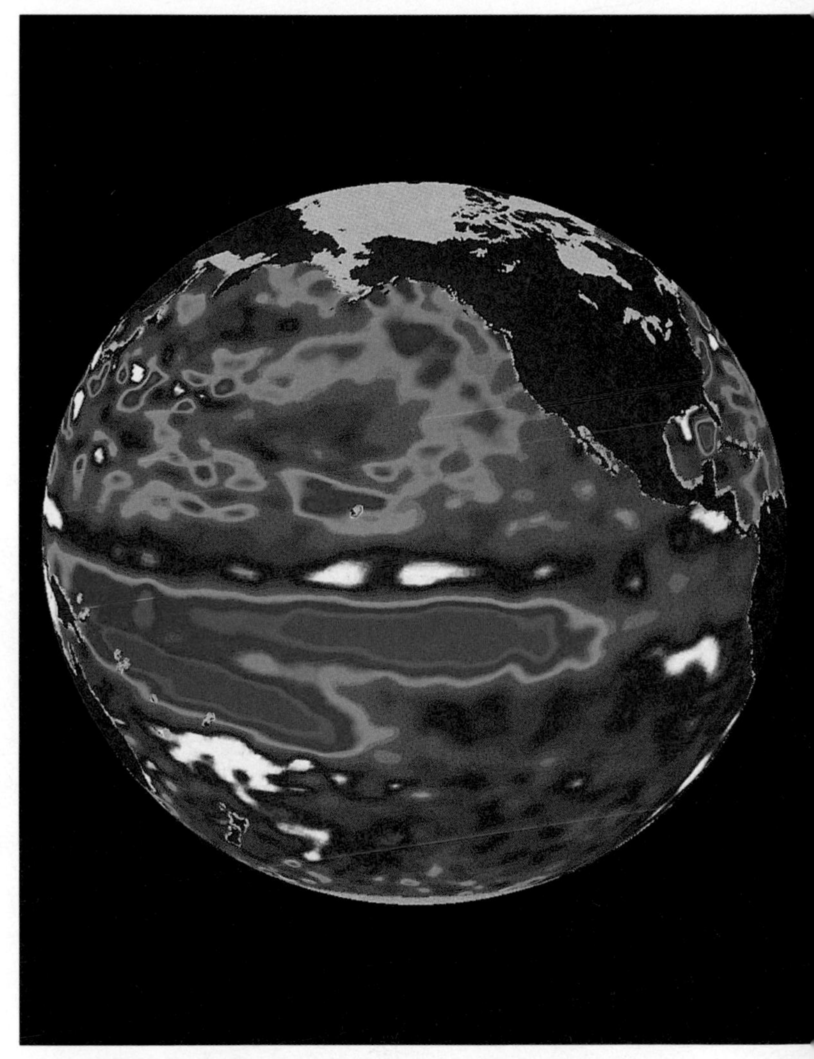

Figure 1.31 *La Niña induced storms in SE Africa*
Source: *NOAA*

La Niña conditions encouraged a very strong wet season in SE Africa in 2000. Flooding was predicted nearly two months before La Niña caused the Mozambique floods. Understanding such long distance interactions between the ocean and atmosphere allows us to begin to predict and prepare.

Linking the ocean and atmospheric processes

El Niño and La Niña form part of a cycle known as **ENSO (El Niño/Southern Oscillation)**. This southern oscillation between normal and El Niño conditions is caused by a change in atmospheric pressure. In order to predict changes in atmospheric pressure up to a year in advance, it is useful to study the ocean. The ocean stores up to a thousand times more of the Sun's heat than the atmosphere, and ocean currents move in slow and predictable ways. Studying sea surface temperature anomalies can help us predict what the atmosphere will be doing in months to come. Since El Niño was discovered, a range of other 'El Niño-type' patterns have been found. These are summarised in Table 1.12.

Scientists now use a combination of satellite imagery and fleets of floating buoys (drifting in major ocean currents) to track variations in ocean climate. Pools of warmer or cooler water embedded in ocean circulations can influence broad weather patterns for whole seasons and thus can be studied for predictive purposes.

Ocean–atmosphere interactions often cause large scale ecosystem changes. The 1997 El Niño resulted in huge population declines of seabirds in Peru. Non-native plant species in the Galapagos have used El Niño years to extend their footholds in the islands. The boom and bust cycles of Canadian and Alaskan salmon fisheries correlate well with the Pacific Decadal Oscillation.

Making use of long term ocean-based forecasts

Peru was badly damaged by the 1982 El Niño. El Niño wrecks the fishing industry, since the warm waters contain few nutrients. Farmers often welcome El Niño's rainfall, but too much can create soil erosion, floods and landslides. Since 1983 the Peruvian Government has been issuing forecasts for the rainy season based on observation of wind and water temperatures in the east Pacific. Forecasts are given on a scale 1–4:

1) near normal conditions
2) weak El Niño – wetter than average growing conditions
3) full El Niño – floods, and fishery decline
4) La Niña – drier than average conditions but good fishing.

Farming choices may be heavily influenced by the forecast. Rice and cotton are both important to Peru's economy. Rice requires wetter conditions so does better in an El Niño year. Cotton grows well in La Niña years. It is not just equatorial nations who will benefit from better predictions of El Niño. Teleconnections between weather in different places means that accurate forecasts of El Niño will benefit billions of people living with a high degree of weather dependency.

Event	Cause	Notable impacts	Timescales
El Niño (ENSO)	• reversal of ocean current related to breakdown and reversal of normal atmospheric conditions	• drought in Australasia • flooding, mudflows and fishery collapse in Peru	• 4–7 years • lasts about 1 year (but up to 2 years in 1990s)
Arctic Oscillation/North Atlantic Oscillation (AO/NAO)	• breakdown of a swirling upper atmosphere wind pattern trapping cold air near the poles • European winters are warm and wet • North Africa and the Middle East have drier winters	• when the vortex breaks down, outflows of polar air into temperate regions bring cold winters to Europe but mild wet conditions in the Mediterranean and North Africa	• can change in days but one mode usually dominates for about a decade. Since 1980 the vortex has mainly remained intact with mild, wet European winters
Antarctic Circumpolar Wave	• alternate pools of warm and cool water circle Antarctica inside the Antarctic Circumpolar Wave	• warm pools near Australia result in warmer, moister winters • cool pools near Australia produce colder drier winters	• alternate warm and cool pools replace one another over a four-year period • they may imprint on top of El Niño effects
Pacific Decadal Oscillation	• oscillation between warm waters along the coast of North America (with cooler waters in the central Pacific), and the reverse condition	• the warm mode brings warm, dry winters to the Northwest Pacific coast • the cold mode brings cool wet conditions to the same area	• the Pacific Decadal Oscillation has a timescale of 20–30 years between mode changes

Table 1.12 *El Niño and other ocean/atmosphere interactions*

Global patterns of climate

With all the different oscillations imprinting on climate, it can be difficult to assess a pattern, but on a global scale key trends can be seen. The most obvious variation in climate is the seasonal migration of the **heat equator**, the region where the sun is directly overhead. The Earth is tilted in its orbit, so at different places in its orbit around the sun it is tilting in different directions, either towards, away from or at right angles to the Sun. On 21 June the sun is directly over the Tropic of Cancer because the northern hemisphere is leaning towards the Sun. On 21 December the situation is reversed and the sun is directly over the Tropic of Capricorn. Between these two dates the position of the heat equator is alternately tracking north and south. The significance of the heat equator moving is that it is the trigger to the global circulation and its accompanying world climate bands (Figure 1.32). When the heat equator moves, the global climate belts move with it.

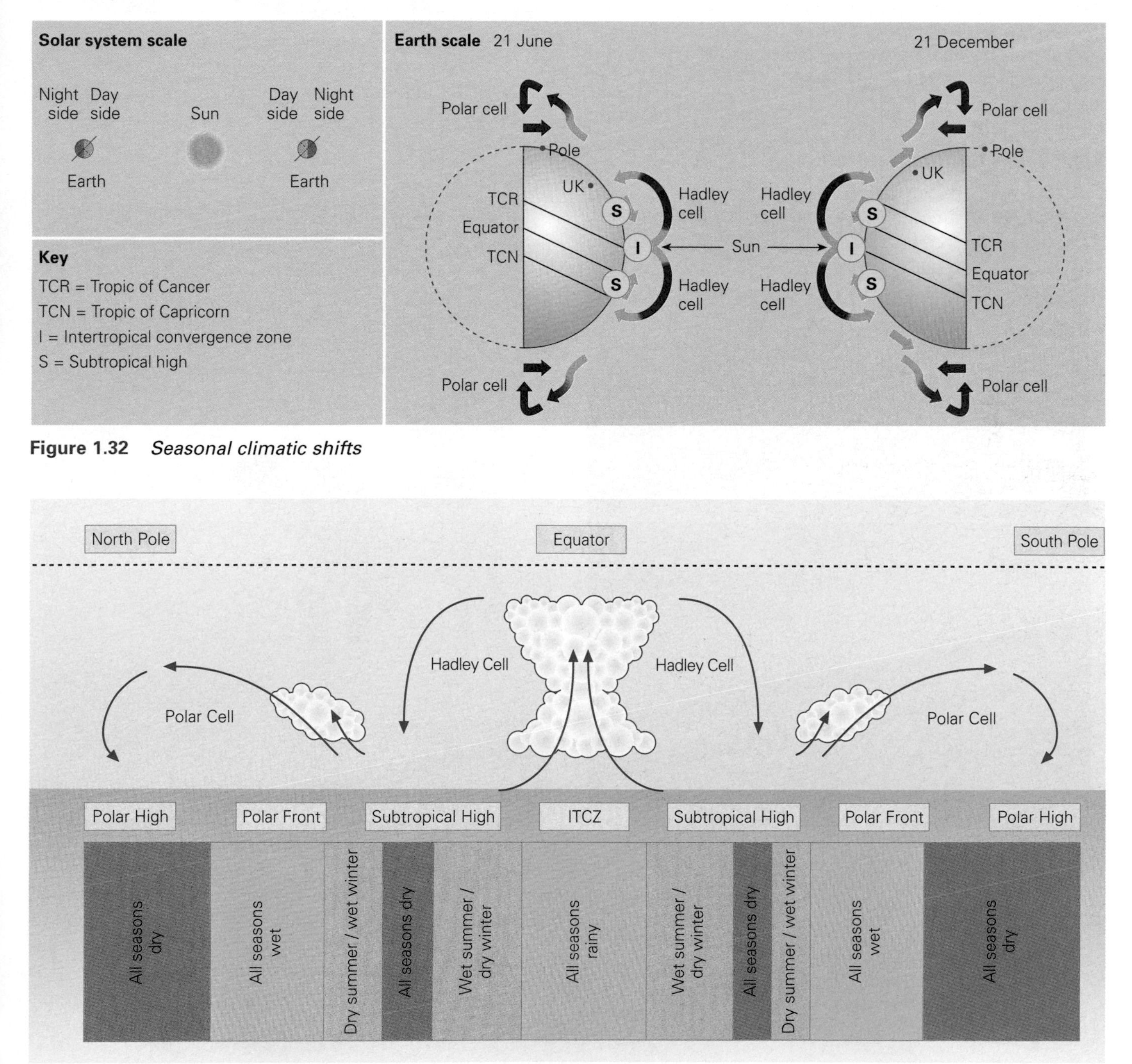

Figure 1.32 *Seasonal climatic shifts*

Figure 1.33 *Global climate regions*

ITCZ migration

On the heat equator, under the overhead sun, lies the ITCZ (Inter Tropical Convergence Zone) (Figures 1.13 and 1.33). In this zone, warm, rising air creates a belt of low pressure which draws in the trade winds from either side of the equator. This warm air creates intense convectional activity, making the ITCZ a region of high rainfall totals (1,500–2,500 mm/yr). Poleward of the ITCZ, near the tropics, the downward cascade of air from the top of the Hadley Cell produces a dry belt, known as the **Subtropical High**. This region of high pressure creates a zone of cloud-free, sunny weather either side of the heat equator. The Hadley cell therefore creates a 'climate sandwich' with a region of high rainfall sandwiched between two adjacent areas of aridity.

ACTIVITIES

1 In which season is:
   a the subtropical high pressure furthest south?
   b polar air over Europe and the UK?
   c heavy rain over the Tropic of Capricorn?
2 In reality, the world's climate regions do not show very clear bands parallel to the equator. Suggest how relief and the distribution of continents/oceans might disrupt the simple bands on the model. Use the climate pages of an atlas to find examples of such disruption.

Adaptations to ITCZ migration

Adapting to high rainfall and high temperature

- near the equator the chief **limiting factor** in an ecosystem is light
- a successful plant strategy is therefore to grow as tall as possible
- trees dominate in this ecosystem

Adapting to seasonal drought

- closer to the tropics the limiting factor is rainfall as rain is delivered in a short wet season
- this environment is difficult for trees as fully grown trees can transpire over 600 litres of water a day. If water is unavailable, the tree will wilt and die
- these semi-arid areas are characterised by plants with a rapid lifecycle that can exploit the short wet season
- grass is well adapted to these conditions

Figure 1.34 *Vegetation adaptations*

Fauna adaptations

The fauna of these contrasting regions is adapted to the climate. Many species inhabiting the dry, tropical grasslands cope by following the seasonal wet weather as the ITCZ moves away. Some species (e.g. rodents) have developed burrowing habits to cope with the high temperatures in the semi-arid regions. In the tropical forests the abundant productivity means that survival is relatively easy. The main competition a species faces is from its own offspring, so tropical forest species often have low breeding rates.

Human adaptations

In areas with short periods of highly seasonal rainfall, if the rain fails to come one year, the population have no chance of recovery until the rains return in a year's time. If the rain fails again it is possible that the ecological and social structure of the area will collapse. In semi-arid areas the most significant water store is the soil. A healthy vegetation cover maintains a healthy soil which, in turn, maintains good vegetation cover. Overuse of soil in marginal areas has resulted in wind and water erosion, leading to desertification. Thinner soils hold less water and therefore recycle less back to the air, discouraging rainfall formation.

Figure 1.35 shows how easily the sensitive link between humans, ecosystems and climate can be disturbed to create a vicious circle of degradation. Figure 1.36 shows the end result, clouds of dust formed as vital topsoil becomes airborne during the dry season.

Figure 1.35 shows that drought is caused by other factors as well as climate. Managing drought can be technically difficult and politically impossible. It involves more than managing water supplies. Table 1.13 (overleaf) illustrates some of the options available.

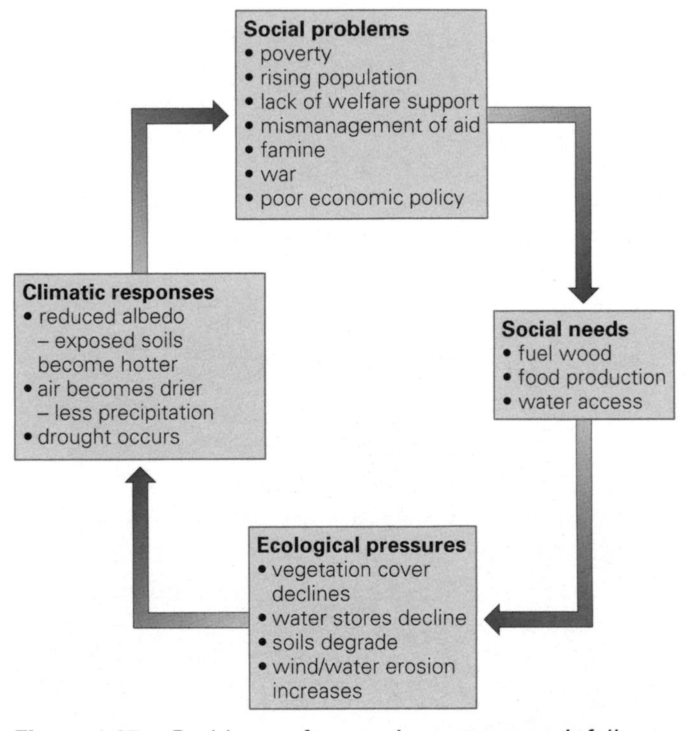

Figure 1.35 *Problems of managing extreme rainfall variations*

Figure 1.36 *Dust clouds over Africa*
Source: *NOAA*

Arid adaptation

The original inhabitants of the Sahel region of Africa were well adapted to the unreliable rainfalls of the region. Based on pastoral farming, tribes such as the Tuareg would move around following the rains. By the 1960s, however, many nations were seeking independence from the colonial European powers. Independence created a strong sense of nationality and a greater concern with borders. Traditional migration routes became hindered by border controls. A combination of factors has reduced the ability of people to cope with the unpredictable rainfalls of the Sahel region. These include:

- government programmes to settle nomads
- reduced infant mortality
- government-sponsored change to a cash cropping economy to fulfil debt service obligations (see Unit 2).

Physical responses	Political responses
• improve existing water storage by improving vegetation cover, building small dams on streams, conserving soil by good farming practice • tap new water stores by exploiting groundwater resources (at rates at or below natural replenishment levels) • alter farming – grow more drought-tolerant crops, reduce livestock numbers	• develop water sharing agreements with neighbouring states • encourage sustainable agriculture based on low rainfalls (rather than relying on irrigation) • set pricing policies for urban/industrial water supplies that reflect the true cost and availability of water
Economic responses	**Social responses**
• invest in rural development • monitor the impact of food prices on food availability • monitor international exchange rates and their impacts on purchasing power • invest in water supply infrastructure	• provide food aid • pipe water from outside the area • improve sanitation to reduce water-borne diseases • set up refugee camps where water supplies are more dependable

Table 1.13 *Managing drought*

In 1999, the International Water Management Institute produced a report, *Water Scarcity in the 21st Century*. The study identified 17 countries facing 'absolute water scarcity' by 2025 (i.e. these countries will not have enough water to maintain 1990 levels of per capita food production, industry, household and environmental needs). The 17 countries are Afghanistan, Egypt, Saudi Arabia, Pakistan, Israel, Jordan, Iran, Iraq, Kuwait, Syria, Tunisia, United Arab Emirates, Yemen, Singapore, South Africa, Oman, Libya (as well as parts of India and China). The study notes that those who will suffer most will be people in the world's poorest nations, who already walk great distances to retrieve water for household needs. The Middle East is a particularly vulnerable region.

Water flashpoint – Middle East

- The area contains 5% of the world's population, but only 1% of the world's fresh water.
- Per capita water availability has fallen 60% in 40 years and is estimated to fall a further 50% from present levels in the next 30 years.
- 87% of fresh water is used in rural agriculture, contributing little to national economy but lots to the health of the rural poor.
- Water losses in urban distribution networks often exceed 50% due to leaky pipes and poor maintenance.
- Nine nations share the Nile's water supplies – one of the major keys to regional development.
- Egypt has already stated it is prepared 'to go to war' to safeguard its water supplies.
- Other nations on the Nile are beginning to get more vociferous about their rights to the Nile's water.
- Global warming predictions for this part of the world suggest reduced rainfall will greatly increase the pressure on the Nile's water supplies.

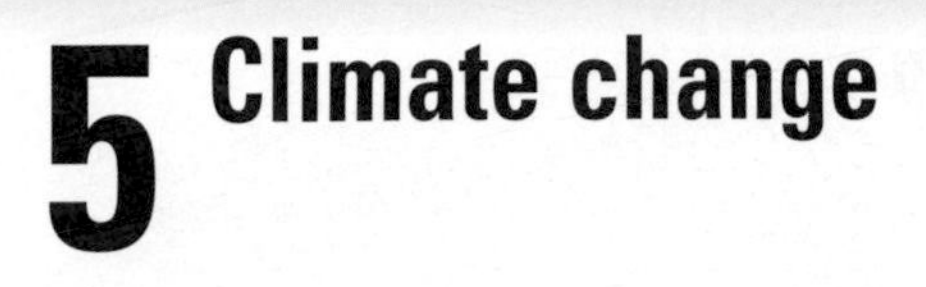

5 Climate change

Climate is never entirely stable. Over long timescales (50 million years), the Earth's climate has experienced gradual changes. Over the last one million years we find huge variations of climate (Figure 1.37).

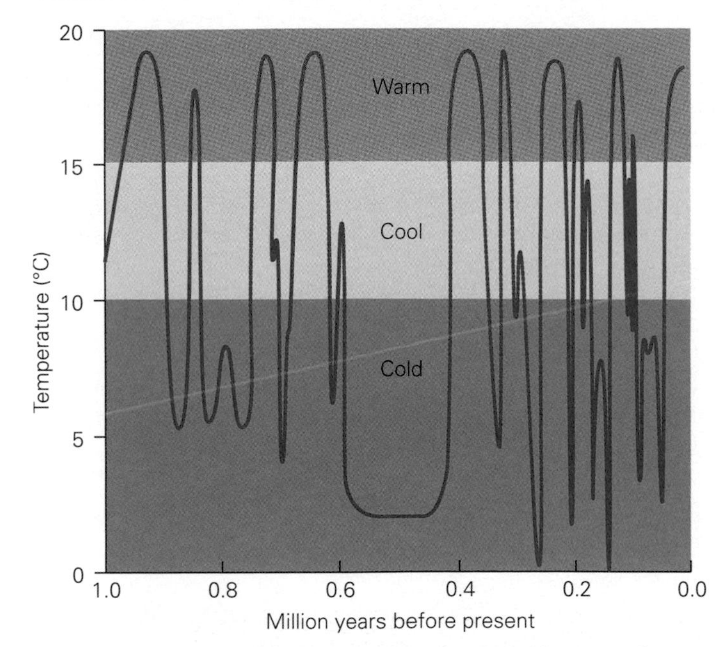

Figure 1.37 *Estimated summer temperatures over the last one million years*

Over historical time climate has also varied. During a warm climate in the tenth century, the Vikings colonised Greenland, at the time a green and hospitable land where they raised sheep and cattle and grew grain. By the fifteenth century the climate was so cold that Greenland was abandoned. Evidence from Greenland suggests temperatures may have been 3°C warmer at the height of its colonisation – a similar temperature rise is predicted for the middle of the next century. Climate is dynamic, it not only varies with time but also with space. It can therefore be difficult to assess whether historical changes were global or regional.

Mechanisms of climate change

We do not fully understand the mechanisms behind climate change but it is clear that the following influence the natural variability of climate:

Regular mechanisms

Variations in Earth's orbit known as the **Milankovitch cycles**.

Milankovitch cycles

Climatic change can be explained in part by changes in the orbit of the Earth. These are known as the Milankovitch cycles and relate to the combined effects of the three orbital variations outlined below.

1 Change in orbital shape
The Earth's orbit around the Sun is an ellipse, but over a 100,000-year cycle it oscillates from being elliptical to circular. This influences the amount and timing of radiation received from the Sun (Figure 1.38).

2 Change in the Earth's tilt
The 23.5° tilt in the Earth's axis as it orbits the Sun is not constant over time. The Earth sometimes tilts more and sometimes less over a cycle of 41,000 years. This influences the extent of seasonal climate change, the smaller the tilt, the less seasonal variation there is between summer and winter.

3 Wobble of Earth around axis
As the Earth rotates on its axis, it wobbles. This occurs over a 22,000-year cycle. This means that summer will occur at a slightly different point in the orbit each year, nearer or further from the sun.

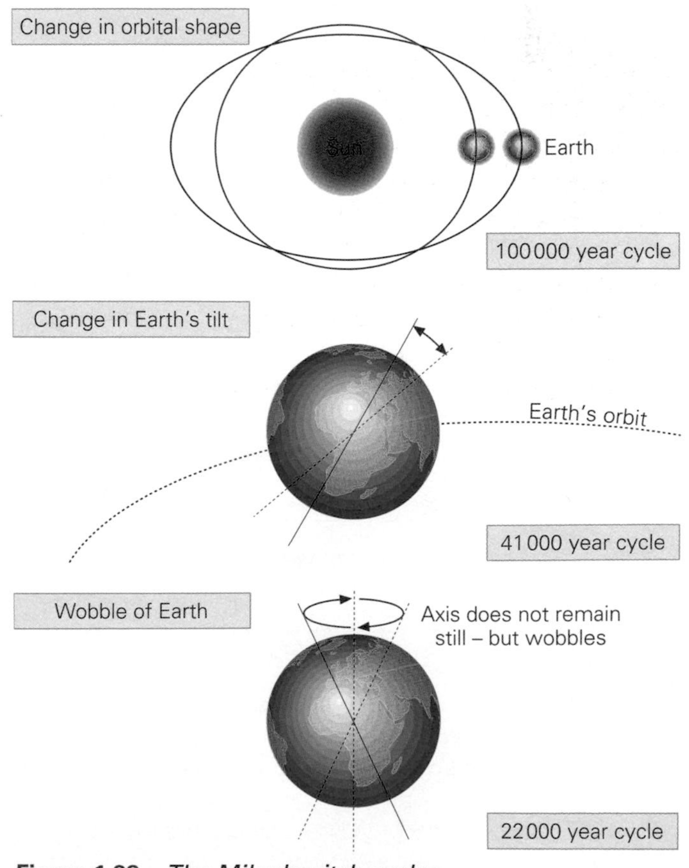

Figure 1.38 *The Milankovitch cycles*

Irregular mechanisms

Volcanic activity and asteroid/comet impact can both cause the atmosphere to become dustier and less transparent to incoming solar radiation, thus reducing temperatures. For example, world-wide cooling was recorded following the eruption of Krakatoa in 1883.

Uncertain mechanisms

Variations in the Sun's activity are known to take place, for example, it is thought that the sun may have been less energetic around the seventeenth and eighteenth centuries. This may explain the **Little Ice Age** which occurred at this time when Western Europe experienced very cold winters.

The challenge for scientists is to separate the normal climatic variability from the influence of humans. The way they do this is shown in Figure 1.39.

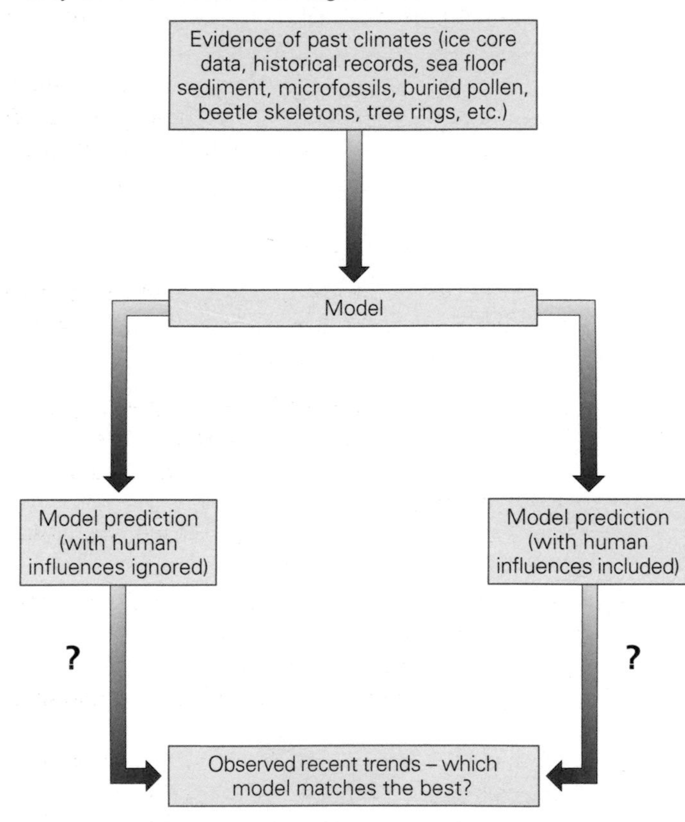

Figure 1.39 *Modelling climatic variability*

ACTIVITIES

1. 'By 2050, Greenland will have the same temperatures that enabled its settlement in the tenth century. Why all the fuss about global warming? We've been there already and survived.'
   Write a short critique of the statement above explaining the weaknesses of the statement.

Global warming

Greenhouse effect – the mechanism by which some of the heat escaping from the Earth's surface is reabsorbed and reflected by certain gases in the atmosphere. This mechanism keeps the planet's average temperatures warm enough to support life.

Enhanced greenhouse effect – the impact of people increasing the greenhouse effect by human activities, notably the use of fossil fuels and deforestation.

Global warming – the consequence of an enhanced greenhouse effect. The planet will continue to warm until a new equilibrium is reached between rate of heat gain and rate of heat loss.

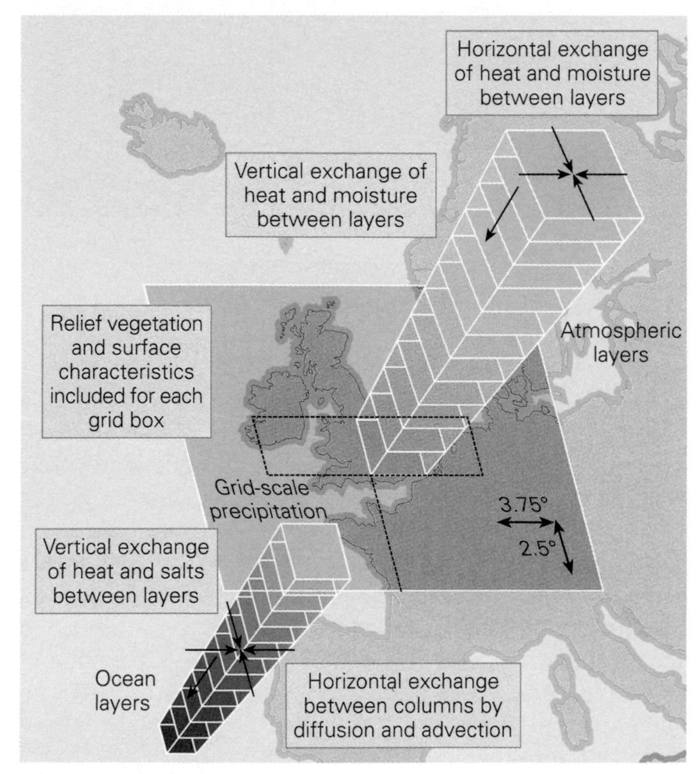

Figure 1.40 *A global climate model*

From the definitions above, it is clear that the greenhouse effect is neither artificial nor bad. In order to determine the nature of human impact on the greenhouse effect we need to separate human influence from natural variability. This can be achieved using computer models of climate (Figure 1.40). In such a model, a region is divided into squares, and different layers of the atmosphere and ocean are incorporated. The interactions between each cell are then calculated for weeks, years and decades ahead. To test the model, known climate conditions are put as a starting point and the model predicts climate for the recent past. The predicted temperature changes are then compared to the actual observations. To test if climatic change is natural or human induced (Figure 1.39), we can run the model twice: 1) with only natural factors built in 2) with twentieth-century pollution levels built in. Results from such modelling suggest that the best correlation is achieved with human pollution included. This implies two things: first, humans are probably influencing climate change; second, the model is probably a reasonable tool for predicting into the middle of the next century. The results of predictions for the UK region are summarised below.

- winter and summer average temperatures will rise between 1.2°C and 1.6°C with greatest warming in the east
- Scotland will show increased precipitation in both seasons (up to 5%) but southern England will experience 5% less summer rainfall, as well as the higher temperatures
- snowfall will decrease
- windspeed will increase
- air quality in cities will decline as hotter summer temperatures encourage increased smog incidence
- sea levels will rise and floods will become more frequent.

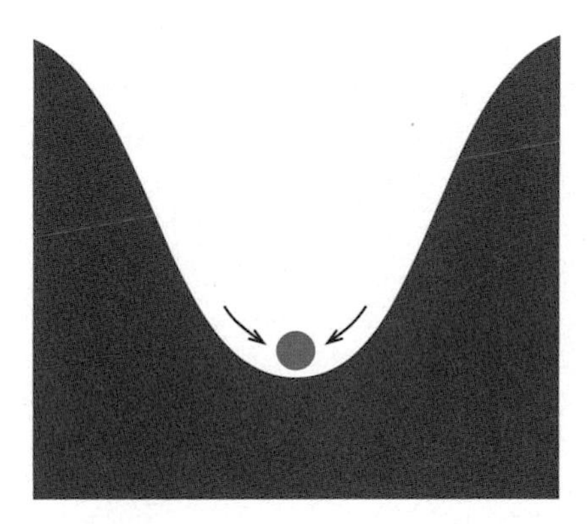

STABLE SYSTEM
Any movement away from the equilibrium position is quickly reversed

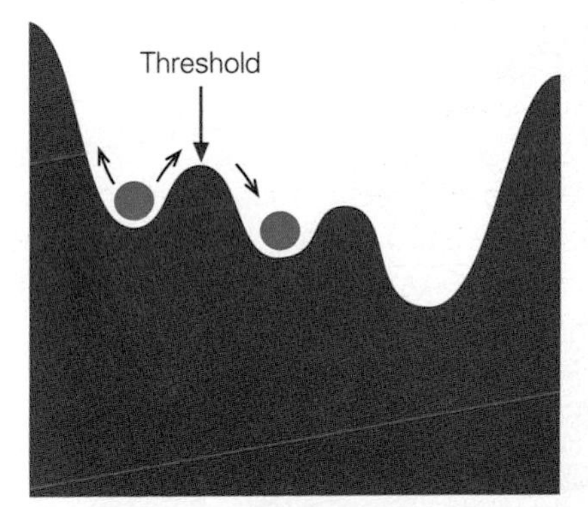

METASTABLE SYSTEM
Small movements from the stable position will easily reverse, but a larger movement may move the system beyond a threshold point to a new, but very different, stable state. The worry with global warming is that we may cross this threshold

Figure 1.41 *Stable and metastable systems*

Climate is a **metastable** system, i.e. it will experience long periods of equilibrium (e.g. an ice age or interglacial) and will suddenly flip to a new state. We do not know what triggers the sudden change. There may be **threshold conditions** (Figure 1.41) which create an irreversible lurch in the climate system. Furthermore, whilst we can anticipate some of the feedback loops in the climate system, three problems remain:

1) we do not know all the feedback loops
2) we do not know the relative priority of feedback loops. For example, more warming melts ice, revealing darker surfaces underneath, which encourage more warming still. But warmer air holds more water, causing higher snowfalls in cold regions. Snow reflects solar radiation resulting in cooling. Which will dominate? Heat induced heating or heat induced cooling? The answers could be very significant so the safest approach is to minimise **anthropogenic** ('human induced') impacts on the atmosphere
3) we cannot predict many of the human impacts which will influence future CO_2 levels, for example, population growth, industrial growth, energy use, deforestation rates.

Wider impacts of global warming

If global warming continues as predicted, it will profoundly affect the environment, societies, politics and economics. Some key concerns are highlighted below:

- 46 million people are affected by flooding each year. This number could double in the next 50 years
- river and coastal floods are already the main causes of death by natural hazards
- some of the worst flooding will be in areas least able to afford protection, e.g. Bangladesh
- low-lying delta regions such as the Yellow River Delta (population 18 million) in China and the Ganges–Brahmaputra delta in Bangladesh are areas of high population density and also highly vulnerable to storm surges
- as the frequency and magnitude of storms increases, there is an increase in the probability of a coastal storm surge coinciding with a river flood and a high tide
- warmer conditions and more climatic extremes will create new opportunities for pests and disease. Droughts encourage pests into agricultural areas. Floods encourage outbreaks of disease
- tropical diseases will expand their range as the disease-carrying organisms move into new territories
- the world's ecosystems will experience high stress levels and some will shrink significantly.

Researching the impacts of global climate change

Many of the most up-to-date resources on global warming are to be found on the Internet. Use the sites listed below to search for some recent predictions. Since website addresses change and new sites are always coming online, hints on constructing an efficient search using a search engine such as Alta Vista are provided.

Sources

The Intergovernmental Panel on Climate Change – www.ipcc.ch/

Carbon Dioxide Information Analysis Centre – cdiac.esd.ornl.gov/cdiac/

Hadley Centre for Climate Prediction and Research – www.met-office.gov.uk/sec5/sec5pg1.html

Environmental Protection Agency – www.epa.gov/globalwarming/impacts/index.html

Ozone action group – www.ozone.org/page20.html

World resources institute – www.wri.org/climate/publications.html

Indian viewpoints – www.oneworld.net/cse/html/cmp/cmp33.htm

Climate change links pages – gcmd.gsfc.nasa.gov/

Hints on using search engines

- Enclose phrases in speech marks (e.g. '**climate change**' is better than **climate change**). This avoids picking up too many irrelevant pages where both words appear, but in unrelated contexts.
- Narrow the number of results by putting a plus sign in front of key words or phrases. Thus +'**global warming**'+**impacts** +**costs** will give a much more finely tuned result than +**'global warming' impacts costs** because the latter will pick out thousands of pages about costs (product costs, holiday costs, etc.) but few will be about global warming costs.
- Narrow the results further by putting a minus sign in front of pages you wish to exclude. A search for +**'global warming'** +**impacts** -**'sea level'** will omit pages with information on sea level rise, allowing you to concentrate on other impacts.

Will global warming create a colder Europe?

Recent climate research has shown that natural climatic changes can take place extremely quickly. At the end of the last ice age (12,000 years ago), evidence from trapped air bubbles in ice cores shows subtle changes in the composition of oxygen which can be accurately related to temperature. The evidence suggests that Europe's mean temperature varied as much as 9°C in the space of 50 years. The speed of this change may have implications for the Gulf Stream, the warm water current which keeps Europe's temperatures so mild for their latitude. Figure 1.42 shows that the flow of the warm Gulf Stream depends on heavy, salty water sinking in the North Atlantic. An increase in air temperature would result in melting of the polar ice and an inundation of fresh water. This additional meltwater flowing into the Arctic Ocean could lead to a breakdown of the Gulf Stream and significant cooling for Western Europe. The complacency that many feel about a hot, sunny 'globally-warmed' Europe would evaporate very quickly if the Gulf Stream turned down!

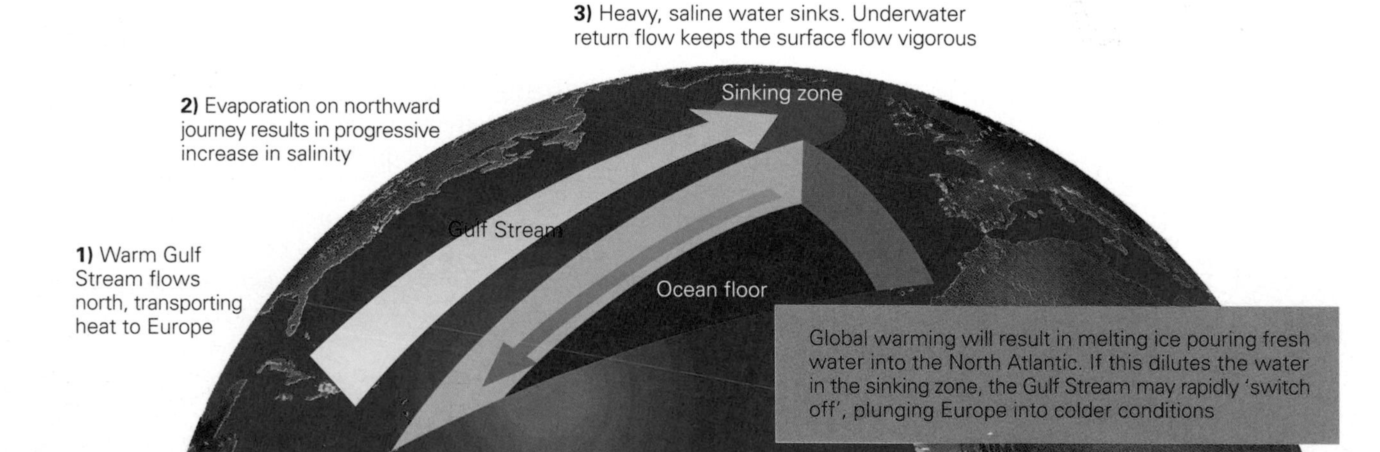

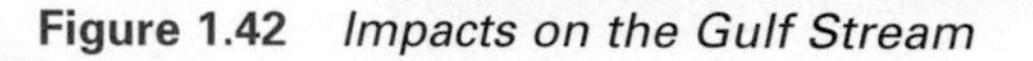
Figure 1.42 *Impacts on the Gulf Stream*

ACTIVITIES

Research the following impacts of global warming and make notes on each.

1. The effect of warming on soil moisture, i.e. it results in severe reductions in semi arid areas.
2. The effects on global biomes, i.e. some will benefit from increased CO_2, temperature or rainfall changes and bands of vegetation will shift on a global scale.
3. The increase in extreme climatic events, e.g. winter storms in Europe or drought in Spain.
4. The rise in sea level, i.e. the implications for low-lying countries. Doubling CO_2 levels could create a 1m rise in sea level.
5. Changing circulation in the ocean. This could have unexpected feedback on temperate regions related to the breakdown of the Gulf Stream.
6. The effects on human health, i.e. the spread of diseases such as malaria and dengue fever.

'(The present heatwave) does not have anything to do with global climate patterns like El Niño'
S R Kalsi, deputy director general of the Indian Meteorological Department

'The heatwave cannot straightaway be linked to global anomalies like El Niño or global warming'
R K Dutta, former head of the National Centre for Medium Range Weather Forecasting in New Delhi

'It can be seen that the maximum number of heatwave days and the human lives lost during May and June over the Indian subcontinent are comparatively large during the years 1983, 1988, 1995 and 1998. These years were preceded by El Niño'
U S De, Director general of meteorology at the Central Observatory, Pune

'(The heatwaves) are initial signals of global warming'
M Lal, chief scientific officer at the Centre for Atmospheric Studies at the Indian Institute of Technology, New Delhi

'Ten of the warmest years on record have all occurred since 1983, with seven of them since 1990'
World Meteorological Organization

'Climate models suggest that both winter and summer rainfall will decline in the Indian subcontinent'
M Lal, chief scientific officer at the Centre for Atmospheric Studies at the Indian Institute of Technology, New Delhi

Figure 1.43 *Heatwaves in India*

Is global warming sabotaging India's climate?

In 1998, heatwaves in India claimed at least 1,350 lives. There is much debate as to whether these heatwaves were caused by global warming. The mean surface temperature in India has increased by 0.4°C in the past 100 years. Figure 1.43 shows a range of informed opinions about the Indian heatwaves.

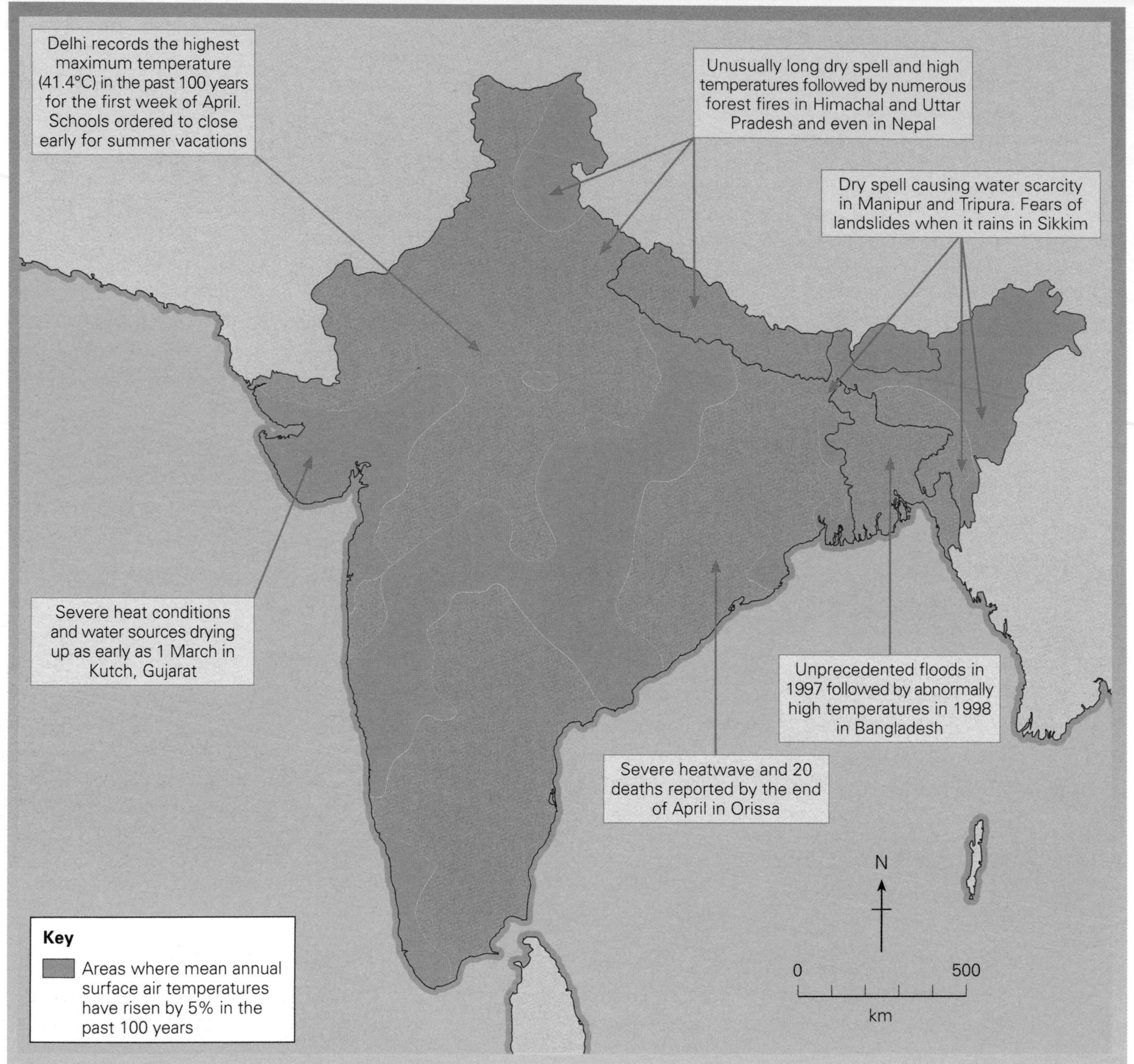

Figure 1.44 *Climatic impacts on India in 1998*

Despite the droughts in India, a significant number of meteorological stations are recording intense rainfalls with associated floods. In the long term, climate models suggest monsoon rainfalls may reduce slightly, with increased potential for drought. If smaller volumes of rainfall are delivered in more experience bursts, India could experience more flooding *and* more drought.

In 1998, cyclone 05B devastated the state of Orissa with heavy rains and torrential flooding. By Spring 2000, drought gripped several Indian states and threatened to resurrect the famines that plagued India 30 years ago. All major towns of north Gujarat and more than one-third of the state's 18,000 villages struggled for a daily supply of drinking water, while over 70% of the state's dams were dry. At the same time, the Tata Chemicals factory in Jamnagar district was extracting 14 million litres of water every day.

ACTIVITIES

1 Justify, with evidence, the statement 'India's future climate is a source of anxiety but it is difficult to make effective predictions as to cause and effect'.

Chapter Two: Ecosystems

1 Defining and valuing ecosystems

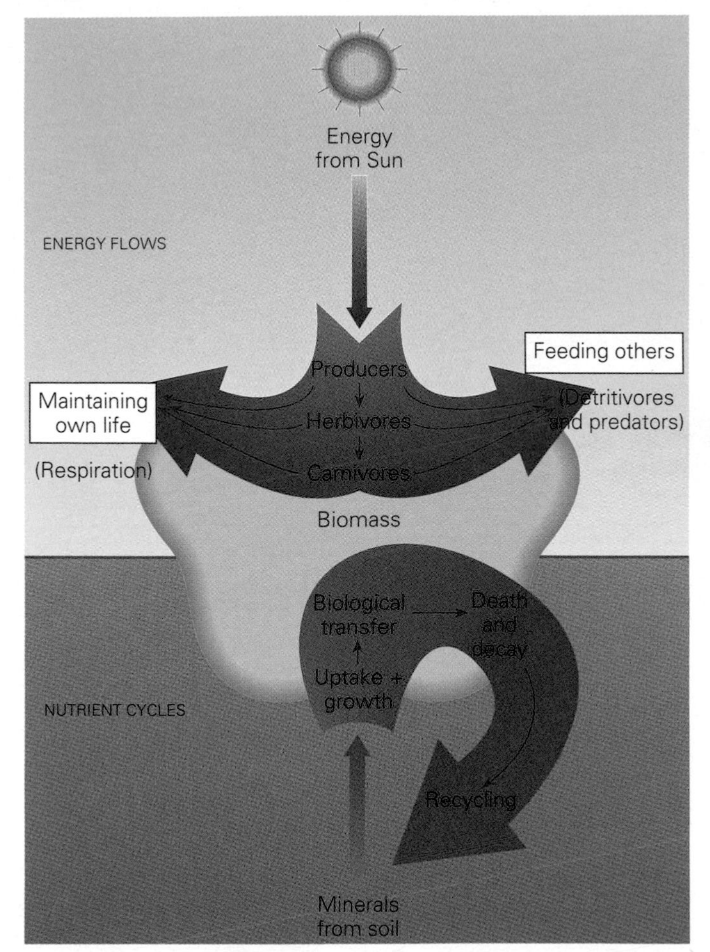

Figure 2.1 *Ecosystems – bridges between systems*

Atmospheric processes

- heat budgets (vegetation colour; evapotranspiration rates; wind friction)
- gas exchange – CO_2 and O_2; global temperature regulation
- moisture budgets – evapotranspiration and interception; rainfall nuclei (sulphur compounds released by oceanic algae); infiltration rates and soil structure

Living organisms

Surface processes

- rock weathering rates (root action, soil pH, etc.)
- river flow rates and hydrograph responses
- erosion rates and stream sediment loads
- coastal sedimentation rates; coastal protection via reefs, mangroves, salt marshes, etc.

Figure 2.2 *Ecosystems as global regulators*

Ecosystems are interacting communities of organisms linked by physical and chemical processes to each other and to their environment (Figure 2.1). An ecosystem has two basic functions:

- to recycle nutrients
- to redistribute energy.

In 1972, James Lovelock published the Gaia hypothesis. This theory suggests that the **biosphere** regulates the environment to keep conditions at an optimum for life's continuation. This process can be seen on a small scale where plant succession transforms a bare rock **lithosere** to a deep soil with forest vegetation over the space of eight or nine decades. On a global scale, ecosystems have an important role in regulating atmospheric and surface processes (Figure 2.2). Humans value ecosystems in terms of their potential resources for consumption and for their ability to provide the planetary systems on which our lives depend.

Global patterns of productivity

At the simplest level, **ecological productivity** (the amount of new biomass produced in a year) depends on four factors:

- temperature – influences the rate of chemical reactions
- moisture – a key component in many chemical reactions and a major transport agent
- nutrients – the raw ingredients of biological tissue
- light – the fundamental requirement of photosynthesis, at the base of most food chains.

Where these four factors are abundant, ecosystems will be highly productive. If any one of the four ingredients is missing it will act as a **limiting factor**, reducing overall production.

The many permutations of light, moisture, temperature and nutrient availability across the globe create distinctive regions where broadly similar conditions attract broadly similar adaptations. This is the concept of a **biome**, a global scale ecosystem (Figures 2.3 and 2.4). Within each biome we can distinguish two important measures of productivity, **net primary production** and **biomass**.

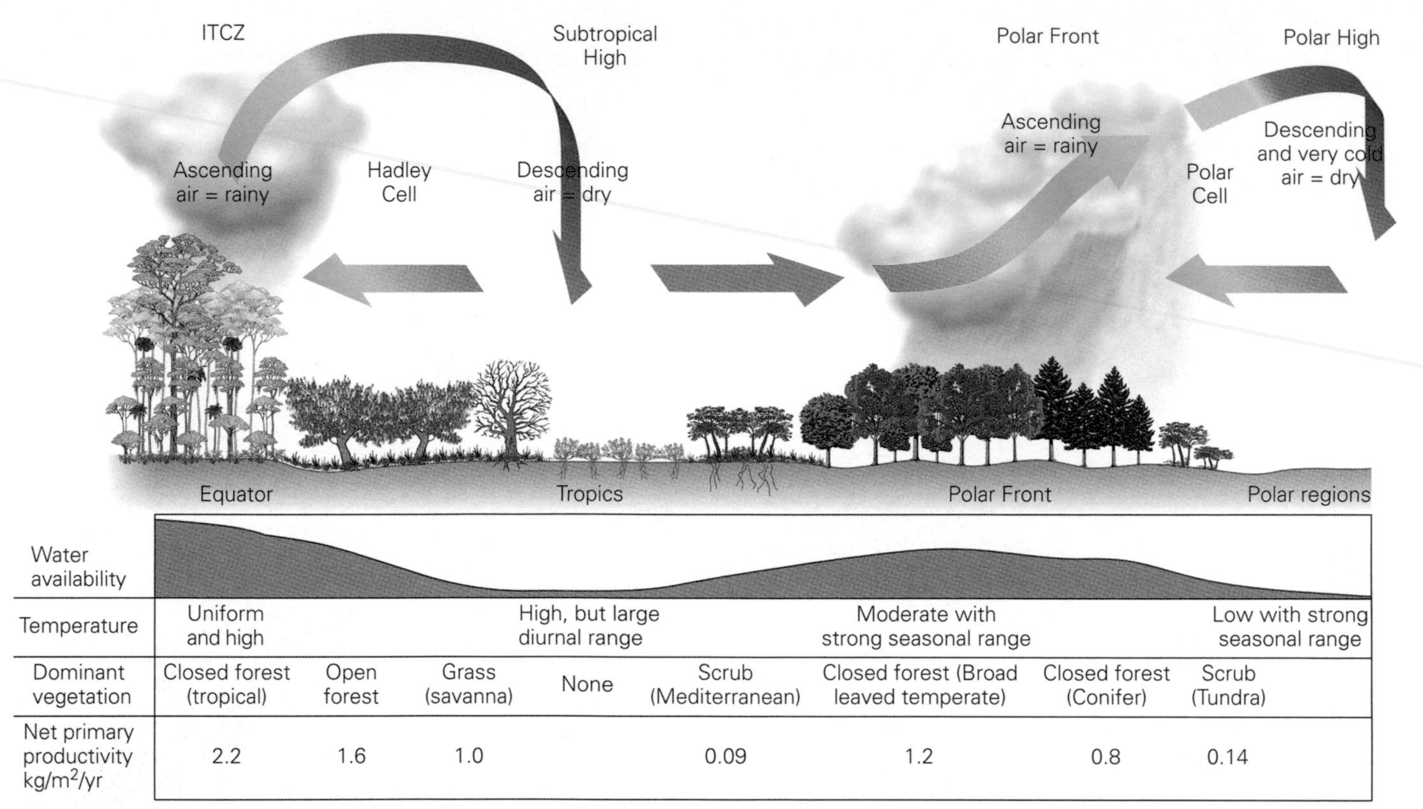

Water availability								
Temperature	Uniform and high			High, but large diurnal range		Moderate with strong seasonal range		Low with strong seasonal range
Dominant vegetation	Closed forest (tropical)	Open forest	Grass (savanna)	None	Scrub (Mediterranean)	Closed forest (Broad leaved temperate)	Closed forest (Conifer)	Scrub (Tundra)
Net primary productivity kg/m²/yr	2.2	1.6	1.0		0.09	1.2	0.8	0.14

Figure 2.3 *The global circulation and ecosystems*

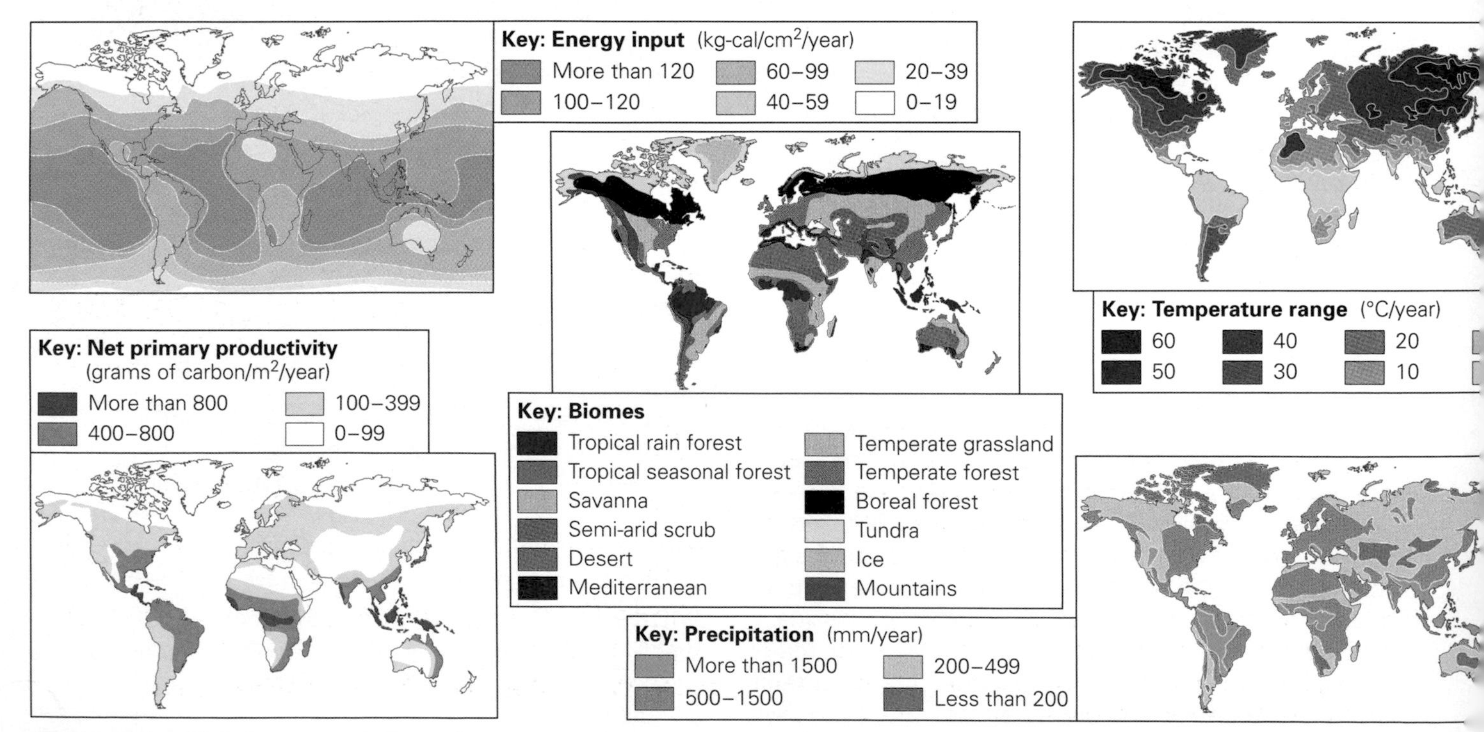

Figure 2.4 *Global patterns influencing ecosystems*

ACTIVITIES

1 Study the maps in Figure 2.4. Which maps best account for:
   a plant productivity
   b the distribution of forest areas
   c the distribution of grassland areas
   d the diversity of bivalve (shellfish) populations?

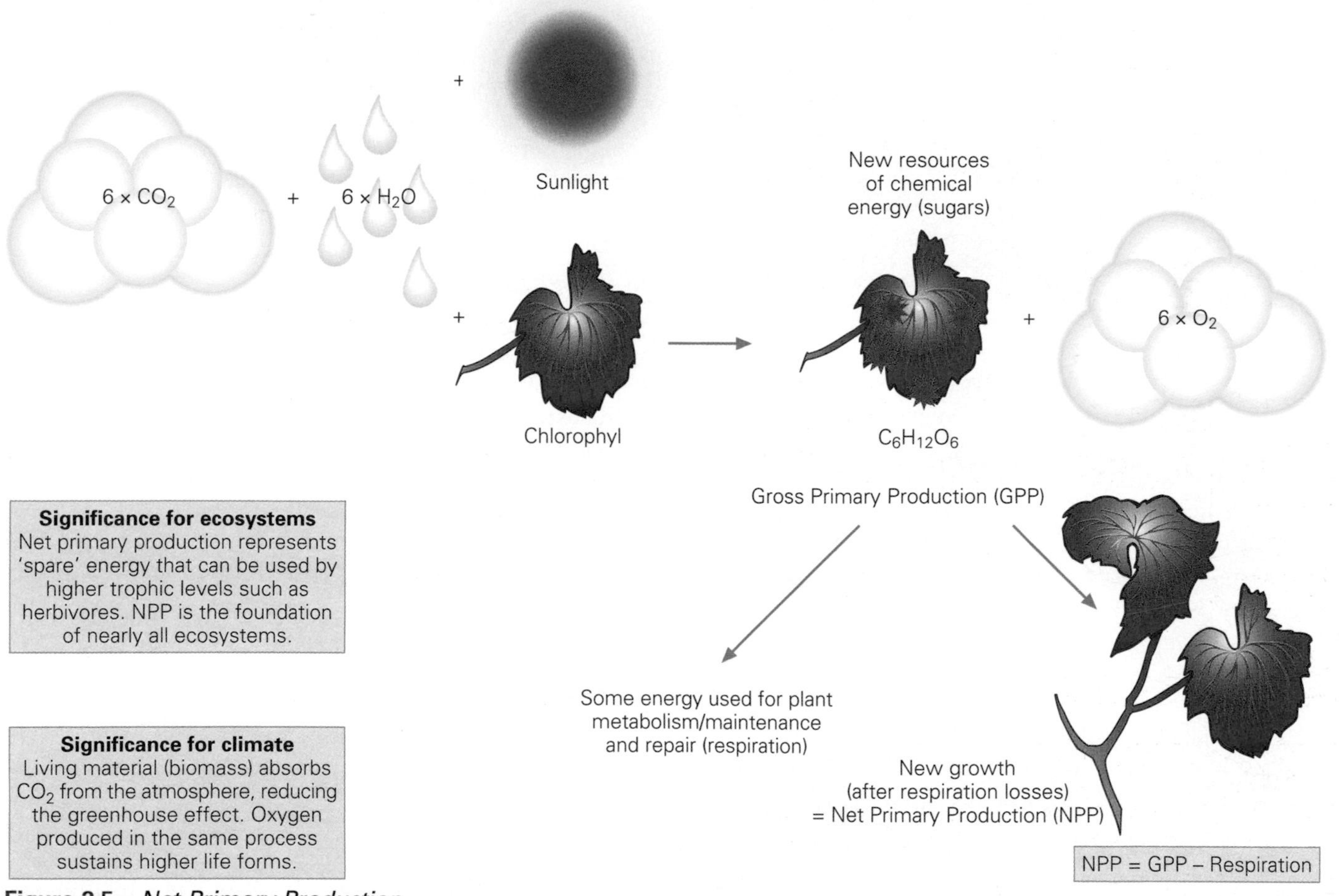

Figure 2.5 *Net Primary Production*

Net Primary Productivity (NPP) is the new growth available for other levels of the food chain to use (Figure 2.5). This can be expressed as NPP = GPP – R

where GPP is Gross Primary Productivity and R represents respiration losses.

Net Primary Productivity is measured as a dry weight of biomass added to the system per unit area, per year. NPP differs from biomass in the same way that a salary differs from savings. NPP is the ecosystem's energy salary. Some ecosystems are good at saving chemical energy in large, long term biological structures (trees), hence the boreal forest has a relatively low energy income (NPP) but a large biomass stored in conifers. Conversely, tropical grasslands have a high energy income in the warm wet season, but a relatively low biomass because grass dies during the dry season so long term storage is low. See Table 2.1.

Biome	NPP (kg/m²/yr)	Biomass (kg/m²)	Ratio of Biomass: NPP
Boreal forest	0.8	20.0	25.0
Temperate deciduous forest	1.2	30.0	25.0
Tropical rain-forest	2.2	45.0	20.5
Prairie (temperate grassland)	0.6	1.6	2.7
Savanna (tropical grassland)	0.9	4.0	4.4

Table 2.1 *NPP and biomass for different biomes*

ACTIVITIES

1 Study Table 2.1. Using climate data from an atlas, suggest reasons for the observed trends in NPP and biomass shown in the table.
2 The images in Figure 2.6 show how there are both seasonal and spatial variations in productivity. The green colour on the satellite images indicates the extent of active photosynthesis over a four month period in Spring, 1995.

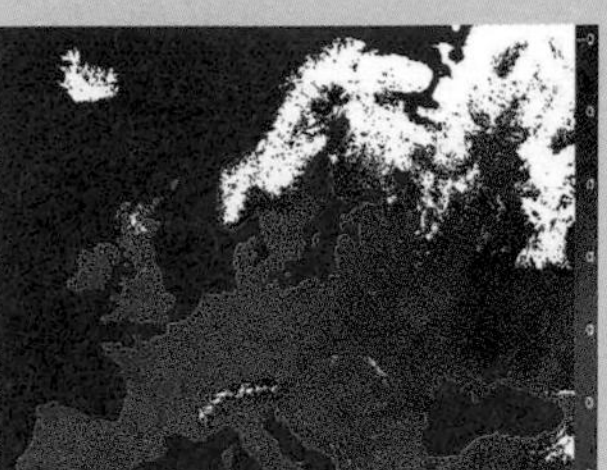

March 1995

April 1995

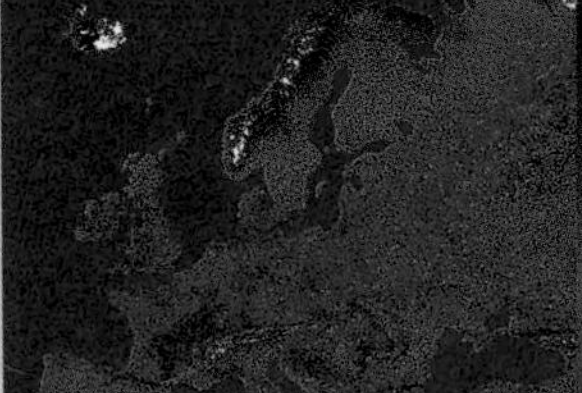

May 1995

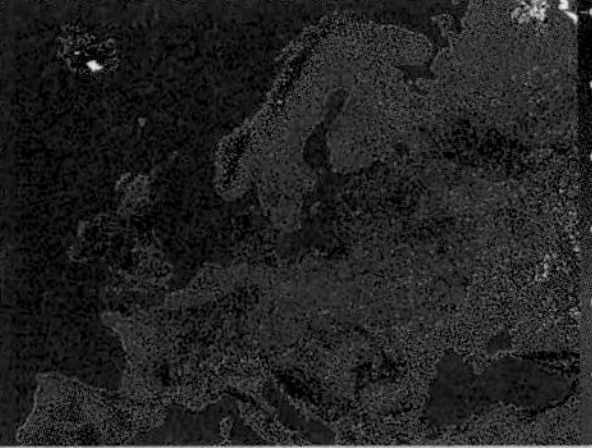

June 1995

Figure 2.6 *Seasonal changes in NPP over Europe*

a Describe the spread of springtime photosynthetic activity.
b Suggest climatic reasons for the pattern of spread observed – consider factors influencing regional temperatures.
c For areas of the maps which show consistently low photosynthetic activity (i.e. brown areas) suggest the limiting factors for each location.

Factors influencing biodiversity

Biome maps such as Figure 2.4 may be misleading and inaccurate because:

- large areas of the biome have already disappeared under agriculture and urban development
- remaining areas of the biome are depleted in species compared to their original populations.

As an example, the woodland areas of the UK used to be home to wild boar, bears, wolves and beaver. Species decline represents a major threat to most biomes. **Biodiversity** (the biological variety within an ecosystem) is declining, sometimes very rapidly.

The biodiversity of an ecosystem depends on the balance of several factors:

Positive factors:

- high temperature and light levels – most species show increased diversity at lower latitudes (Table 2.2)
- ecosystem structure – for a given latitude, habitats with more layers provide a better range of niches for different types of plants and animals (Table 2.3)
- large areas – big biomes support a bigger range of creatures and can accommodate new arrivals without displacing existing species
- long boundaries facing main migration sources – enables greater numbers to migrate
- relief – a large range of altitudes encourages a wider range of ecological niches.

Negative factors:

- limiting factors – the occurrence of a dry or cold season reduces total numbers
- small size and isolation – increase vulnerability to disaster and reduce rates of recovery
- human impacts – by changing ecosystem structures, altering land use and fragmenting large ecosystems, biodiversity is under attack from humans.

Average number of species (terrestrial biomes)			
Latitude (°S and N)	**Birds**	**Mammals**	**Ants**
>60	56	15	10
40–50	105	35	70
<15	469	70	150

Table 2.2 *The influence of latitude on biodiversity*

Habitat	Layers	Average number of bird species
Marsh	1	6
Grassland	1	6
Shrubland	2	14
Coniferous forest	2	17
Deciduous forest	3	24

Table 2.3 *The influence of ecosystem structure on biodiversity*

Why does biodiversity matter?

During the twenty-first century two major losses which could threaten biodiversity are:

- the loss of habitat – every major habitat on which humans depend has suffered widespread degradation. This has particularly hit the poorer sections of communities who tend to depend more directly on locally available resources

- the loss of knowledge – the disappearance and assimilation of native cultures has resulted in huge losses of traditional ecosystem knowledge.

This loss of habitat and knowledge is serious for many reasons, including:

- ignorance – on a global scale there are an estimated 14 million species that inhabit the Earth. Less than 2 million have been scientifically named and described
- loss rate – in North America alone, 200 species of plants and 71 species of vertebrates have become extinct over the past 500 years. A further 750 species are officially listed as endangered or threatened
- riches – we have inherited a treasure trove of unique genetic codes built up over millions of years, but we are destroying them before we have discovered their value, their use or their function
- rarity – this is the only place in the Universe known to have life forms. Recent space research suggests a very low probability of finding anything more advanced than microbes in other solar systems.

Earth's biodiversity may have taken 500 million years to develop and has been shaped by Earth's unique history. The list below represents a selection of ways in which humans have benefited from Earth's ecosystem biodiversity.

Ecosystem biodiversity

- modern agriculture, a $3 trillion global business, relies on wild plant biodiversity for breeding new crop strains, e.g. Teosinte, a wild relative of corn which is resistant to disease
- ecotourism generates $12 billion worldwide in annual revenues
- in 1991, recreation associated with wild birds generated nearly $20 million income and 250,000 jobs in the USA
- in Kenya, the economic value of viewing elephants totalled $25 million in 1989
- in 1988, worldwide commercial trade in wild plants (excluding timber) and animals was approximately $5 billion
- 79 per cent of the top selling 150 prescription drugs in the USA have their origins in natural plant and animal compounds
- the USA imports more than $20 million of rainforest plants per year for their medicinal properties
- traditional herbal remedies provide the only affordable medical treatment for 80 per cent of the world's people
- only 2 per cent of the 250,000 described species of vascular plants have been screened for their chemical compounds and pharmaceutical properties.

Ecosystems with a high biodiversity provide the following:

- hydrological cycling and maintenance of rainfall levels
- the carbon cycle and maintenance of temperature
- pest control. Many pests are created by humans upsetting the balance of native ecosystems. It is no surprise that the ecosystems most dependent on pesticides are those most radically altered by humans, e.g. the crop monocultures of industrialised farming.

We know for certain that living ecosystems provide the functions above. What is less well understood is the role of biodiversity in keeping the ecosystems functioning effectively. How many species can become extinct before the ecosystem fails to perform its normal functions?

Valuing ecosystem services

Ecosystems are under threat as a result of humans using them for income generating activities such as farming and timber production. Our view of economics needs to mature to the point that we examine all costs – social, environmental, long term, short term – rather than assuming that the environment is free and infinite.

All economies would collapse without fertile soil, fresh water and breathable air. In an effort to calculate ecosystem values, a team of researchers from the USA, Argentina, and the Netherlands has attempted to put price tags on the range of services ecosystems provide.

Global ecosystem functions	Value per year (trillion $US)	Global ecosystem functions	Value per year (trillion $US)
Soil formation	17.1	Recreation	3.0
Nutrient cycling	2.3	Water regulation and supply	2.3
Climate regulation (temperature and precipitation)	1.8	Habitat	1.4
Flood and storm protection	1.1	Food and raw material production	0.8
Genetic resources	0.8	Atmospheric gas balance	0.7
Pollination	0.4	All other services	1.6

Table 2.4 *Global ecosystem value*

Source: *Adapted from R. Costanza et al., The Value of the World's Ecosystem Services and Natural Capital,* Nature, *Vol. 387 (1997).*

The values in Table 2.4 represent minimum estimates. For some types of ecosystem, such as deserts and tundra, so little is known that the value assigned to nearly every ecological service was zero, almost certainly an underestimate. Values are also likely to increase as these services become more degraded and scarce in the future.

Why do land use decisions often fail to consider ecosystem values?

- assigning prices to ecosystem services is unrealistic – these services cannot be traded in markets, which is how prices of goods and services are determined
- such prices cannot reflect the full value of these services – there are moral, ethical, and aesthetic reasons to value and protect nature, apart from its benefits to humanity
- most benefits fall outside the marketplace. Services such as nutrient cycling and climate moderation are public goods that contribute immeasurably to human welfare without ever being drawn into the money economy
- traditional economic thinking is mainly based on narrow and incomplete assumptions – for example, valuing forests for the marketable timber they produce ignores the indirect costs to society of their removal: soil erosion, nutrient loss, increased flooding, decline in water quality, reduced carbon storage capacity, changes in regional temperature and rainfall, diminished wildlife habitat and fewer recreational opportunities. A developing nation clearing all its forests can increase its GNP but will lose the benefits of a diverse ecosystem.

The importance of ecosystems as global regulators

The carbon cycle is an excellent example of the way living organisms help to regulate other global systems (Figure 2.7). In the carbon cycle, both marine and terrestrial ecosystems are involved in the recycling of carbon (in long- and short-term time scales). As Figure 2.7 shows, ecosystems form an integral link between oceanic, atmospheric/climatic and tectonic systems. We need to be aware of the consequences of humans on such cycles so that we create only the impacts we are prepared to live with. It is fallacy that population growth is the biggest threat to the global environment. Globalisation is arguably a much greater threat as it divorces human wants from their impacts. Population size is important but a more serious consideration is consumer demand. A society's sustainability can be judged by its '**ecological footprint**', i.e. the demand for water, energy, food, materials and waste disposal that it places on the environment. Not surprisingly, the ecological footprint of a typical European has been estimated to be 60–80 times greater than that for a farmer in rural India. Globalisation allows the wealthy to enjoy a lifestyle that makes high demands on the environments of other nations.

Human impacts on environments can be benign if they are responsive to underlying ecosystem patterns. For example, a 1995 study of the Cree Indians of James Bay, Canada showed that the decisions on what to hunt were related to the relative abundance of the species. Hunting (and diets) would switch from fish to caribou depending on relative abundance. This strategy ensured large animal populations never reached pest status and small populations were left to recover. This is in direct contrast to human impacts in industrialised nations where 'supply and demand economics' and government intervention have repeatedly resulted in the collapse of commercial fisheries. Ecosystems are able to support intelligent human intervention, but not unintelligent political expedience.

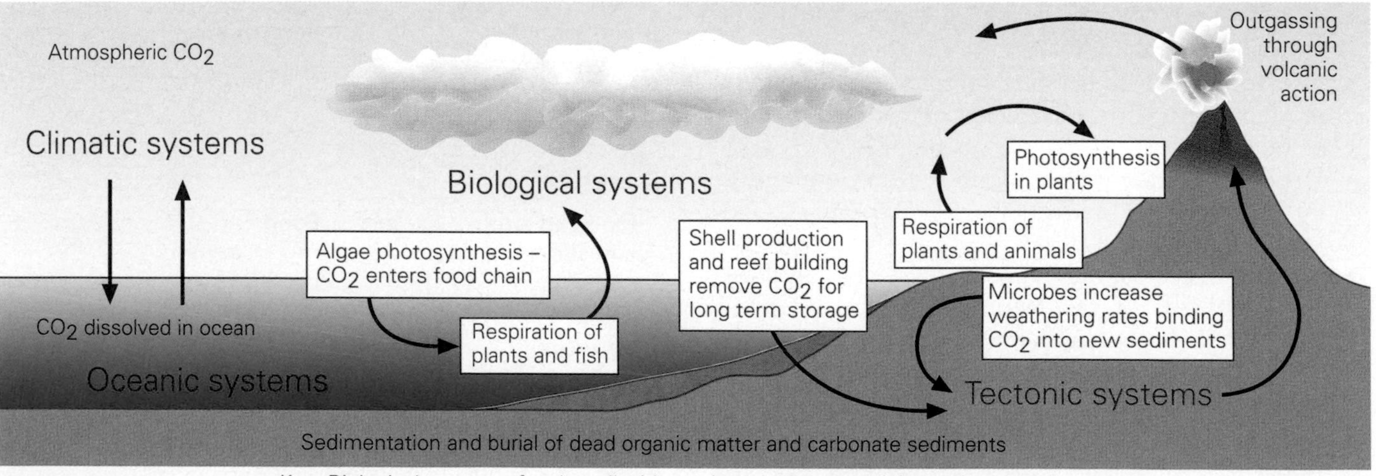

Figure 2.7 *The carbon cycle*

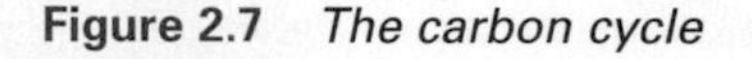

2 Forest ecosystems

Describing forest structure

Forests are biodiverse terrestrial ecosystems. We can describe forests in a variety of ways:

- Age diversity – natural forests have a high age diversity. Different-aged trees provide different ecological niches for insects, birds and animals.
- Biodiversity – the range of species present in an area. Natural forests have higher biodiversity than forests managed for timber production.
- Layering – natural forests may have a herb layer, a scrub layer and a 'canopy' (tree) layer. Each layer provides new habitats, adding to biodiversity.
- Nutrient cycling – forests store large amounts of nutrients in tree biomass.

Introduction

The El Niño that began in March 1997 and continued until mid-1998 is believed to have been one of the most severe in recorded history. It caused drier than normal conditions across a wide range of countries. The dry conditions exaggerated the poor management that characterises so many forest areas. Fires set by the farmers and shifting cultivators to clear land burned out of control. Poor forestry techniques and large-scale land clearance left vast areas with dry dead timber ready to ignite. El Niño's weather disruption was unforgiving in exposing such poor practices. These results are shown in Table 2.5.

ACTIVITIES

1 On an outline map of the world, plot the impacts of the 1997–98 fires, using a suitable graphical technique.

Forests provide us with both goods and services. Figure 2.8 summarises the benefits of forests.

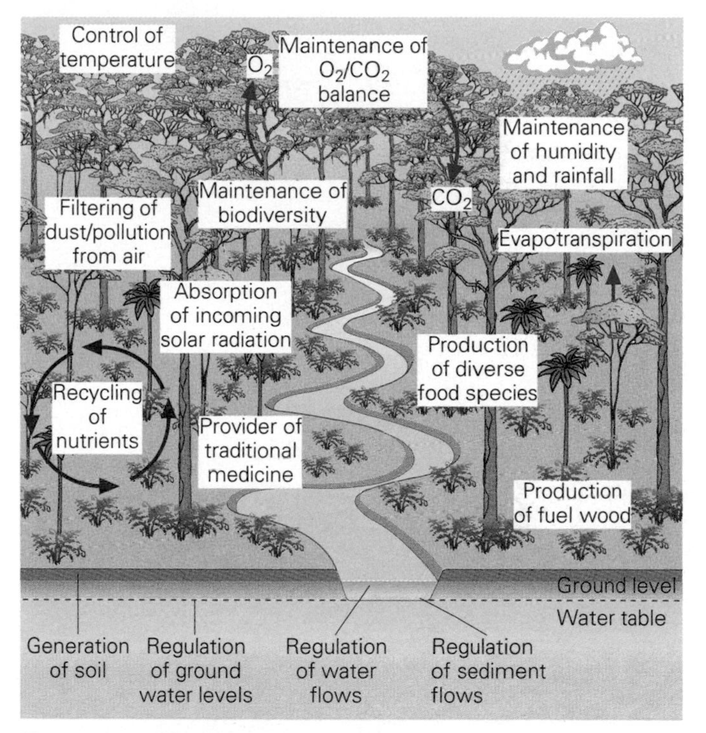

Figure 2.8 *Forest goods and services*

Location	Impacts
Mexico and Central America	• fires burned a reported 1.5 million hectares of land • from January to June 1998, 13,000 fires burned in Mexico alone, killing more than 70 fire-fighters and local residents
Brazil	• over 2 million hectares of rain forest burned
Indonesia	• an estimated 2 million hectares of forest burned • smog from the fires disrupted health, tourism and air travel over the whole of SE Asia
Nicaragua	• between December 1997 and April 1998, more than 13,000 fires burned, destroying more than 800,000 hectares of land
Florida	• 200,000 hectares of forest burned
Greece	• 150,000 hectares of coniferous forest burned
Eastern Russia	• in July 1998, devastating fires burned more than 100,000 hectares of coniferous forest in more than 150 places around Vladivostok, Sakhalin and the Kamchatka Peninsula • fires in the south-west of the Volgograd region destroyed 9,000 hectares of forest, at an estimated cost of US$6 million.

Table 2.5 *Forest fires experienced in the 1997–98 El Niño*

North America
Only 23% of the original forest has been lost. Just over a third of the original tree cover is still pioneer forest, but this is distributed very unevenly with most in Canada. In the lower 48 states of the USA pioneer forest covers only 1% of the original area.

Europe
Nearly 70% of Europe's forest cover has been lost. Remaining pioneer forest accounts for less than 0.5% of the original area. All remaining pioneer forest is under high threat, primarily from logging. Pollution has resulted in a 56% drop in forest health from 1988 to 1995.

Russia
31% of Russia's forest cover has been lost. Remaining pioneer forest accounts for less than a third of the original area. Less than 20% of the remaining pioneer forest is under threat, but changes in Russian politics and economy could influence these figures.

Asia
72% of Asia's forest cover has been lost. Remaining pioneer forest accounts for less than 6% of the original area. 60% of the remaining pioneer forest is under moderate to high threat, mainly from logging and fuelwood/land clearance due to population growth.

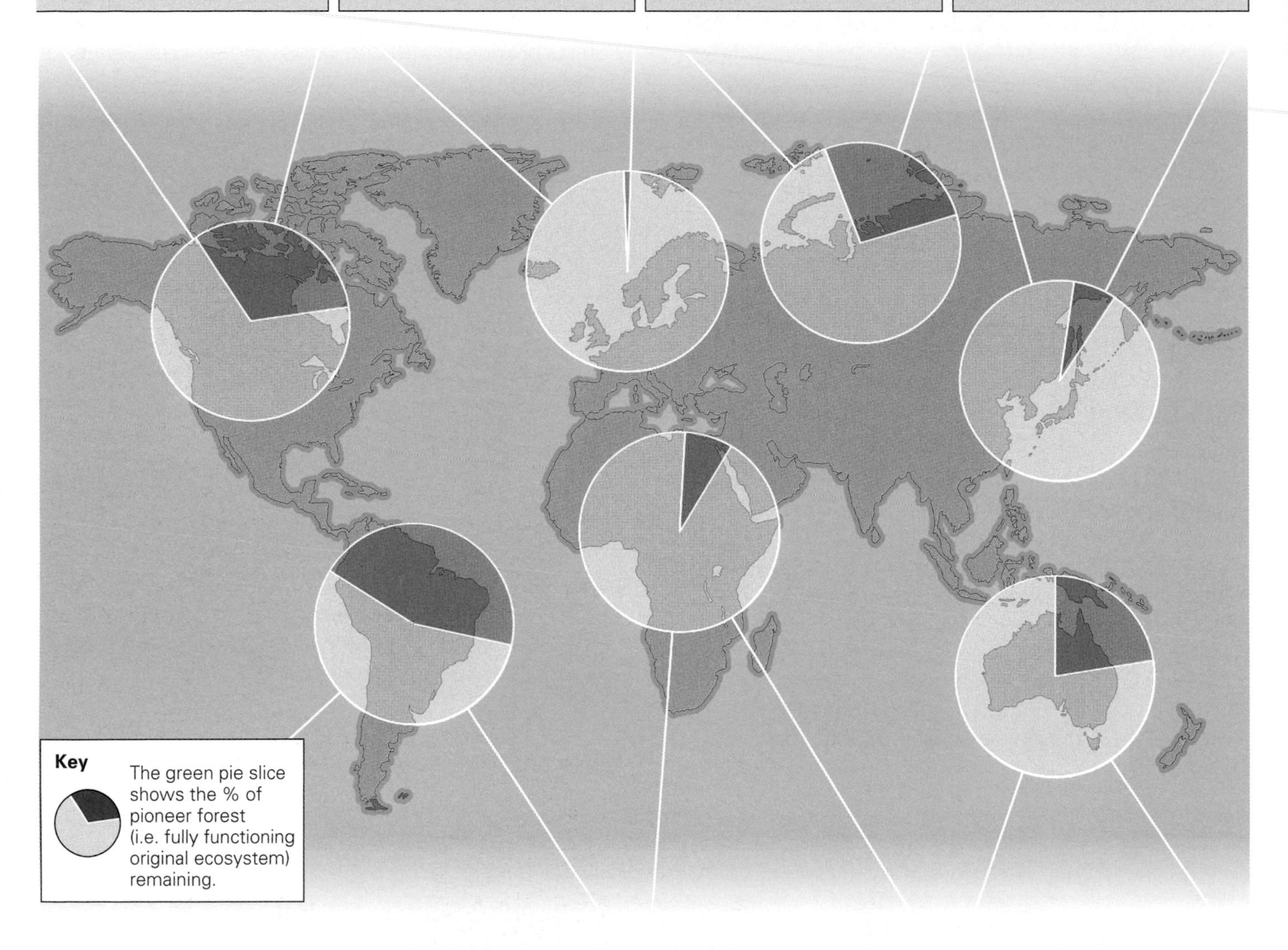

South America
South America is the least threatened area on a global scale. 31% of original cover is now lost and pioneer forests stand at 46% of their original extent. 54% of the current pioneer forest is threatened. The biggest threats are often government initiated – logging, mining and infrastructure development. Government sponsored clearance amounts to 2–3 million hectares per year.

Africa
66% of Africa's forest cover has been lost. Pioneer forest forms only 8% of the original forest. Nearly 80% of pioneer forest is threatened. Main threats are logging and hunting for bushmeat.

Oceania
35% of Oceania's original forest has been lost. Pioneer forest forms only 22% of the original cover and over three quarters of this is under moderate to high threat.

Figure 2.9 *The state of the world's forests*

Our track record of looking after forests leaves much to be desired. Figure 2.9 shows the current state of forests by world region. It distinguishes between forest cover (i.e. areas covered by trees) and **pioneer forest** (i.e. areas with substantially unaltered native forest). In the UK forest covers nearly 11 per cent of the land surface, but the area of pioneer forest is zero. Figure 2.10 shows the key threats to remaining pioneer forests.

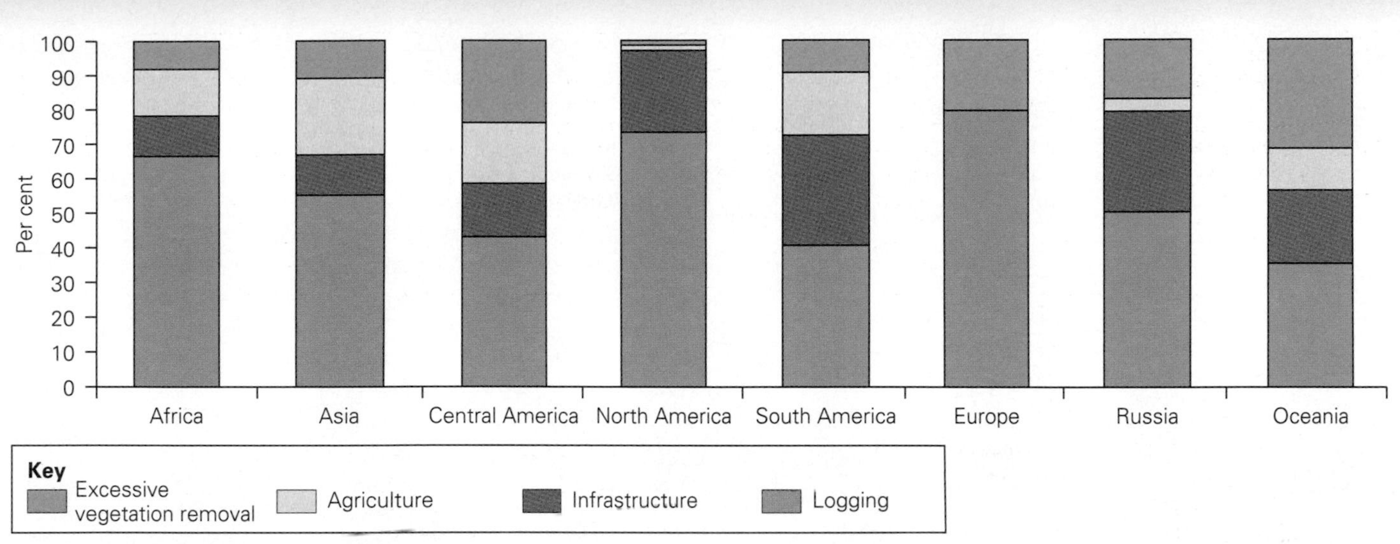

Figure 2.10 *Threats to pioneer forest*

Recent management of forests has had much success. Forest areas in more developed regions are increasing. There are 1 million hectares of forest plantings each year in MEDCs. Different forest areas such as boreal, temperate and tropical forests have different characteristics, pressures, problems and management conflicts.

Boreal forests

Boreal forests are the coniferous forests of the high latitude regions (Figure 2.11).The pressures here vary in type and intensity from place to place, but some of the more significant pressures include:

- competing uses – hydroelectric power, pipeline corridors, urban development, mining, recreation
- inappropriate management practice – herbicides, pesticides, fire suppression, clearcutting, introduction of exotic species
- acid rain – locally produced (e.g. Bratsk, Siberia where 100,000 hectares of forest have been destroyed by air pollution from aluminium smelters, power stations and chemical factories), or from elsewhere (e.g. Norwegian forests stressed by pollution from the UK).

The pressures on the forest are not only ecological. Social pressures on indigenous cultures also have implications for the long term health of the ecosystem.

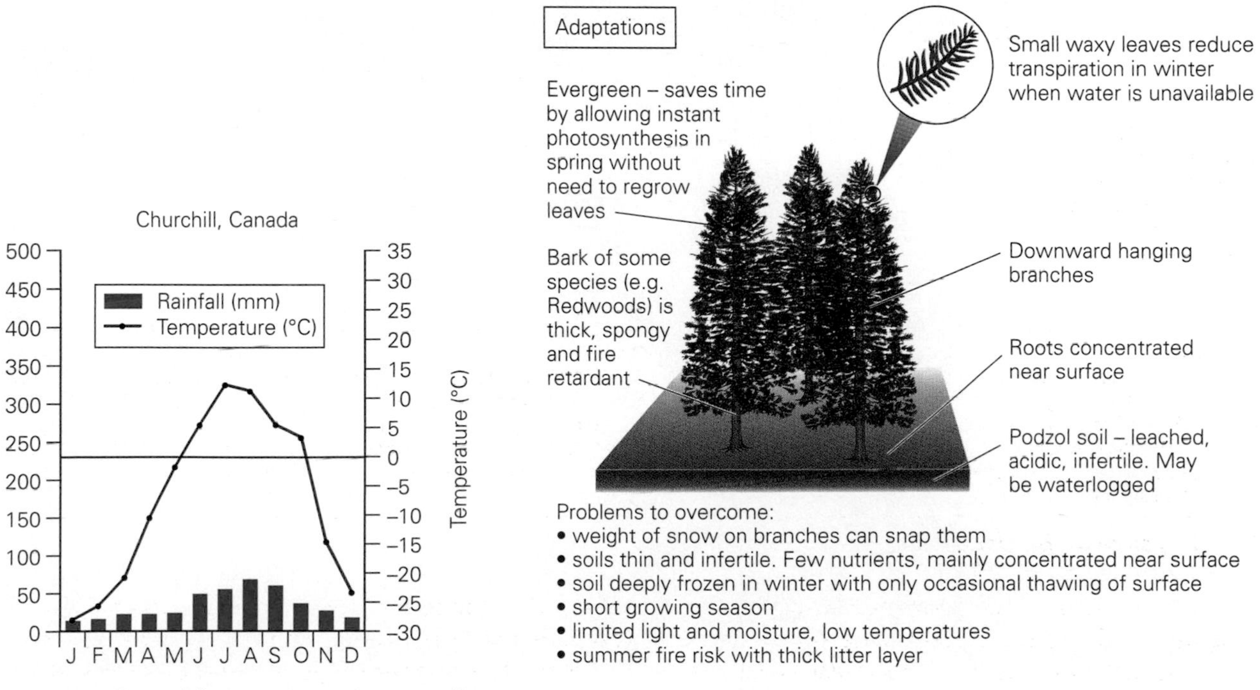

Figure 2.11 *Boreal forest adaptations to climate*

James Bay, Canada

The Boreal forest of Canada is one of the last remaining areas of 'frontier forest'. With 88 per cent of Canada's aboriginal communities living in boreal forests, there are both social and economic issues at stake in effective management of these areas. An example is provided by the conflicts surrounding James Bay and the Cree Nation (Figure 2.12).

The Cree Nation includes about 12,000 aboriginal people, an organised society that has lived, hunted, fished, trapped and harvested in the James Bay area for over 4,000 years. 30 per cent of the Crees continue to live primarily from what the land provides. The James Bay and Northern Quebec Agreement (JBNQA) was signed in 1975 by the governments of Quebec and Canada and the James Bay Cree. It came after years of Cree campaigns against hydroelectric power (HEP) development on their hunting lands. This was a landmark agreement, recognising the rights of indigenous people. The agreement committed the government to the protection of the Cree traditional way of life. The JBNQA does not prevent HEP development, nor place any constraints on commercial forestry in the region but it does require the involvement of the Cree in the decision making. The government of Quebec has three options for development of the area.

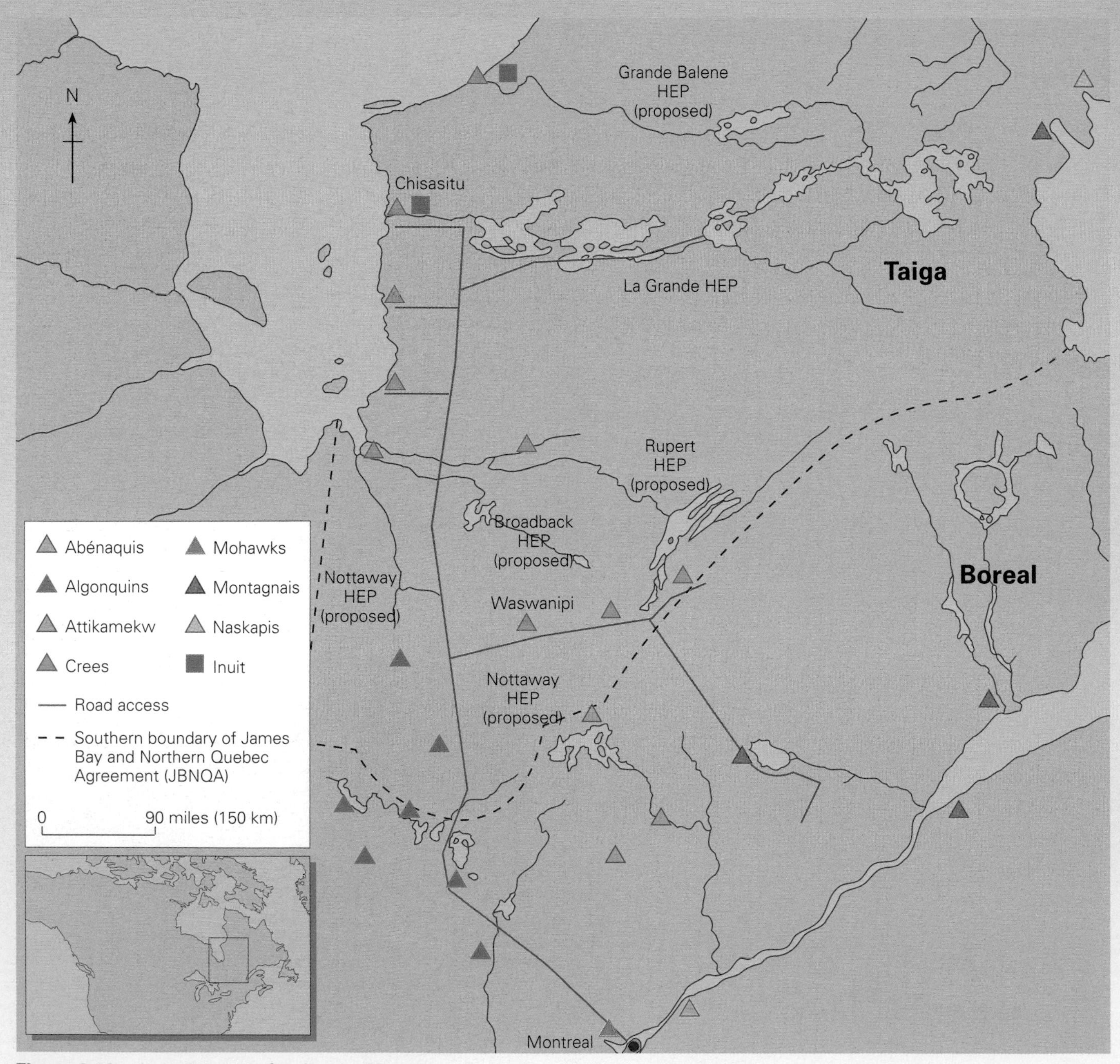

Figure 2.12 *Location map for James Bay area*

Options for development 1: Commercial forestry

In 1995, the value of finished Canadian forest products was assessed at C$71.4 billion. The forest provides employment for 830,000 Canadians (more than 1 in every 17 jobs). Each year, the forest sector pays C$11.1 billion in wages. Forestry is the economic backbone of 337 Canadian communities (Figure 2.13).

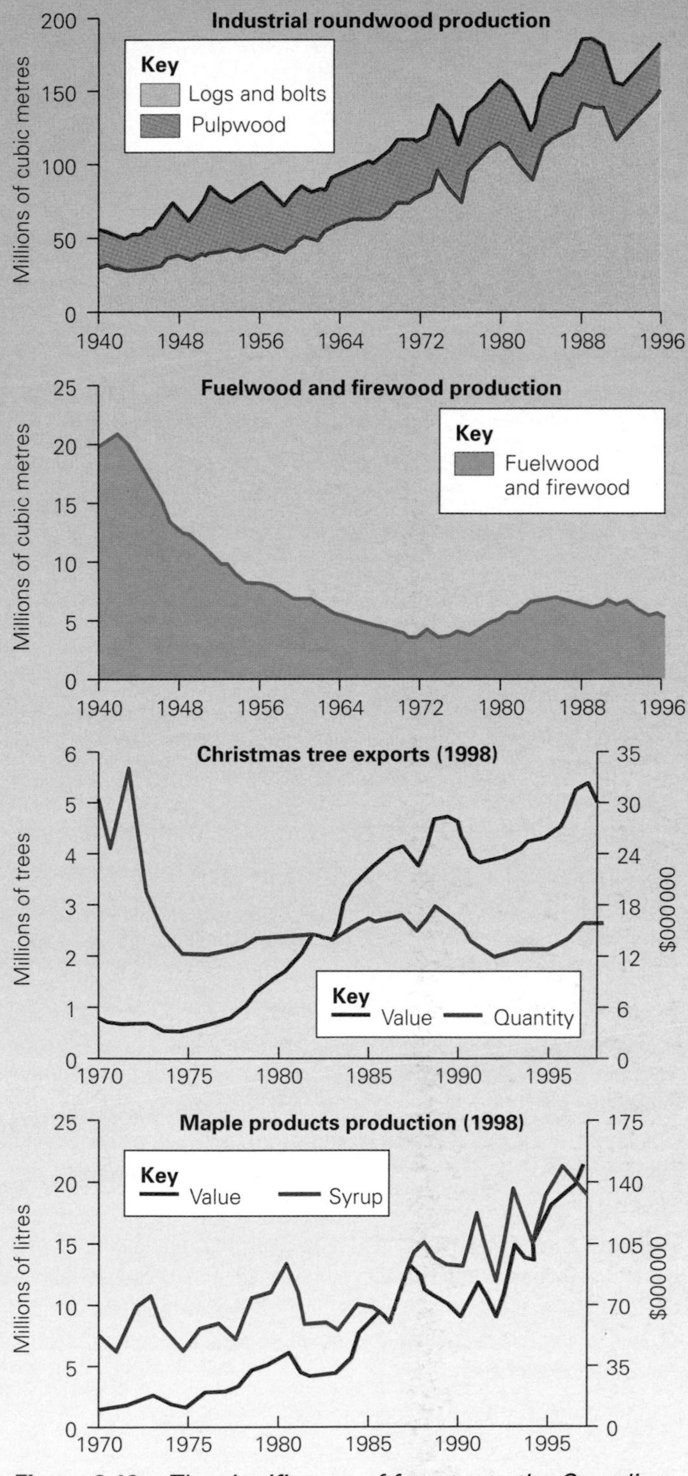

Figure 2.13 *The significance of forestry to the Canadian economy*

James Bay territory includes 5.2 million hectares of boreal forest. The nature of the forest is:

- small trees (~10 metres high)
- slow growth rates
- low yields
- large forest area.

As the more productive forests of southern Canada have been over-exploited, timber companies have increasingly looked to the pioneer forests of the north to keep profits high and shareholders happy.

Arguments for forestry

Forestry is a major source of the region's economy. Forestry is responsible and sustainable and the 1987 Forest Act is based on:

- sustained yield which limits the harvest to the production capacity of the forest and requires regeneration of all harvested areas
- protection of all the resources with part of the landbase to be used for other forest values, e.g. leaving buffers along bodies of water, protecting specific wildlife habitats etc.

The 1996 amendments to the Forest Act incorporated six criteria of sustainable forest management:

- conservation of biological diversity
- maintenance and improvement of the state and productivity of forest ecosystems
- conservation of soils and water
- maintenance of the contribution of forest ecosystems to the major ecological cycles
- maintenance of the many socio-economic benefits of the forests for society
- consideration, in development choices, of the values and needs expressed by the populations concerned.

Co-operation with indigenous people has improved, for example the Trapline Forestry Project in the Waswanipi hunting territories (Figure 2.1) allows affected trappers/hunters to register their concerns and wishes about what they want protected from forestry activities.

Arguments against forestry

- Logging companies clear approximately 500 km^2/year on Cree family hunting areas, greatly reducing their productivity.
- Logging roads fragment ecosystems and give greater access to non-aboriginal people for hunting and fishing in competition with the Cree.
- Legislation is weak and rarely enforced – government approved forestry development is exempt from environmental impact assessment.
- Logging companies are poor at providing information, making it difficult for the Cree to comment on management plans or raise objections in advance.
- Replanting schemes have a high failure rate. Shallow soil freezes and uproots seedlings, winds cause wind-chill and desiccation and nurseries have few seeds from trees of the north.

Options for development 2: Hydroelectric power

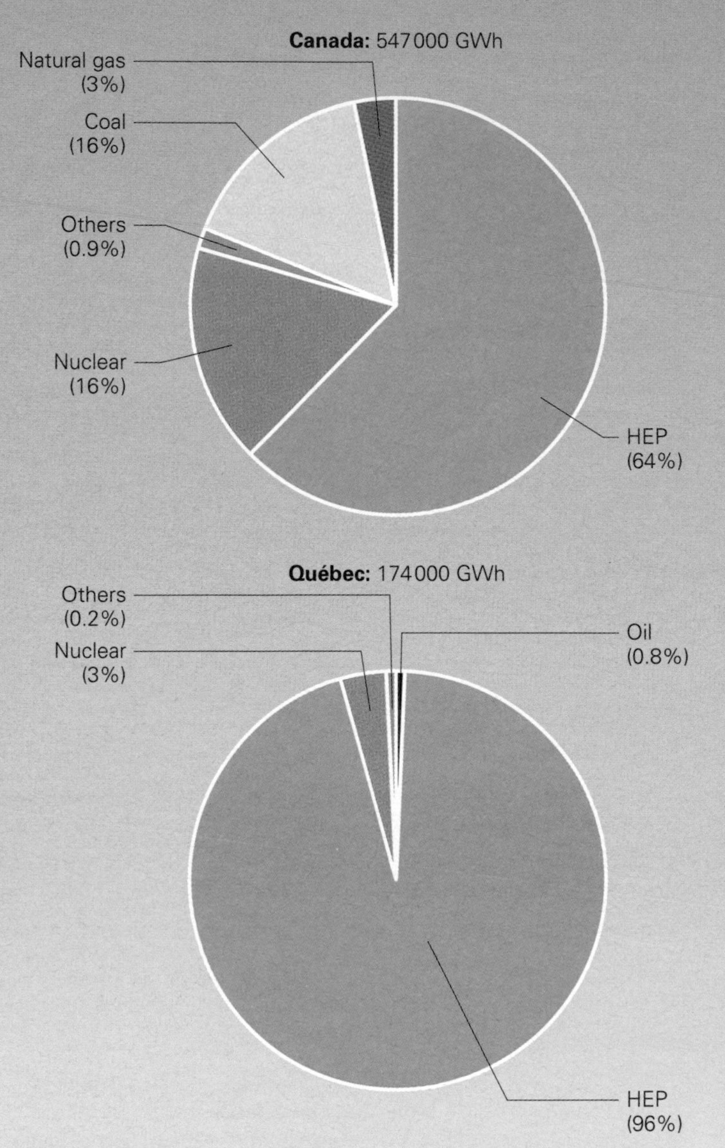

Figure 2.14 *The significance of HEP to Canada and Quebec, 1996*

Figure 2.14 shows the relative contribution of HEP to the energy budgets of Canada and Quebec. In 1997, Canada signed the Kyoto Protocol on greenhouse gas reduction, committing the nation to a 6 per cent reduction in CO_2 compared to 1990 levels. To achieve this target, Canada will need to further develop its HEP potential.

In the James Bay region, 'La Grande project' employs 100,000+ people and produces 15,000 MW of electricity.

Arguments for HEP

- There are huge HEP resources. La Grande project alone supplies over 50 per cent of all Quebec's HEP.
- Compensation to the Cree for new HEP developments on their land can bring great benefit to their communities; the Cree gained C$97 million compensation for La Grande project.
- Associated road infrastructure reduces transport costs, reducing prices of supplies and enabling Crees to benefit both from easier access to hunting grounds and potential tourist incomes.
- As native business expertise and education/training levels have developed, Crees have gained more from employment and contract opportunities.
- Compensation agreements include the training and hire of native people to provide for long term skilled employment. La Grande agreement provides for 150 permanent jobs for the Cree.
- 16 million native seedlings have been planted as mitigation measures to restore environments degraded by construction.

Arguments against HEP

- Environmental impacts of dams affect ecosystems. La Grande complex has displaced up to 8,000 breeding pairs of wildfowl from the area and led to a rise in mercury in ecosystems after reservoir construction.
- Improved infrastructure makes it easier for non-aborigines to get access to Indian hunting grounds for recreation and shooting.
- Jobs are often insecure or temporary. The average length of hiring was only three months in La Grande project. Less than 2 per cent of the potential workforce gained employment.
- Very few benefits of the project accrue to the Cree. La Grande project produced 150 jobs for a population of 12,000.

Both commercial forestry and HEP are large scale projects where the Cree Indians are perceived as very minor players, usually as obstacles to development. Since the initiatives are coming from the outside and based on a foreign culture, even positive impacts (like increased incomes) can be very damaging as shown in Figure 2.15.

Options for development 3: Village scale enterprises

There are nine Cree settlements spread throughout the James Bay region. Each could be the focus for small scale, community based enterprises, using the Cree skills of a deep knowledge of the forest, traditional forest skills and recently acquired business skills.

Example 1: Waswanipi Cree Model Forest is a 209,600 hectare area established in 1997. A sawmill employs over 42 full-time workers from the Waswanipi settlement and has future plans to process the wood, increasing its value and employing a further 54 people. Ultimately the Cree hope to manufacture finished products and possibly develop a school of forestry to raise the skill levels of the Cree.

Example 2: Tourism development. The Cree lands are ideal for many outdoor activities, notably fishing and hunting. The forests are also a destination of tourists who enjoy hiking, river rafting, swimming, snowmobiling, cross-country and downhill skiing, mountain biking, camping and canoeing.

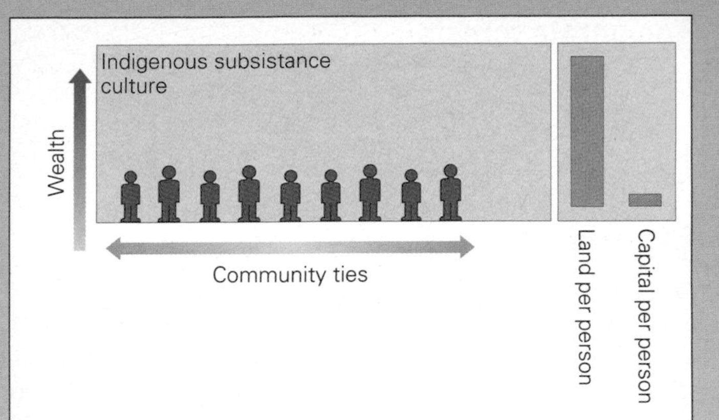

Before:

High degree of community with strong sense of kinship and sustainable reliance on the land. Self sufficient and independent but low level of wealth.

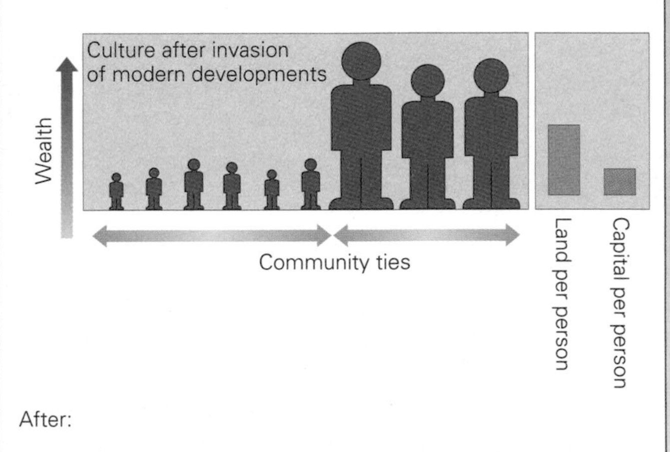

After:

Dislocated community with great inequality between employed and unemployed. New social structures created by wealth – breakdown of traditional relationships. High benefits for a few, but costs affect all (degraded environment). Traditional skills devalued. Move to market economy increases dependency – markets are distant and state aid is needed. Few employers, so unreliable job market. High levels of substance abuse and relationship breakdown may result.

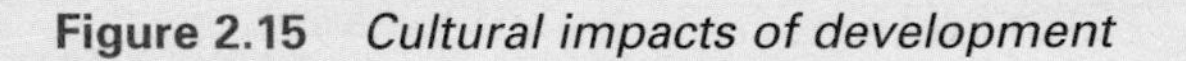

Figure 2.15 *Cultural impacts of development*

Advantages of village enterprise

With small scale village enterprise schemes the initiatives come from the Cree themselves and have the following advantages:

- ensure sustainable use of the land
- generate reliable long term incomes
- allow self sufficiency in the Cree communities and cultural self determination
- ease the process of cultural assimilation.

Disadvantages of village enterprise

Smaller industrial ventures suffer several risk factors:

- Lack of size results in lower economic efficiencies. The Waswanipi sawmill is not expected to make a profit until its third year of operation, by which time a very large debt could accrue.
- It is administratively more expensive for governments to support a large number of small projects than a small number of large projects.
- Fewer benefits will transfer to the South of the country where the government's votes lie. Canadian politics is highly fractured with French/English and Independence/Canadian tensions. No politician can afford to lose votes for a northern minority.

Social issues

The unemployment rate in aboriginal communities is between 80 and 90 per cent so forestry could produce valuable jobs. Clearing forest, however, is culturally foreign in a community based on hunting, fishing and trapping. The Cree have a proven track record of sustainable hunting and are responsive to changes in wildlife. Forestry has a bad reputation with the Cree. Some family lands have lost over 60 per cent of their forest, with dramatic species decline due to logging operations. Some Cree have gained jobs through forestry, but these are normally the lowest paid jobs and they are the first to be fired when the company moves on.

You can follow the Cree case via extensive newspaper and research articles at the Grand Council of the Crees website – www.gcc.ca/Environment/forestry/forestry.htm

ACTIVITIES

1. Use the themes below to create a concept map of the James Bay boreal forest conflicts:
   Land ownership, job creation, job security, sustainability, wealth creation, biodiversity, legislation, cultural conflict, rural development, international trade, long/short term benefits.
2. Summarise the viewpoints of: the Cree; the Canadian government; a Quebec HEP firm; a large commercial timber company.
3. Rank the following considerations from most important to least important, justifying your ranking: economic gain for Quebec; economic gain for the Cree; sustainability for resources; sustainability of habitats/wildlife; respect for Cree land rights; diversification of the economy; social impacts on Cree culture; job security/creation for Canadians; job security/creation for the Cree.
4. Recommend the most appropriate option for the future development of the James Bay region. Where appropriate, modify the three options presented here. Support your arguments with facts and figures from the information here and updates from the website.

Conservation in Boreal forests

The nature of institutions and property rights affects the sustainability of resource use by societies. Unregulated access inevitably leads to resource depletion, whereas private property, communal property, and state property provide mechanisms to regulate resource use and provide for sustainability. To this extent, ecosystem health is dependent on the character (and health) of the social and economic systems. Degraded ecosystems may reflect inadequate socio-economic systems.

In indigenous cultures, communal rights and obligations tend to allow resources to be sustainably shared. Problems only arise if populations grow faster than the capacity of the forest to supply their needs. Business cultures in developed nations work on different principles. They require continuing growth to satisfy shareholder expectations or maintain market position. For large timber companies to operate sustainably, a new approach is needed that does not regard short term profit as the only criterion for decision making. One such approach is through a globally recognised certification scheme like the Forest Stewardship Council.

The Forest Stewardship Council (FSC) started a certification programme in 1993 by which wood products could be guaranteed to be sourced from well-managed forests. This allowed consumers to make informed purchases. The certification scheme has been rigorous, requiring companies to fulfil a number of conditions. These include:

- management plan and supporting documents – management objectives, management systems, harvest rate, species selection, harvesting techniques
- monitoring and assessment – research and data collection to monitor yield, growth, regeneration, flora and fauna, environmental and social impacts of harvesting, costs, productivity and efficiency
- environmental impact – written guidelines for controlling erosion, minimising forest damage during harvesting, road construction, etc., protection of water resources. Representative samples of existing ecosystems within the landscape must be protected in their natural state and recorded on maps. Safeguards must exist to protect rare, threatened and endangered species and their habitats. Conservation zones and protection areas must be established, appropriate to the scale and intensity of operations and the uniqueness of affected resources.

Certification has been very successful in boreal forests – 73 per cent of the world's certified woodland area is from semi-natural boreal forests.

Temperate forests

Temperate forests are the forests of the mid latitudes adapted to well-distributed rainfall and moderate to warm summer temperatures. They are mainly characterised by deciduous species.

Recent developments in UK forestry

Temperate forests are usually cropped sustainably and enjoy a good deal of protection and public support yet their biodiversity is often poor. Forestry in the UK is changing its approach with an increasing emphasis on sustainability and biodiversity. As a result of the 1992 Earth Summit, the UK committed itself to develop national strategies for protecting biodiversity. In 1994 the government published the UK Biodiversity Action Plan (BAP) and the UK Sustainable Forestry Programme (Figure 2.16). The Rio Earth Summit also recognised that sustainability needs grass roots support. A major thread in the UK BAP is the local Biodiversity Action Plan (local BAP). This has the potential to radically alter the way we look at forests and the way we look at decision making. The aim of a local BAP is to address ecological issues (species type, population dynamics, habitat types, habitat fragmentation) as well as management and research issues. It is also designed to be participatory, involving a range of local groups.

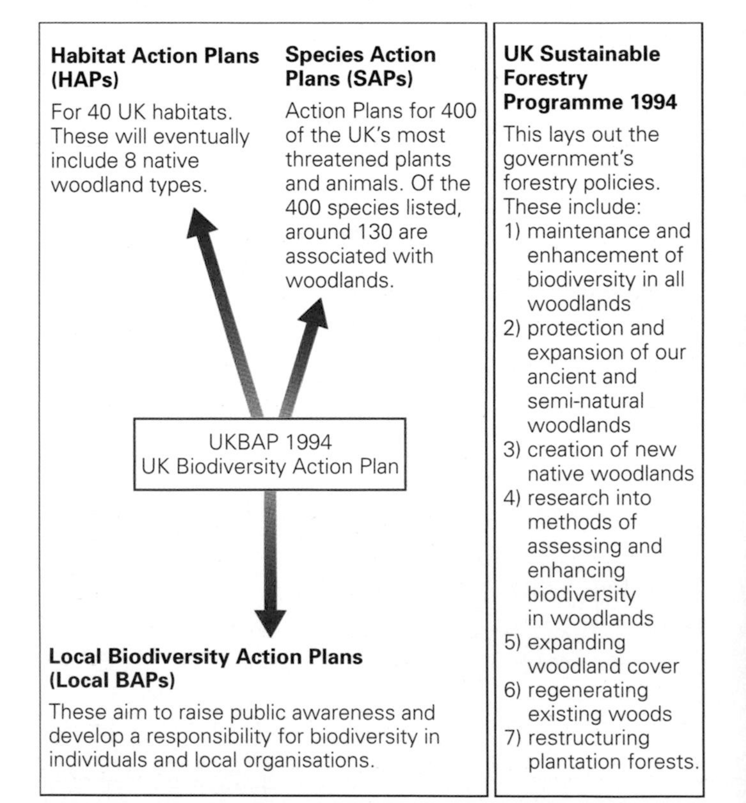

Figure 2.16 *UK Biodiversity Action Plan and UK Sustainable Forestry Programme*

Key data on UK Forestry

In 1994 the UK government's Biodiversity Steering Group identified 400 threatened UK species and 40 habitats at risk.

The forested area of the UK nearly doubled between 1900 and 2000.

Productivity of UK forests has risen from 4 million m^3/yr to nearly 9 million m^3/yr (1998).

Over £1.6 billion was invested in UK sawmills, paper mills and board mills over the last 15 years.

63% of all UK woodland consists of conifer plantation rather than native broadleaved forest. Forestry Commission woodland comprises 88% conifers. Most Forestry Commission planting is non-native and supports very little wildlife.

Forestry Commission objectives

- protect Britain's forests and woodlands
- expand Britain's forest area
- enhance the economic value of our forest resources
- conserve and improve the biodiversity, landscape and cultural heritage of our forests and woodlands
- develop opportunities for woodland recreation
- increase public understanding and community participation in forestry.

Source: Forestry Industry Council of Great Britain yearbook, 1998

	Scotland	Wales	England	UK
1924	5.60%	4.90%	5.10%	5.30%
1947	6.70%	6.20%	5.80%	6.10%
1965	8.50%	9.70%	6.80%	7.70%
1980	11.90%	11.70%	7.30%	9.30%

Table 2.6 *Land under forest*

	Conifer	Broad leaved	Coppice	Other	Total
Forestry Commission	738	46	1	49	834
Private Woodland	801	624	19	162	1606
Total	1539	670	20	211	2440

Table 2.7 *Land under forest – distribution by ecosystem type (thousand hectares), 1998*

	Average yield (m^3)	Average age at harvest	% UK planting
Scots pine	9	65	13
Lodgepole pine	7	55	7
Japanese larch	9	50	6
Norway spruce	12	60	6
Sitka spruce	13	50	28
Sessile oak	5	140	9
Beech	6	115	4
Ash	5	70	4
Silver birch	5	50	4

Table 2.8 *Species diversity in UK forestry, 1998*

ACTIVITIES

1 Study Tables 2.6 to 2.8 to assess the truth of the following statements:
 a 'Forest ecosystems in the UK are a cause for celebration rather than concern.'
 b 'Choice of tree crop is simply a matter of economics. The better the yield, the more you will grow it.'

2 Study Figure 2.16.
 a Explain why a local BAP needs to pay as much attention to habitat as to species.
 b The advantage of a local BAP will be the inclusion of voluntary organisations and non specialists. What will the disadvantages be in this approach?

Figure 2.17 *Eroded footpaths in the New Forest*

Ecological uncertainties

- Minimal critical ecosystem needed by different species
- Nature, extent and suitability of wildlife corridors between forest core and surroundings
- Rates of seral succession in neglected coppice and heathland
- Ecological carrying capacity of different habitats

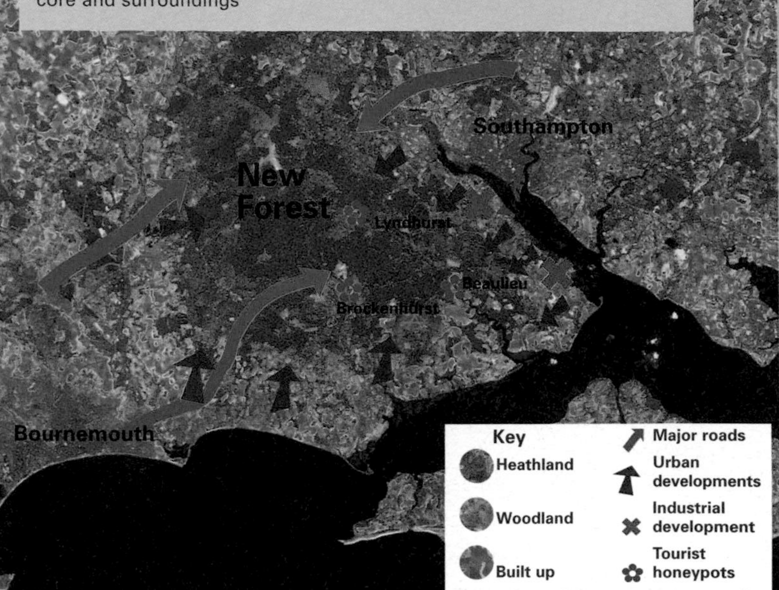

Figure 2.18 *Pressures on the New Forest*

Pressures on temperate woodlands – the New Forest

The New Forest is a landscape of mixed woodland, common lands, farmland and heathland. Norman aristocrats of the eleventh century protected the area for entirely selfish reasons, inadvertently preserving a landscape that millions would later cherish. The New Forest can be valued in a variety of ways as shown below.

Conservation	Recreation
• 90 valley mires – a significant proportion of all that remain in Western Europe • 136 species-rich meadows • 50% of UK species of moths, butterflies and beetles • 30% of all UK breeding dragonfly species • 46+ species of nationally or internationally rare plants are present • riparian woodland (woodland alongside riverbanks) is a nationally rare habitat that is still common in the New Forest	• 16 million visitors a year • wildlife • scenery • historical/cultural tourism **Timber value** • second largest timber producer in the south of England • 46% of the New Forest area is multi-purpose forestry

Management of the New Forest has been weakened by lack of integration. Different agencies were responsible for different aspects of management at different scales and in different places. The New Forest is expected to be a a National Park by 2002 and some of these problems have been resolved. Broadly, there are two complementary ways of protecting the forest biodiversity; effective legislation and enlightened commerce.

Figure 2.19 *Erosion impacts on temperate forest*

Figure 2.18 highlights some of the ecological uncertainties in the New Forest. None of these is beyond solving, but all need active management, preferably with a community-based input. To preserve the value of the New Forest, politically unpopular decisions may need to be taken. Already the banning of mountain bikes from most forest areas has caused conflict, but sustainability implies that the 'freedoms' of one generation should not rob a future generation of its inheritance.

The future of UK forestry

There are a number of large schemes aimed at improving UK forests. These aim to focus on multipurpose forestry but with an emphasis on amenity, wildlife and recreational values. Schemes include:

- the Sussex Wildlife Trust plans a 5,000 hectare Weald Forest, with natural grazers and small scale timber extraction
- The National Forest, sponsored by the Forestry Commission and Countryside Commission, plan a 500 km^2 multipurpose forest in the Midlands with an aim to have 30 per cent forest cover within a huge designated area
- the Trees for Life group plans a 1,500 km^2 Central Highland Forest, ideally with wolves to recreate native forest on a grand scale.

Figure 2.20 *Coppice woodland*

Coppicing – an example of enlightened commerce

Coppicing is an ancient sustainable management technique for woodlands. It involves cutting back the scrub layer of the wood to stimulate high rates of regrowth. Different patches of the wood are cut in rotation, creating a patchwork of different ages with different light levels (Figure 2.20). By returning the ecosystem to an early **seral stage** (scrub stage), higher productivity is encouraged. Coppice can provide:

- home-grown barbecue charcoal (the UK uses an estimated 60,000 tonnes/year, much currently imported from endangered tropical forests)
- fencing hurdles
- thatching spars
- barrel hoops
- rustic garden furniture and walking sticks.

Coppice trees are also a source of CO_2-free energy because they only release what they have already absorbed in growing. Every tonne of dry coppiced wood could generate as much electricity as 650 kg of coal, and save the release of up to 500 kg of carbon into the atmosphere.

The key advantages of coppicing include:

conservation

- a large variety of habitats in a small area
- continuity – wildlife has adapted to millennia of coppice management

employment

- a wood managed by coppice methods will employ at least ten times more people than a wood managed by modern forestry techniques

economic

- economic returns are much quicker than with most other forms of woodland.

Plantation forests now comprise around 135 million hectares globally, with about 75 per cent of existing plantations in temperate regions. Many of the upland coniferous plantations of the last one hundred years were ecological disasters, replacing biologically diverse upland moors with monocultures of exotic species to which few native species could adapt. In the UK, through the 1990s, a trend towards new plantings of broadleaved species began as shown in Figure 2.21.

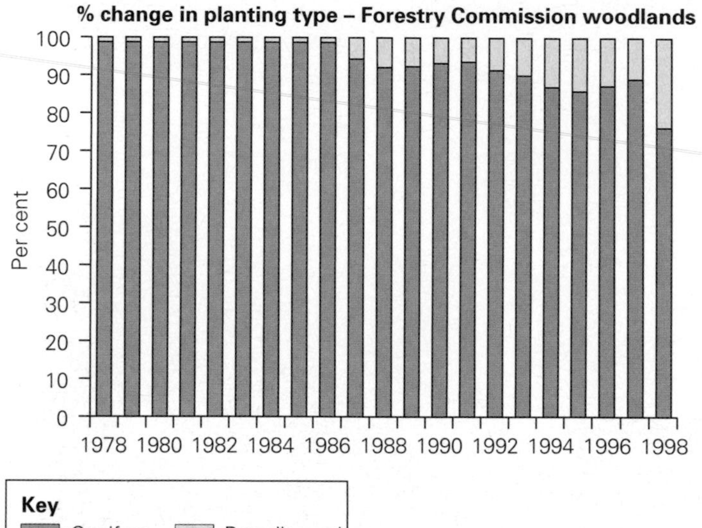

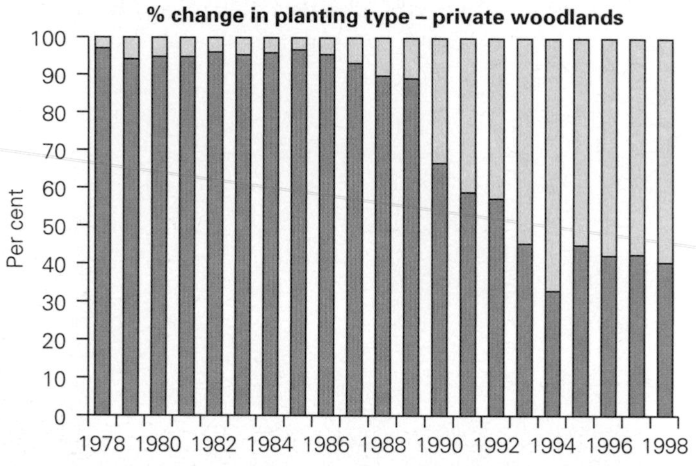

Figure 2.21 *Changing forest composition in the UK*

Kielder Forest management

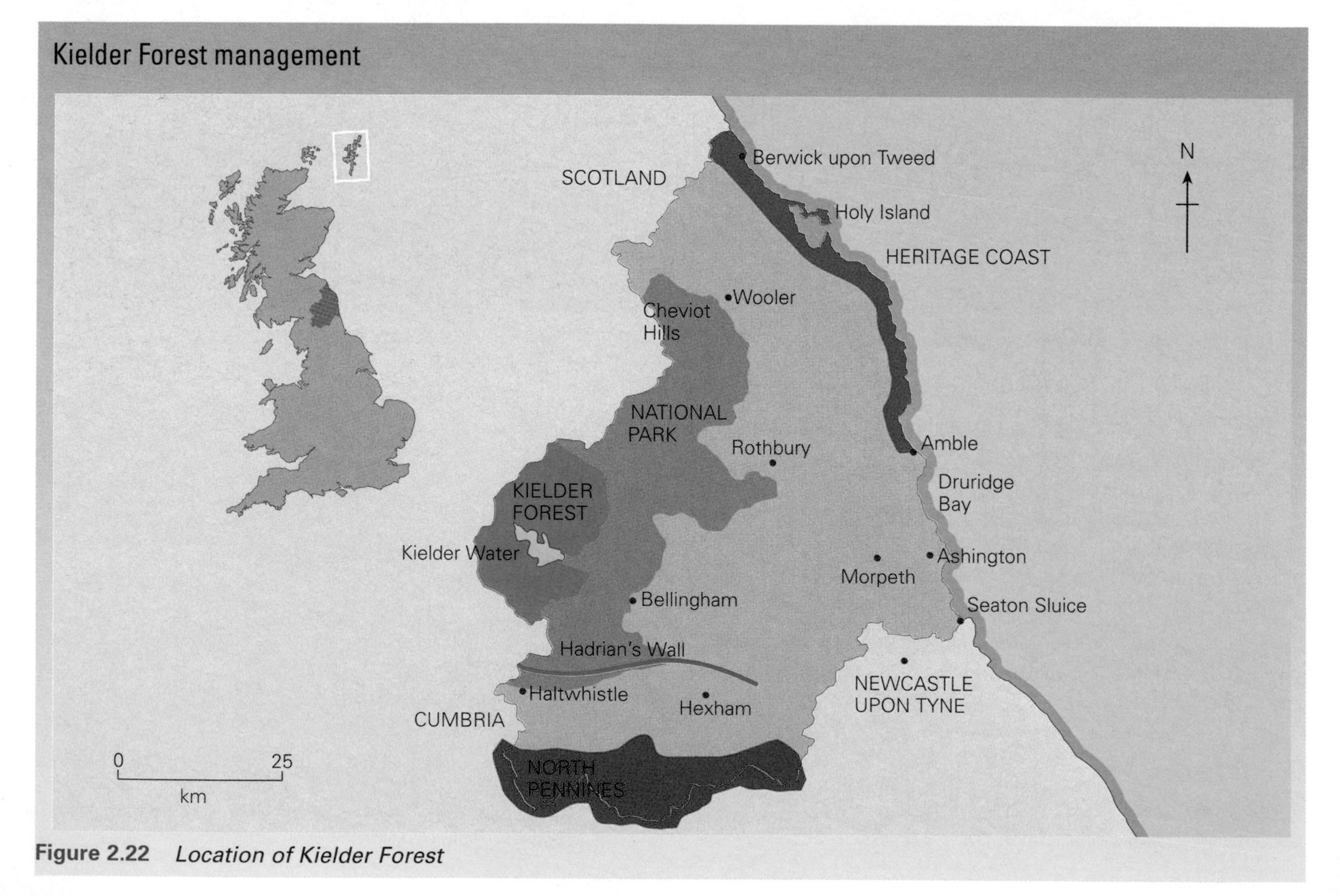

Figure 2.22 *Location of Kielder Forest*

Kielder Forest is the UK's largest forest, covering an area of over 230 square miles (Figure 2.22). Predominantly Sitka and Norway Spruce, the forest is currently being restructured. Hills, rivers and open areas add to the diversity of the forest, one of the few places in England which hosts native red squirrels. There are as many as 6,000 roe deer in the forest. Walking, cycling and horse riding are all well catered for. Kielder currently attracts around 0.5 million visitors per year.

Commercial management of Kielder Forest initially resulted in the following problems:

- non-native ecosystems
- poor age structure – large blocks planted at the same time
- reduced habitat variety due to wetland drainage
- visually intrusive plantings bearing little relation to natural landscape features.

These problems are being resolved by a variety of methods as shown in Figure 2.23.

Remaining problems

Trees have maximum economic value over a narrow age range, so by staggering the cutting (to create more variety) trees are harvested older or younger than the optimum age. The question then becomes how much can one justify losing income in order to improve the conservation value of the woodland. This is not an easy question to answer because, no matter how important biodiversity is, it is difficult to assign it an economic value.

ACTIVITIES

1 Compare and contrast the management issues in Kielder Forest and the New Forest. Refer to ecosystem character, human pressures and future opportunities.

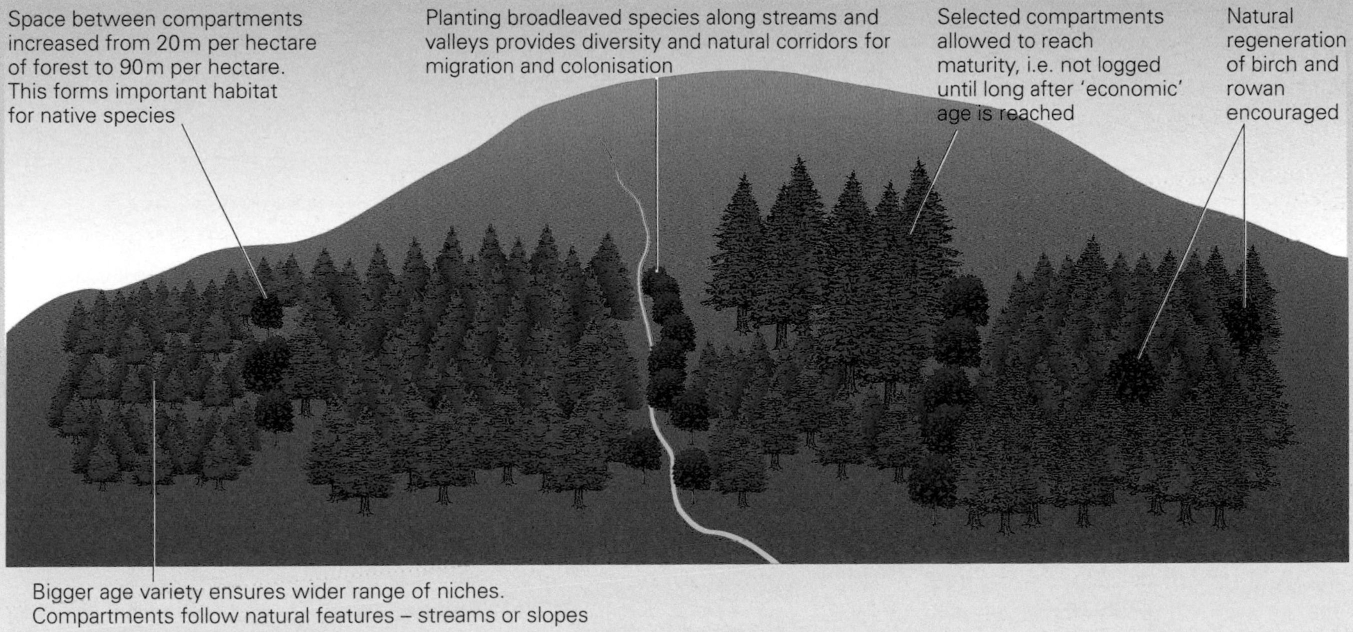

Space between compartments increased from 20 m per hectare of forest to 90 m per hectare. This forms important habitat for native species

Planting broadleaved species along streams and valleys provides diversity and natural corridors for migration and colonisation

Selected compartments allowed to reach maturity, i.e. not logged until long after 'economic' age is reached

Natural regeneration of birch and rowan encouraged

Bigger age variety ensures wider range of niches. Compartments follow natural features – streams or slopes

Figure 2.23 *Kielder Forest management improvements*

Tropical forests

The majority of tropical rainforest areas of the world are in LEDCs. This increases the problems of conservation because additional human factors come into play. Poverty reduces choices and encourages short term solutions rather than long term strategies. The range of pressures on tropical forests includes:

- urban growth
- weak legislation
- government corruption
- HEP schemes
- road building
- mineral exploitation
- climate change
- medicinal collection
- ranching
- logging
- tourism
- plantations.

Conflicting priorities in Borneo – Gunung Mulu National Park

Key details

- largest National Park in Sarawak
- 529 km²
- virgin rainforest
- spectacular underground caves
- difficult access
- home to two indigenous tribes the Berawan and the Penan
- major region being promoted by the Federal and State Tourism Ministries

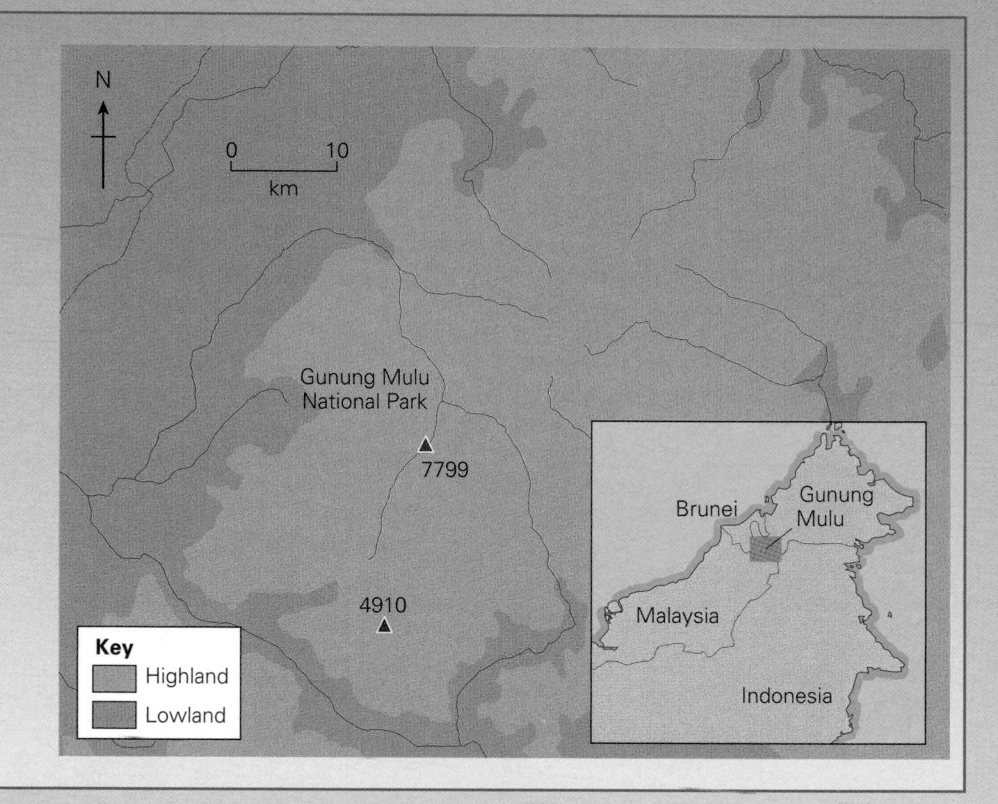

Figure 2.24 *Location of Gunung Mulu*

The Penan are a nomadic tribe, living entirely dependent on the forest. They have no tradition of agriculture or permanent settlement. The Penan have been forcibly resettled on land previously farmed by the Berawan while Penan hunting grounds have been logged.

The Berawan are agriculturists who clear the forests to grow crops for both subsistence and trade. They have experienced an improved standard of living due to tourism.

Conflicts

The need to conserve timber for long term sustainability (7th National Plan (1996–2000) reduced the annual cut by 17%).

Gunung Mulu is an area of virgin forest the government seeks to portray as a major tourist destination.

Malaysian government aims to achieve developed nation status within 20 years. Forestry can generate over US$2.6 billion/year income but the deforestation rate is around 5000 km² a year.

Figure 2.25 *The key conflicts in Gunung Mulu*

Sustainable tropical forestry

Research in the Pasoh Forest, Malaysia involved logging plots in 1955 and surveying them again in 1989.

The main findings show that the logged plots had:

- higher density of smaller trees
- reduction in biodiversity
- increased ultraviolet radiation exposure
- lower humidity
- fewer bird and mammal species.

The researchers concluded:

- the forest would sustain a 70-year logging rotation provided soil erosion was kept to a minimum, but the secondary forest would not have the biodiversity of the original
- conversion to plantations resulted in a massive loss of diversity with only a few of the most adaptable species able to thrive in plantation forest
- small areas of natural forest (164 hectares) had the lowest diversity of mammal species, compared to larger areas of natural forest (10,000 hectares). Less abundant, more wide-ranging or specialist species were unable to cope with habitat fragmentation
- most species were able to survive at least one logging cycle but mammal diversity and numbers changed in logged forest compared with virgin forest. A minority of species were favoured by logging.

The future survival of tropical forests will depend on recognising the multitude of goods and services they provide. Forests must be managed to balance wildlife habitats, timber and non timber production, indigenous development and ecotourism. Intact forest can be worth far more than its timber value, provided intelligent enough economic and political systems exist to evaluate holistic costs and benefits. New management systems will, however, encounter resistance from existing vested interests. Figure 2.26 illustrates a possible future view of tropical forestry.

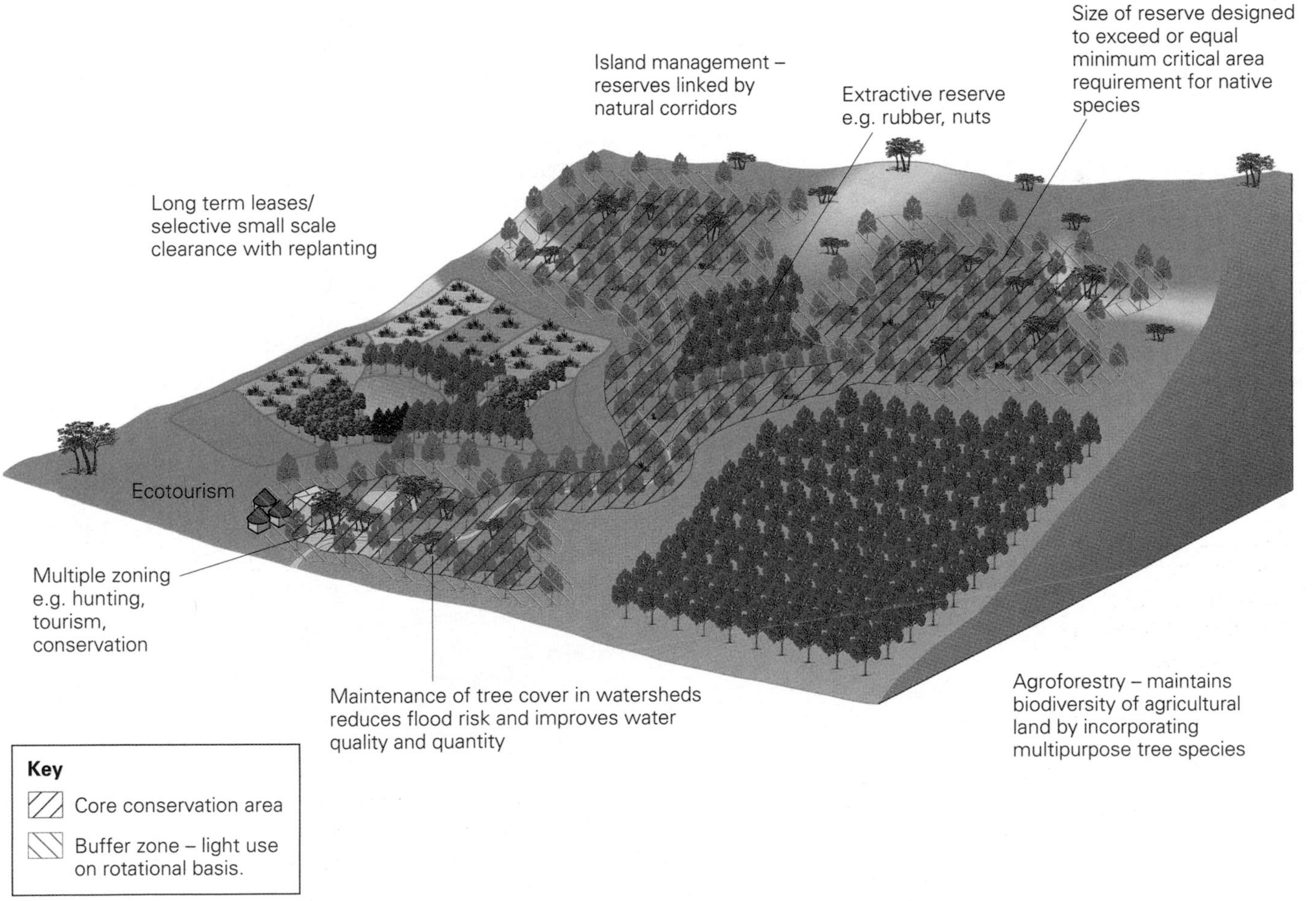

Figure 2.26 *A future view of tropical forestry*

Forest management concepts and techniques

Concepts

- buffer zone – an area around a conservation zone where limited human activity is allowed
- core – the central area of a nature reserve where human disturbance is minimised
- carrying capacity – the amount of pressure an ecosystem can take before deterioration in ecological value takes place
- ecotourism – an approach to conservation that attempts to give an ecosystem economic value by promoting sensitive tourism. Since tourists will come to see the ecosystem, there is an incentive to manage it effectively
- exotic species – species that are not native to an area. Many forest plantations involve planting fast growing exotic species
- minimal critical area – the smallest size of ecosystem needed to maintain a viable population of a given species
- preservation – a 'hard-line' conservation approach where the emphasis is on keeping people away from the environment to preserve its untouched character

Techniques

- agroforestry – a technique combining agricultural production with forest production. Many models of agroforestry offer effective sustainable agriculture with low environmental impacts
- clearfelling – a method of timber production based on total removal of forest over large areas
- coppicing – a method of producing long term sustainable timber yields by cutting trees to root level and allowing regrowth of shoots
- extractive reserve – a form of ecosystem management with emphasis on exploitation of intact ecosystem, e.g. harvesting nuts from wild trees
- island management – a management technique maximising value of small reserves (islands) by linking them along stream corridors or natural routeways
- multiple land use zoning – a management technique that seeks to resolve conflicting demands on an ecosystem by zoning activities
- plantation monoculture – forest management where income is maximised (but ecological value minimised) by planting large areas with one species

In the 1990s there have been major international conservation initiatives. The Intergovernmental Panel on Forestry and the more recent International Forestry Forum have attempted to engage dialogue between the governments of the North and the South. There is, however, little formal involvement of Non Governmental Organisations (NGOs), Indigenous People's Organisations (IPOs) or regional/local representatives in these international bodies. In many countries of the South the views of the government do not necessarily represent either the views or the best interests of rural people.

Resources

Forests as carbon sinks www.wri.org/climate/sinks.html

Greenpeace resources
www.greenpeace.org/~forests/resources/index.htm

Sarawak indigenous people and conflicts
www.rengah.c2o.org/sarawak/index.htm

WWF Forests for Life campaign
www.panda.org/forests4life/

FAO forestry site www.fao.org/forestry/forestry.htm

Forest World www.forestworld.com/

World Resources Institute – frontier forests
www.wri.org/wri/ffi/maps/

Ipassa Mingouli project, Gabon
www.brainforest.org/home.asp

Tropical forests www.wri.org/forests/tropical.html

EXTENSION ACTIVITY

Using a range of resources, including the websites given in Resources, address the following themes.

Question	Themes
What is the global role of rainforests?	What are their impacts on global carbon dioxide/oxygen levels?
What is the regional role of rainforests?	How do they influence regional temperatures and rainfall? Consider Malaysia or Amazonia's climatic trends.
What is the national role of rainforests?	How do they contribute to the economy of a tropical nation? Consider direct and indirect benefits.
What is the local role of rainforests?	How do they contribute to the food, water and fuel requirements of indigenous people or the rural poor?
What is the ecological value of rainforests?	How old are they and how has this influenced their biodiversity? How does the rainforest encourage biodiversity? What are the current extinction issues?
How do the threats to rainforest vary from region to region?	Which region is threatened most by: logging; fuelwood collection; agriculture; infrastructure development?

3 Grassland ecosystems

Grassland areas, by definition, are largely devoid of trees, although many grasslands, in both temperate and tropical regions, are wet enough for some tree species to survive. The trees that do occur in grassland areas are often in distinctive 'firebreak' locations (i.e. along escarpments or in gulleys) suggesting the role of fire may have been important in shaping grassland ecosystems. Fires occur naturally as a result of lightning strikes but also by humans creating hunting opportunities (burned clearings produce a flush of grass to attract grazers to confined spaces). Although the origins of grassland may be climatic, i.e. areas of low rainfall and high evapotranspiration, there is little question that the human imprint is strong. Many consider grassland areas to be anthropogenic biomes caused by the destruction of trees by fire. Grass is present in almost every environment from tropical rainforest to Arctic tundra. Grass is also extremely important to humans, forming the staple food crop of the human race; wheat, rice, oats, millet, sorghum, rye, barley and maize are all grasses, and most meats are derived from grass grazers. Grass owes its success to several adaptations, as shown in Table 2.9.

The main grassland biomes of the world are shown in Figure 2.28. Grassland locations correlate well with continental interiors and tropical wet and dry climates. There are significant differences between the temperate (prairie) and tropical grasslands (savanna), both in terms of their physical characteristics and the issues and conflicts affecting them. These are summarised in Table 2.11 on page 59.

Figure 2.27 *Secondary grassland from degraded forest*

		Grass adaptation				
Environmental problem	**Sample environments**	**Structural toughness**	**Rapid life cycle; high seed yield**	**Dense root network**	**Growth buds underground**	**Vertical leaves**
Cold environment with short growing season	Prairie, tundra, alpine, e.g. Mongolia, North Dakota		✔		✔	
Dry environment with unpredictable rainfall	Prairie, savanna, e.g. Kalahari, Tanzania		✔	✔		
Hot season with high fire risk	Savanna, e.g. Kalahari, Tanzania				✔	
High grazing pressure	Prairie, savanna, e.g. Kalahari	✔				
High trampling pressure	Prairie, savanna, e.g. Kalahari	✔				
Mid–high latitude with low sun angles	Prairie, tundra, e.g. North Dakota, Mongolia					✔

Table 2.9 *Grass adaptations to environmental problems*

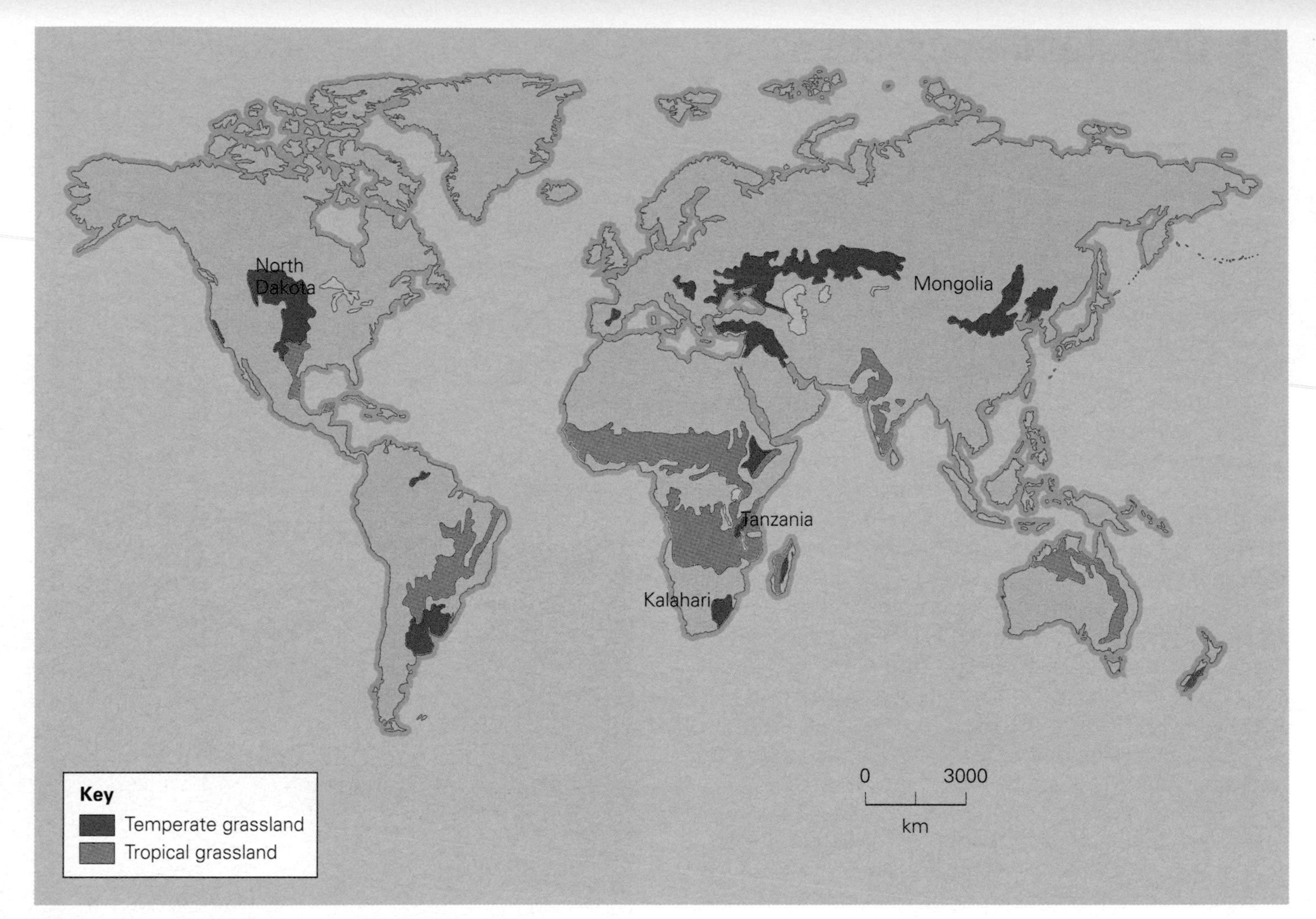

Figure 2.28 *Location of the world's grasslands*

Political impacts have also been apparent. In the latter half of the twentieth century, many grassland areas were created in LEDCs by clearing forests for cash cropping. In MEDCs, agricultural intensification of the grasslands resulted in the dustbowl tragedy in the USA where vast regions suffered from soil erosion, highlighting major gaps in our understanding of sustainable ecosystem management. Table 2.10 shows a summary of world grassland condition, as measured by the quality of the services they provide. Whilst the current state of ecological service is generally fair or good, effective, sustainable management needs to be implemented in such regions in order to maintain this.

Drought risk in grasslands

Ironically, drought poses a bigger risk in the semi-arid grasslands of the world than the deserts. Deserts support small populations highly adapted to drought. By contrast, grassland supports much larger numbers. Political pressures, including debt repayments, have increased settled agriculture in drylands. Unfortunately, the inflexibility of settled agriculture combined with the unreliability of rainfall can lead to devastating drought and famine.

Excellent				
Good			↓	↓
Fair	↓	↓		
Poor				
Bad				
Key: ↓ improving ↑ declining ? uncertain	Food production	Biodiversity	Carbon storage	Recreation

Table 2.10 *The state of the world's grasslands*
Source: *World Resources Institute, 2000-2001*

	Tropical grasslands (savanna habitats)	Temperate grasslands (prairie/steppe habitats)
Climate		
Temperature Precipitation	• 22–32 °C • growing season (2–8 months) limited by lack of moisture during dry season • 250–2000 mm • highly seasonal with distinctive summer maximum	• –20 to +19 °C • growing season (average 5 months) limited by low winter temperatures • 300–600 mm • summer maximum • winter precipitation as snow
Soils		
Type	variable with rock type: • infertile **latosols** – iron rich soils which harden on exposure to air • fertile **tropical red soils** both soil types are sensitive to overuse	• deep, dark, fertile **chernozem** soils
Processes	• fire recycles nutrients • leaching is incomplete and capillary action results in accumulation of iron/aluminium near surface	• leaching incomplete • capillary action results in accumulation of calcium in topsoil
Age	• core areas millions of years old (hence high degree of leaching) • marginal areas younger	• less than 12 000 years old (since end of last ice age)
Land uses	• traditionally herding cultures, e.g. Maasai, Tuareg, Fulani • more recently cash crops grown (e.g. peanut, cotton) or ranching	• traditionally herding or hunting cultures, e.g. North American Indians, Uzbeks of former Soviet Union • more recently intensive arable farming
Plant adaptations	• drought-resistant xerophytes, e.g. thorn scrub and acacia bushes • fire-resistant pyrophytes with underground buds, e.g. grasses or fire-resistant bark, e.g. Baobab tree	• dominated by grasses – extreme winter temperatures kill exposed trees
Conflicts and issues	• cultural/religious significance of herd sizes • national boundaries disrupt tribal migration • population growth pressurises grazing, fuelwood and water supplies • cash cropping reduces amount and quality of grazing • fragmentation of natural habitats • unpredictable rainfall patterns • disease (Tsetse fly) in wetter areas • overstocking in nature reserves • illegal game poaching • impacts on indigenous lifestyles	• ranching and cash crops destroy native habitats and impinge on indigenous lifestyles • agrochemical pollution • introduced species • profitability comes before sustainability, soil erosion and conservation • fragmentation of natural habitats

Table 2.11 *The characteristics of temperate and tropical grasslands*

North Dakota – temperate grassland in a wealthy nation

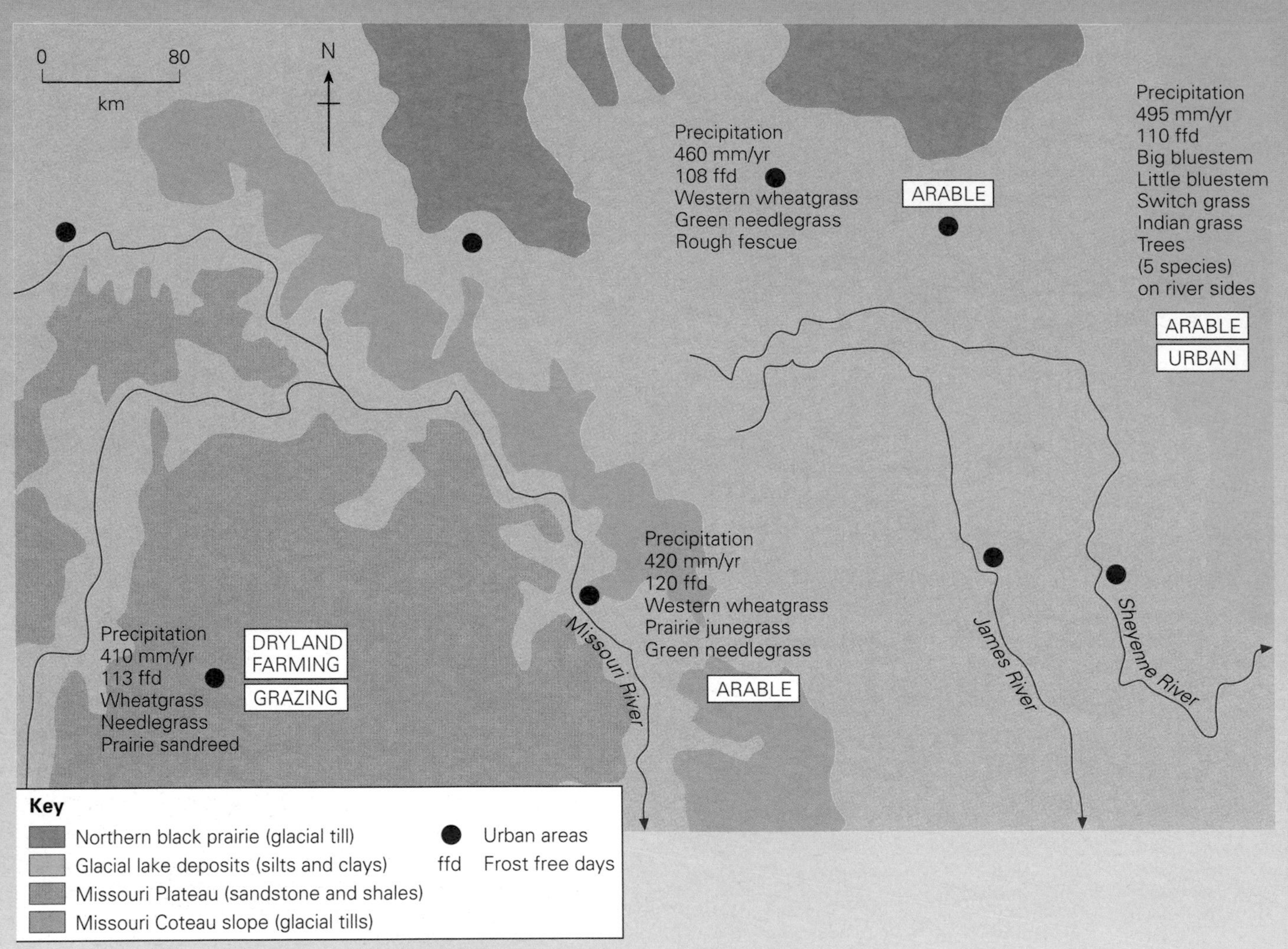

Figure 2.29 *Prairie diversity in North Dakota*

The interior grasslands, or prairies of the North American continent represent an invaluable natural resource.

Main benefits for biodiversity	Main threats
• breeding grounds and feeding areas for migratory birds • wide range of niches related to climate, relief and soil variations (Figure 2.29)	• intensive agriculture • habitat loss • fragmentation • fire suppression • exotic species • altered hydrology • intensive grazing • modified predator communities

A total of 45 distinctly different soil types interact with varying relief and climate to produce a wealth of biodiversity. As Figure 2.29 illustrates, the irregular shapes of these habitats (often reflecting ancient glacial processes) produces an easily fragmented ecosystem making the prairies even more vulnerable.

Approximately 98 per cent of the habitat of the three major species of prairie dogs has been eliminated by disease, agriculture practices and urban development since the early 1900s. The Prairie Pothole Region, a critical nesting area for migratory birds, has been greatly altered by agriculture, resulting in the fragmentation of grassland habitat and increased predation of nests. Large stands of flowering leafy spurge, an invasive alien plant, attract a wide array of insect pollinators with potentially damaging effects for the increasingly small populations of native plants that rely on these same insects for pollination.

The result is that the native ecosystems of North Dakota have largely been replaced with commercial agriculture. Pockets of original prairie ecosystem remain, but in small fragmented areas which are below the minimum critical size of all but the smallest species. Realistically, the prairie ecosystem is extinct except for reserves.

Politics and technology threaten savanna grasslands in the Kalahari

Botswana has been part of the European Union Beef Protocol Agreement since the early 1970s. This has paid above average prices for Botswana's beef. The money has been used for deep borehole drilling technology in order to drill numerous water wells. Consequently, large areas of the Kalahari have changed from low density hunter-gatherer populations to borehole-centred livestock keeping. Ecologically, large herds of wild antelope have been replaced by domestic cattle, creating a threat of wide environmental degradation through overgrazing. In 2004, the Beef Protocol Agreement ends and Botswana is likely to experience lower cattle prices. The obvious response will be to maintain profit by keeping more cattle. This could be disastrous for the savanna ecosystems on which farm incomes depend.

In 1999, CREED (Collaborative Research in the Economics of Environment and Development) studied sustainable livestock management in the Kalahari. Their results illustrate much of the complexity of managing grasslands. There are at least four systems interacting:

- socio-economic systems influence the choices farmers make (how many cattle in the herd? how many boreholes to drill?). If the price is low, farmers need larger herds to make a profit. More boreholes can support larger cattle numbers
- political systems influence the socio-economic systems (legislation on herd density, enforcement of legislation, permits for borehole development)
- ecological systems respond to socio-economic choices. Increases in cattle density result in grassland degrading to nutritionally poor scrub
- climatic systems add unpredictable low rainfalls, superimposed on the other systems. A wetter year might reduce the problems caused by poor management, a drought year might undermine even good management.

Boreholes encourage cattle to congregate in one area, rapidly overwhelming the carrying capacity of the area while underusing grazing land in more isolated areas. Historically, an 8 km borehole spacing led to a few heavily used boreholes with cattle moving long distances between them. This spread out grazing pressure over large areas. Ranchers want to increase the number of boreholes, but this is only sustainable if herd sizes decrease. The government recommends a maximum of 400 'livestock units' (fully grown cattle equivalent) per borehole, but actual figures range from 50 to 1,000 per borehole. When the EU beef subsidy ends, economic pressure will probably increase herd sizes. Figure 2.30 illustrates the factors interacting in the Kalahari to influence grassland degradation.

ACTIVITIES

1 Toss a coin four times to determine the ingredients of possible future scenarios in the Kalahari grasslands based on the table below.

	Heads	Tails
1	EU beef subsidy withdrawn, prices fall	Asian demand for western food pushes up world beef prices
2	Government legislation on herd sizes strictly enforced	Herd size policies not enforced
3	Run of dry years	Run of wet years
4	Borehole permits strictly enforced	Government gives in to pressure for more boreholes

a Using the four scenarios, refer to the graphs in Figure 2.30 and predict the likely outcome in terms of the quality and sustainability of the grassland.

b Suggest other factors that might influence the future of the Kalahari grasslands.

In conclusion, the Kalahari grasslands are under enormous pressure, but there are still areas of intact native grassland ecosystem surviving. The future of many savanna species, including the native grazing animals such as antelope and gazelle, depends on the quality of both conservation and law enforcement in the Kalahari.

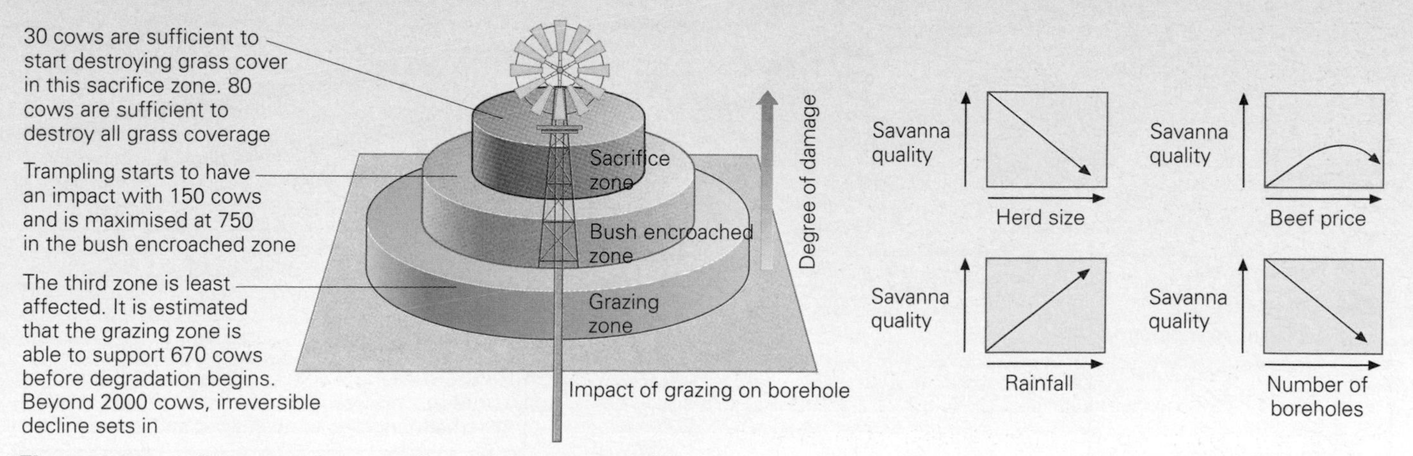

Figure 2.30 *Influences of pastoralism on savanna quality*

Biodiversity and development in an ex-communist nation – the Mongolian experience

Mongolia is a land of extremes, the coldest recorded winter temperatures being –58°C, while summer temperatures climb as high as 40°C. Annual precipitation ranges from 600 mm in the Khentii, Altai, and Khovsgol mountains to less than 100 mm in the Gobi Desert. In this harsh steppe (grassland) environment is one of the most biodiverse countries on Earth with a long tradition of conservation. Mongolia was the first nation in the world to establish a nature reserve – over 200 years ago.

It is estimated that 30 per cent of Mongolia's territory will need conservation protection in order to maintain present biodiversity. The government has planned to fulfil this by 2015. Protected areas already cover 12 per cent of the country but there are real tensions developing. The collapse of the Soviet Union left Mongolia struggling to develop a free market economy and the country is under pressure to develop intensive agricultural practices. The break up of Soviet collective farms in 1991 privatised agriculture, redistributing animals amongst state farm members. This encouraged families to expand their herds, and by the end of 1997 the Mongolian grasslands were carrying over 31 million livestock. Between 25–50 per cent of the rural population are considered to be living in poverty. Poverty threatens sustainability because it can breed a short term approach to problem solving. The threats to the wildlife of the Mongolian steppes include:

- overgrazing
- overexploitation of animal/plant populations
- pollution
- soil erosion
- infrastructure development
- oil and mining
- disruption of migration routes
- habitat destruction in neighbouring China and Russia
- uncontrolled hunting in China and Russia.

The Eastern Steppes (Figure 2.31) are seen as the next region for industrial and agricultural development, but conservationists are working to ensure development is sustainable.

The Global Environment Facility provided funds through the United Nations Development Programme for a seven-year project to ensure sustainable use of biodiversity is achieved through:

- strengthening the management of protected areas – highlighting the need for land-use planning and environmental impact assessments through workshops and regular contacts with government officials at every level. Working towards the recognition of biodiversity affects all land use decisions
- supporting biodiversity conservation and sustainable livelihoods inside and outside protected areas. Encouraging public participation through training and education
- incorporating biodiversity conservation into provincial and local development plans, and ensuring laws, policies and policing support the planning
- supporting research and monitoring of biodiversity and its social context, improving access to conservation funding.

In addition, the Worldwide Fund for Nature (WWF) have the following involvement in the region:

- helping the government establish a nationwide network of protected areas
- encouraging development of sustainable land-use practices such as grazing and cattle breeding
- encouraging traditional metal and leather work, and building a sustainable trade in dairy products
- setting up pilot ecotourism schemes in the national parks closest to the capital, Ulan Bator and the Gobi Altai Mountains, with a view to eventually developing tourism in all eight national parks.

In conclusion, with a large area of steppe and a small population, Mongolia possesses some of the best surviving temperate grassland in the world. It should be feasible to create sustainable conservation-centred development as long as rural poverty can be tackled at the same time.

Weblinks

www.un-mongolia.mn/wildher/index.html – Mongolia's wild heritage

www.un-mongolia.mn/projects/esbp/index.html Eastern Steppe Biodiversity Project

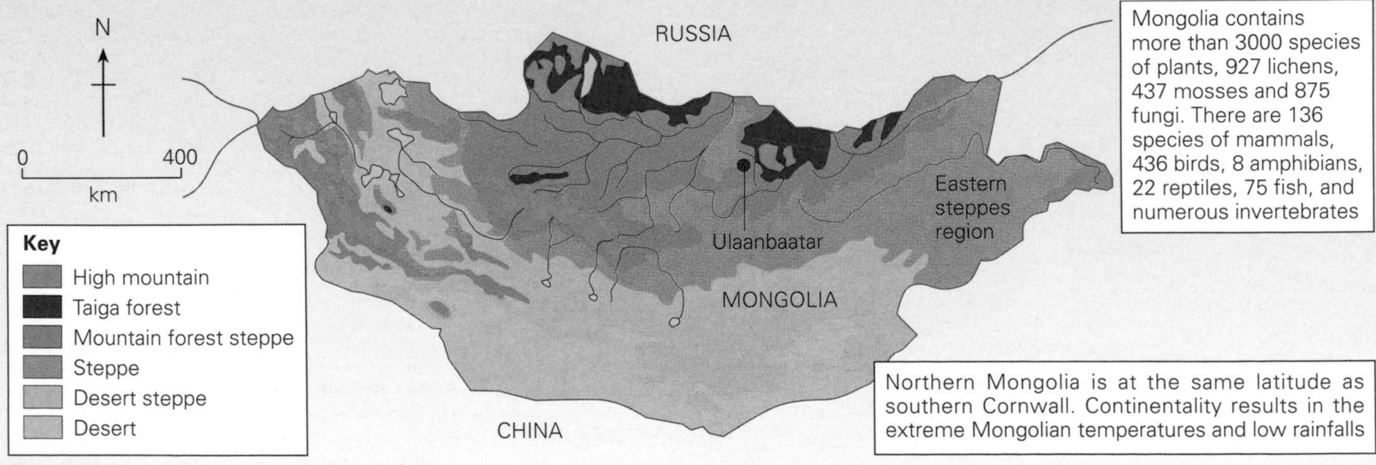

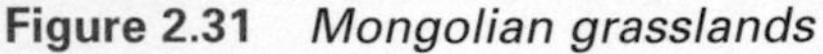
Figure 2.31 *Mongolian grasslands*

Savanna ecotourism in Tanzania

One of the possible ways in which conservation can support both ecosystems and societies is through ecotourism. Tanzania has some of the richest wildlife collections in the world, and a long history of conservation management. A game reserve was established in the Serengeti in 1929.

In 1995, Tanzania was the third poorest country in Africa, its GNP per capita only 17 per cent of Africa's average. Tanzania has an unusual history with a legacy of independence, self reliance and alternative approaches to development, hence whilst GNP ranks 53rd in Africa, daily calorie intake ranks 34th. There has been a strong focus for many years on food crops rather than cash crops.

Agriculture accounts for:

- 57% of GDP
- 85% of exports
- 90% of the work force employment.

Topography and climate limit cultivated crops to only 4 per cent of the land area. Tanzania has few other resources, but with nearly 80 per cent of the country under forest or grassland, there is a great wildlife diversity. Tanzania's population is growing and the government is under huge pressure to exploit national resources, yet there is also a long history of valuing and protecting wildlife. An obvious solution would be to use the natural wildlife resources to make money through sensitive ecotourist developments.

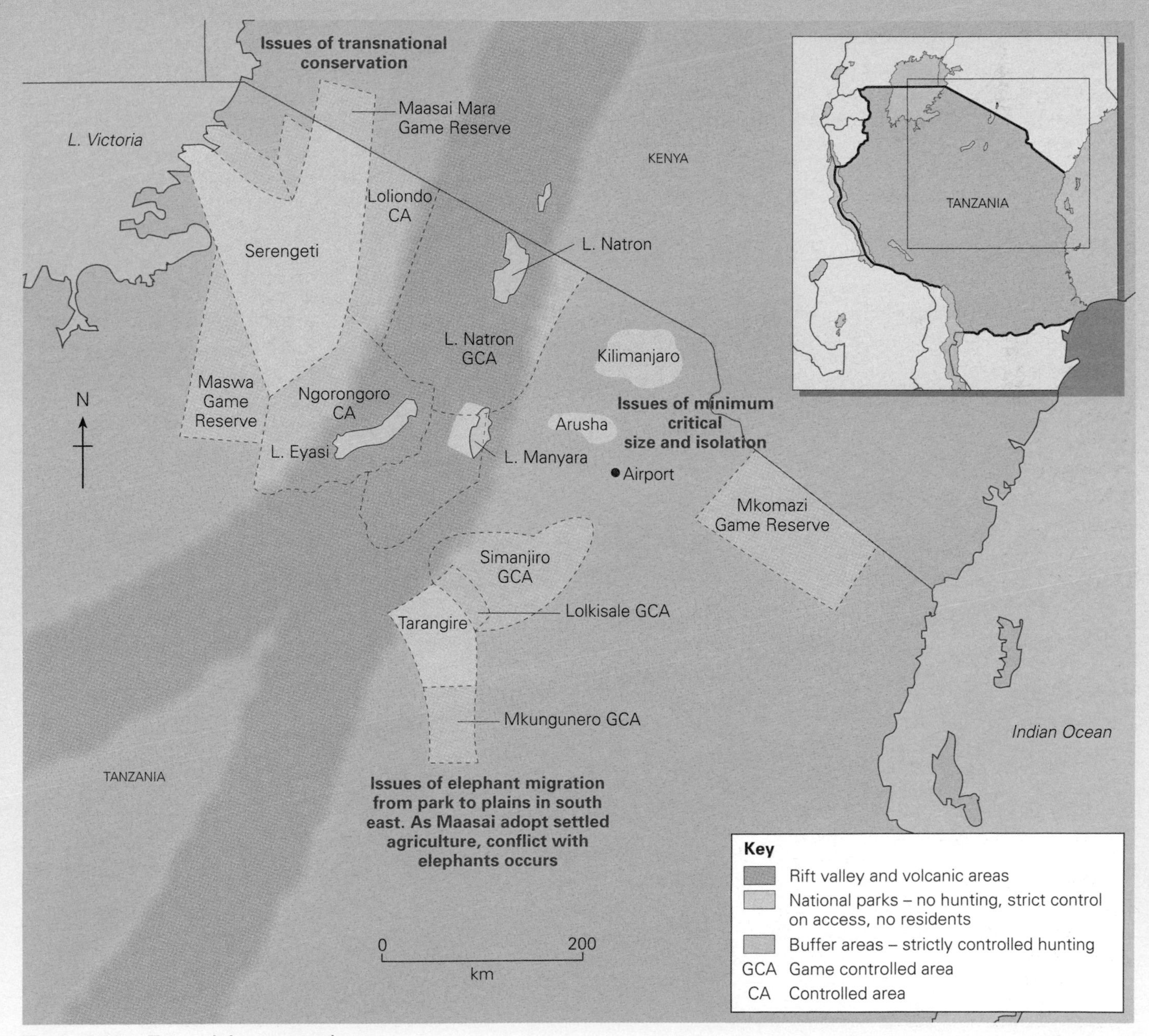

Figure 2.32 *Tanzania's protected areas*

Figure 2.32 shows the areas of Tanzania enjoying protected status. In northern Tanzania a very high level of protection is afforded. The Serengeti National Park covers 14,763 km^2 while the adjacent Ngorongoro Conservation area, a World Biosphere Reserve and Natural World Heritage Site, covers an area of 8,288 km^2. The degree of protection offered is necessary because the climate is strongly seasonal and most of the wildlife migrates over hundreds of kilometres following the rain. The variations in habitat caused by altitude, distance from the sea and soil type creates a spectrum of gradations in habitat (Figure 2.33). The protected areas and buffer zones on Figure 2.32 are not clearly delineated on the ground. No fences can be used due to the animal migration, but the lack of fences makes life easy for potential poachers. Poaching is a major problem in the area.

Ngorongoro Conservation Area

The Ngorongoro Conservation Area (Figures 2.32 and 2.33) is particularly valuable, containing a wide range of habitats. It is also the home of some 20,000–40,000 Maasai, many of whom were relocated here when the neighbouring Serengeti National Park was established in 1951. Ngorongoro exemplifies some of the difficulties in achieving a balance between conservation and development. The key problems are:

- the area has been degraded by trampling, overgrazing and tour vehicles
- poaching is difficult to tackle due to lack of resources
- the rhinoceros population is very small and extremely vulnerable to poaching
- over-stressed grassland is being invaded by alien species
- forest areas are increasingly threatened by local fuel wood gathering
- in response to food scarcity, Maasai were allowed to practise cultivation on a temporary basis. Much took place on areas unsuitable for agriculture, resulting in further habitat degradation.

Since the Ngorongoro Conservation Area Authority (NCAA) formed in 1959, management priorities have included multiple land use zoning, but lack of communication between government officials and resident Maasai plagued the project from the beginning. In 1962, the Tanzanian Government conducted one of the first attempts to reconcile the interests of wildlife, nomadic pastoralists and habitat. In March 1996, the NCAA and the World Conservation Union (IUCN) put forward a new General Management Plan for the area. The plan provided new facilities for the Maasai in a new location. The NCAA claimed the plan had the agreement of the Maasai living in the conservation area but videoed interviews with the Maasai after the meetings suggested a different understanding. The Maasai had only a few days to respond to a complex 160-page document, and most of them are illiterate. Many fear wildlife will be put above their needs and they will be forcibly removed from the Ngorongoro area.

The benefits of ecotourism

Tourism is increasingly important to Tanzania. In 1999 the tourist industry accounted for 16 per cent of the nation's GDP. The government aim is to attract one million tourists by 2004. Ecotourism in Tanzania can take a variety of forms, as shown in Table 2.12.

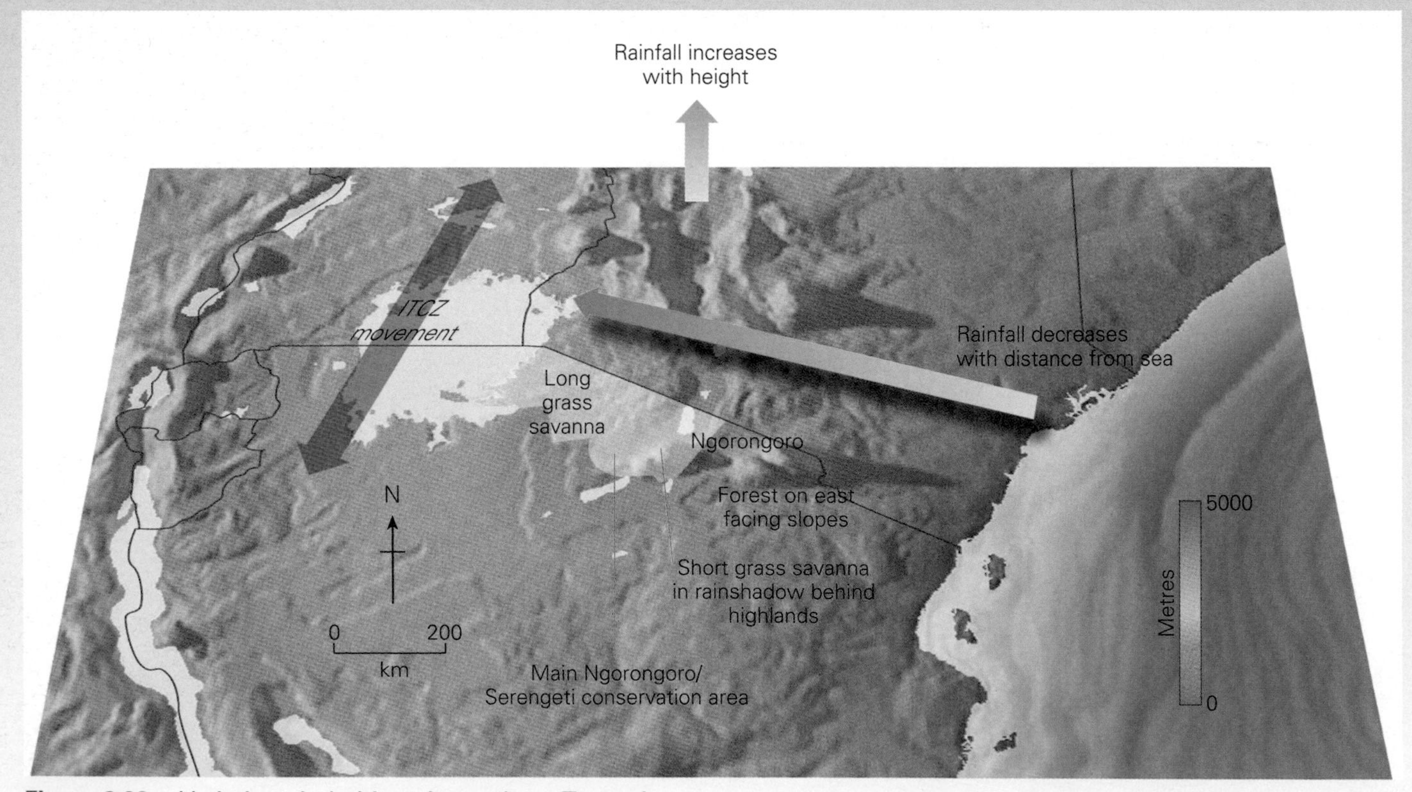

Figure 2.33 *Variations in habitats in northern Tanzania*

Type	Main attraction	Main advantages	Main disadvantages
Wildlife tourism	Seeing wildlife in native habitats.	Brings large number of tourists. Income helps subsidise park management.	Large volume tourism with dense impacts on popular locations. According to recent reports, Northern Tanzania's parks are at saturation point.
Hunting	Some people enjoy stalking and killing large game.	Low impact – very small group sizes. Can fit in to existing management needs, e.g. culling herd sizes. High percentage of money goes directly to native guides.	Small niche markets.
Cultural tourism	Close encounter with native settlements and people.	Large proportion of income directly benefits villagers. Fosters mutual respect and understanding Low impacts on wildlife.	Can disrupt village life, e.g. school interrupted by visitor tours. Can result in voyeur mentality.

Table 2.12 *Ecotourism in Tanzania*

Political integrity is needed to ensure conservation plans are translated into ground level reality. In Tanzania there has been a long term commitment to sustainability and conservation from a centralised government. The government is currently committed to a privatisation programme to improve the economy, but there are worries that opportunistic private business will be able to ignore conservation laws. Whether the government has the power, or indeed the freedom from corruption, to handle an enlarged private sector remains to be seen. Tanzania desperately needs to improve the standard of living of its people. The challenge is to make wildlife a partner in the process rather than a victim.

Figure 2.34 *Savanna themes and issues*

ACTIVITIES

1. Summarise the range of difficulties involved in coming to a genuinely participative agreement with the Maasai on the management of the lands they have used for 200 years.
2. Suggest ways the process might be improved.
3. What are the cost implications of improved participation? What are the costs of ignoring indigenous inhabitants?
4. Refer to Figure 2.34. On a sketch of the images, annotate the main issues, themes and relevant observations.

Web links

www-trees.slu.se/ngorongoro/ngnov95t.html Voices from Ngorongoro.

www.unesco.org/whc/sites/39.htm UNESCO information on Ngorongoro World Heritage Site.

www.unesco.org/mab/br/brdir/africa/tanza2.htm UNESCO information on Ngorongoro/Serengeti Biosphere Reserve.

4 Marine ecosystems

Introduction

Three types of marine ecosystem will be examined in this section – estuaries, mangroves and reefs. Coastal zones are important for a number of reasons:

- three billion people live within 100 km of a coastline
- fish and shellfish provide about one sixth of the animal protein consumed by humans
- one billion people, mostly in LEDCs, depend on fish for protein
- over 65 per cent of cities with a population greater than 2.5 million are on coastlines
- more than half the population of the USA lives within 80 km of the coast
- coastal populations are increasing at a higher rate than the population in general
- world fish harvest (including farmed fish) reached 116 million tonnes in 1996
- of 20,000 known species of fish, around 9,000 are routinely fished
- five species make up 50 per cent of global fisheries – herring, cod, jack, redfish and mackerel
- a recent analysis of fishing trends in 200 species (Food and Agriculture Organisation 1997) indicated that 35 per cent of these species are overfished and 25 per cent are fully exploited
- in 1994, around 8 million tonnes of fish were taken from stocks defined as 'depleted or over-exploited'
- as larger fish have declined in number, smaller varieties lower down the food chain have been targeted for fishing, but their removal influences all species higher up the food chain.

In the late 1990s, attempts were made to place monetary values on ecosystem services. The values (US$ per hectare per year) are shown in Figure 2.35 for marine ecosystems. Note the tropical forest ecosystem shown alongside for comparison.

The traditional way of valuing marine ecosystems is simply by the value of the fish caught. Table 2.13 illustrates some of the potential conflict between the value of an ecosystem for fish, and its broader value for biodiversity and ecological services.

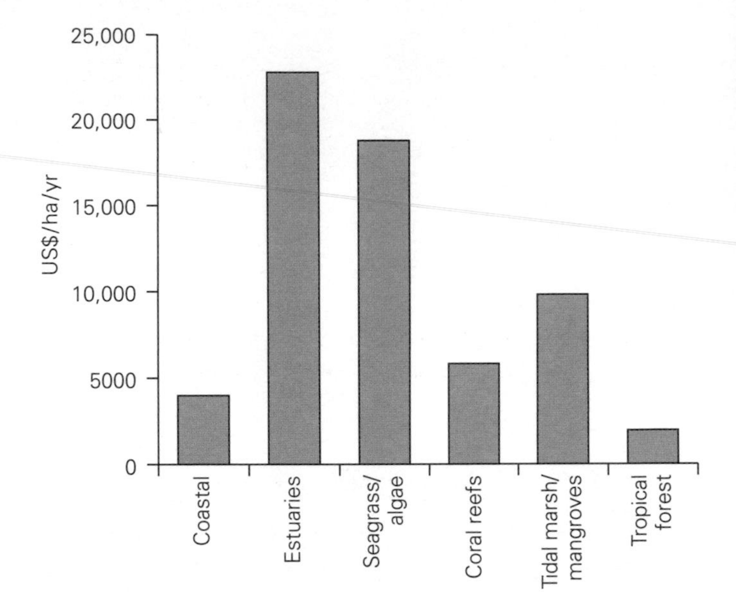

Figure 2.35 *The high value of marine ecosystem services*

	Kg fish/ person/yr	Aquaculture (tonnes/yr)	Fresh water catch ('000 tonnes/yr)	Marine catch ('000 tonnes/yr)
Africa	7	75,681	1,373	3,917
Europe	18	1,472,993	544	17,507
North America	22	464,268	289	6,575
Central America	13	115,818	205	1,512
South America	9	281,800	388	19,751
Asia	13	16,064,067	14,337	40,905
Oceania	22	79,721	16	910
Totals				
LEDCs	10	15,687,518	16,159	58,676
MEDCs	25	2,866,827	994	32,543

Table 2.13 *Worldwide marine output, 1993–1995*

ACTIVITIES

1. Describe and comment on the main patterns emerging from the data in Table 2.13.
2. What further data might you need to answer the question, 'Which region is most vulnerable to overfishing?'.

Pressures on marine ecosystems

Overfishing

One of the most significant features of human management of marine ecosystems is its limited success. The story of the collapse of the North Sea herring fisheries illustrates the point.

1965 Herring forms a major North Sea fishery, peaking at 1.2 million tonnes/yr. The high catches deplete the herring population, taking up to 50 per cent of adult fish in a year and relying on juvenile fish making up the shortfall in subsequent years.

1977 Herring stocks so low that the fishery closed to allow numbers to recover. Numbers slowly increased.

1982 Herring fishing recommences on the basis of **maximum sustainable yield** calculations where fish catch is linked to the population size and likely growth rate.

1992 Herring numbers still low and falling below the **safe biological limit** – the population size where numbers are so small that future breeding success cannot be guaranteed.

1998 Herring fishing continues but on a much more modest level. Catch for 1998 was 39,000 tonnes. As soon as the quota was reached the herring fishery officially closed.

The herring stock is still greatly reduced and may not recover. If smaller catches had been taken in the 1960s to 1980s, there might still be healthy fishing populations today. Much of the problem was caused by fishing quotas based on highly simplistic models of the real world (Figure 2.36). Only as we have researched the nature of marine ecosystems, have we begun to realise the complexity that needs to be considered when setting quotas.

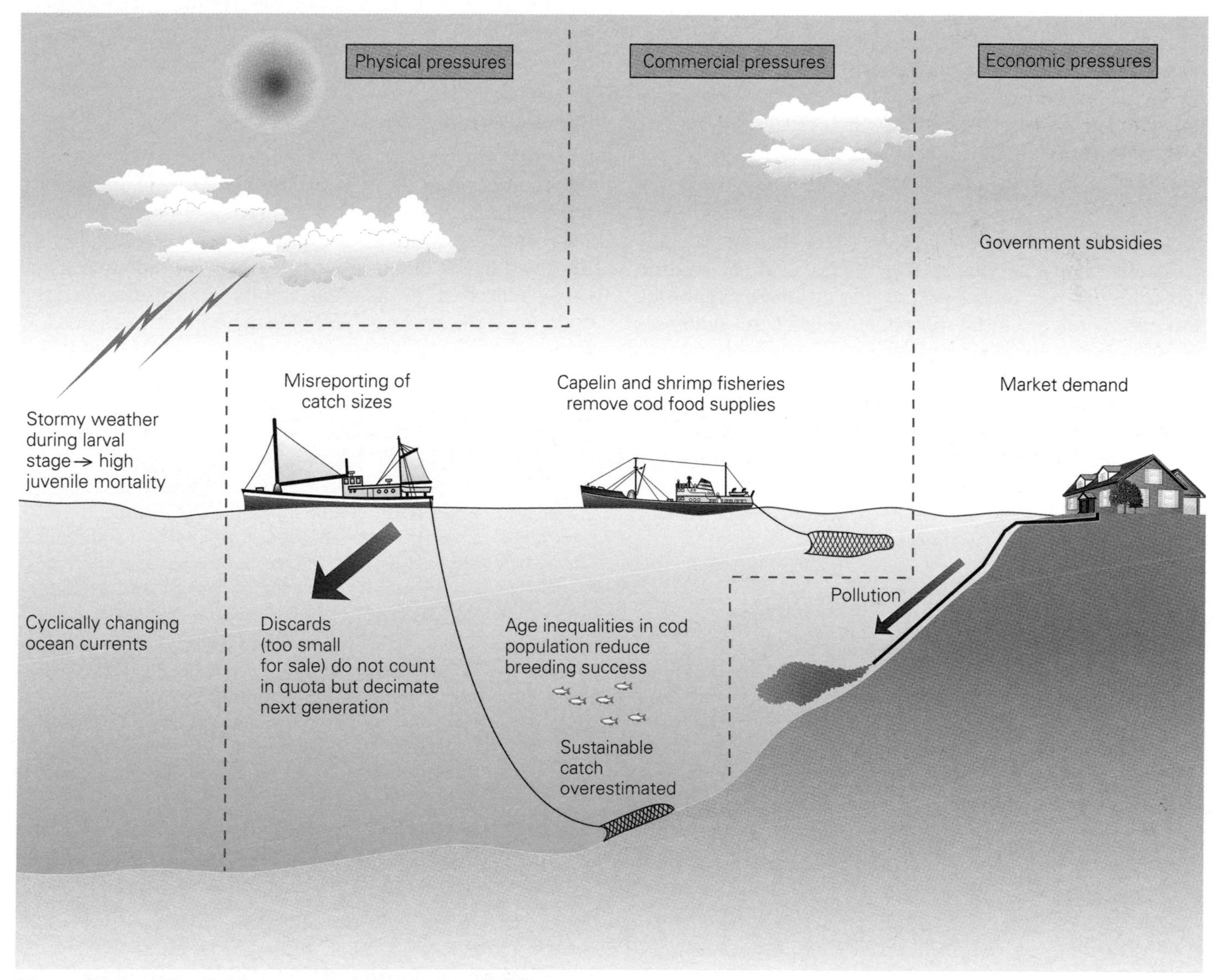

Figure 2.36 *Why fishing quotas failed in the 1980s*

Habitat losses

Coastal development contributes to habitat loss in a number of ways. Urbanisation, industrialisation and agricultural expansion in coastal areas result in the destruction of wetlands and other habitats on land. This causes changes in river flows into the sea, affecting the siltation rates, water temperature and salinity, thus altering the marine environment. The Aswan Dam project on the Nile River led to the erosion of delta habitats and a reduction of nutrient inputs. The dam contributed to the later collapse of eastern Mediterranean fisheries. Intense fishing can destroy not only fish populations but also their habitats, trawling scours seabeds and smothers bottom-dwelling creatures with sediments. Fishing with dynamite is a major threat to coral reefs.

Pollution

Since the oceans are the end point of most rivers, it follows that marine ecosystems are doubly vulnerable because they inherit pollution from the land as well as direct pollution to the sea. There are a number of important concepts to consider when examining marine pollution. These are outlined in Table 2.14.

Marine pollutants vary in their impacts, some are longer lived than others, some are more toxic than others. There is one class of pollution, however, that has particularly insidious impacts on species. The use of certain hydrocarbons is causing sexual disruption to organisms and greatly undermining reproductive rates. Alkylphenols are compounds that are widely used in detergents, plastics and rubber. These compounds mimic the effects of the female hormone oestrogen. Males become 'feminised' and experience breeding difficulties. These impacts have been seen in species as diverse as trout and Beluga whales. It is possible that the decline in human sperm counts observed in developed countries is related to the feminisation of the marine environment.

Sedimentation

Soil erosion on land results in sedimentation in coastal ecosystems. This reduces light penetration to seagrass beds, coral, and other communities dependent on photosynthesis. Sediments settling out choke bottom-dwelling organisms and filter-feeding species. In 1990, United Nations marine pollution experts estimated that, globally, rivers carry volumes of sediment three times higher than the levels expected in 'undeveloped' watersheds, thus creating huge problems for such marine organisms.

Species introduction

Organisms such as borers, plankton and fish larvae, are transported around the world by ships. Exotic species are implicated in the spread of a disease affecting corals in Asia and the Middle East. An American jellyfish first observed in the Black Sea in 1982 is now dominant in the ecosystem and its feeding habits contributed to the collapse of the anchovy fishery in the adjacent Sea of Azov.

Concept	Meaning	Example
Thresholds	Pollution may have very little impact on the environment until a threshold level is reached, beyond which significant impacts occur.	Sewage enrichment can be beneficial for marine ecosystems, but if the sewage input exceeds the capacity of the ecosystem to use the nutrients, decomposition of the excess organic matter causes oxygen levels to plummet. A survey in 1957 found no fish in the Thames from Kew to Gravesend due to sewage loading and oxygen depletion.
Limiting factors	Algal blooms – toxic 'red tides' which can devastate marine life – are held in check by limited nutrient supplies thus inhibiting growth.	In 1981 and 1985, algal blooms caused mass fish kills in Danish waters. Denmark now controls fertiliser use on coastal farms. In 1987, a toxic bloom off the Guatemalan coast resulted in the death of 26 people and serious illness in 200 others.
Biological concentration	Small concentrations of pollutants become more concentrated as they pass up the food chain.	In 1979, organic lead compounds were discharged into the Mersey Estuary. Worms in the mudflats had lead concentrations of 0.2 parts per million (ppm) but wading birds, feeding on the worms, had concentrations of more than 10 ppm.

Table 2.14 *Marine pollution*

Climate change

Ozone depletion could be a significant threat to marine biodiversity. High ultraviolet light levels (induced by a thinner ozone layer) can damage plankton productivity, jeopardising the whole food chain. Global warming could have disruptive effects on already stressed ecosystems, changing ocean currents, salinity and surface temperatures. Rising sea levels could drown estuaries, coastal mangroves and other wetland habitats. Increased water temperatures appear to be a factor in coral bleaching – the progressive reduction in coral growth which, if prolonged, can result in widespread coral death.

ACTIVITIES

1 'Managing marine ecosystems cannot be achieved without international co-operation' – to what extent do you agree with this statement?

Estuarine ecosystems

Figure 2.37 illustrates the main ecosystem functions in an estuary. These foodwebs and nutrient cycles are more complex than in most terrestrial systems because the estuary straddles the marine and terrestrial biomes. Nutrients from the land are washed into the estuary, while nutrients are removed from the sea into terrestrial cycles as a result of fishing.

Estuarine management in the UK

In the UK the Environment Agency is responsible for water quality up to three nautical miles offshore. Coastal water quality is covered by a range of legislation, including:

- EC Bathing Water Directive (1976)
- EC Shellfish Waters Directive (1979)
- EC Directive on Dangerous Substances (1976) and its subsequent 'daughter' directives
- UK Water Resources Act 1991
- Shoreline Management Plans for the UK.

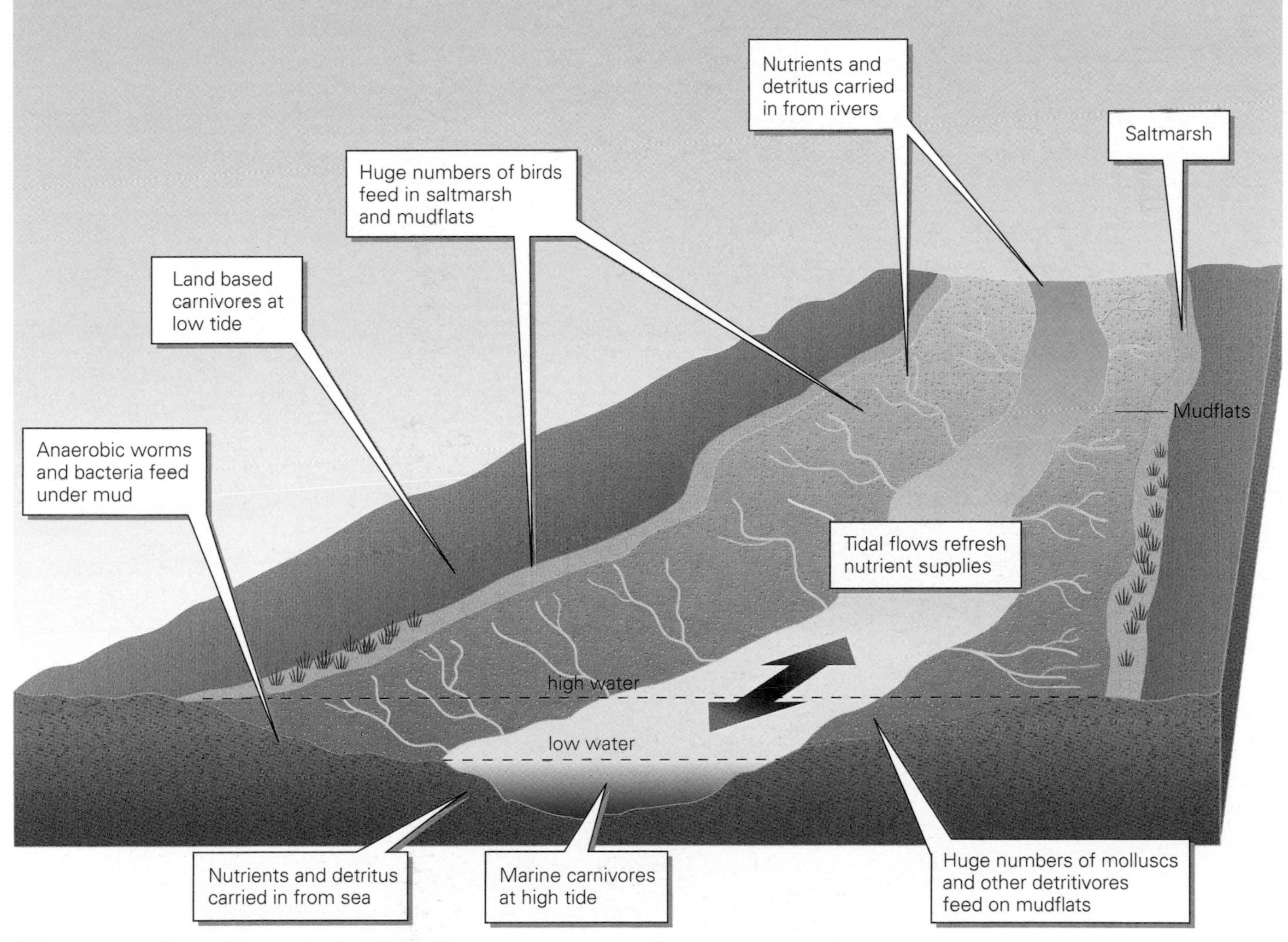

Figure 2.37 *Estuarine ecosystem functions*

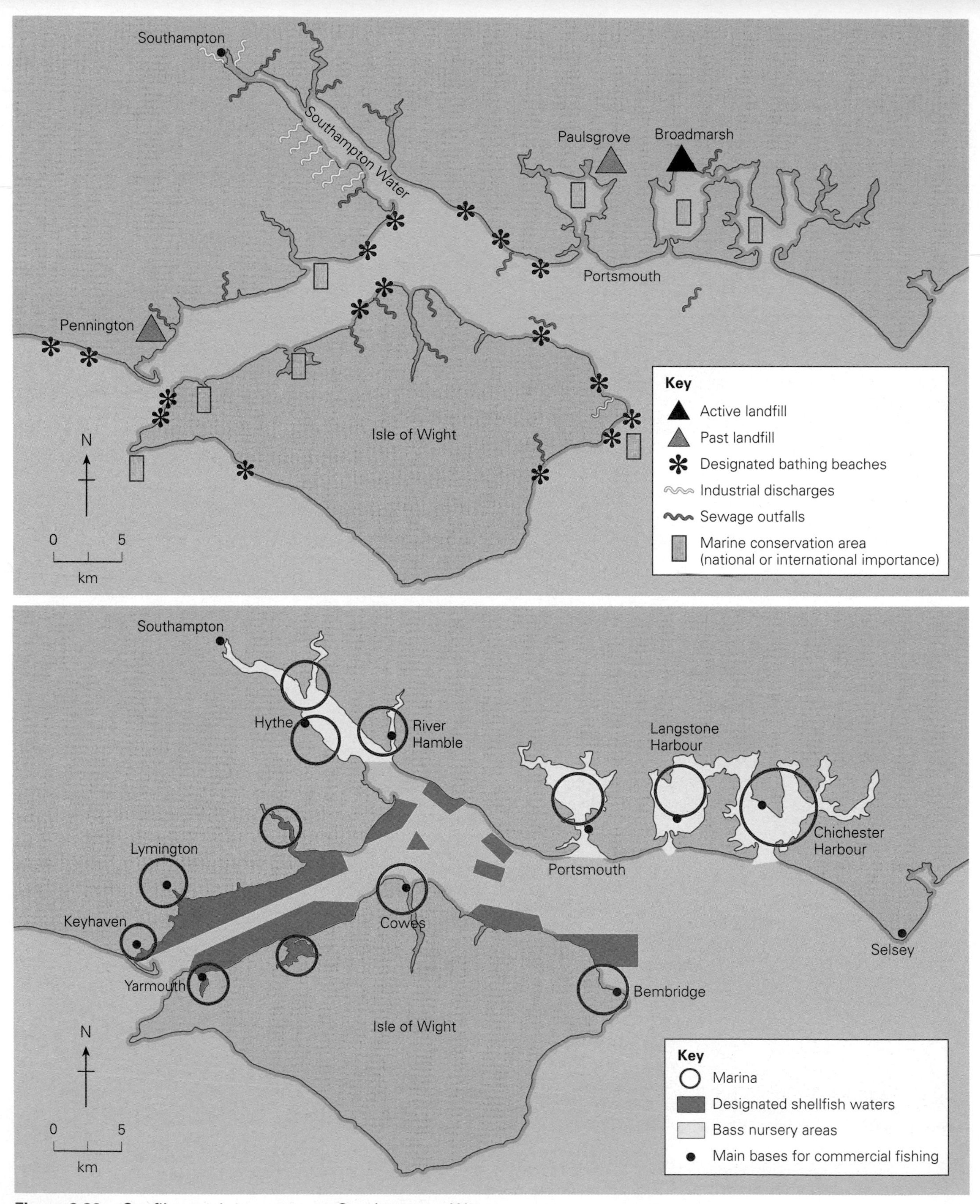

Figure 2.38 *Conflicts and pressures on Southampton Water*

Southampton Water and the Solent – a multi-use estuary

Southampton water is typical of many estuaries in the UK – a lowland river system that has been flooded by a post-glacial rise in sea level. The sheltered waters, high tidal range and numerous tributary river systems provide an ideal range of habitats for wildlife, i.e. breeding grounds for fish and shellfish, wintering and breeding areas for birds. It is also a superb port location with a range of port-side industries, not least the giant Esso Oil Refinery at Fawley. The surrounding area has very good links by air, rail and motorway to the rest of the country, and a thriving economic area has attracted a growing population. The recreational value of these sheltered waters is immense, attracting sailors, wind surfers and divers. An unusual value of the estuary is its record of long term coastal change. Submerged forest and peat beds in the estuary enable accurate carbon dating of different stages in the drowning of these lowland landscapes. In order to model and predict future changes in sea level, we need to have a better understanding of the natural climate and sea level trends of the past 10 000 years.

Pressures on the estuary

The vigorous economy puts many pressures on Southampton Water, ranging from direct discharges from industry to recreational demands, sewage inputs and local fishing industry. The maps in Figure 2.38 show a range of conflicts and pressures on the estuary.

One of the concerns is the eutrophication of the estuary by sewage outflows and agricultural runoff. Eutrophication can be monitored by studying **phytoplankton blooms,** sudden growths of algae in the surface waters. These have been studied by Southampton University Department of Oceanography. Their key findings prove the complexity of marine ecosystems:

- phytoplankton blooms depend on the energy of the system and the time of year
- **spring tides** create greater turbulence in the water, reducing the light available for growth, but **neap tides** (weaker tides with a lower tidal range) encourage phytoplankton blooms
- late spring provides the temperatures to encourage blooms but stormy weather over the neap tide cycle can delay the bloom until June.

There are many unknowns in estuarine ecosystems which make management difficult. A recent report by the Solent Forum has highlighted the following areas as needing more research and understanding:

- ecological interactions between sites
- health of bird populations
- relationships between sediment/invertebrates/birds
- baseline studies of shoreline developments and impacts on bird populations
- impact of gravel extraction on female crab migration
- health of fish stocks – most fishing is from small boats so catches do not need to be registered, but there are worries that a serious decline is going unrecorded as a result
- vulnerability/sensitivity of ecosystems.

Weblinks

www.solentforum.hants.org.uk/solentmaps/solent maps.htm
Dibden Bay issues
www.solentforum.hants.org.uk/solnews/issue3.htm#abp
www.foe.co.uk/campaigns/biodiversity and
habitats/wildplaces/case studies/cs hythe.html site value from FoE
www.hantsweb.org.uk/scrmxn/c31259.html detailed overview by County Council surveyor
www.dibdenterminal.co.uk/FACTS/index.htm detailed proposals from Associated British Ports

Source: *Proceedings in Marine Science, Elsevier,* 1998

Mangrove ecosystems

Figure 2.39 *Typical mangrove growth*

Mangrove ecosystems are composed of low trees and shrubs (Figure 2.39) which grow and spread quickly on tidal mud in tropical regions. Their dense root systems, covered by salt and brackish water at each tide, effectively bind the mud. In this way mangrove plants are adapted to their environment (Table 2.15), but it is estimated that one million hectares of mangrove are lost each year.

Adaptations	Benefits
• 'respiratory roots' (pneumatophores) allow oxygen to reach submerged roots • network of support roots stabilises mangrove against wave action and erosion	• coastal defence • food source • fuel source • building material • nursery habitat for marine life • habitat for terrestrial life • filter sediments and pollution, purifying coastal waters

Table 2.15 *Adaptations and benefits of mangrove ecosystems*

Mangroves in the Caribbean

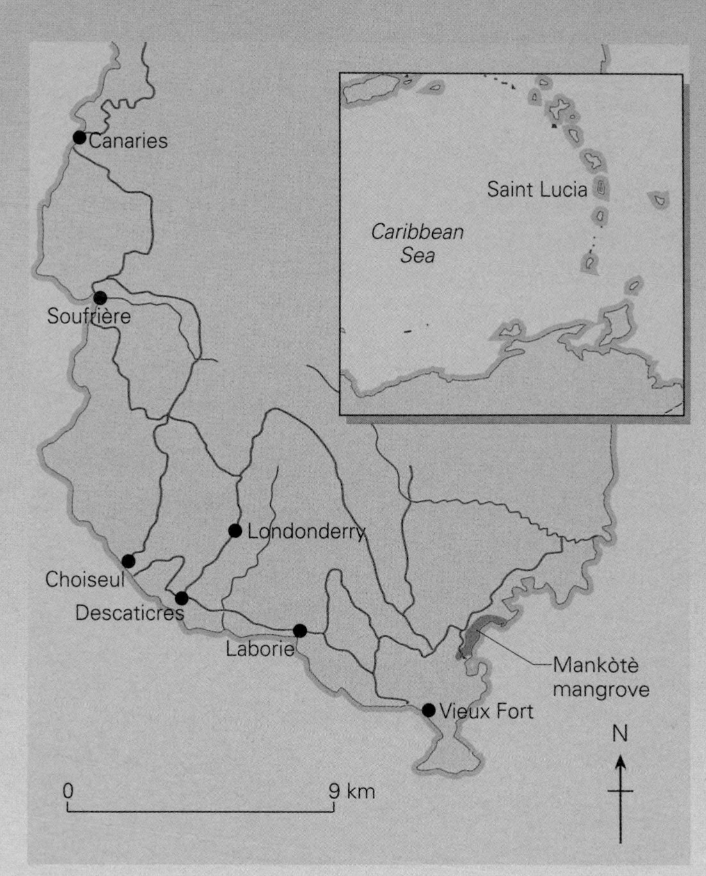

Figure 2.40 *Location of Mankòtè mangrove, St Lucia*

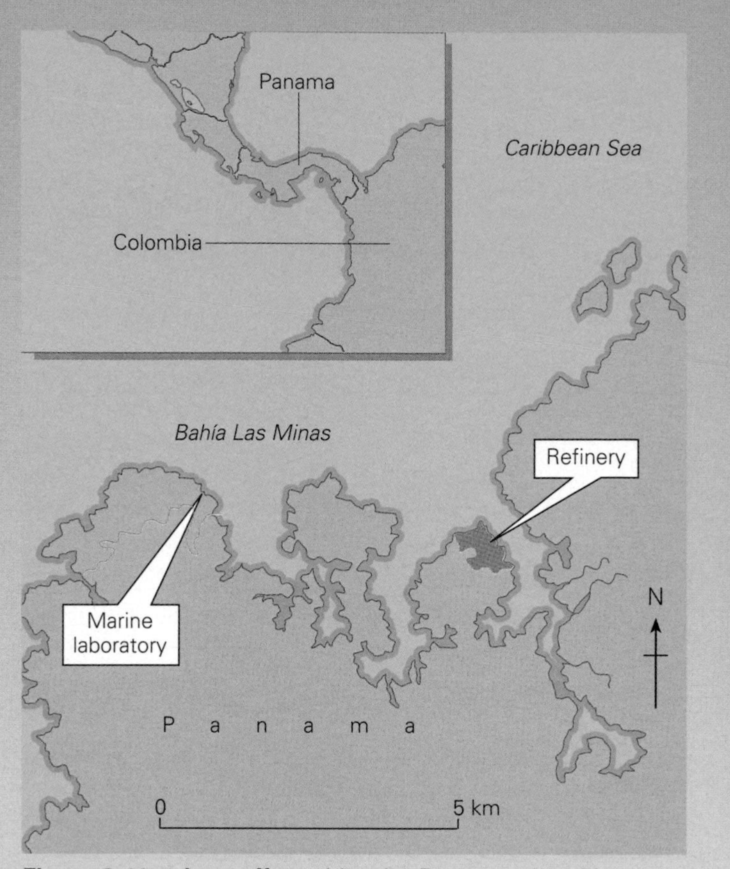

Figure 2.41 *Area affected by the Panama oil spill*

1. St Lucia

The island of St Lucia in the Caribbean has about 200 hectares of mangrove, of which the largest is the Mankòtè mangrove in the south east of the island (Figure 2.40). The changing fortunes of the Mankòtè mangrove illustrate the various influences on habitat conservation with some potentially valuable lessons. Before 1960 very little degradation of the mangrove took place; the area was a US air base with limited access. After the base closed, the area became public land, used for fishing, wood collection, hunting and waste disposal. The unregulated use severely degraded the mangrove. In a system with open access it makes sense to take as much as you can because you don't know if anything will be left next time you return. In 1981 the Mankòtè mangrove was identified as a priority conservation area. One of the major organised uses of the mangrove was by charcoal producers who supplied the nearby town of Vieux Fort (population 15,000). The Caribbean Natural Resources Institute (CANARI) embarked on a strategy to conserve the mangrove. Rather than attempting to reduce the charcoal producers' access to the mangrove, they decided to help them form a co-operative with recognised rights. By creating a sense of property/ownership, the charcoal burners now have a vested interest in managing the resource effectively. They police the use of the area, adopt codes of conservation practice and are committed to sustainable production because it guarantees the future of their livelihood.

2. Panama

There were at least 157 oil spills in the tropics between 1974 and 1990, of which 99 were close to reefs and mangroves. In April 1986, a refinery at Bahia Las Minas on the north coast of Panama leaked between 60,000 and 100,000 barrels of crude oil into the sea (Figure 2.41). The oil washed up on 80 km of mangrove coastline. Around seven per cent of the coastal mangroves were killed by the initial spill but this created a multiplier effect – dead trees left gaps in the forest allowing waves and water to erode the sediment. Higher sediment levels in the water choked the sea grass beds and coral reefs offshore. Even after sediment buried the initial oil slicks, erosion during storms continued to release buried oil, creating new localised slicks.

Five years after the spill, the mangrove death rate on the coastal fringe had climbed from 7 per cent to over 30 per cent and sea urchins, mantis shrimp and grazing fish had disappeared from the nearby reef, leaving it vulnerable to overgrowth by seaweeds. Scientists studying the incident estimated it could take a century for the coastline to recover, and even then the species composition will be significantly changed.

Reef ecosystems

Coral reefs are one of the most highly productive ecosystems in the world. Their ecology is complex, with ingenious inter-relationships between plants, animals and bacteria. The corals themselves consist of a **symbiotic** relationship between **algae** (zooxanthellae) and the anemone-like coral **polyp**. The symbiosis is shown in Figure 2.42.

Benefits of zooxanthellae (algae) to coral	Benefits of coral to zooxanthellae
• removes coral waste • provides nutrients to the coral • accelerates coral skeleton growth	• provides safe habitat out of reach of grazing animals • coral waste products from digestion provide nutrients for algae

Figure 2.42 *Cross section through a reef habitat*

Coral reefs are vertically layered according to the water depth and the wave activity. This provides a large range of niches, increasing the biodiversity of the reef (Figure 2.42). Reefs are important for a number of reasons:

- **Biodiversity** Estimates suggest there may be between one and nine million undocumented species associated with coral reefs, but only 4,000 species of fish and 800 species of reef-building corals are scientifically described, less than 0.5 per cent of the most conservative estimate.
- **Seafood** Reef species provide the main source of protein for many of the world's poor. Properly managed reefs can provide 15 tonnes of seafood per square kilometre per year.
- **Tourism** The tourist industry on Australia's Great Barrier Reef is estimated to be worth £800 million per year. Florida's reefs (being more accessible) bring in over £1 billion per year from tourism. Caribbean countries derive approximately half their GNP from the beach and reef tourism.
- **Pharmaceuticals** Biodiversity influences genetic variety, so it is clear that biodiverse habitats can provide a multitude of molecular compounds. Each new chemical compound has a pharmaceutical potential. Corals are used for bone grafts, and virus research. Half of all new cancer drug research is based on marine organisms.
- **Coastal protection** Coral reefs provide an offshore frictional surface to reduce storm wave energy. By protecting adjacent coastlines, other habitats requiring low energy levels can develop. These include mangroves and wetlands, both important nursery areas for fisheries.
- **Other products** Coral reefs provide a range of other economic goods from shells to live aquarium fish. Coral is also used in the construction industry.

Coral is threatened by numerous factors, particularly when reefs are in close proximity to the following:

- areas of high population density
- airports and military bases
- mines
- tourist resorts
- ports and shipping routes
- oil tanks and wells
- areas of blast fishing or poison fishing
- eroding drainage basins (producing high sediment loads)
- polluted river systems.

In addition to these 'area based' threats there is also evidence that coral is being affected by global warming and its impact on marine temperatures. On a global scale, the key threats to reefs are shown in Table 2.16.

Threat	% global reef area affected
Overexploitation	36
Coastal development	30
Inland pollution/erosion	22
Coastal pollution	12

Table 2.16 *Global threats to reefs*

Source: *Reefs at Risk,* World Resources Institute, 1998

ACTIVITIES

1. Some threats to reefs are very localised, while others originate a long distance away. Decide which threats in Table 2.16 are local and which are distant.
2. What are the implications of long distance threats for the management and conservation of reef areas?

Managing reefs to deal with different types of pressure

According to the World Bank, the cost to Indonesia of large scale poison-fishing on reefs (using poison to catch and kill fish) is more than US$10 million a year. A single kilometre of reef can be worth from US$137,000 to almost US$1.2 million over a 25-year period. These estimates are based on the value of the reef for fisheries, tourism, and coastal protection. If managed effectively, Indonesia's reefs could support a US$320 million/year industry, employing 10,000 people.

Different reefs have different types of pressure and therefore different management issues. Three contrasting examples are given in Tables 2.17 to 2.19.

Threats	Management	Successes
• overfishing • organic pollution • sedimentation • tourist trampling • ecosystem disruption has favoured burrowing sea urchins which has undermined corals	Since 1989 the area has been managed as a marine park. Management includes: • beach cleaning • regulation of tourist activities • maintenance of moorings	Surveys since 1988 have shown: • major increase in fin fish size, abundance, and diversity • coral area has increased from 8 to 30 per cent • sea urchin numbers have decreased • nesting sea turtles have increased

Table 2.17 *Management of reefs in Mombasa, Indian Ocean*

Threats	Management	Successes
• from the mid 1970s, catches of key reef species declined significantly due to overfishing • grouper fish catches dropped over 60 per cent in a ten-year period • careless fishing methods damaged reef structures • recreational boats anchoring in reef areas damaged the reef	• tourist-related businesses pressurised the government to close the fishing industry in 1990 • fishers were compensated for the cost of their gear and lost revenue	• while the $2 million/yr fishing industry has closed, the $9 million/yr tourist industry has blossomed • biodiversity has been maintained

Table 2.18 *Management of reefs in Bermuda, Atlantic Ocean*

Threats	Management	Successes
• in the late 1980s, overfishing and destructive fishing practices reduced coral by 50 per cent over a five-year period • reef biodiversity rapidly reduced	• in 1988 a national marine park was established. It was later recognised as a UNESCO World Heritage Site • fishing activities banned in 1997 • rangers conducted patrols to stop illegal fishing • environmental education materials produced and distributed • dive tourism industry installing anchor buoys to stop anchor damage to reef	• coral reef substrate has recovered significantly since 1989 • diversity of fish is exceptionally high

Table 2.19 *Management of reefs in the Sulu Sea, Philippines*

There are three main approaches to marine conservation as shown in Table 2.20.

Approach	Scale	Advantages	Disadvantages
Protected areas	Small	• affordable • achievable (33 per cent are achieving their management objectives) • flexible (27 per cent of biosphere reserves include marine protected areas)	• many globally unique habitats receive no protection whatsoever • unevenly distributed (50 per cent are located within Asia and Oceania) • many are smaller than the minimum critical size requirements of the species they protect, half are less than 1,000 hectares in size, much too small to include the breeding, nursery, and feeding areas of many species
Bioregional management	Medium	• integrated coastal management balances coastal development, fishing and conservation in a holistic way	• scientific understanding on which decisions are made is incomplete • vested interests in development and fishing can outweigh conservation needs
International agreements	Large	• many species are migratory therefore depend on different habitats at different stages of their life cycle • international agreements provide legislative protection	• not all countries choose to sign international agreements. Even if they do, different countries apply the law with different amounts of vigour

Table 2.20 *Approaches to marine conservation*

Managing the Great Barrier Reef, Australia

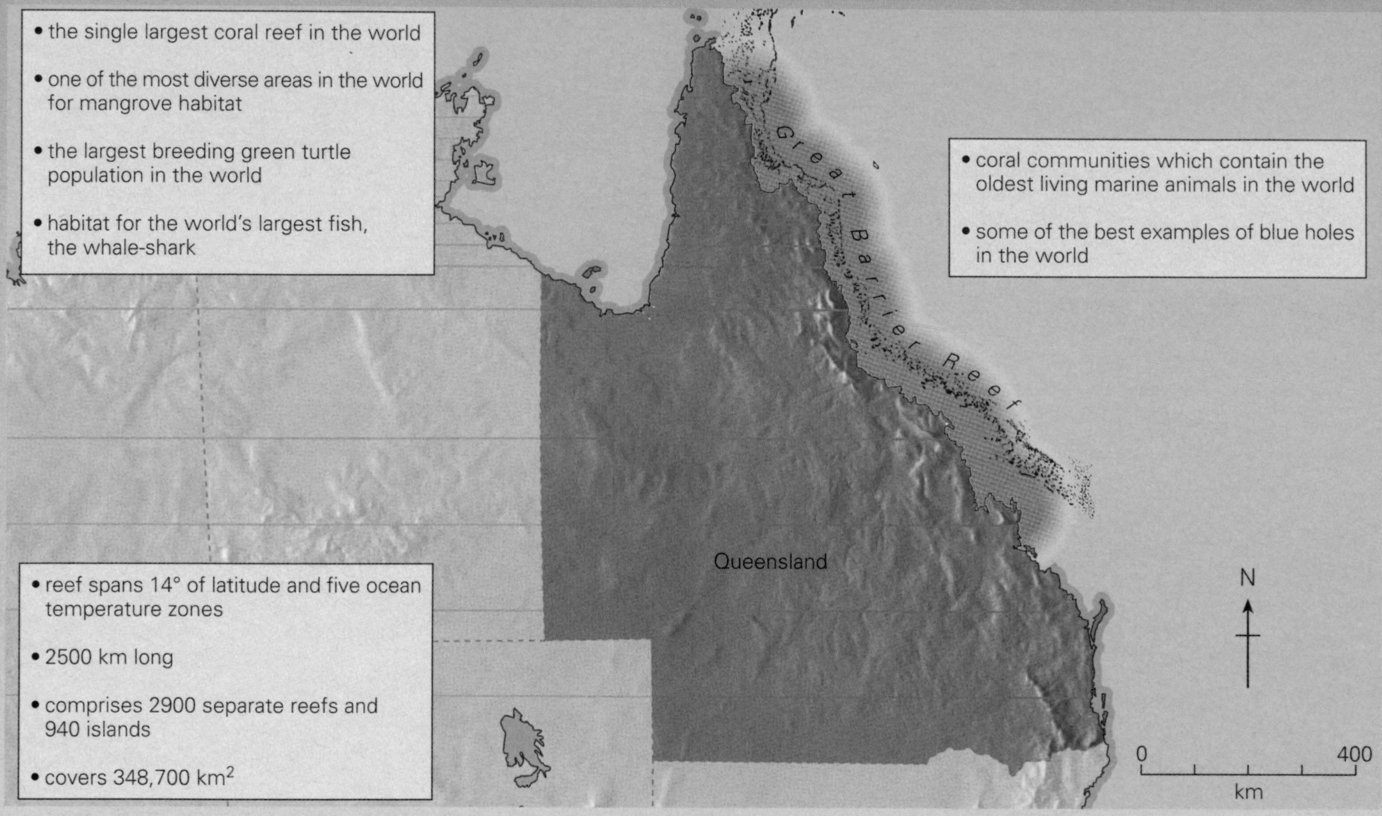

Figure 2.43 *The Great Barrier Reef*

The Great Barrier Reef World Heritage Area encompasses a huge range of habitats with great biodiversity (Figure 2.43). It is managed by the Great Barrier Reef Marine Park Authority, with the Queensland Department of Environment and Heritage responsible for day-to-day management. Its economic value is over A$1 billion per annum.

Unusually for an ecosystem of this size, the Great Barrier Reef lies within one country. Even more unusually, it lies within a wealthy nation with the resources to manage the reef.

There are numerous international conservation agreements which apply to the reef (Table 2.21). The justification for this degree of protection is the Great Barrier Reef's unusual diversity and scale (Figure 2.43).

Convention	Relevance to Great Barrier Reef
Convention on the Conservation of Migratory Species of Wild Animals (1979)	The reef is a habitat for migratory species such as sea turtles.
China and Australia Migratory Birds Agreement – CAMBA (1986)	Many bird species depend on the Great Barrier Reef for part of their migration.
Japan and Australia Migratory Birds Agreement – JAMBA (1979)	Many bird species depend on the Great Barrier Reef for part of their migration.
Convention on International Trade in Endangered Species of Wild Fauna and Flora – CITES (1973)	A wide range of endangered species is found in the Great Barrier Reef area.
Convention on Wetlands of International Importance Especially as Waterfowl Habitat (1971)	Bowling Green Bay and Shoalwater Bay are recognised as important water-bird habitats.
Convention on Biological Diversity (1992)	Australia is committed to preserving the biodiversity of the reef.
Convention Concerning the Protection of the World Cultural and Natural Heritage (the World Heritage Convention) (1975)	The area is recognised as being of 'outstanding universal value' as a World Heritage Site.

Table 2.21 *Conservation of the Great Barrier Reef*

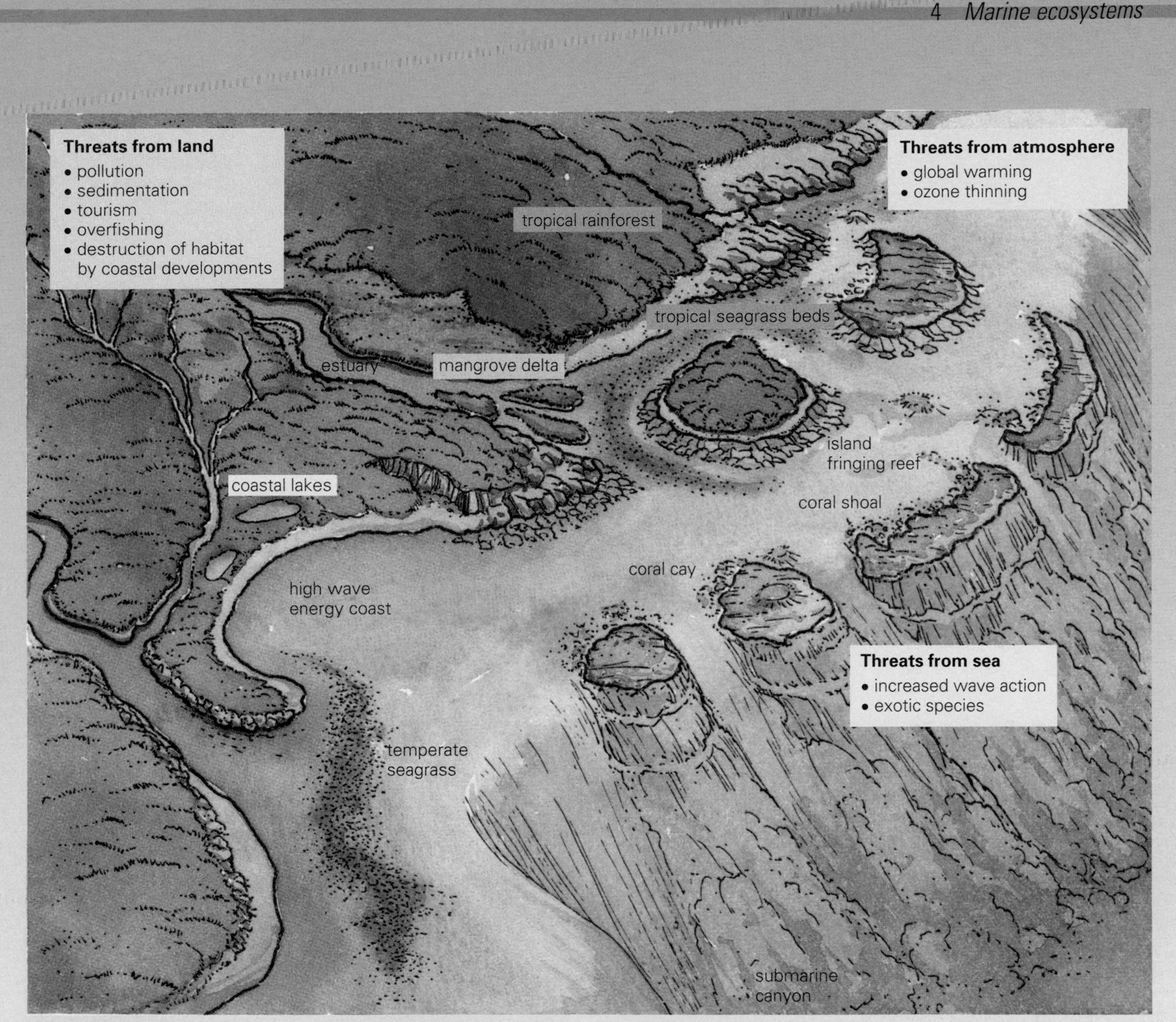

Figure 2.44 *The reef under threat*

The main threats to the Great Barrier Reef World Heritage Area are shown in Figure 2.44 and include:

1 Pollution and sedimentation from adjacent land areas
- eutrophication due to agrochemicals
- domestic sewage from urban areas and tourist developments on land
- increased sediment loads in streams due to agricultural activity, woodland clearance and mining
- mangrove disturbance and clearance.

2 Pollution from boats within the Great Barrier Reef
- oil spills from large vessels
- sewage from boats.

3 Unintended effects of development and tourism
- increased boating activity creating both direct and indirect disturbances
- destruction of natural beauty through development scars
- overfishing pressures.

4 Climate change
- rising sea temperatures causing coral bleaching.

Management of the reef

To manage the huge visitor pressure effectively, land use zoning is used extensively in the Great Barrier Reef area. Indigenous people have been consulted to try to balance their traditional hunting/fishing activities on the reef with the need to conserve increasingly threatened species. Figure 2.45 shows an educational poster explaining how migration of indigenous people has resulted in varying levels of threat to dugong populations. Traditional fishing with traditional methods is highly targeted and has little impact on reefs, but indigenous people are increasingly tempted to use poisons and explosives to increase the quantity of their kills.

Perhaps the greatest management challenge for the Great Barrier Reef World Heritage Area still lies ahead. Global warming is raising sea temperatures. When corals undergo certain kinds of stress, the zooxanthellae (the symbiotic algae that provide coral polyps with nutrients) are expelled from the coral tissue. The coral takes on a bleached appearance as the green algae disappears. Ultimately, bleached corals may die. Scientific studies have linked bleaching events to temporary areas of unusually high temperatures. During the El Niño event of 1982–3, bleaching killed more than 50 per cent of corals on some reefs. Corals are more vulnerable in areas where human activity has already resulted in large scale ecological disruption. Such disruption is seen in the explosive growth of coral predators such as the Crown of Thorns starfish.

The 1997–8 El Niño event was particularly severe. Aerial surveys indicated more than 88 per cent of inshore reefs suffered bleaching. Future climate scenarios suggest that by 2070 air temperatures could be up to 2.7°C higher than present. Higher temperatures would bleach more coral. Higher rainfalls associated with more frequent and extreme El Niños would increase river flow into the Great Barrier Reef coast, increasing sedimentation and decreasing salinity, both major stresses for corals. Increased storm activity could increase the physical battering corals receive from waves.

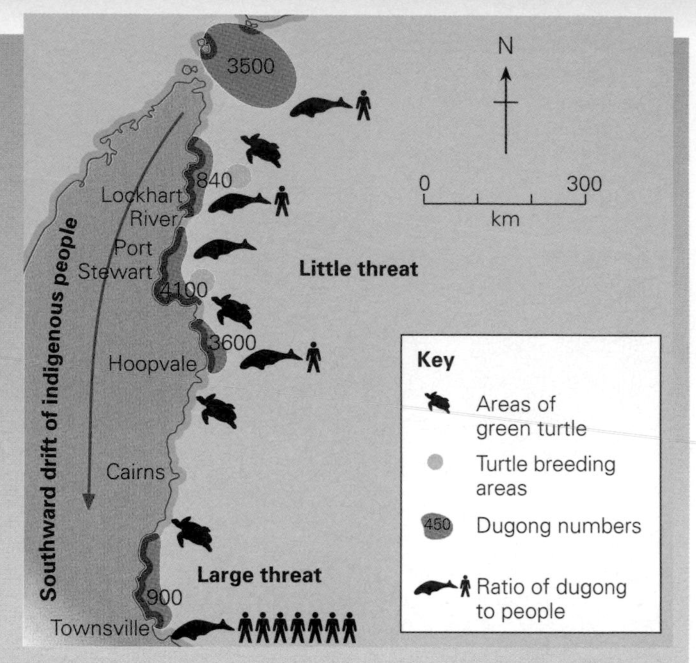

Figure 2.45 *Indigenous self regulation of the reef*

ACTIVITIES

1 In a small group, make a list of the threats facing the Great Barrier Reef and rank each threat from 1–5 according to: **a** its potential impact and **b** its ease of management. Discuss your findings and report back.

Artificial reefs

A potentially exciting development is the use of appropriate waste material to create artificial reefs. This can be an effective way of recycling and reducing on-land disposal problems. For example, quarry dust in a slurry is a potential pollution problem, but, by turning the dust into cement-stabilised blocks and placing them offshore, a potential lobster fishing reef can be created, benefitting the environment twice.

Artificial reefs and habitat protection

Artificial reefs have been used effectively as a means of protecting *Posidonia* meadows off the Spanish Mediterranean coast. By building artificial reefs with material designed to snag and tear fishing nets (for example, waste concrete telegraph poles), it is easy to discourage fishing from areas that might otherwise be overexploited. The safe habitat allows fish stock to recover – ultimately benefiting fishermen.

Artificial reefs and biodiversity

By building artificial reefs, planners and coastal managers have another management option – for example, artificial reefs can create buffer zones around real reefs, marine reserves, or "honeypot structures" for diving tourism. Equally they can be used as physical barriers to protect endangered habitat from illegal trawling.

Figure 2.46 *Artificial reef*

5 Conservation and sustainability

Figure 2.47 illustrates some of the issues surrounding the practical application of sustainability and conservation.

Individual value systems	Perceived costs	Media appeal – how good a story?
Scientific knowledge	Community value systems	Perceived benefits
Political structures	Cultural background – traditional attitudes to wildlife	Emotional appeal – pandas have it, snakes don't!
Socio-economic group	Pressure group activities	Relevance to locality

Figure 2.47 *Issues surrounding sustainability*

Level of influence	Involvement
Individual	Buy fair trade produce, organic produce, FSC certified wood, dolphin friendly tuna, GM free produce, recycled paper, high efficiency electrical goods, durable items, etc.
	Read quality reporting on environmental matters, both sides of arguments, small print on labels, recycling information on purchased goods.
	Watch documentaries on environmental policies and practice.
	Recycle paper, tins, plastic, glass, clothes, books, organic waste, etc.
	Support active organisations whose work has environmental impacts, e.g. WWF, Sustrans, FoE, Greenpeace, National Trust, RSPB, BTCV, Tear Fund, Oxfam, Christian Aid, Farm Africa, Water Aid.
	Enjoy wilderness areas, attractive environments, walking, cycling, sharing lifts.
Government and international	Write regarding sustainability, environment, recycling, transport policies, agricultural policies, transport policies, housing policies, social policies, foreign policies.
	Vote for more than self interest, for standard of life rather than standard of living.
	Become involved as a member of a global pressure group.

Table 2.22 *Individual and government involvement in conservation*

Each of the issues in Figure 2.47 will interact with several of the others. Some of the issues vary from place to place, for example wild bird shooting is culturally acceptable in Spain but not in the UK. Others change through time; factory smoke was a symbol of industrial vigour in the nineteenth century – now it would be regarded as a symbol of inefficiency.

There is a spectrum of potential involvement. Anyone can make sustainability happen and it is often an accumulation of small changes that has a bigger effect on the environment than one or two high profile campaigns that soon become yesterday's news. Table 2.22 illustrates a range of ways people can be involved both as decision makers and in influencing decision makers.

Conservation and sustainability are not simple issues. There are often many complex factors interacting and the answer is not always clear, as the following paradoxes show:

Paradox 1

In March 1999, three California Gray whales became stranded in ice on Alaska's frozen north coast. Their plight attracted widespread media coverage as hundreds of volunteers converged on the area to help keep air holes open in the ice. An icebreaker (ship) was chartered to clear a route back to the open ocean. The North American people excelled themselves at showing commitment to these three whales, yet the USA will not ratify the Kyoto Protocol committing the nation to reducing CO_2 emissions.

Paradox 2

In June 1999, a group of Beluga whales were trapped by shifting ice in the Canadian Arctic. The whales surfaced around a small ice hole to breathe, but up to 13 polar bears gathered round the hole to pounce on the whales. Some had already been killed by the bears, others were wounded. Conservationists broke extra holes in the ice to allow the whales to surface away from the bear ambush. Polar bears are also a threatened species. Were the conservationists saving whales or robbing bears of their food?

Small scale ecosystem management: Magdalen Hill Down

Magdalen Hill Down is an area of traditional grass downland on a south-facing chalk scarp east of Winchester. Being too steep to plough, the land has been used for grazing for millennia. In the 1980s, changes in agricultural prices meant the land was uneconomic to graze. This posed a major threat to the value of the ecosystem because grazing favours low, slow-growing specialist plants. Traditional chalk grassland can support over 25 species per square metre, but if grazing is stopped, a small number of competitive species rapidly dominate, destroying the variety.

The British Butterfly Conservation Society successfully restored the downland using a number of approaches.

Management approaches

- clear scrub and invading trees, mainly by hand
- fence the area into paddocks to allow controlled grazing. Find farmers willing to graze sheep according to a strict timetable and stocking ratio
- monitor butterfly numbers as a 'health indicator' of the downland habitat
- continue to expand the reserve area where possible in order to increase the minimum critical size of the ecosystem and provide continuity with nearby isolated downland areas
- use leaflets and interpretation boards to educate visitors as to the significance of the site.

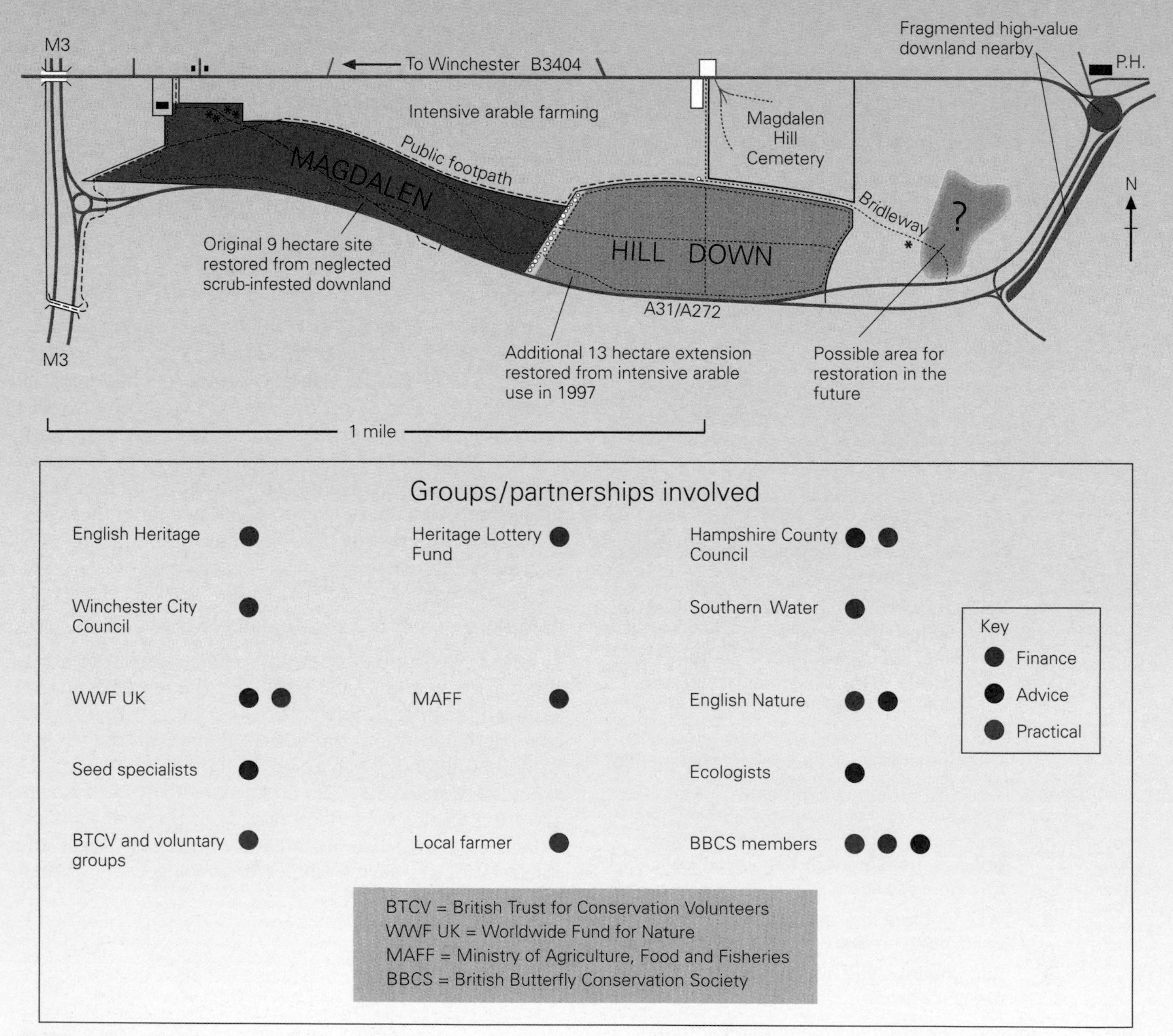

Figure 2.48 *Location of Magdalen Hill Down nature reserve*

Conservation on an international scale

Wildlife is seldom restricted to a single nation. Humans have traded plants, animals and their products internationally since prehistoric times. Many species are migratory, travelling through different countries as part of their life cycle. Conservation therefore needs to be international if it is to succeed.

In 1973, 96 countries signed CITES – the Convention on the International Trade in Endangered Species of Wild Flora and Fauna. The agreement recognised two groups of species – Appendix 1 (species in danger of extinction; all trade banned) and Appendix 2 (species not yet endangered but soon could be; trade limited and monitored). This agreement has its advantages, but it also has disadvantages (Table 2.23).

CITES – the good news	CITES – the bad news
96 countries signed – truly international protection offered	Countries can claim a 'reservation' on any species at the time of signing – this allows them to continue trading, even in Appendix 1 species.
Trade controls for both live species and 'readily recognisable' derivatives, e.g. seeds, skins	Readily recognisable derivatives have been interpreted differently by different countries. For example, Hong Kong claimed that ivory was not a readily recognisable elephant product, so continued to trade

Table 2.23 *The pros and cons of CITES*

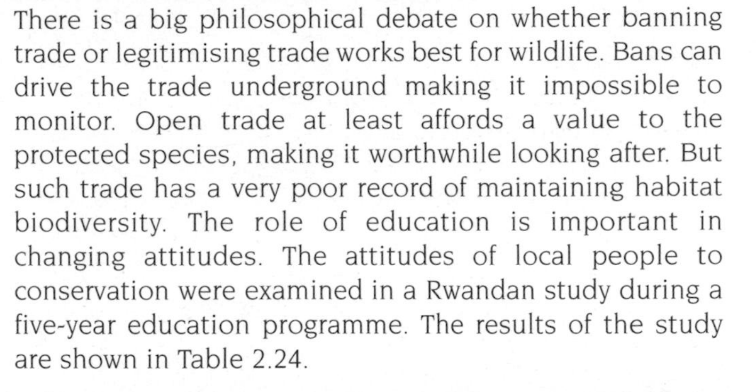

There is a big philosophical debate on whether banning trade or legitimising trade works best for wildlife. Bans can drive the trade underground making it impossible to monitor. Open trade at least affords a value to the protected species, making it worthwhile looking after. But such trade has a very poor record of maintaining habitat biodiversity. The role of education is important in changing attitudes. The attitudes of local people to conservation were examined in a Rwandan study during a five-year education programme. The results of the study are shown in Table 2.24.

Statement	% agreeing after year 1 of education programme	% agreeing after year 5 of education programme
There is some use in conserving forest	49	81
Wildlife protection has benefits to people	41	63
Forests benefit water supply	49	86
The reserve area should be converted to agriculture	51	18

Table 2.24 *Attitudes to conservation before and after educational programme*

ACTIVITIES

1 'By giving wildlife a commercial value, there is greater incentive to preserve it.'
'Experience of commercial whaling and fishing proves that commercialisation of wildlife increases the likelihood of extinctions.'
In pairs, find evidence to support each of the arguments. On balance, which do you find more convincing?

Figure 2.49 *Ivory on sale*

Figure 2.50 *An iguana for sale in a petshop in the UK*

Figure 2.51 *Plants imported from South-East Asia*

Conserving the whale

The whaling industry was one of the first to demonstrate the failure of industrialised self-interest to manage natural resources. The continuing defiance of Norwegian and Japanese fleets in the face of international legislation banning whaling casts doubt on the ability of industries to regulate themselves responsibly – but the success of environmental groups in bringing the debate to the public eye is itself a sign of hope.

The whaling industry was originally a significant resource for maritime nations (Table 2.25).

Part of the whale	Uses
Intestines	Used in scent and high quality soaps
Baleen bones	Corsets, umbrellas, brooms, whips and riding crops
Blood	Fertiliser
Skin	Leather for bicycle saddles, handbags, cases and shoes
Natural oils	Cold creams, lipsticks, shaving creams, ointments, lubricating oil, varnishes, linoleum, printing inks, margarine, cooking fat, lard
Tendons	Tennis racket strings, surgical stitches
Meat	Human food, pet food, animal feed

Table 2.25 *The whale as an industrial resource*

The range of uses gave great economic credibility to whaling during the twentieth century. The first signs of overexploitation emerged in the 1920s. The key dates in the development of whale legislation are shown below:

1925 League of Nations recommends whaling to be regulated from over-hunting

1930 Bureau of International Whaling Statistics established

1931 Convention for the regulation of whaling, signed by 22 nations

1937 Minimum size limits set for Fin, Blue, Humpback and Sperm whales to be hunted

1946 International convention for regulation of whaling

1949 International Whaling Commission (IWC) established with 14 member countries

1965 Blue whale gains full protection

1974 Catch quotas set on individual stocks and species

1979 Entire Indian Ocean declared a whale sanctuary and whaling prohibited for a minimum of 10 years

1994 Southern Ocean whale sanctuary put into operation. Japan ignores the ban on whaling in the sanctuary, claiming a need to hunt 440 Minke Whales for scientific purposes. The IWC ruled that the Japanese whaling did not meet legitimate scientific goals

1998 Japan's scientific whaling program produced 1,700 tons of whale meat from the Southern Ocean whale sanctuary (retail value approximately £56 million). In contrast, the whale-watching tourist industry nets an estimated £300 million per year and benefits whale sustainability. There could be a strong argument for whaling nations to develop whale based tourism as an alternative to slaughter.

The impacts of hunting whales have been severe (Figure 2.52). Recovery rates have been very slow for some species. The more depleted the species, the slower the recovery rate is likely to be. There are estimated to be no more than 300 surviving Northern Right whales, a desperately vulnerable population size. The population of Sperm whales near the Galápagos Islands is barely growing because few males survived the whaling years. Yet Norway and Japan continue to hunt. They campaigned for resumption of sustainable whaling in the April 2000 CITES conference but were defeated 69 to 46.

There are three new perspectives developing in the whaling debate; an ethical perspective, a resource perspective and an environmental management perspective.

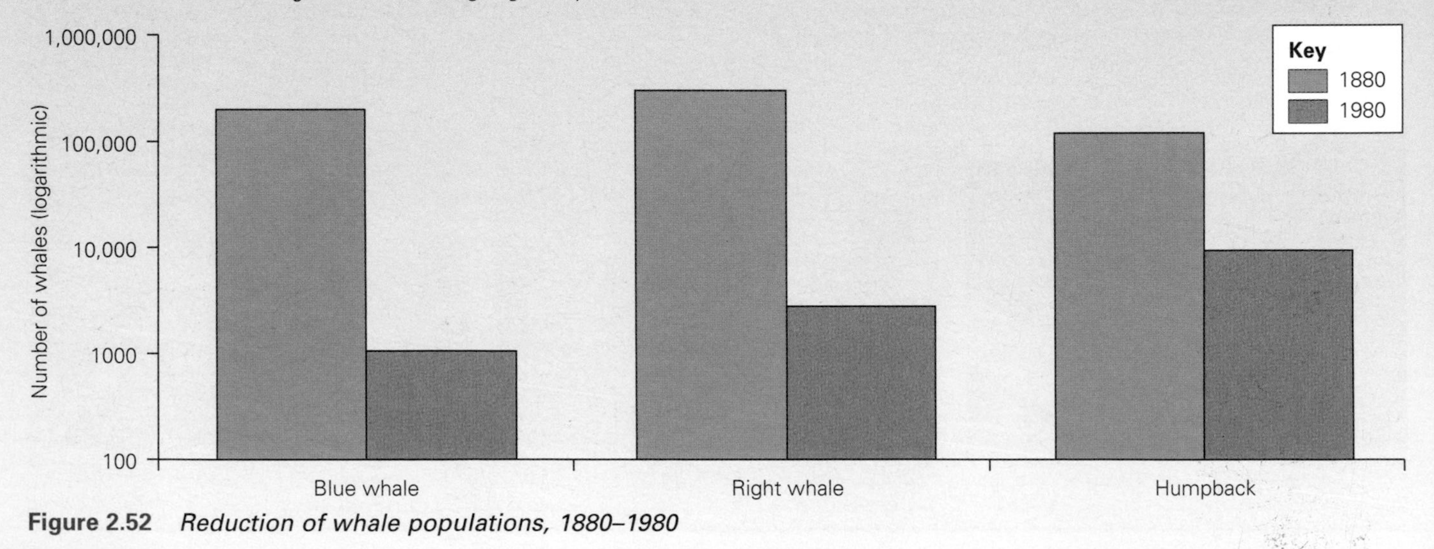

Figure 2.52 *Reduction of whale populations, 1880–1980*

The ethical perspective	The resource perspective	The environmental management perspective
Whales are highly intelligent species with well developed social structures and a complex language. Whale hunting is not necessary for society as alternatives exist for all whale products. To systematically hunt and kill intelligent creatures for no obvious need other than to satisfy the food tastes of minority nations is unethical and immoral. Whale watching is a growing ecotourist attraction.	Whales are wild food resources like any other. Now that whale stocks have had a chance to recover we should use scientific knowledge to hunt them in a sustainable manner. By allowing whaling to continue, we benefit the livelihoods of thousands who are employed directly or indirectly in the whaling industry. It is hypocrisy to defend the intelligent whale yet continue to farm and eat the intelligent pig.	Whaling is no longer the biggest threat to whales. The following factors are increasingly significant: • entanglement in fishing nets • habitat degradation • chemical pollution • noise pollution • global climate change • accidents and disturbance. Whaling is obviously a further pressure but the demise of the whales will come about more quickly if these other factors are ignored.

The impacts of pressure groups on conservation

One of the encouraging phenomena of the late twentieth century was the growth of peaceful, creative environmental protest. The development of communication technology has been very important in this cause in several ways:

- direct actions can be broadcast live to the embarrassment of offending industries
- the Internet has provided an ideal medium for reaching a global audience
- email allows rapid building of online communities
- global positioning systems (GPS) allow easy navigation in wilderness regions where research or monitoring may be taking place.

Despite the role of technology, the success of a group is very often due to the boldness and imagination of individuals on the ground.

Greenpeace versus Japan (December 1999 – January 2000)

Greenpeace perspective

Japan's Antarctic whaling programme was in violation of articles 65 and 120 of the United Nations Convention on the Law of the Seas, (UNCLOS) that requires all states to co-operate with the International Whaling Commission (IWC) in the matter of whale protection.

The Greenpeace vessel MV Arctic Sunrise tracked the Japanese whaling fleet illegally hunting whales inside the Southern Ocean Whale Sanctuary. Greenpeace activists used peaceful means to protest illegal whaling on at least 11 occasions. Selected highlights are shown below:

20 December Crew members sailed an inflatable boat between the Nisshin-maru (a factory ship that processes whale meat) and the Yushin-maru (a 'catcher' ship that hunts whales) while the Japanese were transferring their catch. By disrupting the transfer of dead whales they interfered with the hunt because catcher ships can only carry two whales at a time.

21 December The Nisshin-maru rammed the Greenpeace boat M/V Arctic Sunrise.

29 December The M/V Arctic Sunrise surprised the Japanese whaling fleet and managed to prevent two catcher ships from hunting whales for almost five hours.

9 January The crew of the M/V Arctic Sunrise used a vertical spray of water to prevent a Japanese whaling ship from targeting and hunting whales.

11 January Rough weather prevented the crew of the M/V Arctic Sunrise from launching inflatables, but the Greenpeace camera crew was able to document Japan's illegal whaling from the ship's helicopter.

12 January Greenpeace activists in an inflatable boat were captured and dragged up the stern ramp of the Japanese factory ship Nisshin-maru.

The appeal of the Greenpeace campaigns is primarily in the courage of the campaigners. Riding a small inflatable boat in Antarctic seas between large vessels that are prepared to use force is either foolhardy or immensely courageous. It also shows that when all else fails the courage of individuals can make a difference. Greenpeace have also contributed to their success by taking research seriously and communicating the results of research effectively.

The Japanese perspective

The Japanese believe themselves also to be taking research seriously. The extracts below are taken from a letter from Seiji Ohsumi (Director General of Japan's Institute of Cetacean Research) to the Prime Minister of New Zealand:

- The issue of scientific research on whales is of vital importance to the IWC ... Japan's research program in the Antarctic ... has contributed valuable scientific information related to estimation of trends in abundance and biological parameters to improve the stock management of the Southern Hemisphere Minke whale.
- ... the IWC Scientific Committee has commended both the quality and quantity of data resulting from this program.
- Japan's research program in the Antarctic will ... [only] take ... 440 Minke whales from a stock of over 760,000 animals.
- ... the Scientific Committee has agreed that Minke whales in the Antarctic and elsewhere ... are increasing.
- [The New Zealand Prime Minister's] statements about 'serious decline in whale numbers' and that 'whale numbers were only around five per cent of what they were a hundred years ago' are simply untrue.
- Greenpeace has carried out a dangerous and violent campaign which has, among other things, caused a collision with our research vessel.
- Whales in the world's oceans consume approximately three to six times the amount of resources as is harvested for human consumption ... [people] dependent on the fishing industry understand the serious implications of this.
- ... there was no scientific basis for the establishment of the IWC Southern Ocean Sanctuary.

Greenpeace Southern Ocean action

www.greenpeace.org/-oceans/whales/onboardstories.htm

Letter to New Zealand

ens.lycos.com/e-wire/Jan00/Jan270002.html

ACTIVITY

1 Compare and contrast the accounts of Greenpeace and Japan. How many differences seem to be due to:
- factual disagreements
- disagreements concerning the issues?

Elephants in Africa

In 1989 the members of CITES agreed to ban international trade in African elephant ivory. In the previous two decades, poaching had reduced African elephant numbers from several million to 500,000 at most. Immediately after the ban, elephant poaching appeared to drop substantially. The demand for ivory, particularly in East Asia, remained strong so prices rose, making poaching more attractive. Coupled with this, several African countries, including the Democratic Republic of Congo (formerly Zaire) experienced political instability, so government priorities moved away from antipoaching efforts. Poaching intensity gradually increased, and illegal elephant kills were reported regularly. Elephants can be dangerous pests (e.g. rampaging villages in Bangladesh) and a number of countries have campaigned for the lifting of the 1989 ivory ban. Even a restored ivory trade will benefit few people if mismanagement leads to extinction. Whatever safeguards are placed on the trade of ivory, poachers will see the sales as a signal to resume the slaughter.

Elephant slaughter in the Congo, December 1997

David Barritt, African Director for the International Fund for Animal Welfare, reported the discovery of 280 rotting elephant corpses near Congo's border with Gabon. The herd, including calves and pregnant females, was shot in a forest clearing by locals who had been hired by a poaching gang, and were paid as little as $10 for their work. The poachers told the local inhabitants, whom they hired, that it was all right to kill the elephants because next year the trade in ivory was going to be resumed legally. Many conservation groups oppose lifting the ban because it would be impossible to distinguish between legally obtained ivory and poached ivory. Africa Resources Trust, a pro-ivory trade conservation group, argue differently - the way to save elephants is to accord them a value so that the local population will regard them as assets and continue to conserve the species.

Habitat not trade is the issue

CITES protects species by banning international trade but the biggest threat to most species is not poaching but habitat loss. CITES does not require countries to protect habitats - only to refrain from trade in endangered species. Even the Convention on Biological Diversity (CBD) signed by 169 countries after the Rio Earth summit (1992) only partly addresses this problem. Signatories to the CBD must prepare national strategies for conserving biodiversity. The main approach countries have taken has been to establish national parks and protected areas.

Elephants are not endangered in Namibia so lift the trade ban

During the 1997 CITES meeting in Zimbabwe, Namibia, Botswana and Zimbabwe requested that African elephants were taken off the protected list so international ivory trade could resume. It was accepted that elephants in these countries are no longer threatened and limited trade could resume.

The Namibian elephant population was estimated to be 7,684 (+/- 18%) in 1995, occupying up to 100,000 km^2. In some areas the population required culling in 1983 and 1985, and has remained stable since then.

The future of conservation

For conservation in the future to be successful, we will need to learn to think in new ways. It is not adequate to debate whether people are more important than the environment because the truth is that degraded environments impoverish people, reduce health and fracture societies. There are three main areas where our understanding needs to improve:

- **understanding ecosystems** so we manage them from knowledge rather than ignorance
- **accounting for ecosystems**, i.e. assigning values to ecosystems so that cost benefit analysis works on real (and long term) costs and benefits
- creating **flexible societies** where the aspirations of individuals and the promises of politicians are realistic and sustainable rather than exploitative and damaging.

Understanding ecosystems

Recent research in DNA clinical methods allows ecologists to gain information about species, sex, blood ties and health of animals in an ecosystem. By gathering dung and analysing DNA from cells, highly relevant information can be rapidly gathered. In 1992 scientists from the University of Munich used fresh dung to investigate a population of European Brown bears in the Brenta region of northern Italy. The bear population was thought to be dwindling but field monitoring was difficult in this remote area. The authorities wanted to know whether they should import more bears from the nearby Balkans. From DNA studies on the bear dung, the Munich researchers found:

- males and females were still present in the population so the community could breed
- the population was very small and isolated
- the DNA was more similar to bears from Slovenia than Croatia or Bosnia
- plant remains in the dung showed the food plants the bears relied on in summer.

The insights into bear ecology that this study provided allowed intelligent management decisions to be made. Such studies could be used in many ecosystems in order to unravel the requirements and vulnerability of many endangered species.

On a completely different scale, radio tracking of penguins by GPS satellites has provided the Falkland Island Government with surprising results in their search to understand unstable penguin populations. Daily tracking revealed the penguins swam up to 1,000 miles from the Falklands on winter migrations to feeding grounds off the coast of Argentina near Buenos Aires. Consequently, fluctuations in penguin numbers were not necessarily due to commercial fishing near the Falklands but possibly related to the environment of the winter feeding grounds one thousand miles away (Figure 2.55).

This shows how improved understanding of the ecosystem allows management to focus on the key issues – in this case pollution in Argentine rivers – as much as overfishing in the open ocean.

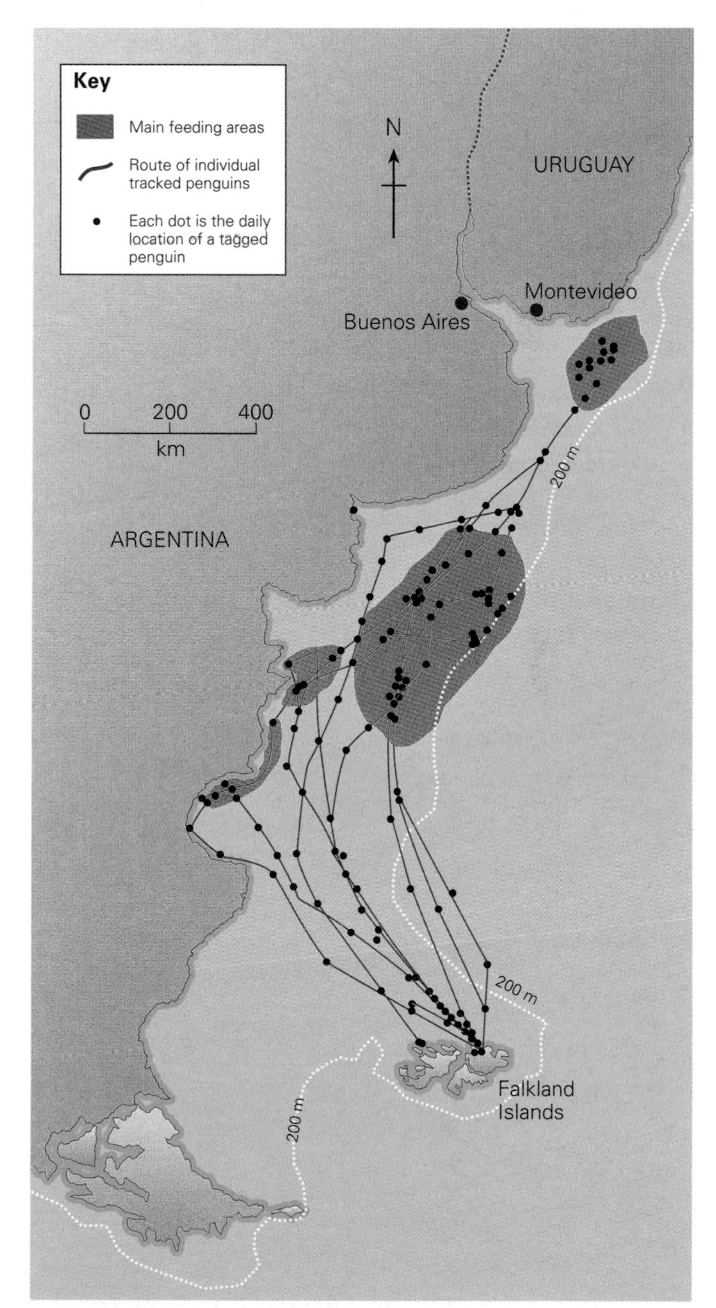

Figure 2.55 *Penguin migration patterns revealed by GPS*

Accounting for ecosystems

Values for ecosystem accounting have been given in Table 2.4, and the following two examples show ecological economics in action.

New York City

Need improved water supply and purification.

Modern economics Spend up to US$8 billion in constructing new water treatment plants to cope with low quality water supplies.

Ecological economics Spend US$1.5 billion in buying land around reservoirs and stream sources. Protect native ecosystems which naturally purify the water.

Additional benefits Recreation, wildlife.

Hadejia-Jama'are flood plain, Nigeria

Need Agricultural development.

Modern economics Build dam and irrigation scheme to improve cash cropping. Net benefit = US$29 per hectare.

Ecological economics Value existing activities of locals (many of which do not enter the cash economy). Value of farming, fishing, grazing livestock, fuelwood and other wild products = US$167 per hectare.

Additional benefits By dropping dam schemes, wetland is preserved for wildlife and no new national debt is taken on.

The graphs in Figure 2.56 illustrate two alternative approaches to ecosystem valuation. The first is based on the value per hectare, the second on the total area of that ecosystem. What is surprising is how some of our most threatened ecosystems (like wetlands) have such high values.

Flexible societies

There comes a point in ecosystem management where it is more cost effective and sustainable for us to adapt to nature rather than attempt to adapt nature to our needs. Political power needs to be localised if people are to make sustainable choices, yet it also needs to be centralised, as ecosystems do not restrict themselves to political boundaries. Democracies are poor institutions for encouraging long term political thinking, particularly those involving unpopular sacrifices, yet autocracies have among the worst environmental records on the planet.

Even our view of conservation needs to be flexible. The World Wide Fund for Nature has recently reviewed its role in Africa and has decided that it is not sustainable for Western organisations to be mounting conservation, protection and policing operations in LEDCs. The emphasis will now be to influence policymakers in LEDCs so that local communities will be encouraged to take on both the responsibility for conservation and the benefits from conservation. The WWF admit this is a high risk strategy but feel that there are no alternatives – if local people are not gamekeepers they are likely to be poachers.

EXTENSION ACTIVITY

Table 2.26 shows a variety of ways in which humans currently influence ecosystems. Select case studies from this book and other resources to exemplify different sections of the table.

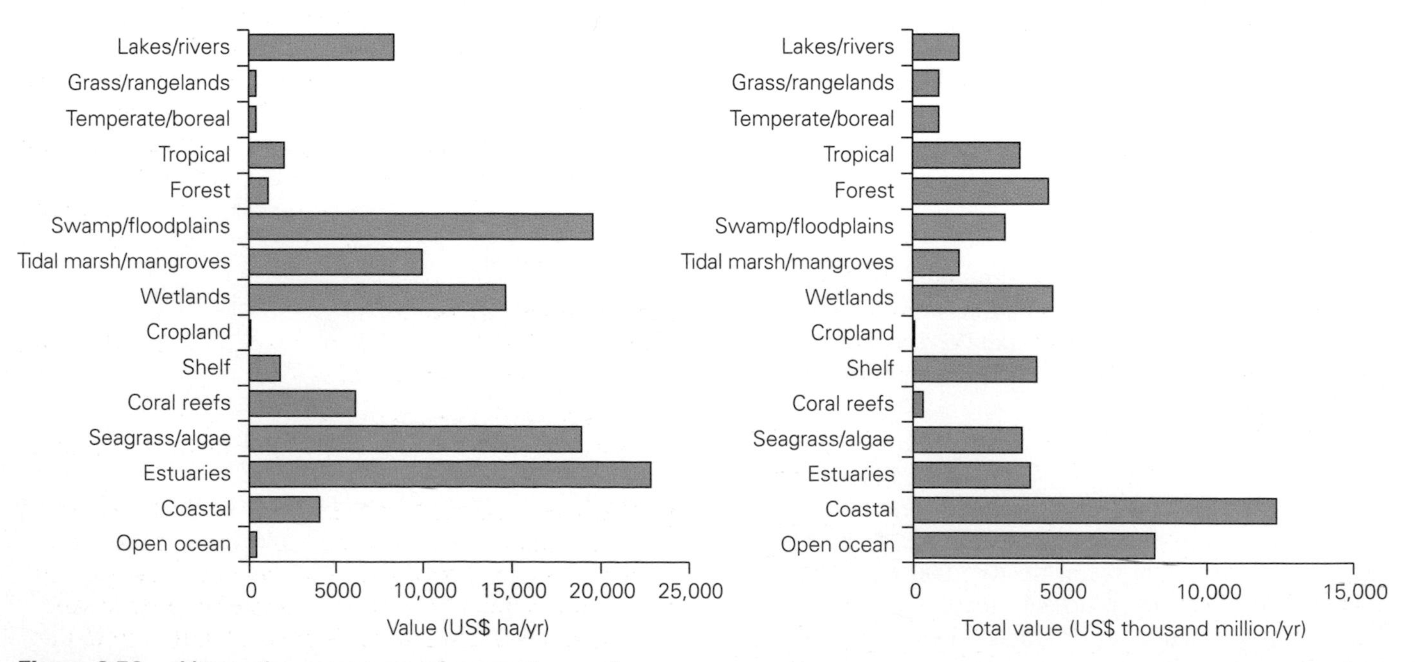

Figure 2.56 *Alternative measures of ecosystem value*

	Nature of influence	Terrestrial examples	Marine/freshwater examples
Biotic factors	**Composition** Additions Subtractions	 • agricultural crops; exotic introductions • extinction; over hunting/collecting	 • fish farming • overfishing
	Structure Simplified foodwebs Reduced layering Fragmentation	 • deforestation; agriculture • deforestation; grazing • transport routes; housing development	 • reef degradation; marsh reclamation; overfishing • regulated river flows; tidal barrages • dams and weirs; tidal barrages
Abiotic factors	**Climate** Changing climate patterns	 • global warming and biome shifts	 • global warming and ocean current shifts; El Niño/La Niña
	Nutrients Too many Too few	 • agricultural improvements • soil erosion, soil structure decline	 • eutrophication; sewage dumping; siltation of reefs • acid rain in freshwater ecosystems
	Pollution Air pollution	 • acid rain damage to forests	 • acid rain damage to freshwater ecosystems; CO_2, global warming and reef bleaching; ozone thinning and enhanced UV exposure on plankton
	Water pollution	• pesticide pollution; eutrophication; 'feminising' hormones; radioactive waste	• tanker spills; agricultural runoff; 'feminising' hormones; radioactive waste

Table 2.26 *Human threats to ecosystems*

Conclusion

The good news

- one billion hectares of the Earth's surface is designated as protected
- protected lands safeguard 40 species of the fauna of east and southern Africa, including giraffes, hyenas and wildebeest that would otherwise be close to extinction
- between 1990 and 1995 the global protected area grew by the addition of 1431 new reserves, totalling 224 million hectares.

The bad news

- protected areas do not always target sites of high biological diversity. Mountains are obvious places for national parks due to their scenery and lack of development pressure. But they contain little biodiversity
- much of the land given protected status between 1990 and 1995 was in scarcely populated desert and high mountain areas, with small biodiversity
- many highly diverse ecosystems, from tropical dry forest to temperate river basins, continue to receive little formal protection
- many national parks exist only on paper with no protection or management being implemented on the ground. This is especially true in developing nations where funds are scarce. Such 'paper parks' can be worse than having no protection at all because the political pressure to do something reduces once a park has been decreed
- some reserve areas are 'decommissioned' if the opportunity arises to exploit resources. Recent Indian examples include the Melghat Tiger Reserve, which was reduced in size by one third in 1992 to allow timber exploitation and dam building, and the Narayan Sarovar Sanctuary, reduced in size by 40 per cent in 1995 to allow mining. The area previously had a rich biodiversity with the largest known population of Indian gazelle.

Essentials for the future

There are three principles of sustainability which are essential for long term sustainability:

- substances produced by society must not systematically increase in ecosystems (i.e. substances should biodegrade or be recycled)
- the physical basis for the productivity and diversity of nature must not be systematically diminished (i.e. ecosystem diversity and health must be maintained)
- resources must be used fairly and efficiently to meet human needs. In the words of Gandhi, the world has sufficient for everyone's need but not their greed.

UNIT TWO Population and the economy

Chapter Three: Global population and migration

1 Introducing the challenges

On 12 October 1999, the world passed a milestone in its history. Six billion people were living on the Earth, twice as many as in 1960, three times as many as in 1927 and four times as many as in 1900. The last billion people were added to the global population in just over 12 years. Clearly, the twentieth century witnessed a population explosion of immense proportions. This increase was largely the outcome of a spectacular dip in death rates. This was prompted, amongst other things, by:

- better medicine and treatment of disease
- better access to health care
- better sanitation and personal hygiene
- better diet and food supply.

In 1990, the annual increase in the size of the world's population reached a peak of 86 million extra people. Today, it is around 75 million and falling. But despite this fall in the annual growth rate, global numbers continue to rise and are expected to reach 9 billion by 2050. Global population is unlikely to level out much before 2200, by which time it will have reached at least 11 billion. Our crowded planet is set to become even more crowded.

This mushrooming of global population has given rise to a range of issues and problems which are likely to worsen before they improve. The more important of these are outlined below and examined in detail later in this chapter.

Evening things out

In 1900, approximately two-thirds of the 1.5 billion people inhabiting the Earth lived in the less economically developed countries (LEDCs) of Asia, Africa and Latin America. Today, well over three-quarters of the global population are found in such countries (Table 3.1).

About 90 per cent of the babies born each day will be raised in LEDCs. Of the 4.8 billion now living there:

- 60 per cent lack basic sanitation
- 30 per cent are without clean water
- 25 per cent do not have adequate housing
- 20 per cent have no access to health services.

World population (bn)	1950 2.5	2000 6.0	2050 9.0 (estimate)
% shares			
MEDCs	32	20	13
LEDCs	68	80	87
Africa	9	13	20
Asia	56	60	59
Europe	22	12	7
Latin America and Caribbean	6	9	9
North America	7	5	4
Oceania	<1	1	1

Table 3.1 *Global population (1950–2050)*

The challenge: to reduce the disparity between more economically developed countries (MEDCs) and LEDCs.

Cutting consumption

If malnutrition and starvation are to be avoided, more food needs to be produced. This challenge is intensified by the fact that most of the extra people to be fed are being born in LEDCs. They are swelling the populations of countries where the ability and opportunity to raise food production are very limited.

But the problem does not end there. As wealth increases, new needs are created. Demand is also increased by the rise in the number of households, as people live longer and family break-up becomes more common. This growth in consumption is greatest in the MEDCs, but many of the required resources are being stripped from LEDCs. Figure 3.1 illustrates this inequality of consumption between the richest and poorest sectors of global population. In the future, technology will have to deliver major improvements in resource productivity and massive reductions in waste.

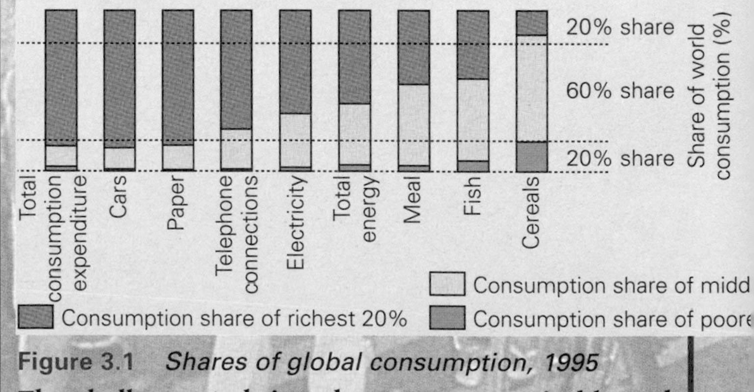

Figure 3.1 *Shares of global consumption, 1995*

The challenge: to bring about a more equitable and efficient use of resources.

Sparing the planet

The need to produce more food has an impact on the environment. It encourages farming to spread into marginal and wilderness areas, regardless of the long-term environmental consequences. But the growing consumption demands of the more affluent sectors of global population also have environmental impacts. Non-renewable resources, such as minerals and fossil fuels, are put under increased pressure.

Since 1970, the World Wide Fund for Nature (WWF) has been producing a living planet index. This is a measure of the health of the Earth's forest, freshwater and marine environments. What does Figure 3.2 show?

The challenge: to achieve a sustainable mode of development.

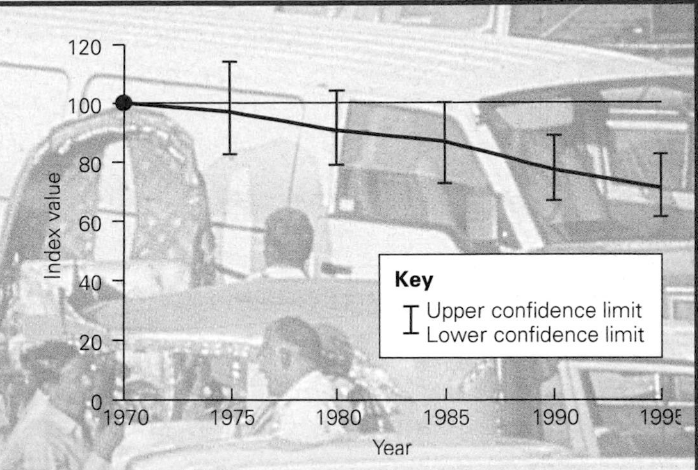

Figure 3.2 *WWF living planet index (1970–95)*
Source: *WWF Living Planet Report*, 1998.

Easing the flow

The history of the human race is full of examples of migrations. Some have been set in motion by hazards, often triggered by human abuse and over-use of the environment, e.g. famine. Oppression of minority groups and war have been, and still are, major contributors to the global refugee map (Figure 3.3). One in every 200 people in today's world is a refugee.

While migration has the potential to bring about a better balance between numbers of people, resources and the environment, it has become a hot political issue. This is especially true where people are forced to cross national boundaries.

The challenge: to loosen the barriers to migration.

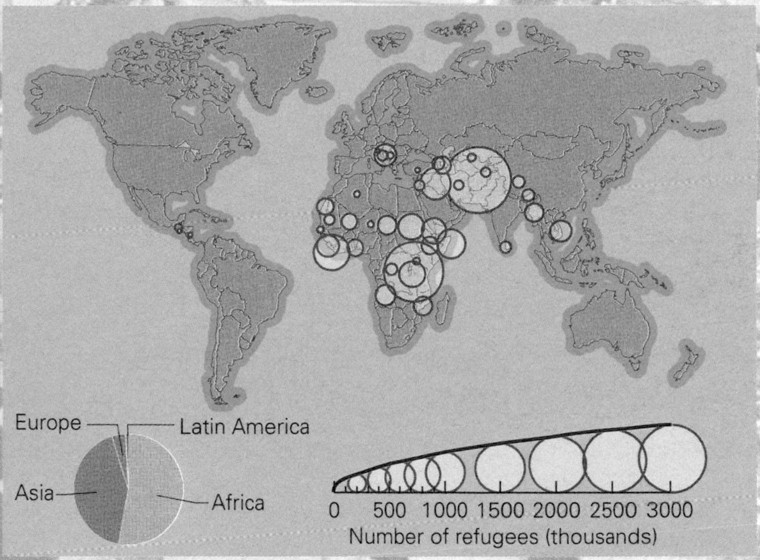

Europe
Latin America
Asia
Africa
0 500 1000 1500 2000 2500 3000
Number of refugees (thousands)

Figure 3.3 *Origins of the world's refugees, 1995* Source: Boyle et al, *Exploring Contemporary Migration*, Longman, 1997.

Shrinking the family

This topical issue may seem less geographical, but it is important to the future of human population. The global birth rate fell by about one-third during the second half of the twentieth century, and the death rate more than halved. As a result, the latter cancelled out the former and the rate of natural increase remains high. The world now needs lower fertility rates. Only when this happens will it achieve a stable population size. High fertility is not universal, however, and some MEDCs are becoming alarmed because their populations have become too infertile.

In LEDCs it is common for women to start bearing children too early and continue for too long. In order to lower fertility rates, education about birth control and more gender equality is required in such countries.

The challenge: to lower fertility rates by voluntary means.

Figure 3.4 *A teenage mother in Burkina Faso – how many more children will she bear?*

ACTIVITIES

1. Discuss in groups which is the most important challenge on pages 90-91. Report and justify your conclusions.
2. Explain the link between wealth and resource consumption.
3. Describe two ways in which MEDCs might adversely affect the environment in LEDCs.
4. Suggest a recent example of migration triggered by: war; environmental hazard; ethnic cleansing.

What are the components of population change?

The central focus of population geography is the distribution of people over the Earth. The population distribution map (Figure 3.5) shows how population densities vary from place to place. However, any population distribution map is simply a snapshot. Like the camera, it 'freezes' the situation as it was when the census that provides the data was carried out. Population distribution is not static; it is constantly changing. The changes are often quite complex, for example, while the total population of a country is rising or falling, there may be contrary trends both between and within its regions. Loss and gain, growth and decline may exist side by side.

Population as a system

Population change is the outcome of two processes: **natural change** and **migrational change**. It is an **open system** (Figure 3.6). The inputs are births and inward migration (**immigration**), and the outputs are deaths and outward migration (**emigration**). Whether the number of people rises or falls depends on the nature of the net balance between all the inputs and outputs. When births exceed deaths, there is a **natural increase**. **Natural decrease** occurs when the balance is reversed. Similarly, migration can result in either an increase or decrease in population. **Net migration gain** happens when more people are moving into an area than leaving it. The result is population growth. When departures exceed arrivals, there is **net migration loss** and population may decline. So natural change and migration are the processes of the system, and the people are its stores.

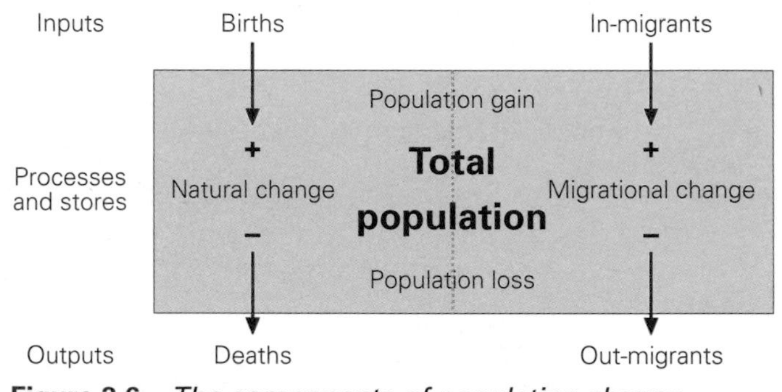

Figure 3.6 *The components of population change*

ACTIVITIES

Study Figure 3.5.

1. Which regions of the world show the highest population densities? Suggest reasons for these high densities.
2. Are the regions that most increased their share of global population between 1950 and 2000 (study also Table 3.1) regions with high population densities? Suggest reasons for your answer.

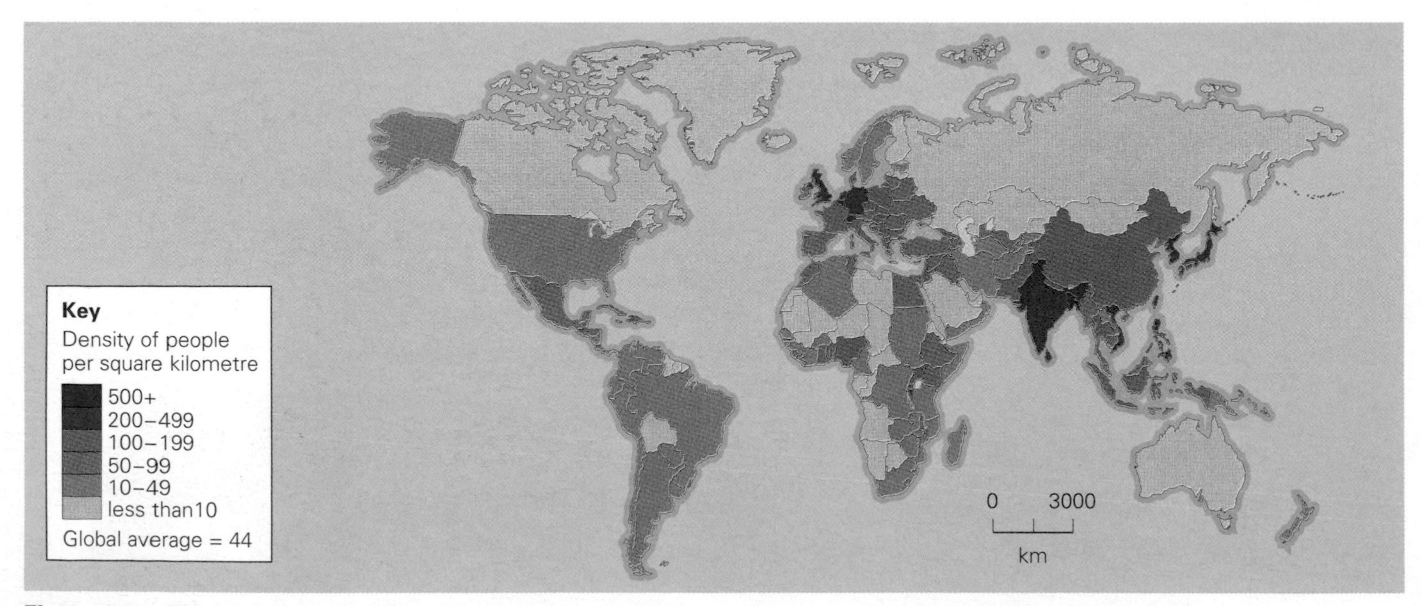

Figure 3.5 *The global distribution of population, 1997* Source: *Philip's Modern School Atlas, 92nd Edition,* 1998.

Given these two processes of population change, it is possible to outline different scenarios of population change which affect the system's stores (Figure 3.7):

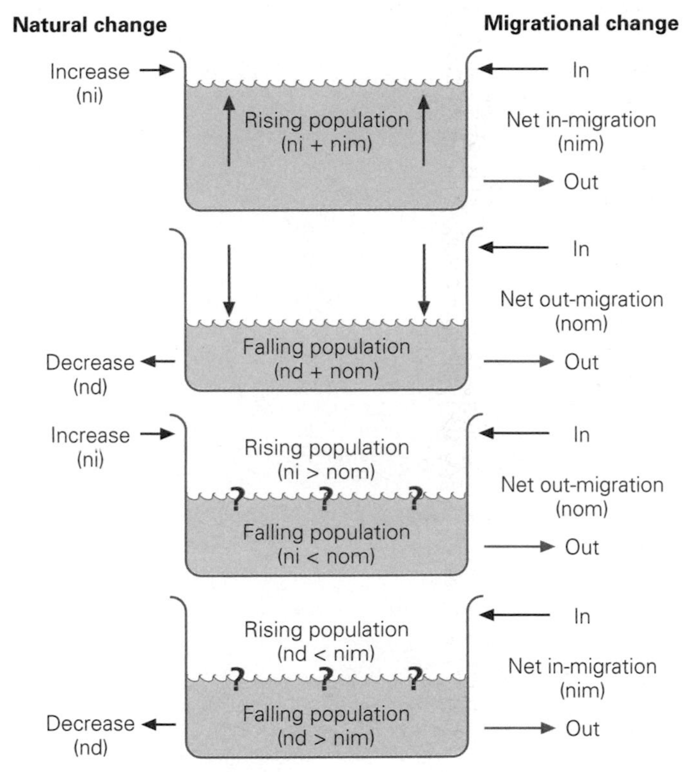

Figure 3.7 *Different scenarios of population change*

- **inputs exceed outputs** There is both natural increase and net migration gain. Since both the elements are positive, the population increase could be quite large.
- **outputs exceed inputs** Population change will be negative. Natural decrease combined with net migration loss can quickly lower the population level.
- **contrary trends** The two elements of change work against each other. Either natural increase is paired with net migration loss, or natural decrease is paired with net migration gain. The net change is likely to be slow population change, either positive or negative. The two contrary elements might balance each other and thereby create a no-change or stationary situation.

ACTIVITIES

1 Which is the more important element of population change – natural change or migration? Justify your view.
2 Suggest parts of the world which are experiencing:
  - natural population decrease
  - net out-migration
  - a stationary population
  - the highest rates of population growth.

Natural change

One of the two components of population change is natural change. Investigations of natural change, particularly of its scale and speed, require information about its inputs (births) and outputs (deaths) (Figure 3.6). These elements are often referred to respectively as **fertility** and **mortality**. Rather than use total numbers, the number of births and deaths recorded in a year are expressed in ratio form, most often as per 1,000 people living in the area under investigation. Such ratios are known as **crude birth** and **crude death rates**. They are of limited value since neither takes into account the age structure of the population or possible differences in the ratio of males to females. In the case of births, it is important to have some idea of the proportion of a population in the reproductive age range. In the case of deaths, sex differences need to be taken into consideration; women generally live longer than men.

Measures of fertility

standardised birth rate The birth rate for a particular area is calculated, assuming that its age structure is identical to that of the nation as a whole. Attention then focuses on the difference between this standardised birth rate and the actual birth rate recorded by that area.

general fertility rate The number of births in a year per 100 women of reproductive age (generally given as being between 15 and 45).

Measures of mortality

standardised death rate The death rate for a particular area is calculated, assuming that its age structure is identical to that of the nation as a whole. Attention then focuses on the difference between this standardised death rate and the actual death rate recorded by that area.

infant mortality rate The number of deaths of children under the age of one year per 1,000 live births in a given year.

ACTIVITY

1 Explain why:
  - it is better to use standardised rates than crude rates when studying natural change
  - it is important to take the age structure of a population into account
  - standardised rates are particularly useful in geographical studies.

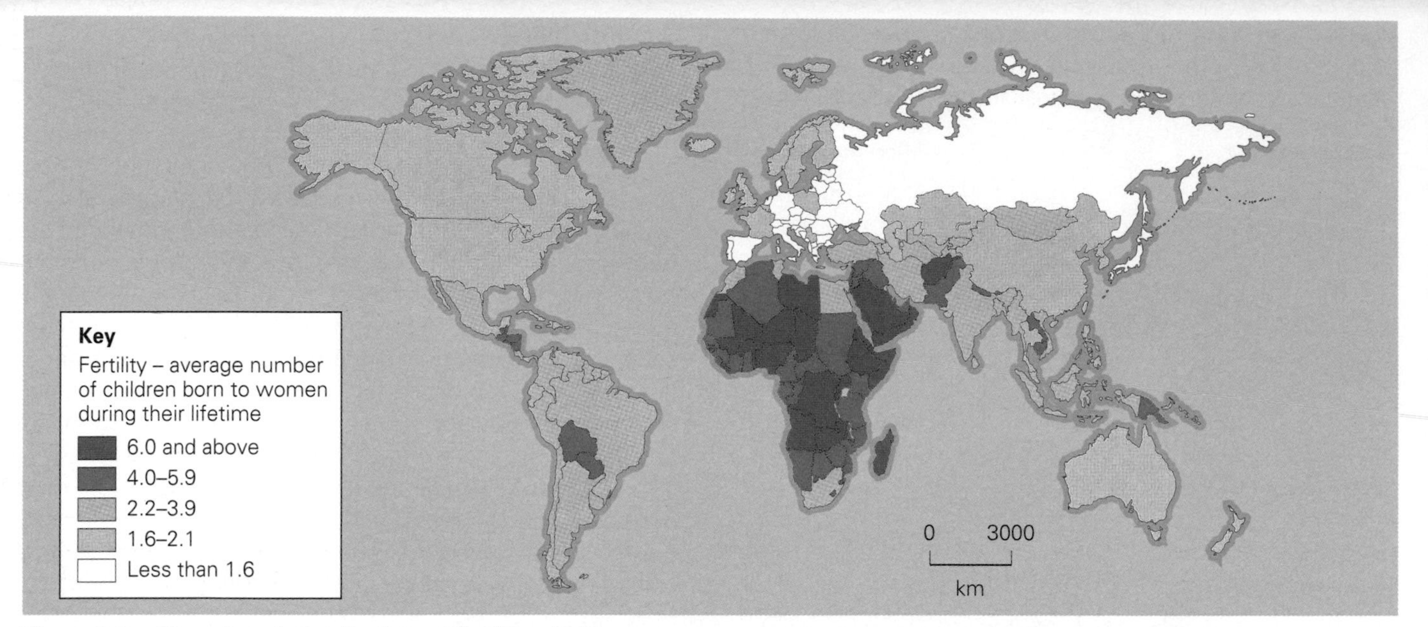

Figure 3.8 *The global distribution of fertility, 1995* Source: Ross et al, *Essential AS Geography*, Stanley Thornes, 2000.

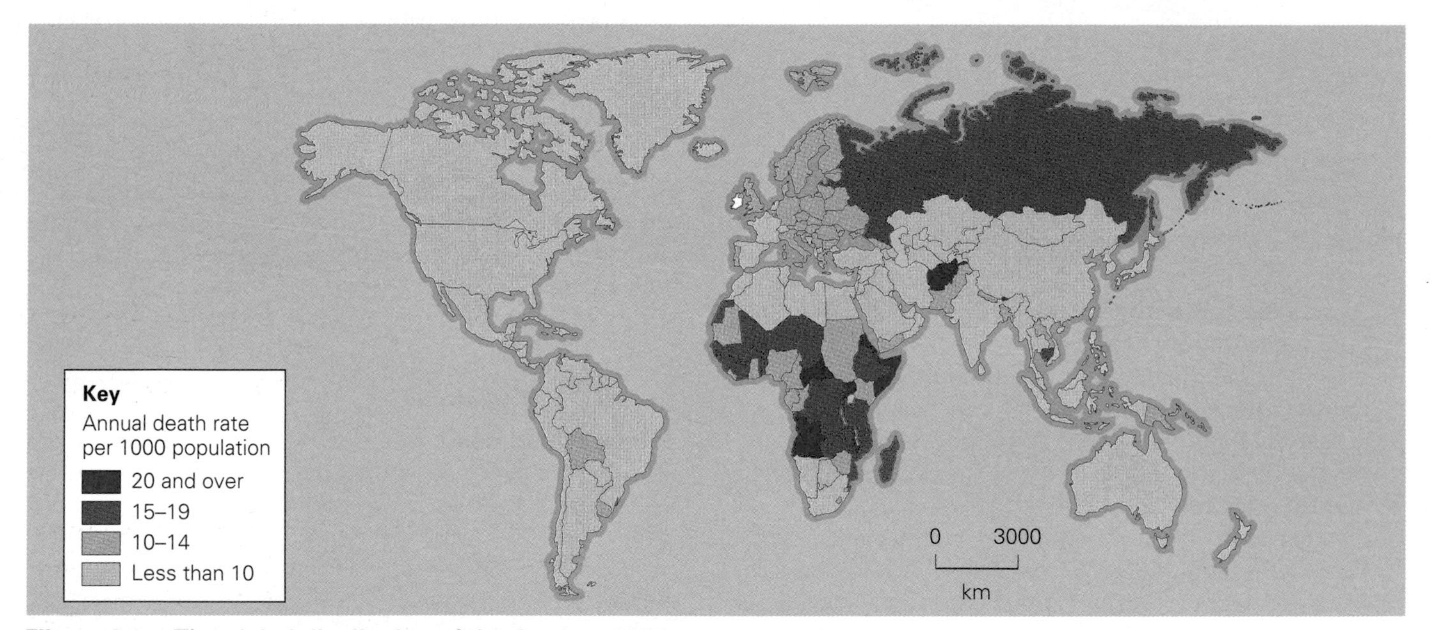

Fiigure 3.9 *The global distribution of death rates, 1995* Source: Ross et al, *Essential AS Geography*, Stanley Thornes, 2000.

Figures 3.8 and 3.9 give a global picture of the incidence of births and deaths respectively. In the former, a more refined measure than the crude birth rate is used. In the latter, use of an equivalent measure is prevented by the absence in many countries of the raw data needed for calculation, and the limitations of crude rates should be borne in mind. In Figure 3.8, high fertility in Africa and the Middle East is apparent. In Figure 3.9, much of Africa also appears to have a particularly high death rate. Are there good reasons why these two opposing situations are found together? The relatively high death rate in Russia may come as a surprise.

Figures 3.8 and 3.9 present snapshot views of global fertility and mortality as it was in 1995. It is important to remember, however, that these measures vary both from place to place and from time to time. This can be demonstrated by looking at the changes in crude birth and death rates experienced by a sample of countries over the relatively short time span of 50 years (Figure 3.10). While there are considerable differences in the birth rates between Ethiopia and the UK, crude birth rates for all the selected countries are lower today than they were in 1950. Two similar observations can be made for crude death rates. Large international differences are apparent, but in all countries shown, the trend is downwards. Remember that the relationship between the two rates is critical. Natural increase results when birth rates are higher than death rates; natural decrease sets in as soon as the positions are reversed. There are relatively few countries in the latter situation, but with a birth rate of 11 per 1,000 and a death rate of 16 per 1,000, Russia is clearly one of them.

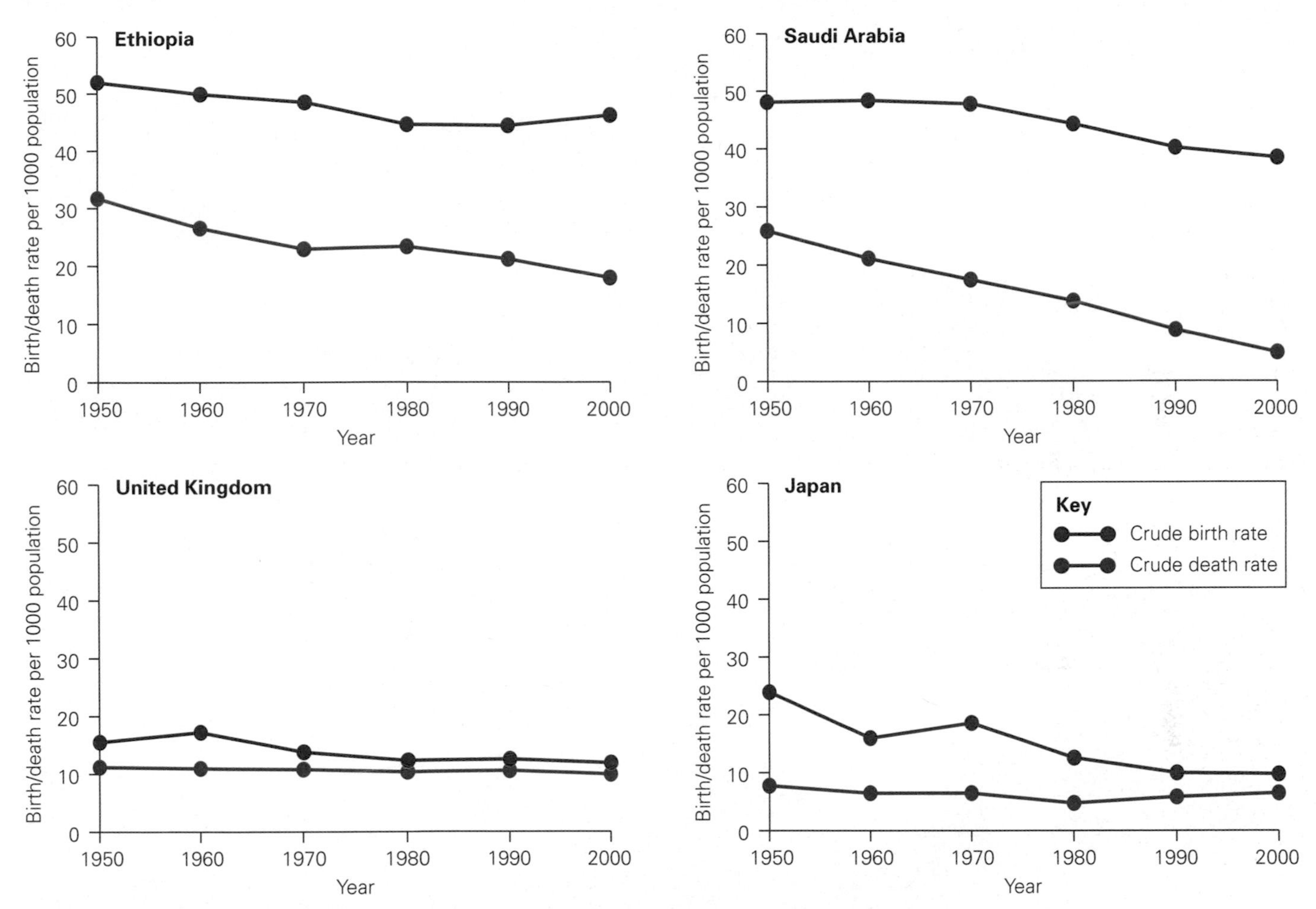

Figure 3.10 *Crude birth rates and death rates for selected countries (1950–2000)*

'Russia's population goes into free fall'

This was a recent headline in the British press. Russia is facing a demographic crisis as the birth rate plummets and the death rate climbs steeply. The plunge in the birth rate has been brought on largely by a crumbling pre-natal healthcare system. Only one in ten pregnancies results in a normal birth, and less than a third of recorded pregnancies produces a live birth (abortion is widely used as a form of birth control). Anaemia, heart problems, malnutrition and excessive consumption of cigarettes and alcohol lie behind the rising death rate.

If present trends persist, the number of 13–16 year olds will fall from 30 to 22 million by 2015. The overall population has already fallen by 6 million in 10 years. It could fall by another 39 million by 2025. At that point Russia would then have the population of Japan spread over 11 time zones.

ACTIVITIES

1. Identify the key features of the distribution patterns shown in Figures 3.8 and 3.9.
2. What similarities, if any, do you detect in the two distribution patterns?
3. Discuss the long-term consequences of Russia's population decline.
4. Identify the key features shown by the graphs in Figure 3.10. What conclusions might be drawn about the nature of population change in these countries?

EXTENSION ACTIVITY

Figures 3.11 and 3.12 are maps of population change in the British Isles in 1995. Figure 3.11 shows the pattern of natural change; Figure 3.12 the pattern of net migration between counties within the British Isles (it excludes overseas migration).

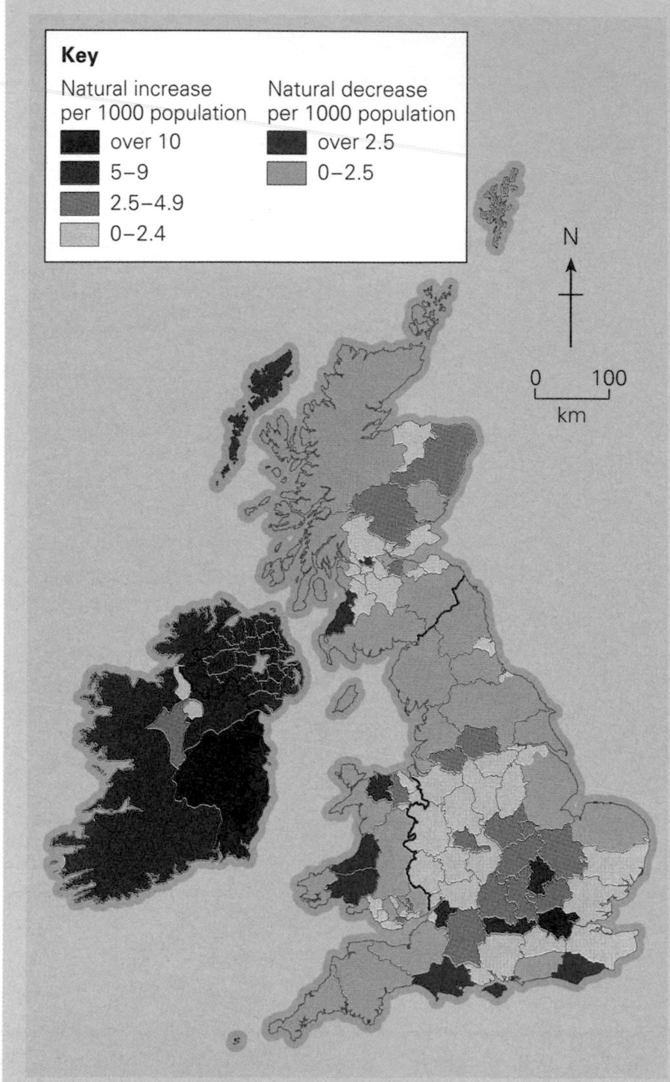

Figure 3.11 *Natural population change in the British Isles, 1995*
Source: *Philip's Modern School Atlas, 92nd Edition*, 1998.

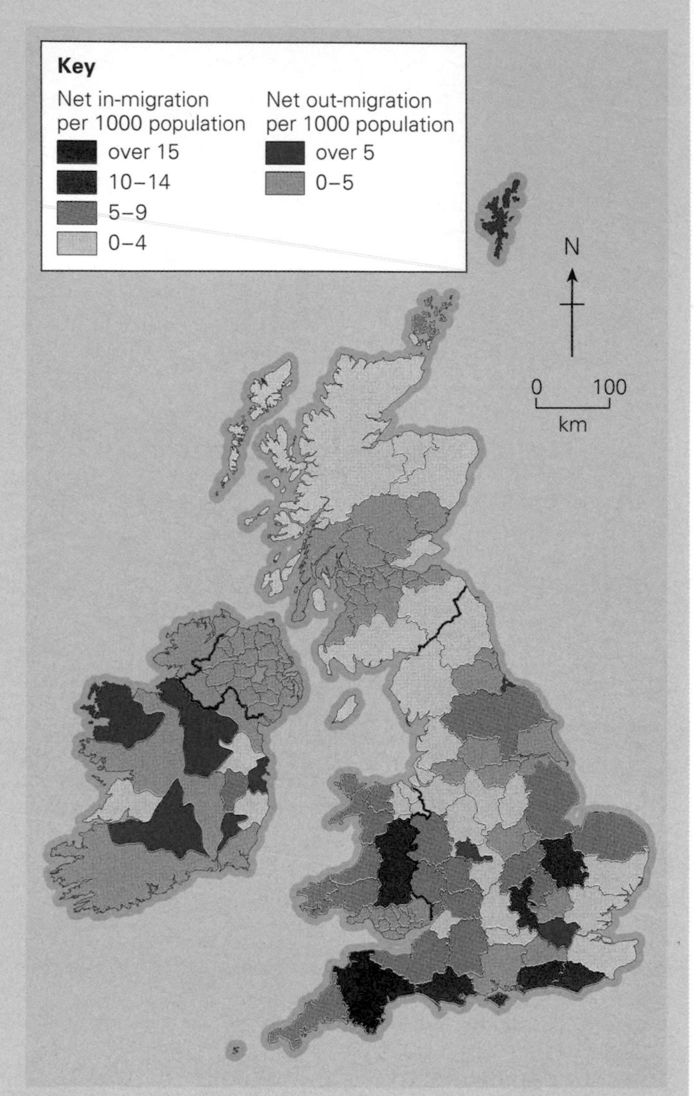

Figure 3.12 *Internal migration change in the British Isles, 1995*
Source: *Philip's Modern School Atlas, 92nd Edition*, 1998.

a Produce your own map which classifies the counties as follows:
- **marked growth** – natural increase and net in-migration
- **little change** – natural increase and net out-migration
- **little change** – natural decrease and net in-migration
- **marked decline** – natural decrease and net out-migration.

b Annotate your map to highlight key features.

c Suggest possible reasons for each of the four different scenarios.

d Make a more detailed study of the situation in your home county. Data can be obtained from the Office of National Statistics (www.statistics.gov.uk). You might work under the following headings:
- natural change during the last inter-censal period
- trends in birth and death rates during that period
- migration balances during that period.

For each of these lines of enquiry, you should
- produce a map or diagram
- write a brief report, drawing attention to the key features and offering some explanation for them
- compare what you find in your county with the national situation.

2 Measuring population change

Census data and measures of change

The basic need in population geography is for accurate information about key aspects of the world's population (Figure 3.13). Three categories of information are particularly important:

- population **distribution** – numbers and where they occur
- population **structure** – age, sex, marital status, ethnic origins
- population **change** – changing numbers, shifts in the relative importance of natural and migrational change, alterations in structure.

Ideally, data for each of these three categories is needed for the whole range of spatial scales: for continents, countries, regions within those countries, for towns and small areas within them and rural districts.

Figure 3.13 *A global challenge – keeping count of the world's population*

In nearly all cases, the responsibility for collecting and publishing population data rests with national governments. MEDCs have the resources and organisations to collect large quantities of reliable information about their people. Information in LEDCs is often less reliable. Since the middle of the twentieth century, the United Nations Organisation (UNO), has done much to improve the supply of information about LEDC populations. The UNO has also tried to standardise data by encouraging all countries to collect the same types of information in their censuses, and to do so at regular intervals. Such co-ordination of the census efforts of individual countries should produce a much clearer picture of global population.

Lines of census enquiry, as recommended by the UNO

- total population and its distribution within the country
- sex, age and marital status
- place of birth and nationality
- mother tongue and literacy
- occupation
- residential location (urban or rural)
- household or family size and structure
- fertility.

While the national census is the most common way of collecting population data, there are three important differences. These relate to:

- the **method of collection** – people are 'counted' either where they are at a precise moment in time (*de facto*), or according to their normal place of residence (*de jure*)
- the **frequency** – a census taken every 10 years is a common practice; some countries manage every 5 years, others much less frequently
- the **extent** – either the whole population is surveyed or it is sampled (e.g. 10 per cent of the population is sampled) and general conclusions are then derived about the whole population

Change is the aspect of population that most concerns governments and other decision-makers. Reliable data on change is only found when there is consistency over time; that is, in the type of data collected and in the spatial divisions used in its collection. Clearly, when it comes to monitoring change, frequency is a key issue. It is generally agreed that a census taken every 10 years allows most countries to gain an adequate overview. But why is this monitoring of change so important? The simple answer is that it allows trends to be identified. These trends, in turn, allow forecasts to be made, and future situations anticipated. How many more people are likely to be living in an area in 10 years' time? How many new houses will have to be built? What will the extra demand be for jobs and shops, schools and hospitals? In short, the monitoring of population is essential to good government, proper planning and sound decision-making in many types of business.

ACTIVITIES

1. What are the relative merits of the *de facto* and *de jure* census methods? Which method was used by the UK's 2001 Census?
2. Find out about the UK Census – its frequency, extent and the spatial units used in the collection of data.
3. Identify other aspects of planning that benefit from having information about population change.
4. Complete Table 3.2 by working out the rates of natural change for 1990 and 2000. Produce graphs to show the data. Study your completed table and graphs and come to a reasoned conclusion about:
   - the soundness of distinguishing between LEDCs and MEDCs on the basis of population change characteristics
   - the degree to which the countries in each grouping share the same demographic characteristics.

	Total population (million)		**Crude birth rate** (per 1000)		**Crude death rate** (per 1000)		**Rate of natural change** (per 1000)	
	1990	2000	1990	2000	1990	2000	1990	2000
LEDCs								
Brazil	145	160	31	20	8	9		
China	1155	1215	21	17	8	7		
Ethiopia	46	59	45	46	24	18		
India	835	980	32	25	13	9		
Mexico	86	98	32	26	6	5		
Saudi Arabia	15	19	43	38	9	5		
MEDCs								
Australia	17	19	14	14	7	7		
Bulgaria	9	9	13	8	12	14		
Japan	124	126	11	10	7	8		
Singapore	3	3	17	16	5	5		
UK	57	59	14	13	11	11		
USA	250	268	16	15	9	9		

Table 3.2 *Indices of population change for a selection of countries, 1990–2000*

Portraying distribution, density and change

Most often, investigations of population distribution start with a map to show where exactly people are to be found within a given area. Two different types of map might be produced.

1 Distribution

The first involves taking a base map of the area under investigation, probably a topographic map, and locating people on it by means of a standard symbol. This might be:

- a dot representing a given number of people (Figure 3.14a)
- a circle whose radius is proportional to the number of people being represented (Figure 3.14b)

A map might use both types of **located symbol**, for instance with villages shown by proportional circles and the intervening dispersed farmhouses by standard dots.

This last approach may give a good and accurate picture of the actual distribution, but it does involve detailed investigation, painstaking plotting and is time consuming to prepare. So unless there is an acute need for detail and precision, other methods are available that are easier and quicker to use and yet give a good visual impression of population distribution.

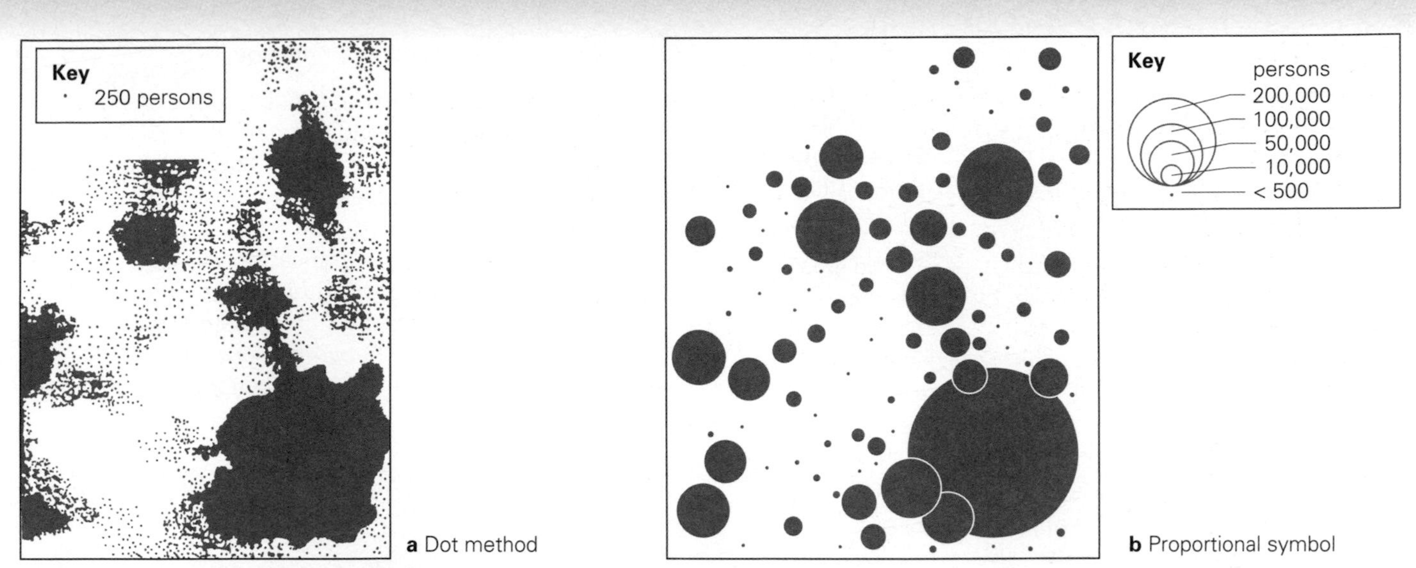

Figure 3.14 *Cartographic methods for showing the distribution of population: a = dot method; b = proportional symbol*
Source: *Derived from* Witherick, *Population Geography*, Longman, 1990.

The topological map is another variant used to show the distribution of population. In the case of Figure 3.15, each country is represented by means of a rectangular shape, the area of which is proportional to its total population. The map is accurate with respect to this one variable, but reality is stretched by the relative positioning of countries on the map, and by ignoring their actual shapes and areas. Nonetheless, it gives an interesting view of the way in which the world's population is distributed.

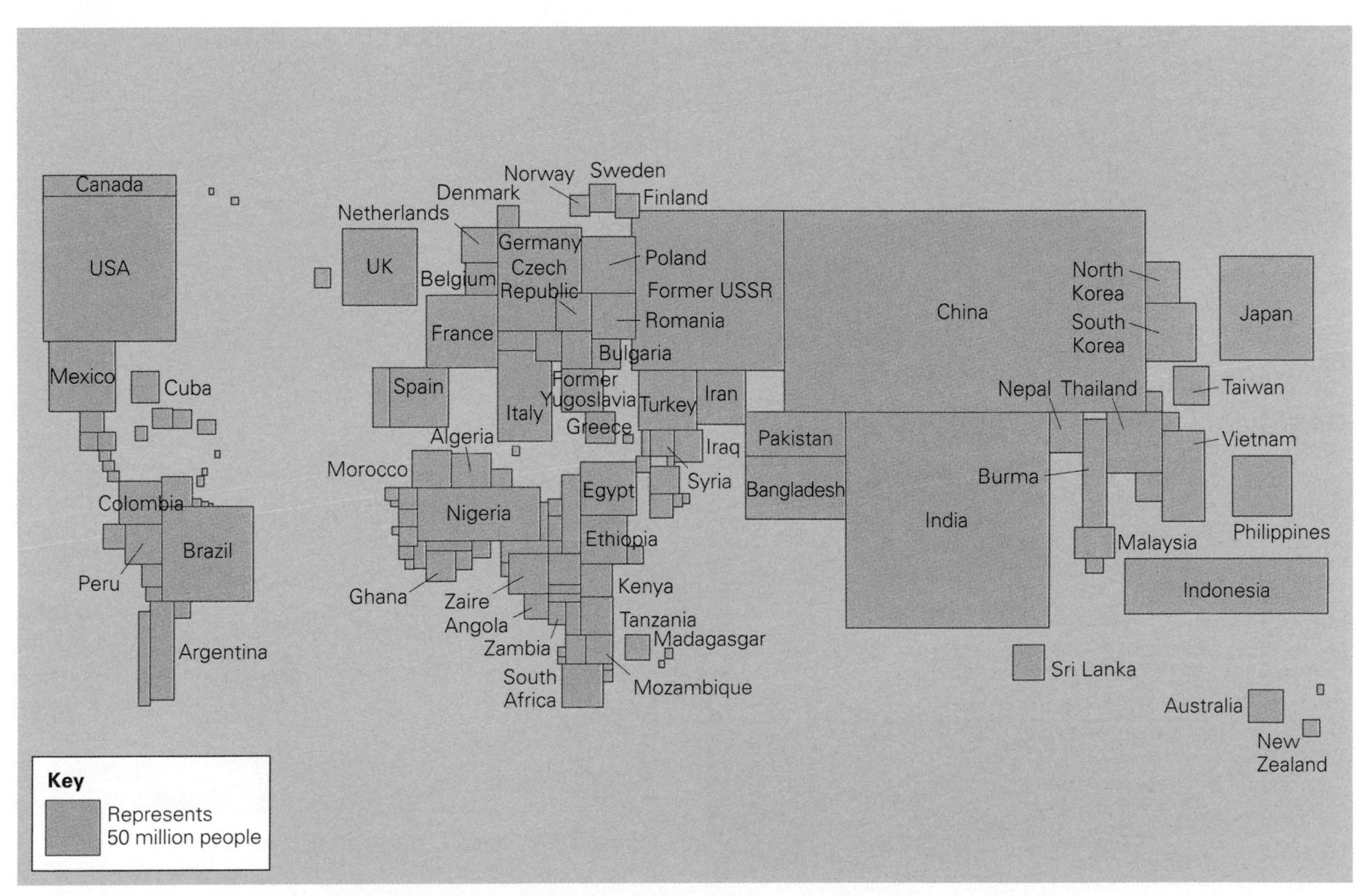

Figure 3.15 *A topological map of global population* Source: Witherick, *Environment and People*, Stanley Thornes, 1998.

2 Density

A second mapping strategy is to plot the distribution of people in terms of the relationship between numbers and area. This measure is usually referred to as **population density** and the technique widely used to map it is known as the **choropleth** method.

- Mean density values for subdivisions of the area under investigation are shown by a scheme of graded colours or shading.
- The greater the density, the greater the intensity of colour or shading (Figure 3.16).
- The scale of spatial units used in the plotting of data depends on the scale of the investigation. For example, in studying the distribution of population within a city, it would be appropriate to plot the density values for the city's wards, while for a global study, national values would be more suitable.

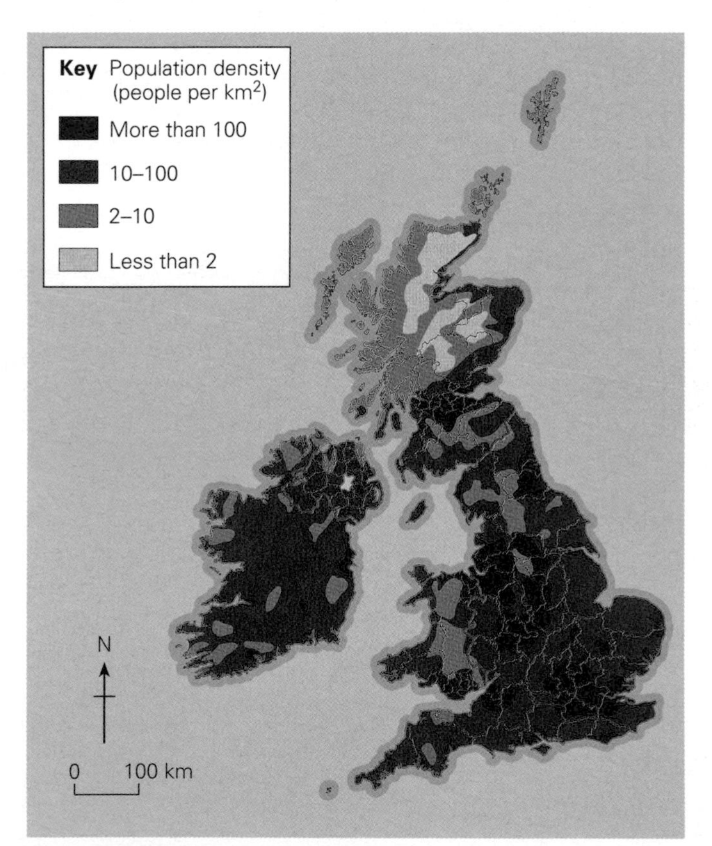

Figure 3.16 *Choropleth map*
Source: Witherick, *Population Geography*, Longman, 1990.

ACTIVITIES

1. Of the three methods shown in Figures 3.14 and 3.16 which do you prefer? Give your reasons.
2. Assess the relative merits of Figures 3.5 and 3.15 as ways of showing the global distribution of population.

Choropleth maps have some limitations:

- No matter what the spatial scale, these maps represent only the average value for each of the units.
- Mean values are generalisations; they conceal spatial variations within the areas they represent. The larger the spatial unit used in the plotting of data, the greater the degree of generalisation.
- Where neighbouring spatial units have different densities, the map gives the impression of a sudden break at the boundary between them. In reality, changes in population densities are gradual and gentle.

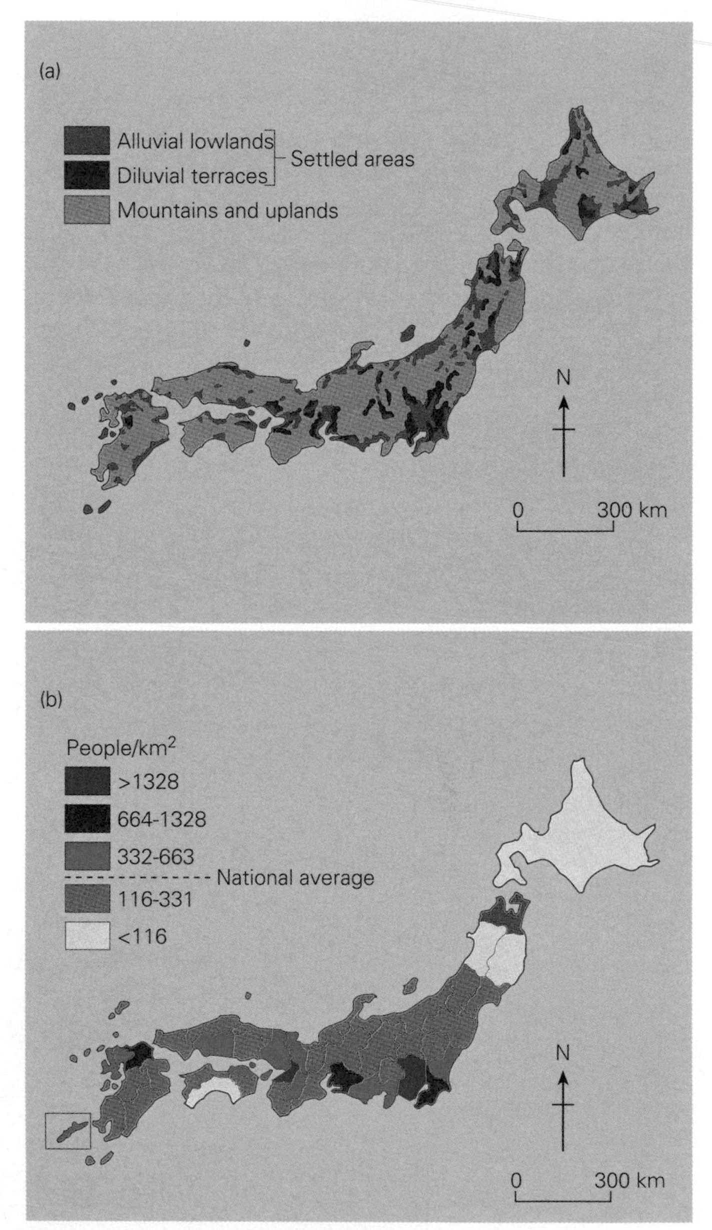

Figure 3.17 *Japan, showing a) physical terrain and b) population distribution, 1990* Source: Witherick and Carr, *The Changing Face of Japan*, Hodder & Stoughton, 1993.

- The use of mean density values is flawed in another way. For example, a figure of 334 persons per km² for the whole of Japan seriously understates the actual density of population. Over two-thirds of the country is made up of inhospitable mountain terrain (Figure 3.17a). The settled lowland and terrace areas are not only small and fragmented, but many have very high densities, well in excess of 1,000 people per km². Here, as in many other parts of the world, it would be better to calculate density as the number of people per unit of habitable space rather than total space. This would certainly produce a more accurate picture than Figure 3.17b where each of the administrative divisions of Japan is represented by a crude mean value.

ACTIVITY

1 Suggest reasons for the variations in population density shown on Figure 3.17b.

Although the choropleth map is a widely used technique for showing density distribution, there are some technical problems associated with drawing it. Two vital questions have to be faced:

- How many different density classes should be recognised? Ideally the scheme might comprise from four to eight different classes. Where less than four categories are used, the map becomes too generalised; more than eight and it becomes too difficult for the eye to 'digest'.
- How are these classes delimited? There are a number of options. The simplest is to divide the range of values in the dataset into a number of equal classes (Figure 3.12). Alternatively, the scheme might follow a geometric progression (Figure 3.11). In both approaches, the scheme may take into account the overall mean of the dataset (Figure 3.17b). Incorporating this mean value can be very useful, particularly when it comes to comparing areas.

ACTIVITIES

1 When would it be more appropriate to use a geometric scale in the construction of a choropleth map?

2 Explain the advantages of using the mean of the data set in the definition of density classes.

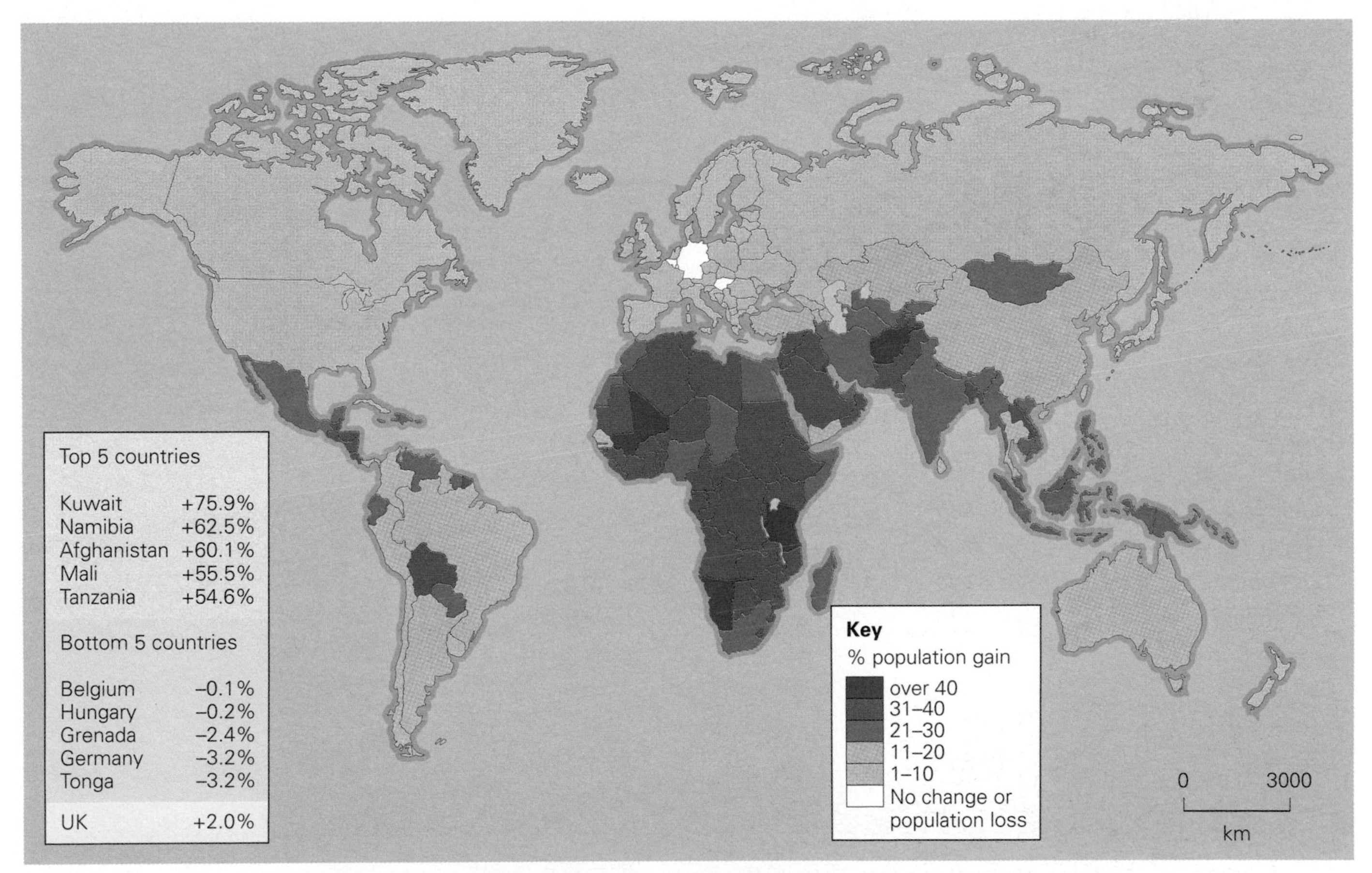

Figure 3.18 *Global population change, 1990–2000.* Source: *Philip's Modern School Atlas, 92nd Edition,* 1998.

Change

When it comes to the mapping of population change, many of the above techniques may be used. Figure 3.18 illustrates that the choropleth technique can be used to show the spatial pattern of changes in density. Graphs also have an equally important part to play in demonstrating how aspects of population vary over time, i.e. changes in numbers and densities; variations in birth and death rates (Figure 3.10). In general, it is best to measure change in percentage rather than absolute terms. In many cases, calculating a mean annual rate provides a good standardised indicator of the rate and scale of change. Population pyramids are also helpful in analysing change in age and gender structures (page 121).

ACTIVITIES

1. Explain the benefits of using percentage values in the measurement of change.
2. For your local area, extract population data at a ward level from the SCAMP CD.
   - produce maps to show a) the distribution of population, and b) the percentage change during the last inter-censal period
   - write a brief account pointing out the key features of each map
   - to what extent do the mean values for the whole of your local area conceal important spatial differences within it?
3. Identify the key features of Figure 3.18. To what extent does this pattern fit with the broader sequence of population change shown in Table 3.1?

EXTENSION ACTIVITY

Table 3.3 gives information about population change in SE Asia.

a Which of the three variables do you think provides the best measure of change?

b Represent the data of your chosen measure using three different cartographic techniques.

c Compare your three maps in terms of:
- their effectiveness
- the time and effort involved in their preparation
- any particular problems encountered.

Population change (1990–1997)

	Increase in numbers (thousands)	Mean annual increase (%)	Increase in mean density (people per km²)
Brunei	47	1.7	9
Cambodia	1932	3.5	10
China	54,595	0.9	5
Hong Kong	795	1.5	97
Indonesia	23,670	1.8	13
Japan	2363	0.3	6
Laos	998	3.3	5
Malaysia	3136	2.2	10
North Korea	2726	1.7	22
Philippines	12,020	2.4	41
Singapore	495	2.5	812
South Korea	3181	1.1	32
Taiwan	1347	0.9	38
Thailand	4718	0.9	9
Vietnam	10,867	2.1	34

Table 3.3 *Measures of population change in the countries of SE Asia*

3 Rates of natural population change

The global population is highly prone to change. Over much of the world, the dominant trend is population growth. The rate at which this growth takes place varies over space (Figure 3.18) and time (Figure 3.26). These two dimensions of change are largely the outcome of changes in birth rates (**fertility**) and death rates (**mortality**), as well as shifts in the relationship between those two rates (**natural change**). For the moment, let us focus on these three aspects of change. In doing so, we should not forget that, although it is of much less significance, migration also contributes to overall population change (Figure 3.6). Rural-urban migration can have very important consequences within individual countries.

Changing fertility

Figure 3.8 illustrates that birth rates and fertility vary from place to place, while Figure 3.10 indicates that there is also change over time. In general, fertility has been declining throughout most of the world for much of the last 100 years. Between 1950 and 2000, the world's crude birth rate fell from 38 to 25 per 1,000. Why does fertility vary in time and space? There are many, often linked, reasons.

Birth control is one factor of vital importance today. It includes contraception, sterilisation, abortion and abstention. The level of knowledge about modern birth control methods differs between MEDCs and LEDCs. Development and its ramifications would seem to be a key factor, but this is not the only explanation for the marked differences in the degree to which use is made of such methods. The whole status of birth control is influenced by a complex web of linked factors (Figure 3.19).

The age structure of a population has a clear and direct bearing on fertility. In general, the greater the proportion of a population in the reproductive age range (normally taken as 15 to 45 years), the greater the expectation of fertility (Table 3.4). Higher rates of fertility are likely to be reflected in a high proportion of young people in the population. High infant mortality possibly encourages a higher level of fertility and larger families (Figure 3.20). A fertility rate of just over 2 is known as the **replacement level**. A couple will in a sense 'replace' themselves when they die if they have had two children. If they, and most other couples in the population, have had more, then population will grow; if fewer, then population declines.

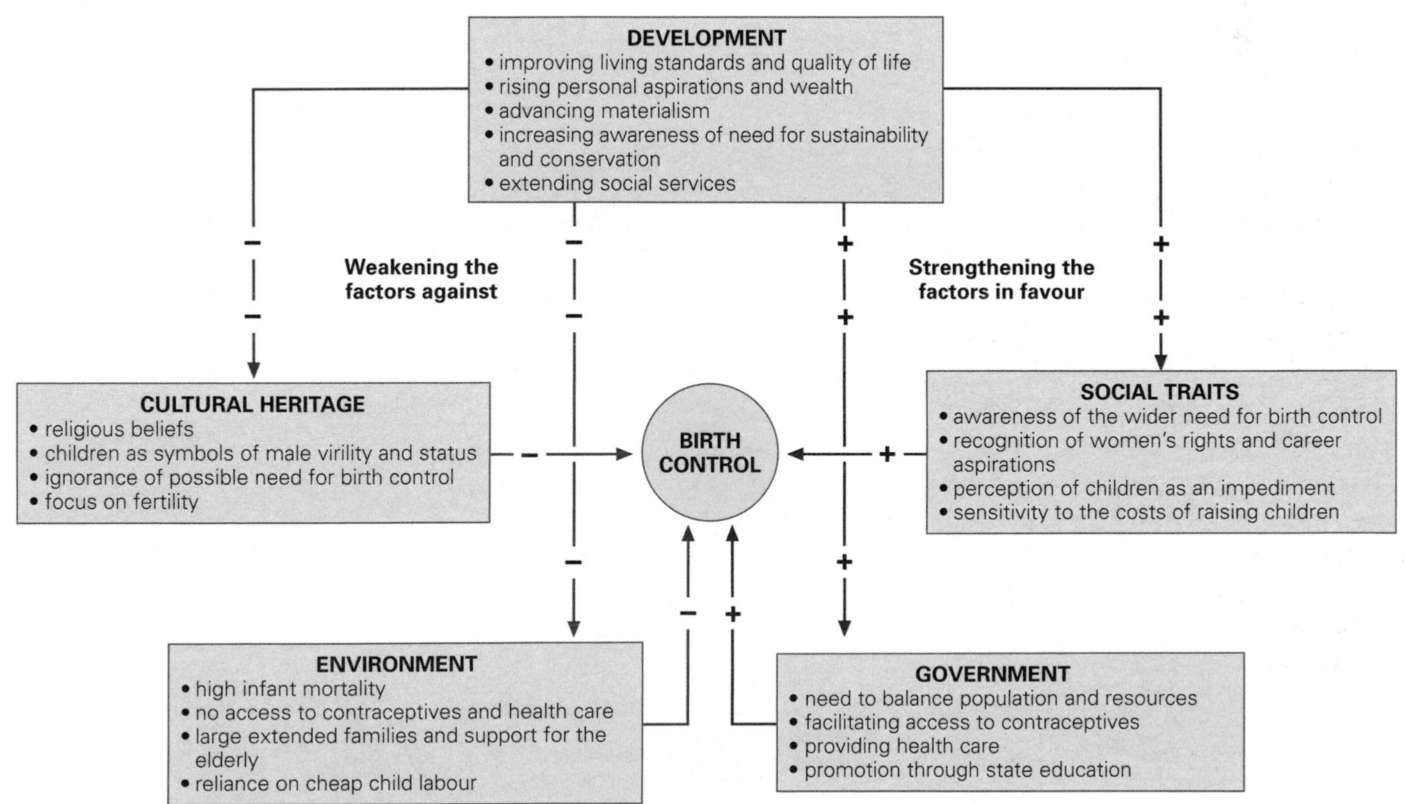

Figure 3.19 *Factors affecting birth control*

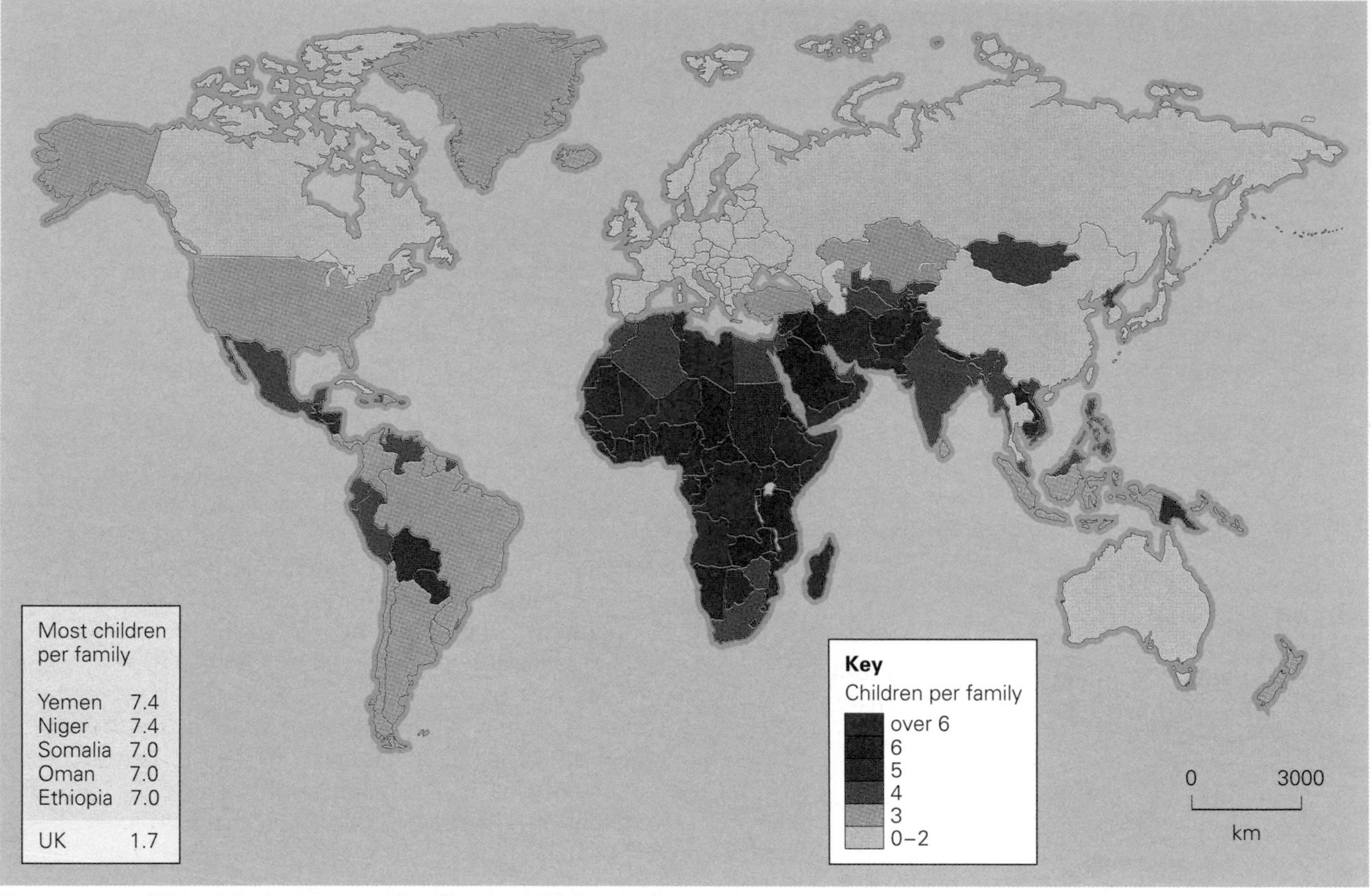

Figure 3.20 *The global pattern of family size, 1995*
Source: *Philip's Modern School Atlas, 92nd Edition*, 1998.

	Fertility rate (children per female)	**Population aged under 15** (%)	**Population aged 15–50** (%)	**Family size** (average number of children)
LEDCs				
Brazil	2.4	35	52	2
China	1.9	27	58	1
Ethiopia	7.0	45	45	7
India	3.2	37	49	3
Mexico	3.0	37	52	3
Saudi Arabia	6.2	45	46	6
MEDCs				
Australia	1.9	22	53	1
Bulgaria	1.2	20	56	1
Japan	1.5	18	53	1
Singapore	1.7	23	62	2
UK	1.7	19	51	1
USA	2.1	21	53	2

Table 3.4 *Fertility and related measures for a sample of countries, 1995*

ACTIVITIES

1. Study Figure 3.19.
   - Explain the links shown.
   - Are there any other bullet points that should be added to the boxes? Give your reasoning.
2. Use an appropriate statistical test to measure the degree of relationship between the variables in Table 3.4. Write a short account of your findings.

'Our young mothers are getting older every day'

The average age at which women in England and Wales have children topped 30 for the first time in 1999. Official figures show that, despite growing public concern about teenage pregnancy, the birth rate has been falling among all age groups, apart from women in their thirties, where rates have risen steadily since the early 1970s. The only other time in the twentieth century that the average age of motherhood has been close to 30 was during the Second World War, when it rose because so many young men were away fighting.

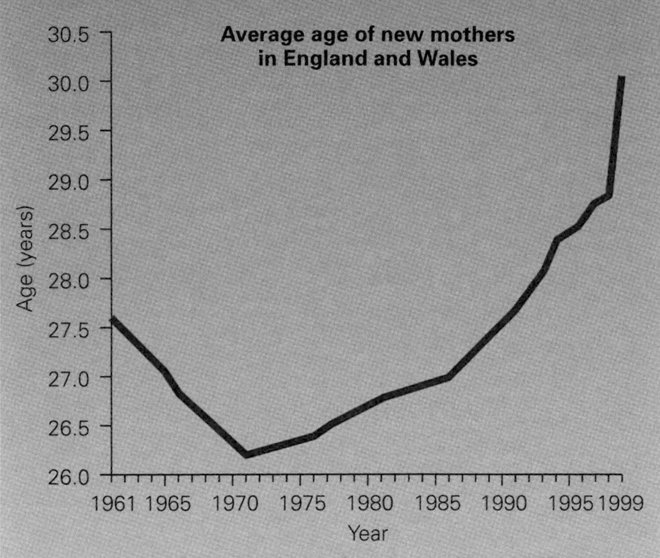

Figure 3.21 *Average age of new mothers in England and Wales, 1961–1999*

Source: *Office of National Statistics, Social Trends*, 1998.

It is now clear that women are settling down to start their families roughly ten years later than they did a century ago. This is partly a result of the growing availability and use of contraceptive devices. It is also partly to do with the fact that women now have better medical support. Previously it would have been unthinkable for a woman to postpone having children until her mid-thirties, because she would have been risking her life. But quite apart from medical advances, many women are busy developing their careers in their twenties and early thirties.

Teenage pregnancies in Britain

The Government has launched a high-profile campaign to reduce Britain's high rate of teenage pregnancies. With 46,000 teenagers giving birth each year, Britain has the highest rate of teenage pregnancy in Europe. Although rates have declined in most other western countries in the past 20 years, in the UK they have stuck at the same level as in the 1980s. Despite government pleas to authority figures to preach the message of abstinence or safe sex, the latest figures show the pregnancy rate among under-16s actually rose slightly from 8,300 to 8,400 between 1991 and 1998.

'I'm not selfish – I just don't want children'

Lysette is getting angry. 'It really does get me going when people say that I am being selfish,' says the 38-year-old nurse from Bedford. 'I believe I have made the decision for the right reasons.' Lysette is one of a growing band of women who have decided not to become mothers. 'It is less selfish not to have children if that is what you want. Everyone else is producing enough. My husband said he wanted me, not children. I just felt that it wasn't for me. I love children so long as I can give them back. I suppose I don't want the responsibility. I have a good career and I want my freedom. My husband and I pay the taxes that financially support those who do have children. We don't consume resources in the way that families with children do.'

'Two's enough, why do I need more?'

That was the question asked by 24-year-old Santhamani, a barely literate housewife whose husband rides a scooter rickshaw in Madras (India). She was in a small health centre recovering from a tubectomy operation performed after having her second child. What she has done represents a very radical break from the traditional view in India and many other parts of the world, that it is ordained by their religion for women to have as many children as possible. She has shown remarkable assertiveness. She has had the operation that will release her from the endless cycle of child-bearing and poverty she watched her mother go through.

In many parts of the world, marriage still has a direct bearing on fertility rates. A marriage contracted when people are in their 'teens is likely to yield more children than if the marriage takes place much later. Bigamy may be expected to raise the level of fertility in those societies which permit it. It is interesting to speculate about the possible impact in MEDCs of the increasing tendency for couples to live together without contracting a marriage. Is the number of children produced necessarily linked to the length of time a couple live together, their commitment to each other and their legal status?

ACTIVITIES

1. In groups, discuss the possible impact on rates of fertility of the following:
   - sex equality and equal opportunities
   - the rise in cohabitation in preference to marriage
   - the increasing number of single-parent families.

   Share your ideas with the whole class.
2. 'Fertility in Britain shows some conflicting trends.' Identify those trends and suggest reasons for them.

Changing mortality

Global variations in death rates are noticeably smaller than in birth rates. In 1995, national crude birth rates ranged from 8 (Bulgaria) to 54 (Niger) per 1,000, whereas crude death rates ranged only from 4 (Paraguay) to 25 (Malawi) per 1,000 (Figure 3.9). A global view of mortality patterns is best gained by looking at the distribution patterns of three different measures:

- crude death rates
- life expectancy
- infant mortality rates.

Figure 3.9 shows some unexpected features. For example, the distinction between MEDCs and LEDCs is much less clear-cut than is the case with crude birth rates (Figure 3.8). Clearly, high rates of mortality prevail over Africa and some parts of SE Asia. At the other extreme, however, the lowest mortality rates do not include all of the most advanced MEDCs. Look at the situation in the UK and Scandinavia where relatively high mortality rates are found. These anomalies support the point made earlier that crude death rates are a poor measure of mortality, because they do not take age structure into account. The higher than expected values for the UK and Scandinavia are a reflection of the fact that their populations are relatively old. The existence of a large 'silvering' population will inflate the death rate.

Figure 3.22 shows the global pattern of life expectancy and gives a more reliable picture of mortality. The inhabitants of the most advanced MEDCs (Western Europe, North America, Australasia and Japan), have a life expectancy of more than 75 years. In stark contrast, life expectancy over much of Africa is less than 50 years. In Malawi it is only 35 years. Afghanistan is the only country outside Africa to rank in the lowest category of life expectancy. Remember, of course, that this map shows average life expectancy. Throughout most countries there will be marked contrasts, e.g. between rich and poor people, rural and urban areas.

ACTIVITY

1 Explain:
- **a** Why life expectancy may be a more reliable measure of mortality than crude death rates.
- **b** Why death rates only make sense when the age structure of a population is taken into account.
- **c** Why infant mortality is such an important aspect of population.

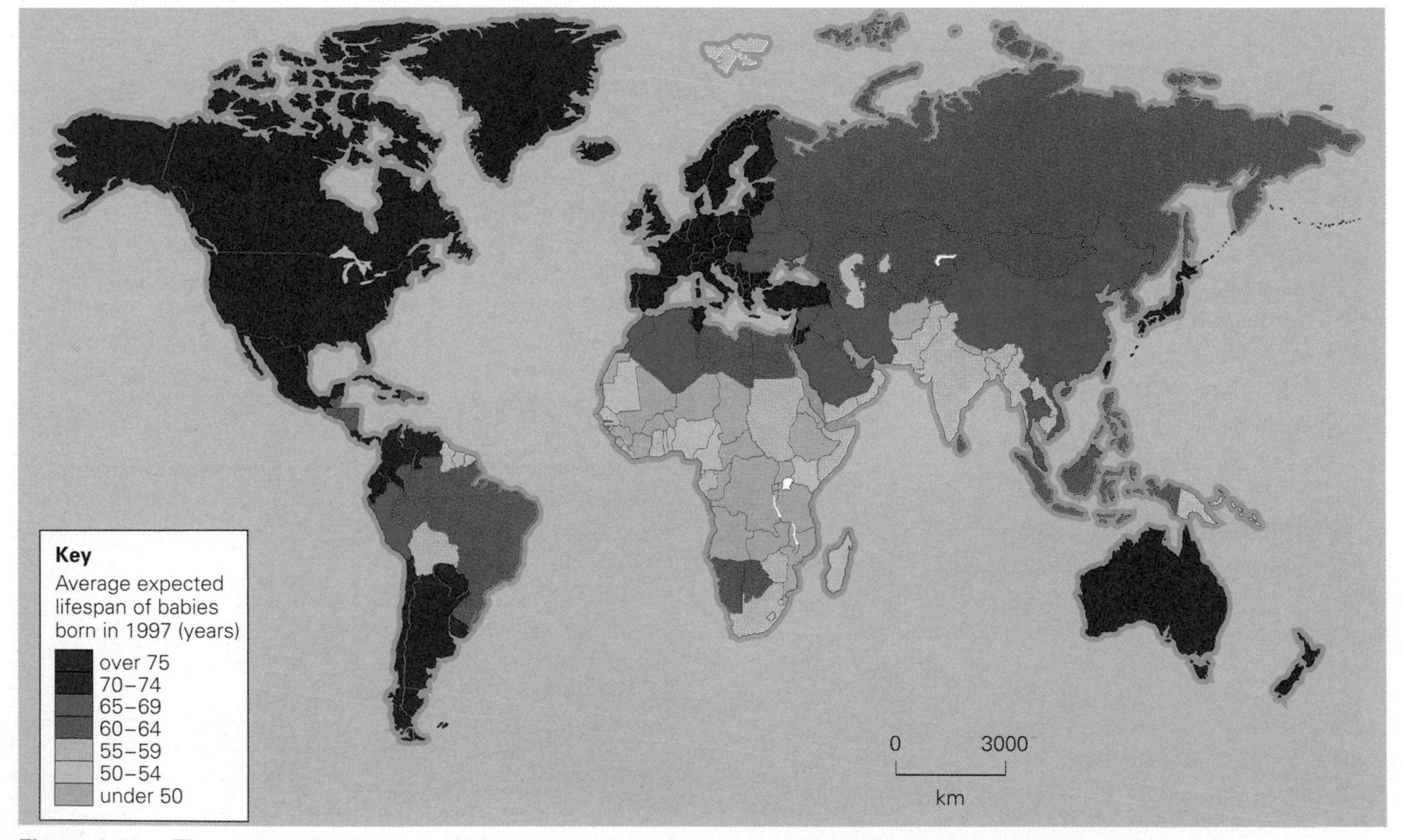

Figure 3.22 *The global distribution of life expectancy, 1997* Source: *Philip's Modern School Atlas, 92nd Edition*, 1998.

	Infant mortality (per 1,000 live births)	Life expectancy (years)		Population per doctor	Food intake (calories per day)
LEDCs		M	F		
Brazil	53	57	66	844	2824
China	38	69	72	1063	2727
Ethiopia	122	45	48	32,499	1610
India	69	60	61	2459	2395
Mexico	24	70	78	615	3146
Saudi Arabia	44	68	71	749	2735
MEDCs					
Australia	5	77	83	500	3179
Bulgaria	15	67	5	306	2831
Japan	4	77	83	608	2903
Singapore	5	75	82	714	nd
UK	6	74	79	300	3317
USA	7	73	79	421	3732

KEY M = Male F = Female

Table 3.5 *Mortality and related measures for a sample of countries*

There are some basic similarities between the distributions of life expectancy and infant mortality (Table 3.5). Figure 3.23 shows that the lowest infant mortality rates are recorded in North America, Western Europe, Australasia and Japan. In these areas, the rate is less than one-tenth of what it is over much of Africa, the Middle East and SE Asia. In short, the overall pattern conforms with the broad distinction between MEDCs and LEDCs.

Over the last three centuries, the trend in global mortality rates has been downward. During that time, however, the trend has been neither steady nor exactly the same the world over. The first marked fall occurred during the later stages of the Industrial Revolution and was confined to the MEDCs of Europe, North America and Australasia. Major contributors to the decline were the advances in medical science, better housing and sanitation, together with improved food and water supplies. A second marked fall occurred during the second half of the twentieth century, but this time it was mainly experienced by LEDCs. Here, a combination of economic development, aid from MEDCs and effective medical campaigns against infectious diseases led to a marked decline in mortality. At the same time, death rates in many MEDCs levelled out. For example, the death rate in the UK has now hovered around the 12 per 1,000 mark for approximately 50 years.

This two-phased 'retreat from death' has had two important impacts:

- the death rate differences between MEDCs and LEDCs are now much less than they were
- life expectancy has increased, slightly more so for women than men.

It could well be, however, that we are now on the brink of a possible global up-turn in death rates. The accelerating spread of Aids in many parts of the world could bring this about. The key thing to remember is that because Aids hits those in the reproductive ages hardest; it not only raises mortality, but it also depresses fertility.

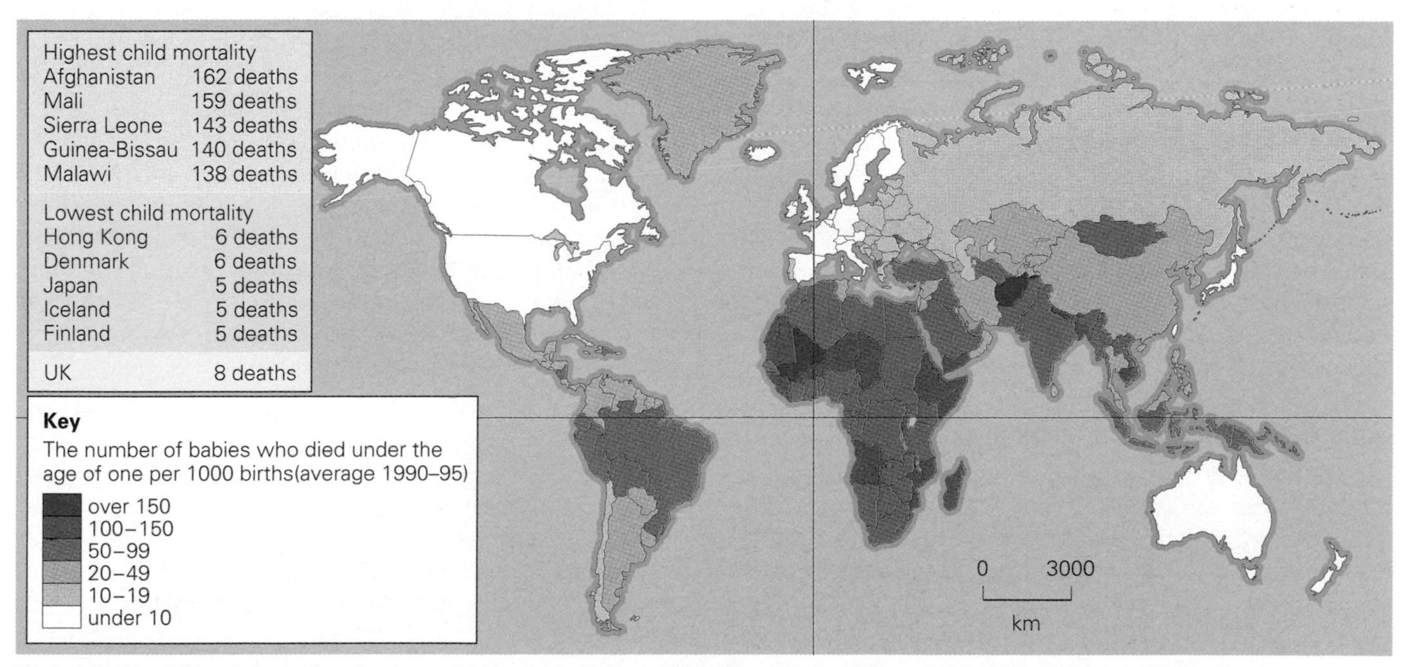

Figure 3.23 *The global distribution of infant mortality, 1990–95* Source: *Philip's Modern School Atlas, 92nd Edition,* 1998.

The spread of Aids

In 1999 more than 33 million people around the world had been infected by Aids. Figures published for countries where the disease is spreading fast paint a bleak picture. China estimates that 400,000 of its population are now HIV positive. India, Russia and Nigeria have a rapidly rising number of HIV carriers, and catastrophic increases in deaths are forecast. India accounts for 60 per cent of all Aids cases in Asia, and admits that 3.5 million people are carrying the virus. In Russia over 23,500 cases were reported in 1999 compared with 2,617 three years before. In Nigeria one person per minute is being infected, and by 2003, an estimated 4.3 million will be carrying the virus.

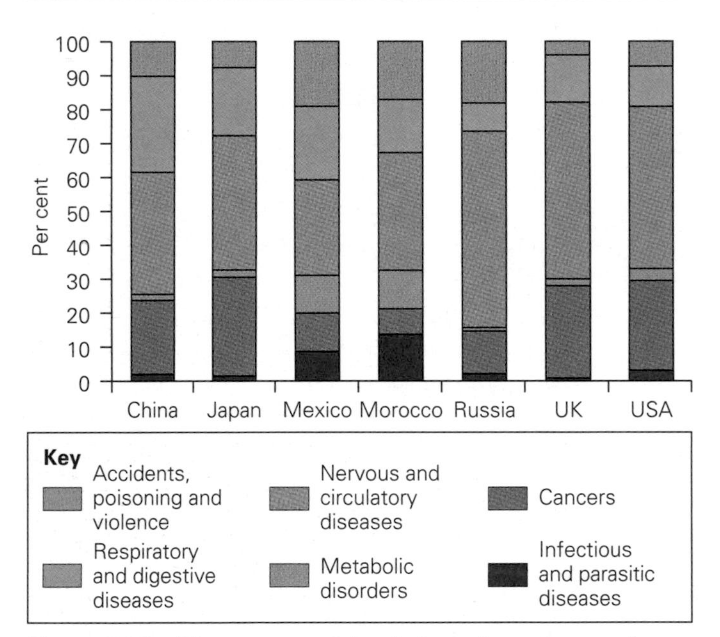

Figure 3.24 *The causes of death for selected countries, 1992–4* Source: *Philip's Modern School Atlas, 92nd Edition*, 1998

No discussion of mortality would be complete without some reference to the causes of death. These vary over time and space and so contribute to variations in mortality rates (Figure 3.24). The causes of death fall broadly into two categories. First, there are **endogenetic causes**. This means that they are either **congenital** (such as deformities and diseases dating from birth) or **degenerative** (associated with ageing and the gradual wearing out of the mind and body). Secondly, there are **exogenetic** causes, that is those which result from environmental conditions. These include infectious, respiratory and digestive diseases which are linked with climate, diet, housing conditions, pollution, and social habits such as smoking, drinking, drugs, promiscuity and urban living (stress). Also included are deaths caused by natural hazards, war, road accidents and so on.

ACTIVITIES

1 Explain:
   - the link between mortality rates and life expectancy
   - how and why housing conditions affect mortality
   - why death rates are not always inversely proportional to food intake (Tables 3.2 and 3.5).
2 Use an appropriate statistical test to measure the degree of relationship between the variables in Table 3.5. Write a short account of your findings.
2 Identify the main features shown in Figure 3.24 and suggest possible reasons for the international differences.

Natural change

Just as fertility and mortality vary from place to place and from time to time, so does the relationship between them and natural change (the difference between births and deaths). Since population change is primarily the outcome of natural change, the fact that Figure 3.18 takes migration into account should not prevent it from giving some pointers about the global pattern of natural change. Despite high rates of mortality, the level of fertility in Africa makes that continent stand out as the present power base of global population growth. The Middle East and SE Asia may also be seen as a major growth axis. In contrast, not only are there very low rates of growth in Europe and North America, but during the 1990s there were a handful of countries, including Belgium, Germany and Hungary, that actually experienced a decline in population. This came about through a combination of declining fertility and stable mortality.

Just 500 Japanese and an empty Europe

By the year 3000, the population of Japan will be 500 and by the year 3500, the population will be 1. These are the mathematical certainties if Japanese women, on average, carry on having just 1.4 children each, and if Japan does not change its immigration policy.

Japan and the UK are just two of 61 countries that are not having enough babies to replace their populations. Fertility rates are below the critical 2.1 replacement level. In the UK, the current average is 1.7 children. One in four women is opting to have no children at all. Spanish women have the lowest fertility rate in the world; 1.15 children. Throughout much of the EU, fertility is now so low that populations are set to decline.

It should also be pointed out that this 'birth dearth' is even spreading to some LEDCs. Women in India now have fewer babies than US women did in the 1950s, while in China, Cuba and Thailand fertility rates have fallen below the replacement level.

After a century of population growth, and warnings about the 'population explosion', most MEDCs are now facing a 'population bust'. The prospect of steadily declining populations is fast becoming a real one.

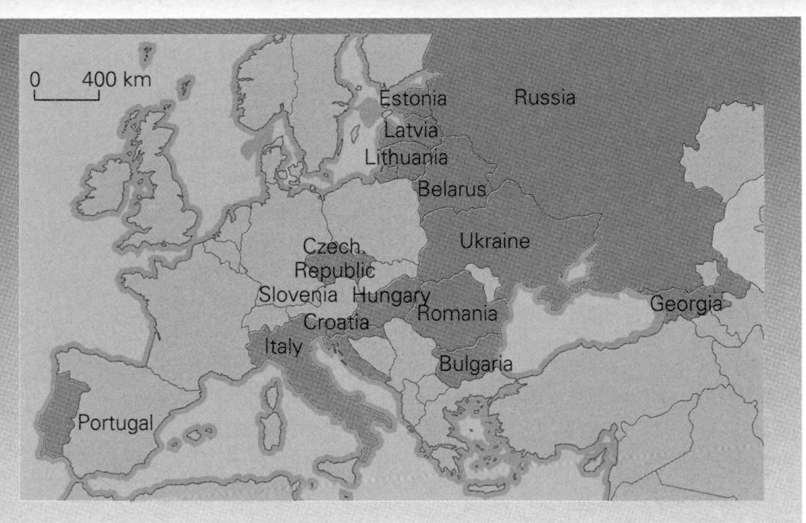

Figure 3.25 *Countries where population has already begun to fall, 1998*
Source: *Independent*, 12/01/98

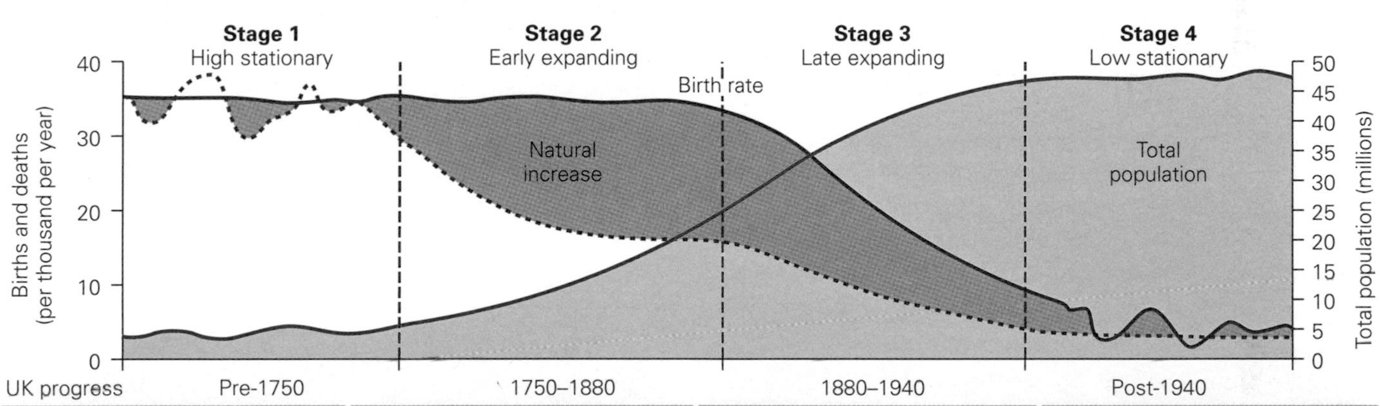

Stage 1	Stage 2	Stage 3	Stage 4
Population change fluctuates between growth and decline.	Population growth accelerates.	The rate of population growth begins to ease.	Population growth flattens out at a low level; intermittent decline.
High birth rates due to: • no birth control • children needed to work on the land • high infant mortality • religious and social beliefs.	High birth rates continue for the same reasons as in Stage 1.	Birth rates fall due to: • birth control • lower infant mortality • desire for smaller families • greater wish for material possessions.	Birth rates remain low due to: • birth control • more career women • awareness of pressures on environment.
High death rates due to: • disease • famine and malnutrition • poor hygiene • no health care.	Death rates fall due to: • better housing • better food and water • modest health care • lower infant mortality.	Death rates continue to fall for the same reasons as in Stage 2.	Death rates stabilise. Advances in medicine cancelled out by a increase of degenerative diseases in an ageing population .
Dependency ratios tip towards the young due to low life expectancy. Large extended families.	'Young' population with high levels of child dependency. The extended family persists.	Dependency ratios begin to tip towards the elderly due to increased life expectancy. Family size declines. Extended families diminish.	'Old' population with high elderly dependency. Family size begins to fall below replacement level. Nuclear families prevail.
Primary sector dominant. Emphasis on self-sufficiency.	Birth of agricultural specialisation and manu-facturing. Trade in primary products and processed goods.	Industrial growth and diversification. Service sector expansion. Trade in both goods and services.	Service sector becomes dominant due to increased affluence. Trade in information and technology.

Figure 3.26 *A global view of progress along the demographic transition, 1995*

ACTIVITY

1 The world is divided into two parts: one where population growth is slowing as fertility falls, and one where population growth is slowing as mortality rises. Explain and provide examples for this statement.

The demographic transition

Observations of changing levels of fertility and mortality over time, their changing balances and their net effect on rates of natural change have led to the generation of a model known as the demographic transition model. These demographic changes may be tentatively linked with the broad development process over a sequence of four stages (Figure 3.26).

Figure 3.27 attempts to give a global picture of progress along the demographic transition. It needs to be stressed, however, that this model is a broad generalisation. The MEDCs which have followed the transition have done so at different rates. It took Japan a quarter of the time that it took the UK. Furthermore, the fact that many of today's MEDCs have experienced this type of transition does not necessarily mean that all LEDCs will. Some may make the transition much more quickly or slowly, while others might show different trend patterns due to differences of culture, economy and technology. For them, the past of others may well not be the key to their future. There is another aspect of the future that is uncertain; are we to assume that once reached, Stage 4 will last forever? Looking at the most recent trends in some MEDCs, a fifth stage seems to be coming over the horizon – a low contracting stage. This will be characterised by low mortality, fertility below the replacement level, and therefore natural population decrease.

EXTENSION ACTIVITY

You have to report to an international body on contrasts in demographic change. In preparing your report you must:

a Analyse the data given for Ethiopia, Mexico, Bulgaria and the UK given in Tables 3.2, 3.4 and 3.5.

b Assess what stage each country has reached in the demographic transition. Give evidence to support your conclusions.

c Say to what extent you agree that Mexico is an LEDC and Bulgaria an MEDC. Justify your viewpoint.

d Identify the key issues (demographic, economic and social) facing each country. You might find out more about these countries from the Internet (try www.cia.gov/cia/publications/factbook/ etc.). Focus on environment, food, employment, health and welfare issues.

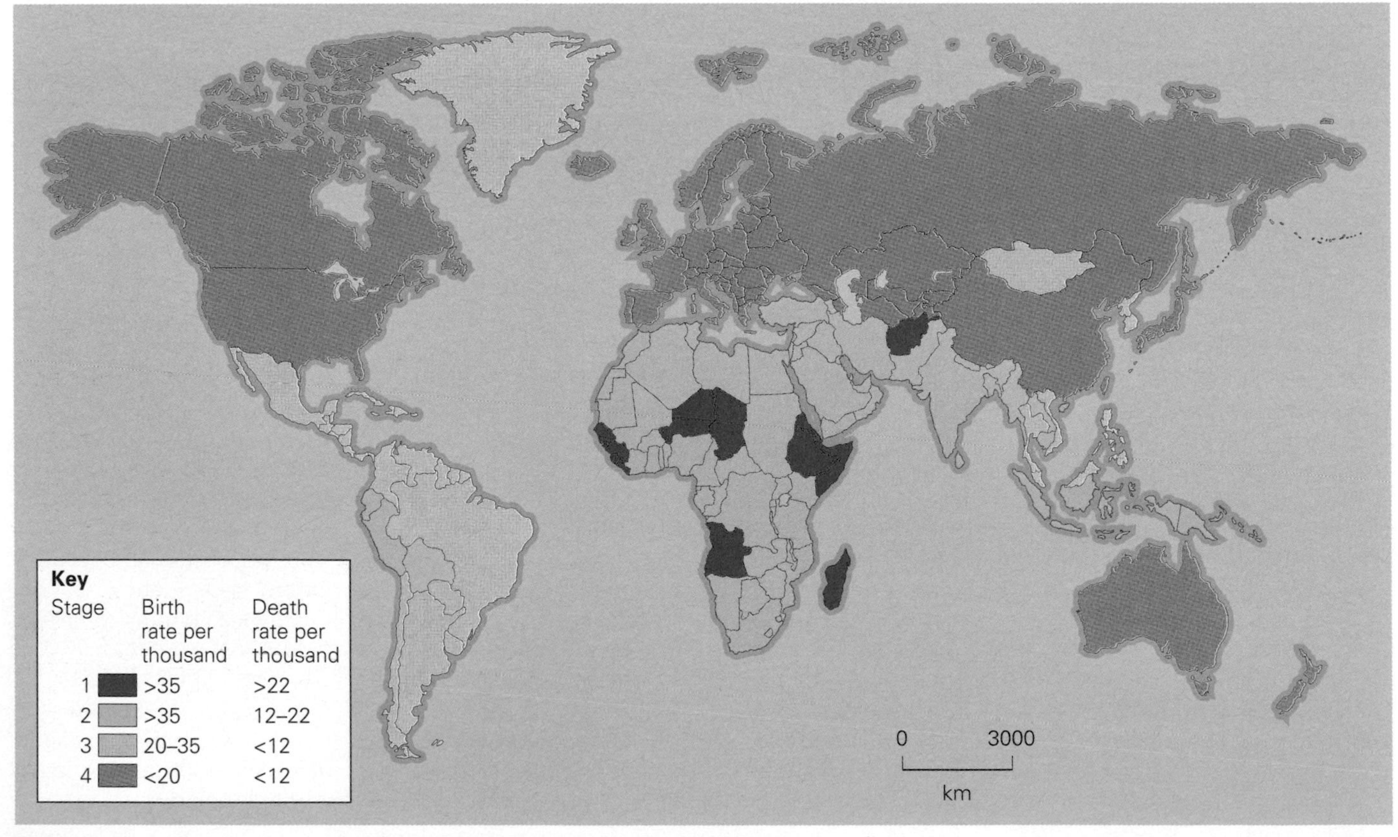

Figure 3.27 *Stages of the demographic transition model (DTM)*

4 Global challenges of population change

World population growth – past, present and future

On 13 October 1999, the Secretary-General of the United Nations welcomed the birth of the world's six billionth inhabitant. The spotlight fell on the new-born son of a Bosnian Muslim woman at Kosovo Hospital. Figure 3.28 shows global population rising exponentially to this demographic milestone.

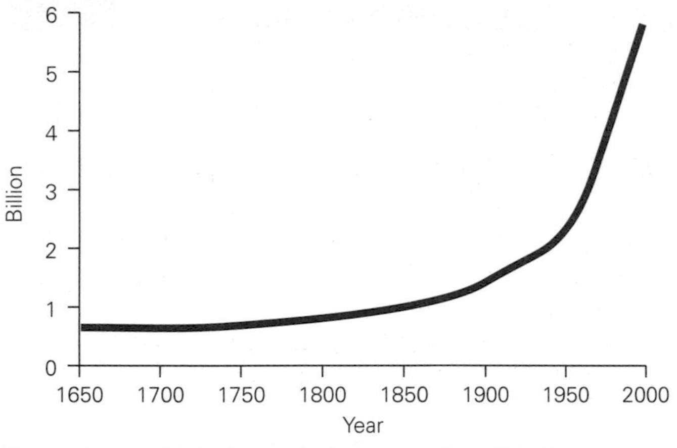

Figure 3.28 *Global population growth, 1650–2000*

Given that the first national census was not taken until 200 years ago, it follows that any assessment of the scale and rate of population growth before that time must be largely guesswork. It has been estimated that the global population in 1500 was around 500 million. Since 1650 population growth has increased at an exponential rate (Figure 3.28). It doubled between 1650 and 1850; it doubled again between 1850 and 1950; and it doubled yet again between 1950 and 2000. The second population explosion was largely ignited by the Agricultural and Industrial Revolutions.

	% of total population							
	1650	1700	1750	1800	1850	1900	1950	2000
Africa	20	16	14	10	9	8	8	13
Asia	57	63	64	66	62	56	55	60
Europe	20	18	20	21	24	27	23	12
Latin America	2	2	1	1	3	4	6	9
North America	<1	<1	<1	1	2	5	7	5
Oceania	<1	<1	<1	<1	<1	<1	<1	1

Table 3.6 *Shifts in global population, 1650–2000*

ACTIVITIES

1. Explain what is meant by the term 'exponential growth'. Identify what you consider to be the key factors behind the exponential growth of global population.
2. Explain the significance of the Agricultural and Industrial Revolutions to population growth.
3. Study Table 3.6.
   - Plot the data by means of an appropriate technique.
   - Highlight the main changes that have taken place, and suggest possible reasons.
   - Relate your findings to Figure 3.18.

It is now possible that the era of exponential population growth is coming to an end. In 1995, demographers were forecasting that global population would continue to rise and reach a peak of nearly 11 billion by the year 2150 (Table 3.7). This forecast assumed that the fertility rate would fall to replacement level by 2050. This is happening much faster and it is even being suggested that global population might peak 100 years sooner, at just under 8 billion. By 2150, it could be that global population is close to today's figure. The good news is that global population growth is slowing for the first time.

Forecast	Assumed fertility rate in 2050–2055	2150 population (billions)
Low	1.6	3.6
Medium–low	1.9	6.4
Middle	2.1	10.8
Medium–high	2.3	18.3
High	2.6	27.0

Table 3.7 *United Nations 1996 population projections to 2150*

The main reason for the downward revision of population forecasts has been the dramatic fall in fertility rates, particularly in LEDCs. Across Africa and Asia millions of people are confounding predictions by reducing family sizes. It used to be said that, without the strong imposition of birth control, childbearing only declines when economic conditions improve (Figure 3.26). During the 1990s, however, a number of LEDCs disproved this.

Bangladesh, which once had a breeding population out of control, cut its fertility rate in the 1990s from 6.2 children per woman to 3.4 within a decade. Despite extreme poverty and illiteracy, the fall in fertility was largely due to contraception. Fertility rates in many African countries, though still high, are also falling fast as the practice of birth control is implemented. The fall is thought to be 'crisis-led' and assumes that people choose to have smaller families when faced by increasing hardship, particularly food shortages.

The important point is that today more and more people in LEDCs have the means to put that choice into effect. In North America and the Caribbean, Europe and SE Asia, fertility rates are now below the critical 2.1 replacement level. Recent estimates indicate that 18 countries, including Russia and Japan, will lose more than 15 per cent of their population by 2050.

Figure 3.29 *Women in Bangladesh being told about family planning*

The Cairo Conference

This huge conference on 'Population and Development' took place in September 1994. It was held against a backdrop of fear about what was seen as the never-ending advance in global numbers. It involved 180 governments and hundreds of non-governmental organisations. Its end-product was a 20-year Programme of Action, much of it aimed at women. Specific goals included:

- increasing investment in women's reproductive health, particularly in good family planning services, in better care during pregnancy and childbirth and in fighting sexually-transmitted diseases
- reducing the number of unsafe abortions
- eliminating female genital mutilation, a common practice in Africa
- enforcing laws on the minimum age of marriage
- improving sex education for teenagers, particularly for girls
- increasing the opportunities for women to earn and contribute to the economy.

The thinking underlying the Programme was that, with women more in command of their own destinies, the choice of the majority would be to have fewer children. This would come about through:

- a proper recognition of their rights
- better access to reliable contraception and safe abortion
- a reduced need to have children to replace those lost through still-births and infant mortality
- opportunities to earn money outside the home and so help with family budgets.

Clearly, much of this Programme cuts across culturally sensitive areas. For example, the Vatican opposes contraception and abortion. Many Muslims fear an erosion of their values, particularly so far as women are concerned.

Is it stretching things too much to claim that the 'birth dearth' is a sign that the Programme is already producing results? Certainly, it has done much to raise awareness of the need to cut fertility and respect the wishes of women.

Figure 3.30 *Meeting of minds?*
Source: *Habitat,* 30 October 1994.

While the birth dearth is the major contributor to the population slow-down, there is another. In sub-Saharan Africa, death rates are rising due to the alarming spread of HIV and Aids. In some countries, at least a quarter of the population is infected. For South Africa, the figure may be as high as 40 per cent. Life expectancy in Botswana, for example, has already fallen from 62 to 40 years, and in Zimbabwe from 61 to 39 years.

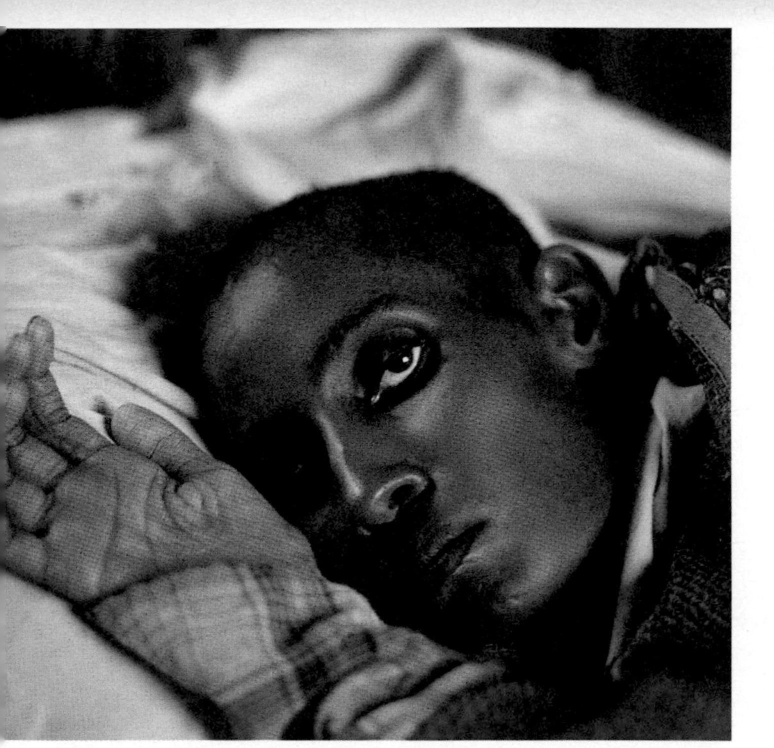

Figure 3.31 *A young Aids victim waits to die*

What will be the outcomes of this birth dearth and the Aids pandemic (affecting people on a global scale)? In those countries relatively unaffected by Aids, there will be a marked 'wrinkling' of the population. Elderly people may even outnumber children. In Europe, about one in five of the population is over 60. By the end of the next century, it could be as high as one in two. This will create huge challenges in such areas as health care and leisure. The economic impact will be enormous, unless managed properly. Rampant ageing is expected to sap a nation's vital energy. Businesses will be starved of innovative ideas and the dynamism of a young workforce. A 'grey, conformist society' is anticipated and certainly population numbers will decline.

For those countries badly afflicted by Aids, there will be a spectacular collapse of population as affected parents and their HIV-positive children are wiped out. There will be at least two generations of greatly reduced reproduction. Much will depend on how quickly science can discover and supply affordable vaccines.

ACTIVITIES

1. With others in your class, discuss one of the following propositions:
   - population forecasting is an inexact science
   - the decline of the human empire is close at hand.

   Write a brief essay based on the discussion of your chosen assertion.
2. Refer to the Cairo Conference section and for each of the second set of bullet points, explain the link to reduced fertility.
3. Explain the message conveyed in Figure 3.30.
4. Research the arguments of the Roman Catholic Church and other 'pro-life' groups in their stance against birth control and abortion.
5. For an LEDC, find out what progress has been made in implementing the Cairo Conference Programme of Action.

Population and resources

Shifting the focus back to the present, remember that today's world is still in a population growth mode. Accumulation of this growth, particularly over the last 50 years, has thrown up the issue of the relationship between population and resources. The key question is whether or not the world is capable of supporting its present population in a sustainable and satisfactory way. Trying to answer this question requires examining the concept of **optimum population**, and a sound grasp of the nature of the **development** process and **resources**.

Key terms

Resource Something that can be used to satisfy a human need or want. A resource is something of value to people. Resources can be **natural resources**, derived from the environment (e.g. minerals, energy, climate, soils), but it is possible to recognise **human resources** (the mental and physical abilities of people) as well as capital **resources** (aids to production and living, i.e. machines, money, houses – all created by people).

An important distinction is drawn with respect to natural resources. **Non-renewable resources** have been built up over geological time and cannot be used without depleting the stock (coal, oil and gas). **Renewable resources** have a natural rate of availability and flow continuously (water power, solar energy). In most cases, they can be consumed without endangering future supply.

Development The use of resources and available technology to bring about an increase in the living standards and quality of life of a population. Earlier views stressed economic growth, increased output and technological change as the essence of development. Today, a rather broader view prevails which also includes social and cultural advancement.

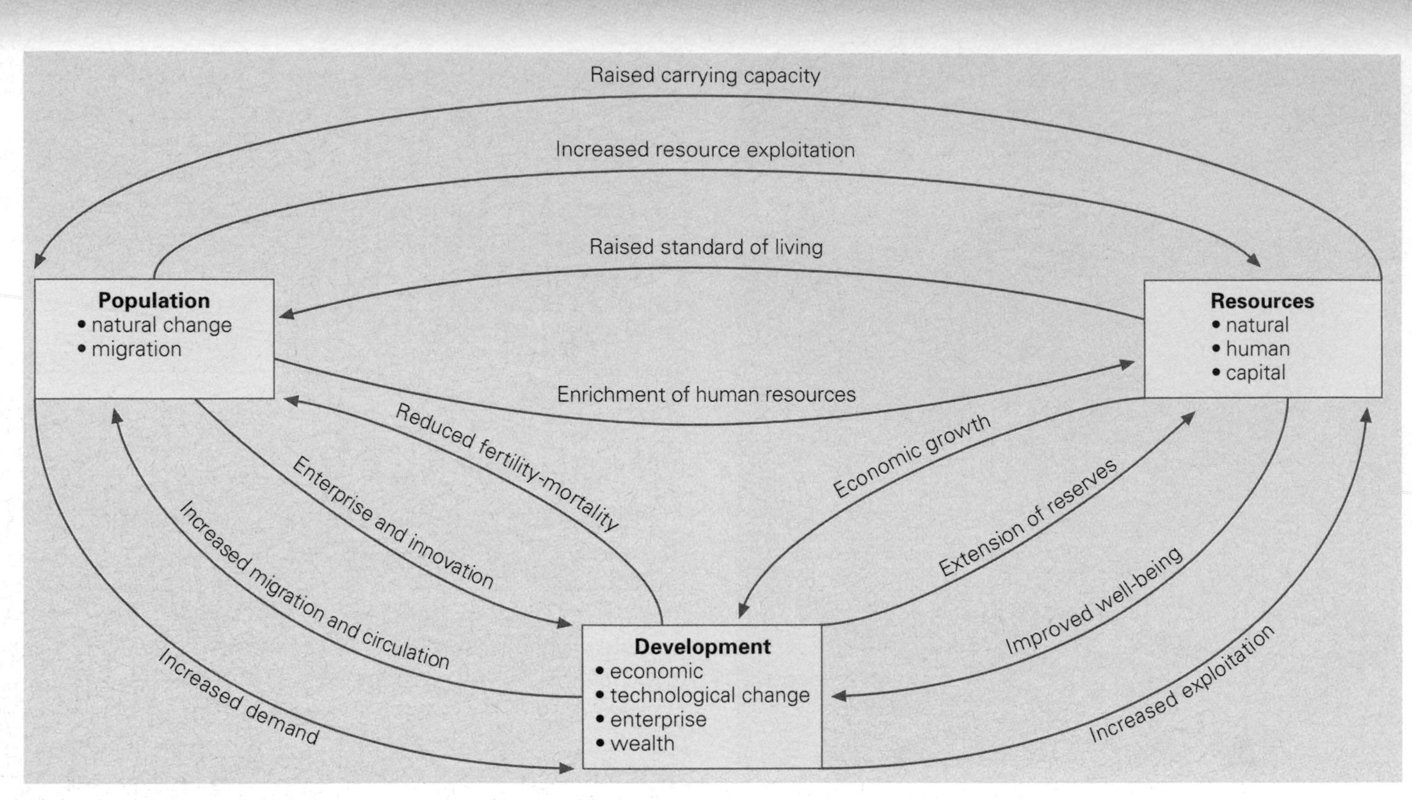

Figure 3.32 *The relationships between population, resources and development*
Source: *Witherick, Population Geography,* Longman, 1990.

In analysing the relationship between population, resources and development, it is easiest if we imagine a balance existing between the first two, with the precise nature of that balance strongly conditioned by the state of development (Figure 3.32). The link between people and resources is mainly through the medium of food supply. In primitive societies, resource exploitation is largely to do with subsistence and survival. In advanced societies, there are more options. Resource exploitation might be to do with high levels of food production; equally, it might involve providing raw materials for manufacturing, producing goods or providing services; or there might be a mix of these options. Clearly, development leads to higher levels of resource exploitation which, in turn, raise the **carrying capacity** and therefore the number of people who can be supported.

There is a strict balance between the number of people in an area and the amount of food that can be provided by whatever means. In reality, there is frequently a mismatch. **Overpopulation** is said to occur when the number of people exceeds the supporting capacities of the resources (Figure 3.33a). The consequences of overpopulation are often painful: the symptoms include a lower standard of living, malnutrition and starvation, disease and poverty. Overpopulation tends to be most felt by the weakest and poorest members of society. It usually brings environmental as well as human costs.

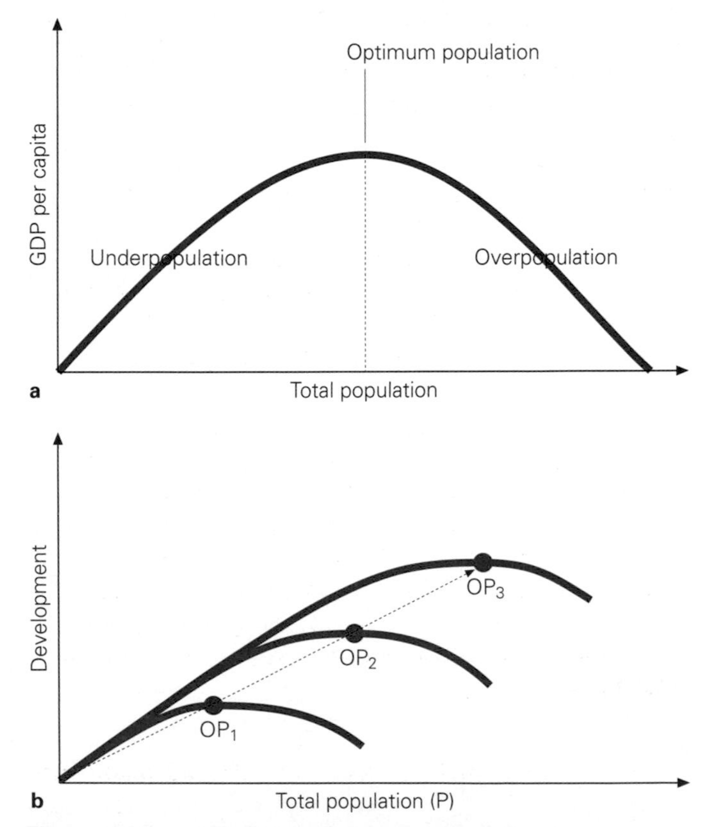

Figure 3.33 *a) Defining optimum population; b) The impact of development on optimum population*
Source: Witherick, *Population Geography,* Longman, 1990.

Is Australia becoming overpopulated?

Australia, known as the 'empty continent', accounts for 5 per cent of the world's land area, 0.3 per cent of its population and 1 per cent of its economy. Can a land of over 7 million km² and 18 million people living at a mean density of less than 3 people per km² really be in danger of becoming overpopulated?

Figure 3.34 *It is difficult to believe that Australia is overpopulated*

The root of the matter is that Australia is largely desert and agriculture lies at the heart of its economy. There are only 700,000 km² of arable land, and most on this is marginal because of thin soil and lack of water. In its reliance on agriculture, Australia may be likened to an LEDC. Without exports of food, wool and some minerals, it would not be able to import the many foreign goods it needs to sustain its affluent lifestyle.

At present, the Australian population is growing by over a quarter of a million people per year; nearly half of this is due to immigration. This makes for an annual growth rate of 1.1 per cent, way above that for most MEDCs. If recent immigration and birth rates persist, Australia's projected total by 2050 will be 30 million. In order to cope with this increased population, Australian farmers will have to increase agricultural output from marginal land. Australia needs to stop the threat of overpopulation as it is fast approaching its carrying capacity.

Much less common in today's world is **underpopulation** (Figure 3.33a). This exists where resources and development could support a larger population without any lowering of living standards. It also occurs where a population is too small to develop its resources effectively.

Is Amazonia underpopulated?

With a population density of less than 1 person per km², plus a wealth of resources ranging from timber to minerals, there is no doubt that this vast region could support a much larger population. Furthermore, a better standard of living than at present would be virtually guaranteed. So yes, in this sense, the Amazon lowlands are underpopulated.

Figure 3.35 *A Yanomani family – a scarce resource in Amazonia*

However, any scaling up of settlement and development would have considerable impact on the rainforest that still covers much of the area. More forest would be felled for a variety of reasons; for timber, for improving access to mineral resources and new settlements and for creating farmland. That loss could have serious consequences for global weather and climate, as well as for biodiversity. The vastness of the region means that any programme of colonisation and settlement requires a huge 'up-front' investment in physical and social infrastructure, much more than has already been provided by the Brazilian Government and transnational companies. It is unlikely that such investment would ever be justified by the increase in population and economic output, no matter how large that might eventually be.

Between the extremes of overpopulation and underpopulation, there exists a third condition. This is referred to this as **optimum population**. It is defined as: the size of population which, for a given area, allows the sustainable utilisation of resources, and achieves the greatest per capita output, and the highest standards of living. It is a critical point on the population growth curve (Figure 33.3a). That point will depend on a range of factors, such as the size of the area, its resource base and the state of development. Equally, the optimum population of an area will vary over time, particularly with development (Figure 3.33b).

ACTIVITIES

1. Population growth racing ahead of economic development is the most common cause of overpopulation (in China, Indonesia and Puerto Rico). Can you think of at least two other overpopulation scenarios? Cite an actual example of each scenario.
2. Give examples of two different scenarios of underpopulation. In what ways are the symptoms different from those of overpopulation?
3. What measures might you use to decide whether or not a country or region has an optimum population?
4. Discuss with your fellow students the question posed by each of the case studies on page 115. What are your answers and why? Share your findings with the class.
5. Define **sustainability** as used in the contexts of population growth and development.

The relationship between population growth and resources (particularly food supply) has been of interest and concern for centuries. Three different views have emerged:

Three different views of global population growth

Malthus (1798) based his theory on two principles:

- in the absence of any checks, human population has the potential to grow at a geometric rate (2, 4, 8, 16 and so on). In other words, a population can double every 25 years
- even in the most favourable circumstances, agricultural production can only be expected to increase at an arithmetic rate (1, 2, 3, 4 and so on) (Figure 3.36a).

Thus, population growth may be expected to outstrip food supply. Furthermore, the ability of every country to

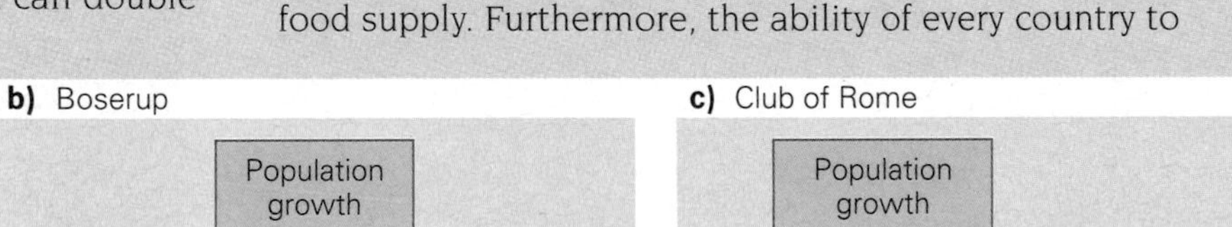

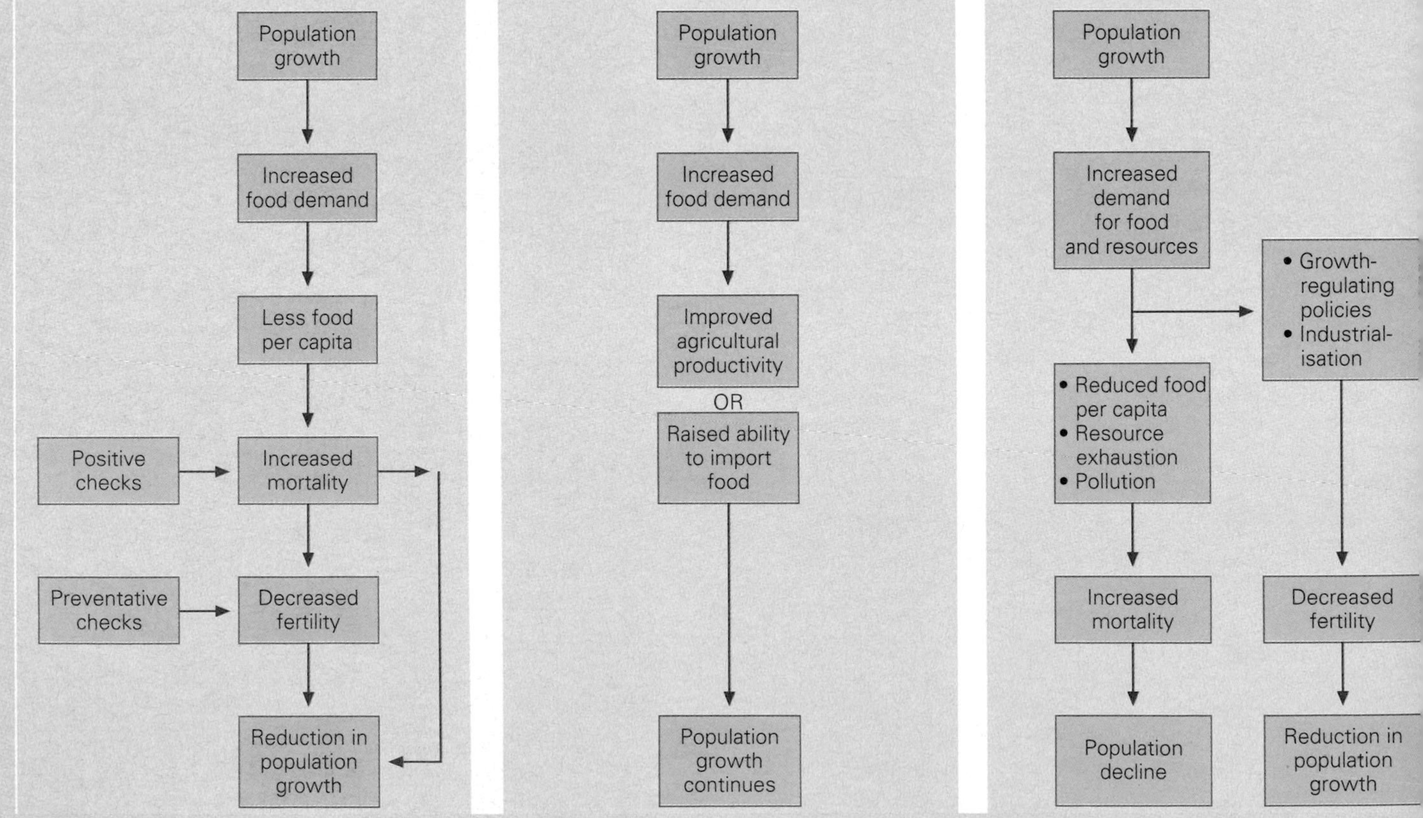

The whole relationship between people and resources in today's world appears to be producing two distinct geographies – one of hunger and the other of plenty. The terms 'hunger' and 'plenty' are used in a much broader sense than just food supply. They are intended to convey the basic idea that spatial contrasts exist between areas of shortage and deprivation and those of surplus and wealth. The boundary between the two geographies is much more complicated than the dividing line between LEDCs and MEDCs. There are pockets of plenty in poorer countries, just as there are regions of hunger in more affluent nations.

ACTIVITIES

1. Think of some of the things that have stopped the predictions of Malthus coming true. Try brainstorming in a small group.
2. Justify the claim that Boserup's view is more optimistic than that of Malthus.
3. What signs are there, if any, that progress is being made in introducing the growth-regulating policies advocated by the Club of Rome?
4. Do you think that there are areas of 'hunger' in the UK? If you think there are, suggest some examples. If you think there are not, justify your viewpoint.
5. Can you think of some examples of pockets of plenty to be found in LEDCs?

produce food has a finite limit, and this sets a 'ceiling' on population growth. As a population begins to reach this ceiling, two different types of check come into play that stop population growth. **Preventive checks** include abstinence from, or delay in the timing of, marriage. This helps to lower fertility rates. **Positive checks** include famine, disease, war and infanticide, all of which help to raise death rates.

Boserup (1965) based her theory on the argument that in an agricultural society, an increase in population stimulates an improvement in agricultural techniques, so that more food can be produced (Figure 3.36b). In more advanced societies, the production of goods and the provision of services allows food to be purchased from external sources.

The Club of Rome (1972) produced a report entitled 'Limits to Growth'. They stated that if current trends in the growth of global population, industrialisation, pollution, food production and resource depletion continued unchanged, the limits to growth on Earth would be reached sometime in the next 100 years. However, they argued that it is still possible to alter these growth trends and to establish an equilibrium that is sustainable far into the future (Figure 3.36c). In this way, people have a choice. If they prefer the second scenario, the sooner they begin working to attain it, the greater will be the chances of success.

Figure 3.36 *The views of a) Malthus, b) Boserup, c) The Club of Rome*

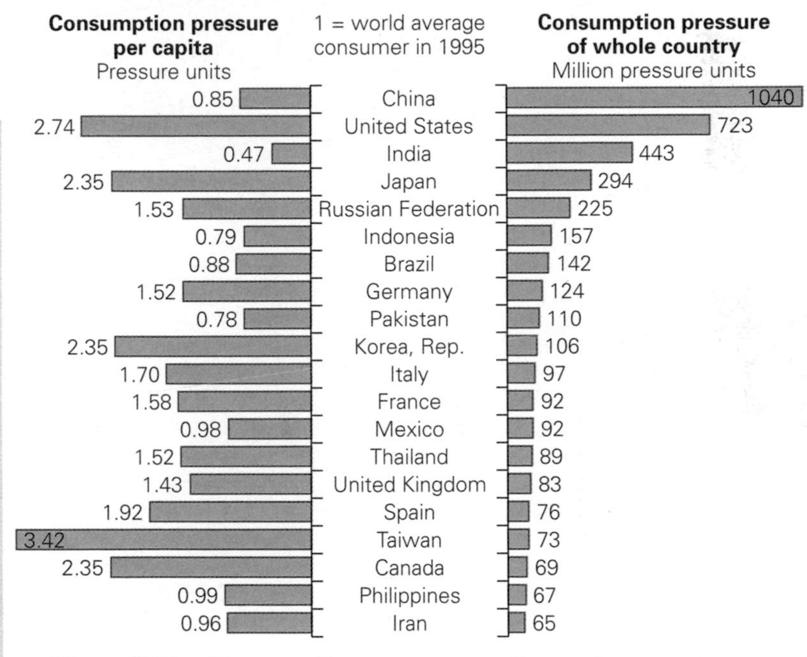

Figure 3.37 *Consumption pressure on the environment, 1995* Source: *WWF Living Planet Report*, 1998.

Figure 3.37 looks at the population resources equation in terms of the burden placed on the environment by people as they consume the resources of land and water ecosystems. The right-hand side of the diagram shows that consumption pressure at a national level is directly related to population size. The left-hand side suggests that the same countries are ranked rather differently when consumption pressure is measured in per capita terms.

ACTIVITIES

1. Redraw the left-hand side of Figure 3.37 ranking the countries according to consumption pressure per capita.
2. Compare the two rankings and identify any significant differences.

5 National challenges of population change

Coping with population growth and loss

The message conveyed by Figure 3.18 is that high rates of population growth prevailed over much of Africa, the Middle East and southern Asia, where population grew by over 40 per cent during the 1990s. The issues raised by such an unsustainable population explosion are many and immense. Figure 3.38 attempts to identify some of the more important repercussions.

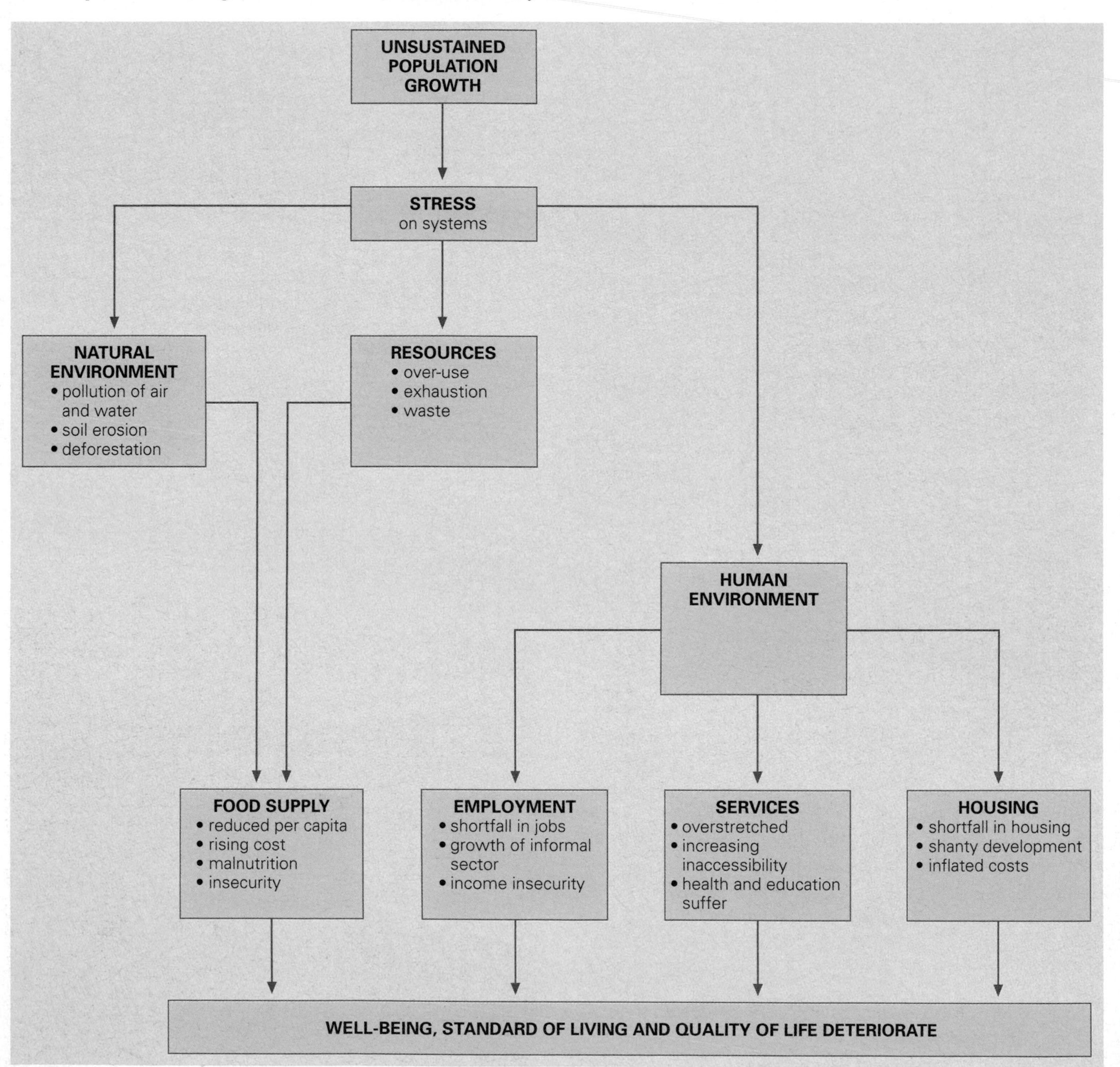

Figure 3.38 *Cascading consequences of unsustained population growth*

Hiatus in Haiti

The population of Haiti, currently 7.5 million people, has been growing at an average rate of 1.7 per cent per year since 1970. The huge growth in the demand for food has led to the clearance of most of the nation's forests. Since two-thirds of the land area slopes by more than 20°, soil erosion is both widespread and severe. As a result of this environmental damage, food production is low and around 1.5 million people have left their rural homelands. Some have emigrated to other Caribbean islands, some to North America and others have moved into city slums.

Cité Soleil is said to be one of the most densely populated slums in the western hemisphere. Covering 5 km² on the northern edge of Haiti's capital city, Port-au-Prince, it is now home to 300,000 Haitians, most of them recently arrived from the countryside. Living conditions here, as in other squatter settlements, are appalling. People live in small homes made of cardboard packing cases, boards and abandoned metal sheeting. Inside the homes, beds are typically raised above the ground, since rainwater mixed with sewage gushes thigh-high into homes during the rainy season.

Unemployment is high, reaching 70 per cent, but local residents try to earn a living by becoming part of a highly active informal sector. Charcoal vendors and women selling imported plastic goods or big pots of goat stew crowd the tiny passageways of the slum. Profits of US$1 a day are considered satisfactory in a country where 60 per cent of the population earn less than US$100 a year.

Within the slum, polluted water, contaminated rubbish and faecal matter cause epidemics of malaria, typhoid and chronic diarrhoea. Together with malnutrition, these diseases result in only one-third of all children born here ever reaching the age of five.

Despite these appalling conditions, some people survive, and hope that things might get better. Their hopes are set no higher than, for example, that one child might be sent to school or that another might find a temporary income, thus ensuring the family's survival for another week. Deprived of their land, rural migrants want jobs, food for their families and a future for their children. But who cares? Is anything being done to meet these basic needs? Is this human suffering the price to be paid for unsustainable population growth?

ACTIVITIES

1. Suggest possible revisions that might be made to Figure 3.38. Does the case of Haiti fit the diagram?
2. You are required to advise the government of Haiti on improving conditions in rural areas, improving agriculture, providing urban housing, and giving cities a proper infrastructure. Write a brief report to the government, making sure you justify the points you make.

Figure 3.39 *Cité Soleil, Port-au-Prince, Haiti*

Gender

It is politically correct these days to distinguish between sex and gender. Sex is a biological fact; you are born either male or female. Gender is something shaped by society and culture. It relates to the roles that males and females play in society. In many parts of the world, the gender role for a woman is still to have children, run the home and be dependent on a 'bread-winning' male. This traditional allocation of roles is being increasingly challenged.

Two examples illustrate the difference between sex and gender. The fact that the relative numbers of males and females in a population (the **sex ratio**) changes with age is a biological fact (Figure 3.46). It is explained by the fact that women have a greater life expectancy. The fact that more women today work outside the home is a change to do with gender roles and shifts in society (Figure 3.47).

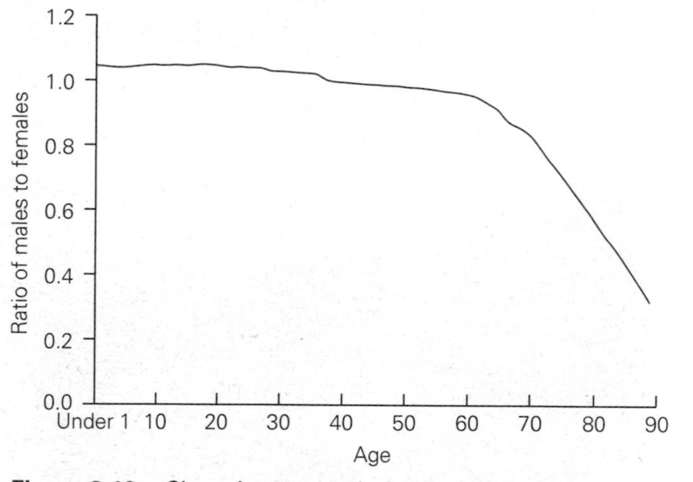

Figure 3.46 *Changing sex ratio in the UK, by age*
Source: *Office of National Statistics, Social Trends*, 1998.

	Female (millions)			Male (millions)		
Year	Full-time	Part-time	All economically active	Full-time	Part-time	All economically active
1984	5.5	4.4	9.9	13.4	0.6	14.1
1997	6.6	5.4	12.0	13.4	1.3	14.7

Table 3.9 *The economically- active population of the UK, 1984–97* Source: *Office of National Statistics, Social Trends*, 1998.

Much of the scope of the Cairo Conference, 1994 (page 112), focused on gender, particularly the status and rights of women in LEDCs. The case studies below illustrate two traditional attitudes towards women that need to change. They involve practices rooted in culture and religion that have demographic consequences.

Sold into slavery

Mercy Senahe was 9 years old when her parents gave her as a 'wife' to the priest of the local shrine in the Volta district of Ghana. This was to 'appease the gods' after one of her family had been accused of stealing. Her typical day at the shrine was to get up at 5 am, fetch water and work on the farm until 3 pm. From then, she was free to cut firewood which she could sell in order to buy food. She was given no money, food or clothes by the shrine. Often such girls were forced to stay at the shrines for the rest of their lives. In Mercy's case, she was finally released when she was 21 in exchange for two sheep, two goats, six bottles of liquor and some cash.

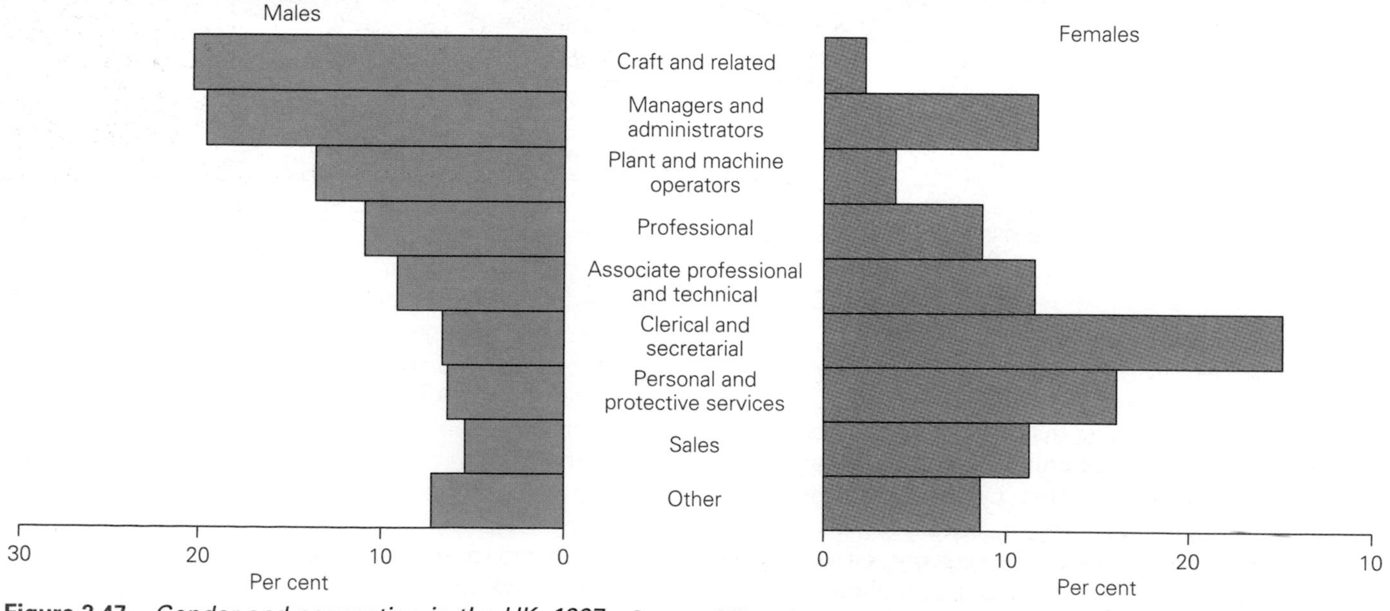

Figure 3.47 *Gender and occupation in the UK, 1997* Source: *Office of National Statistics, Social Trends*, 1998.

Missing girls

Up to 100 million girls are 'missing' from the global population, victims of sex-selected abortion and neglect.

The killing of girl babies, a practice that was once quite widespread, has not completely disappeared. The gender ratio in China has been rising steeply in recent years, from the normal 105 males per 100 females, to 120 males per 100 females. In India and South Korea the selective abortion of female foetuses has also raised the gender ratios. Unhappily, modern advances in prenatal diagnosis are being abused to satisfy the traditional preference for sons.

That preference is also pursued in another way. Analysis of infant mortality rates in these and other countries also show a sinister bias towards males. Given the fact that females are the biologically stronger sex, we should expect mortality to be consistently lower for females. When the situation is found to be otherwise, there are suspicions that girls are not enjoying the same level of health care as boys. Indeed, they may even be fed less well. Clearly, actions of this kind can have significant demographic effects.

Unequal opportunities

Women make up two-thirds of the one billion illiterate adults in the world. They fare much worse than men in terms of secondary and higher education. Female enrolment at secondary level is only 14 per cent in Africa and 26 per cent in Asia. The prospect of universal schooling remains a distant prospect for most LEDCs outside East Asia, Latin America and the Caribbean, unless the education of girls is given a much higher priority.

The problem is partly rooted in costs and partly in traditional attitudes towards females. Even where primary schooling is said to be free, there are the 'hidden' costs of having to buy exercise books, pens and school uniforms. When poor parents are forced to select which of their children should go to school, in most societies the boys will be preferred. Indeed, parents often do not see that a primary school has much of value to offer their female children. This is particularly the case if the expected role for girls is that they help run the home and grow food.

Figure 3.48 *Only four girls in a class of thirty*

ACTIVITIES

1. Describe and explain the trend shown in Table 3.8.
2. Write a short analytical account based on the information contained in Figures 3.46, 3.47 and Table 3.9.
3. Try to explain why in many societies the tradition is:
   - to prefer boys to girls
   - to treat women as second-class citizens.
4. Think of some of the benefits of ensuring that girls receive an education similar to that of boys.

Marriage, families and households

These three aspects of population are closely related, as will be seen from the following case studies. Their interaction has a direct impact on population structure, as well as on practical matters such as housing and services.

Untying the knot in Britain

Changes in society over time have had a marked effect on attitudes and expectations regarding marriage. Up to the late eighteenth and early nineteenth centuries, parents encouraged their sons and daughters to marry a partner of equal or higher social status. The idea was that such a person would provide economic support and stability. Divorce was difficult to obtain and was granted only in extreme cases of violence and adultery. In modern times, however, most people are more independent and have the freedom to select a partner. For a growing number of people, cohabitation is preferred to the formality of a marriage (Figure 3.49).

Many would argue that relationship satisfaction is now the overriding criterion within marriage. It is failure on this count that is at the root of divorce. It is now easier for women to gain financial and social independence, and there is less of a stigma attached to divorce. So if two people are no longer in love, there is little to hold them together, save possibly their children.

Figure 3.49 *The church wedding – a quaint old custom?*

The Fourth World of the one-parent family

The breakdown of the family is a world-wide phenomenon. The most visible symptom of this is that one-quarter of all households are now managed by women without the support of a male partner. This global total conceals wide disparities. In Europe, Asia and North Africa, the figure is approximately one-fifth, whereas in Latin America, the Caribbean and sub-Saharan Africa it is nearer one third. The figure is rising all over the world. For example, in the USA during the 1980s, one-parent families almost doubled from 12 to 23 per cent of all families with dependent children. In Ghana, one-parent families increased from 26 to 32 per cent between 1960 and 1985, and in Brazil from 13 to 20 per cent over the same time period.

One-parent families now account for just over 20 per cent of all families with dependent children in the UK. This is three times the proportion in 1971. Most such families are headed by a lone mother. Of these, 38 per cent are single women, 24 per cent separated, 33 per cent divorced and six per cent widowed. The rise of such families is the outcome of several important shifts in British society:

- a rise in the incidence of divorce
- more cohabitation but on a short-term basis
- the greater independence of women.

One-parent families create a particular set of needs. These include:

- income support
- low-cost housing
- child-minding facilities
- employment with flexible working hours
- pre-school and nursery education.

In themselves, one-parent families are not necessarily a bad thing. But what is very evident is that households headed by women are amongst the poorest: they form a growing underclass (termed the **Fourth World**) and cry out for, but do not necessarily get, state support.

Figure 3.50 *A single mother with her children in Saigon, Vietnam*

Single-person households

Today over a quarter of UK households comprise only one person and this proportion is expected to rise to 40 per cent by 2010 (Table 3.10). This is the product of a number of factors:

- people are marrying later
- more women are pursuing full-time careers
- more people are working from home
- the divorce rate is rising
- widowed people are preferring to live alone for as long as possible.

There are important repercussions from the increase in single-person households, particularly so far as housing is concerned. It is not just that more smaller households mean more dwellings, but an increasing number of these single-person households, particularly the younger ones, are not content as they once were to live in bed-sits, flats or maisonettes. They are moving into three- and four-bedroomed houses. A significant number of these single persons are career-oriented; they earn high salaries and are regarded as very 'mortgage-worthy' by banks and building societies. They are adding to a demand for housing that in many parts of Britain outstrips supply. By so doing, they are helping to inflate house prices and may also be seen as contributing to urban sprawl and the loss of countryside. The irony is that while the UK's population scarcely increases, the number of households does so quite markedly.

Household size	1961 (%)	1996 (%)
One person	14	27
Two persons	30	34
Three persons	23	16
Four persons	18	15
Five persons	9	5
Six or more persons	7	2
Number of households (millions)	16.3	23.5
Average size (persons)	3.1	2.4

Table 3.10 *Changing household dimensions, 1961–1996*
Source: *Office of National Statistics, Social Trends*, 1998.

ACTIVITIES

1 Summarise the recent changes that have taken place in UK society with respect to:
  - marriage
  - the family
  - households.

2 Show how these three sets of changes might be linked.
3 Identify the impact that each set of changes is having on the demand for housing and services.
4 Outline the reasons for the emergence of the Fourth World.

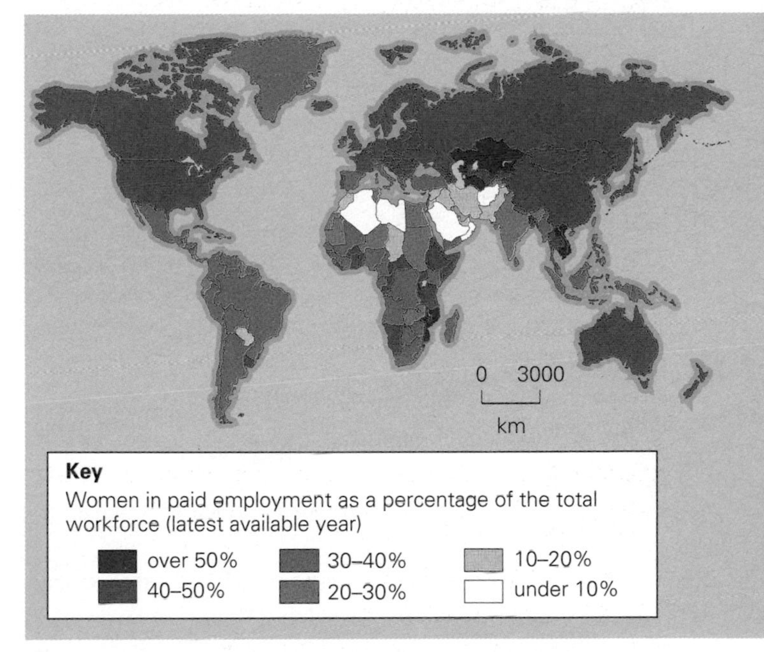

Figure 3.51 *The global distribution of women in the workforce* Source: *Philips Modern School Atlas, 92nd Edition*, 1998.

EXTENSION ACTIVITIES

1 For an LEDC:
  a) Find out what the situation is with respect to two of the following:
  - dependency
  - women in the workforce
  - marriage and divorce
  - lone-parent families
  - single-person households.

  b) Identify and try to explain the ways in which the situations differ from those in the UK.

2 Describe and explain the pattern found in Figure 3.51.

6 Managing population change

Controlling numbers

Most responsible governments accept that achieving a sustainable equilibrium between population, resources and development should be amongst their top priorities (Figure 3.32). In theory, there are three possible ways of adjusting the triangular relationship:

- by managing the development process, but as we shall see in Chapter 4, this is also controlled by the global economy and the TNCs
- by achieving a more efficient use of resources or increasing a country's ability to import resources from abroad. Raising the carrying capacity allows more people to be supported in a sustainable way
- by controlling population numbers. Since the need is to lower rates of growth and lower population levels, an attack on fertility rather than mortality is appropriate.

There are a number of well documented examples of government action taking the last route, for example in the world's two most populous countries, China and India. Singapore had a 'please stop at two' policy but was forced to abandon it because population growth quickly fell below replacement level.

China's one-child family policy

For the first 30 years of its existence (from 1949), the People's Republic of China blew hot and cold about birth control. In that time, the mammoth population nearly doubled and almost reached the 1 billion mark. During the 1960s the growth rate averaged at a staggering 2.4 per cent per year. The alarm bells began to ring and in 1979 China launched its one-child family campaign to reduce the rate of population growth. The general idea is to use coercion and penalties to persuade couples not to have more than one child. One-child families are given preferential treatment in education, healthcare, housing and wages. Couples with 'unauthorised' children are subjected to a range of economic, social and political sanctions.

The indications are that the policy has been successful. Mean annual growth rates fell to 1.3 in the 1980s and to 0.9 in the 1990s. The policy appears to have done well in cities, but less so in rural areas. Resistance in the countryside seems to stem from:

- the continuing need for security in old age
- the abandonment of the cooperative farming system, meaning child labour is important
- the perception that girls are no good in either respect, because they marry and leave home.

There was a time in the 1980s when it looked as if the birth rate was beginning to rise again (having fallen from 37 to 17 per 1000). It was thought that the degree of coercion to keep strictly to one child should be raised by:

- more peer pressure from mothers toeing the party line
- compulsory abortion of any second child, followed by either sterilisation or the insertion of an IU device.

The one-child policy seems to have at least three serious backlashes:

- It has encouraged sex-selective abortion. The traditional wish amongst Chinese fathers, as elsewhere in the world, is to produce a son and heir. Fulfilling this desire has been given added urgency by the one-child policy.
- Another, little publicised, consequence has been the high rate of divorce involving women whose one child turns out to be a girl. It has been used as grounds for divorce. Recently, however, the law has changed so a man is not allowed to have another child if he divorces his wife for having a girl. But there appear to be ways around this legislation. The husband can beat his wife, so she divorces him on these grounds instead.
- A third and perhaps better known outcome of the one-child policy is the 'little emperor' syndrome. Because boys are so sought after by would-be parents, when they do arrive they are treated like royalty.

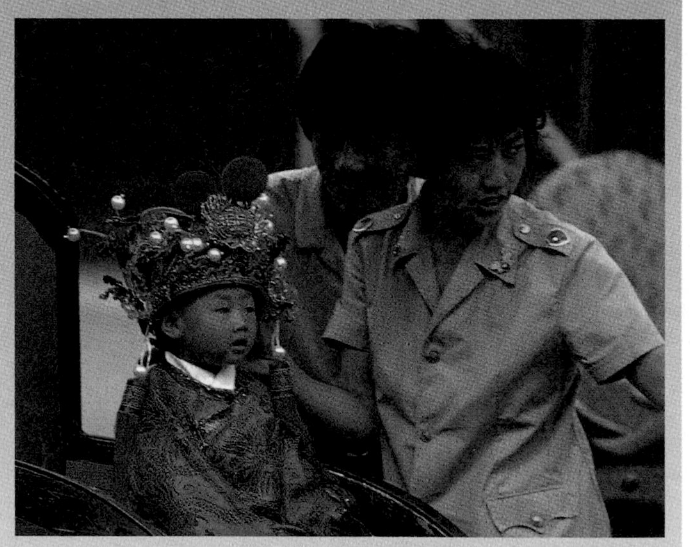

Figure 3.52 *One of China's little emperors*

ACTIVITIES

1. Do you think that China had any option other than a policy of strictly enforced birth control?
2. Before 1979, some people, who were against introducing a national birth control campaign, pointed out that China's greatest resource was its people. Explain what they may have meant.

India's attempts to control fertility

The Indian Government has tried to promote family planning by:

- spreading information about the techniques of birth control
- distributing condoms
- encouraging surgical sterilisation, particularly of men, by offering cash and other incentives.

One of India's problems, apart from the size of its population, is that it has a much more devolved form of government than China. Much of the governing is done by the 22 states and 9 territories into which India is divided. Each tends to be more concerned about its own well-being and status, and less aware of the national need. So the success or otherwise of birth control programmes is rather patchy. Some states made sterilisation compulsory for men with two or more children. Others denied access to public housing for those families with more than two children, unless the husband was sterilised. Perhaps a little more encouraging is the discovery that effective birth control is more easily achieved if campaigns are targeted at the poorest families. In these instances, the secret seems to lie in promoting primary education and raising literacy, as well as improving access to healthcare.

India has a long way to go before its population explosion subsides. Throughout the period 1950–2000, the mean annual growth rate has fluctuated around the 2.2 per cent mark, and is currently running at 2.5 per cent. In May 2000, India joined China as a nation of a billion people. The way things are going, in 50 years time India will have passed China as the world's most populous country.

Figure 3.53 *India is poised to overtake China as the world's most populous nation*

ACTIVITY

1. Why do you think that China's birth control campaign has been more successful than India's? Brainstorm your ideas and share them with others in your class.

It is perhaps less well known that there have been instances of governments encouraging population growth. Germany, Italy and Japan did so before the Second World War (1939–1945) for political reasons. After the war, France and the UK did so in order to compensate for population lost. The former Soviet Union and Australia have done so to supply people for the opening up of pioneer areas. During the 1980s, abortions were banned in Romania and contraception was allowed only if a woman had borne more than five children. There are also major religions, and many people outside those specific religions, who are morally opposed to birth control.

There are instances where government actions have indirectly encouraged population growth. For example, investing in services such as ante-natal clinics, special classes for expectant mothers and maternity hospitals have reduced the incidence of stillbirths and infant mortality. Similarly, better healthcare, education about healthy life styles, special housing and services for the elderly have all helped to lower mortality rates and raise life expectancy. The outcome, intentionally or not, has been population growth.

Most interventions, whether they are aimed at fertility or mortality, have both short- and long-term consequences. The most obvious example is when fertility rates are cut back. The undercutting at the base of the population pyramid then gradually works its way up, so that there comes a time when the reduction in numbers passes through the economically-active age range. This can create a shortage of labour. A further reduction of fertility is almost certain, because it is the people in the lower part of the economically-active age range who normally produce the next generation. So automatically there is a second attack on fertility. At this point, there is also the problem of supporting the increasingly elderly population, who were born ahead of the birth control campaign. In short, intervention can have unwanted consequences.

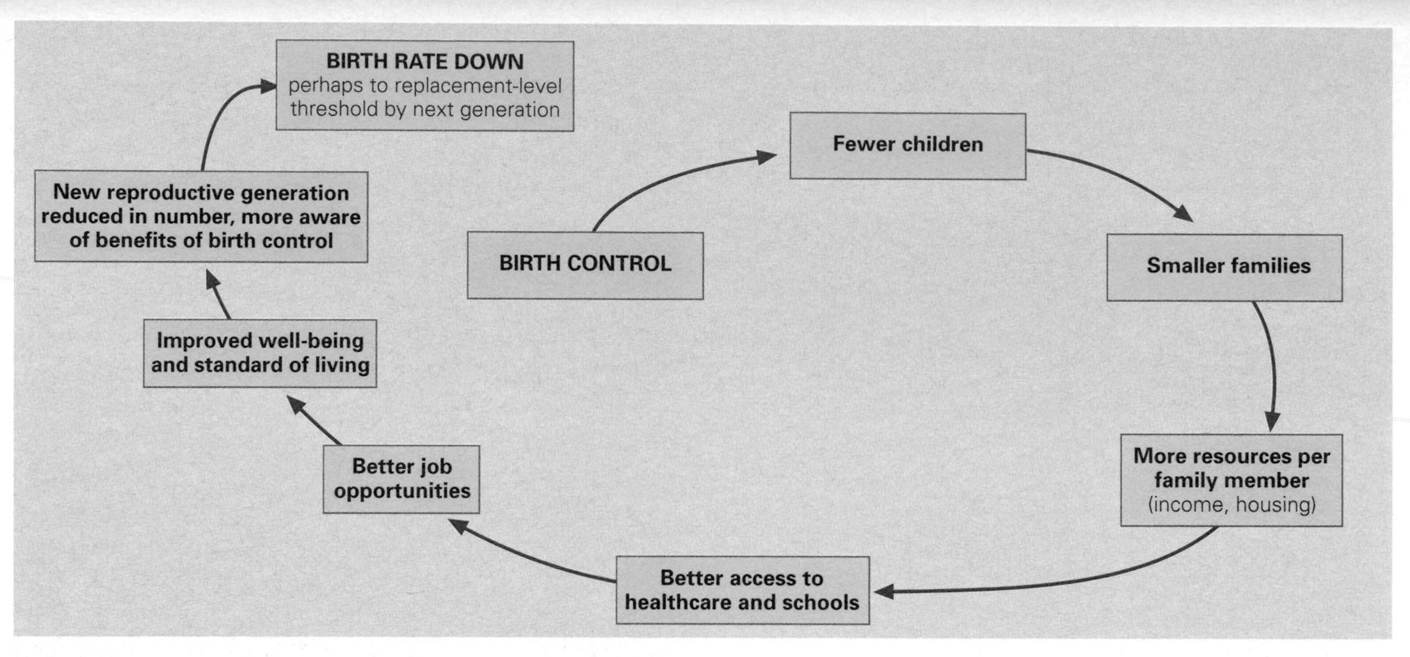

Figure 3.54 *The virtuous upward spiral of birth control*

ACTIVITIES

1 Explain the links between the boxes in Figure 3.54.
2 Find out what was done in the UK after the Second World War to encourage couples to have more children. Are there any direct incentives today? Or are there any disincentives?

Mauritius shows the way

Thirty years ago the island of Mauritius in the Indian Ocean was being overwhelmed by a population growth rate of more than 3 per cent per year. Mean population density was more than 320 persons per km^2 and poverty and illness were rampant. Today the island is economically booming and enjoying a high level of social well-being. Fertility is around the replacement level and mortality rates are more like those of Europe than Africa. Per capita GDP is now US $3,380 (higher than in Russia).

What has brought about this spectacular turn-around? Two achievements have been critical. First, fertility declined from 6.2 to 3.2 children per woman within a period of 10 years (Figure 3.55). It did so on a voluntary basis rather than by coercion and the decline in fertility has since continued. Second, during the 1980s, Mauritius experienced remarkable economic growth based on export-oriented industries, mostly textiles. Since then the economy has been boosted still further by international tourism and by foreign investment in labour-intensive industries, such as electronics.

Why did fertility decline so rapidly in those first ten years when the island's economy was still stagnant? The answer lies in a combination of social development (especially promoting female education), family planning campaigns and legal reform (especially establishing the rights of women).

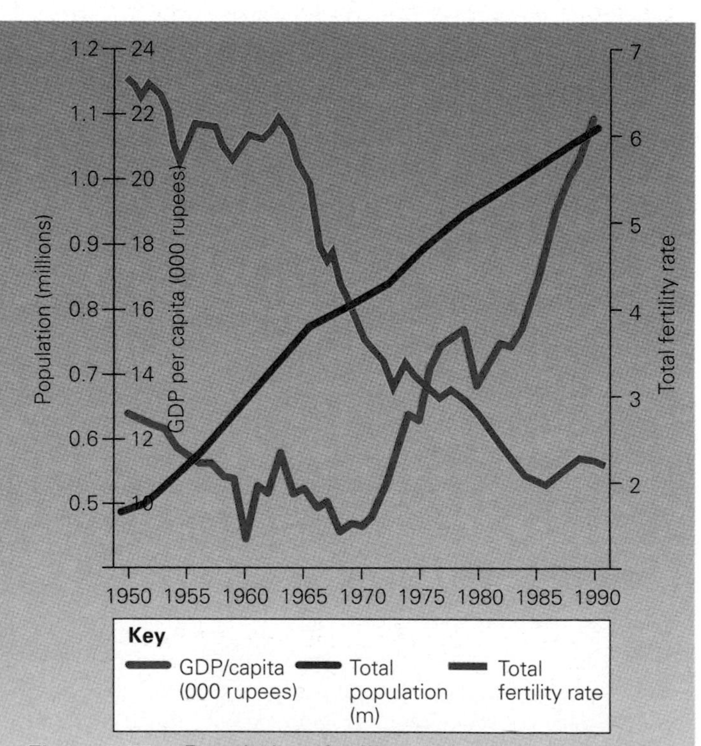

Figure 3.55 *Population, fertility and per capita GDP in Mauritius, 1950–2000* Source: *People and the Planet*, 3 March 1994.

What Mauritius has clearly shown is an inverse relationship between female literacy and fertility (Figures 3.55 and 3.56). Making the education of women a top priority has yielded a whole range of benefits:

- more awareness of the need for birth control
- more openness towards using contraceptives
- delayed marriage
- strengthened the position of women in society
- reduced the desired family size
- more women in the workforce.

So, although the population continues to increase (now over 1 million, more than twice what it was 50 years ago), there can be no doubting that Mauritius is coping with population growth. It is moving nearer to achieving sustainable equilibrium between population, resources and development. Mauritius has achieved all this by gentle persuasion rather than brute force, and by getting its priorities right. It challenges the traditional view that economic growth is a prerequisite of declining fertility.

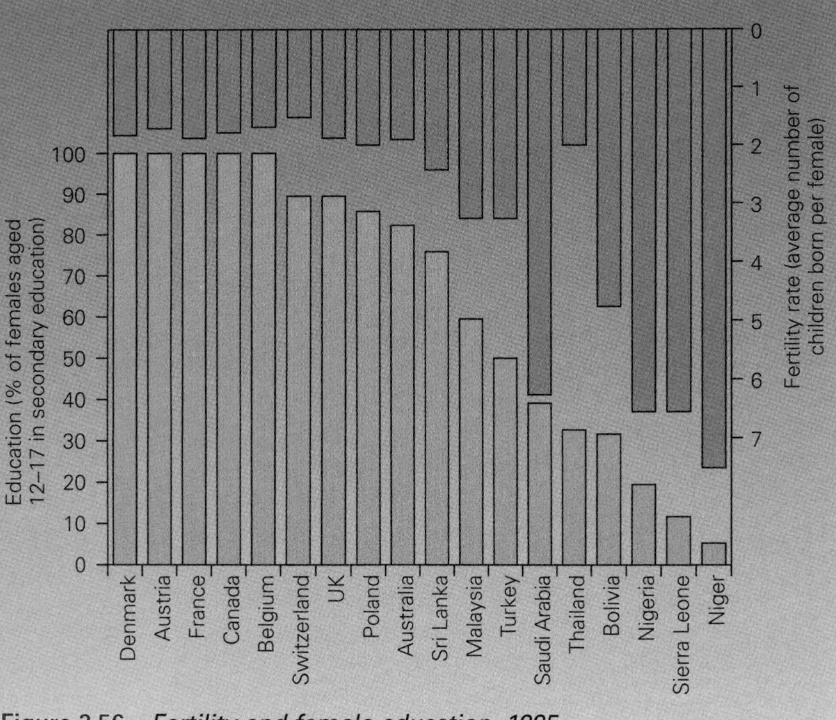

Figure 3.56 *Fertility and female education, 1995*
Source: *Philips Modern School Atlas, 92nd Edition*, 1998.

The education effect

Educating women is the single most important step governments can take to improve the health of their citizens and their economies. This is because:

- **educated women are more economically productive**
  In Morocco, an extra year of education is linked with a 16 per cent increase in women's earnings.
- **educated women are more confident**
  Studies in Nepal, Nigeria and India found literate women expected and received better treatment at clinics and hospitals.
- **educated women marry later**
  The World Fertility Survey found that women with over seven years of schooling married around four years later than uneducated women.
- **educated women use family planning**
  Uneducated women in Brazil have three times as many children as those who graduate from secondary school.
- **educated women have healthier children**
  A study of four Latin American countries found educated women are more likely to attend ante-natal clinics, have their births supervised by a trained person, and take their babies to be immunised.

ACTIVITIES

1. In what ways might the small size of Mauritius have contributed to the success of its population programme?
2. Explain each of the five points shown in 'The education effect'. Look elsewhere in this chapter for other examples to support these points.

Controlling movement

It is possible that in the above discussion we might have forgotten that population change has a second component – migration (Figure 3.6). This is examined in detail in the next section, but for the moment it needs to be understood that migration is much more managed than natural change. Migration can be a highly sensitive issue, particularly where the flows of people cross national boundaries and when the flows involve people of different ethnic backgrounds. Migration also occurs within national boundaries and can be equally controversial. In the following case studies, the aim is to illustrate some of the different motives behind the control of migration and some of the ways it has been achieved (Table 3.11).

Motives	International migration	Internal migration
Political	• US selective immigration • expulsion of Ugandan Asians • Vietnamese boat people	• Israeli settlement of West Bank • China's Cultural Revolution • Westminster Council's displacement of tenants
Social	• Manx policy to attract wealthy immigrants • export of UK orphans to colonies in nineteenth century	• post-war overspill in UK • kibbutz movement in Israel
Ethnic/ religious	• evacuation of Ethiopian Jews • immigration control in UK • partition of India	• apartheid in South Africa • ethnic cleansing in former Yugoslavia • movement of Kurds in Iraq
Economic	• labour recruitment in Venezuela • Australia's populate or perish policy • Turkish guest- workers in Germany	• Ethiopian villagisation • Indonesian transmigration • control of movement in Romania

Table 3.11 *A matrix to illustrate different types of government-led migration*

USA – international migration and politics

There are people in most Caribbean countries who try to migrate to the USA, but emigrants from Cuba and Haiti receive very different treatment from the USA. Cubans who try to leave their country, mainly by boat, are given every help to complete the escape. They are called political refugees. In contrast, those leaving Haiti are labelled economic migrants. If intercepted on their way to the USA, they are immediately returned to Haiti.

The reasons for this discrimination lie in US foreign policy. Since the Second World War, this policy has been anti-communist. Those seeking to flee a communist country, such as Cuba, are welcomed, as by leaving their homeland they are seen as condemning communism and underlining the superiority of American democracy. In short, allowing Cuban migrants into the USA has propaganda value. Haiti, however, is a staunch supporter of the USA and it is Haiti's wish to retain its population and stem the flow of emigrants. The USA is happy to cooperate.

Figure 3.57 *US Coastguards intercepting and helping Cuban 'boat people'*

Ethiopia – international migration and religion

The Falashas, or Ethiopian Jews, are a mountain tribe that first settled in NW Ethiopia around 300 BC. Because they preferred to live in isolation, they subsequently became known as 'the lost tribe of Israel'. They first hit the headlines in 1984 when the Israeli Government had 12,000 of them airlifted to Israel. 'Operation Moses', as it was called, was undertaken because Israel feared that this unique tribe (they were Jewish, black and did not speak a Semitic language) was likely to be lost through the process of assimilation into Ethiopian society. In 1994 the situation for the remaining Falashas became dangerous as a civil war began in Ethiopia. Israel negotiated directly with the Ethiopian Government. Eventually, Israel agreed to pay $20 million to secure the release of 16,000 Falashas who were quickly airlifted to Jerusalem.

At first, the Falashas received much public support. Subsequently, however, they faced racism and discrimination. Because of their extended family structure (households of more than 20 being quite common), there were serious housing difficulties, and because of their inability to speak Hebrew, they found it difficult to find work. They were also surprised by the laxness of modern Judaism compared with their own traditional and strict observance of the faith.

United Kingdom – internal migration and social engineering

The New Towns programme was launched in 1946, immediately after the end of the Second World War. It was driven by the government's wish to:

- curb the expansion of London and other large conurbations
- improve the lot of poor people condemned to live in inner-city slums
- create new urban environments which offered social justice and attractive living conditions, i.e. modern housing, jobs and good services.

The aim was to trigger a voluntary movement from old cities to new towns (Figure 3.58). In addition to the attractions that the new towns had to offer, incentives were used as gentle persuaders. Hundreds of thousands of people took advantage of the chance of a new and hopefully better life offered in two generations of new towns.

The make-up of the population of the new towns as a whole, and of their constituent neighbourhood units was carefully managed.

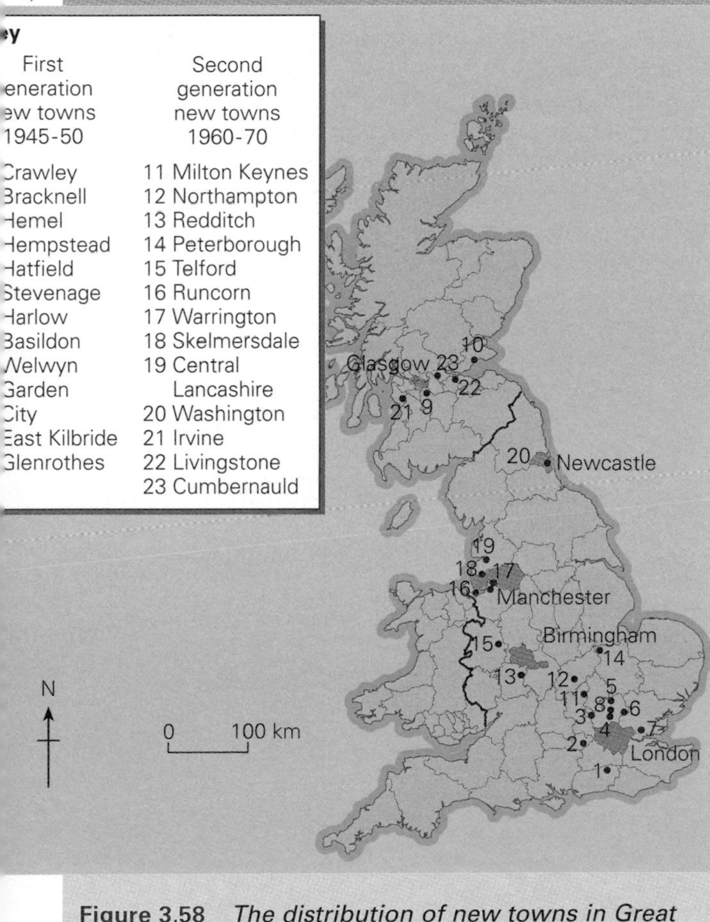

Figure 3.58 *The distribution of new towns in Great Britain*

Indonesia – internal migration and economic engineering

Indonesia's transmigration programme was launched because the government wished to stimulate economic development in its more peripheral islands. Sixty per cent of Indonesia's 205 million people live on the island of Java at densities of up to 2000 people per km². In stark contrast, the outer islands of Sumatra, Borneo (Kalimantan) and Celebes (Sulawesi) are underpopulated, with vast tracts of land occupied at very low densities.

Since 1950 over three million people have been sponsored to relocate, and over 7,000 km² of rainforest on these outlying islands has been cleared to accommodate them. The World Bank has invested over $500 million, the road networks have been extended by 50 per cent and many airstrips built. Numerous new settlements with schools, clinics, religious facilities and markets have been established and the programme has created over half a million permanent jobs. Migration is encouraged by government sponsorship. This involves support for up to five years, the provision of housing and land, and access to transport and social services.

Figure 3.59 *One environmental cost: loss of tropical rainforest*

The fact that Java's shares of GDP, agricultural output and manufacturing have declined indicates that the programme has had some success, but the rapidly growing population on Java has not dropped. On the debit side there is immense environmental damage caused by rainforest clearance in the outlying islands (Figure 3.59). The native people in the resettlement areas have been badly treated and lost their land rights. Research has shown that many transmigrants end up on lower incomes than the average for the area they have left. Too few migrants have been selected for their enterprise. In East Timor, annexed by Indonesia in 1976, transmigration was used to help suppress the independence movement. Happily, in 1999, it regained its independence and many transmigrants, fearful for their safety, moved out.

ACTIVITIES

1 With your class, debate the propositions:
- 'The global population problem is as much to do with distribution as with numbers.'
- 'When it comes to controlling population numbers and migration, coercion is best.'

2 Plan an essay on one of the propositions and ask a partner to write a critical analysis of your plan.

7 Causes of international migration

Classification of migration

Population movements from place to place range in scale and distance. They can vary from the movement of a single person from one bedsit to another within the same town, to mass movements of people across national frontiers and between continents. They can also differ in time. Some movements are continuous and regular, such as commuting to and from work. Other movements are one-off and permanent, as when Jewish people in North America and Europe emigrate to Israel.

It is common practice to refer to all population movements as **migration**. However, the UN has recommended that in national censuses, the term **migration** should only be used when:

- population moves from one administrative area to another
- the result is a change of permanent residence.

For other movements, the term **circulation** is used. This typically includes movements that are short-term and circular in nature. They include shopping trips, holidays abroad, going away to university and commuting.

Given that population movements can be so diverse, it is useful to have some sort of classification. This helps us to put the individual movement into context, to see how it relates to or compares with other movements. Unfortunately, there is as yet no scheme that is widely accepted. Figure 3.60 suggests one possible scheme. The first division or tier in the classification is between migration and circulation. Circulation is subdivided according to its frequency: daily, weekly, monthly, seasonal and long-term. It would be equally valid to subdivide circulation on the basis of purpose: employment, shopping, education, leisure and recreation, etc.

The classification of migration is rather more complicated. There are a number of possible criteria. Distance, volume, motive and nature are four that immediately spring to mind. Who is to say which criterion is most important? National boundaries are important in migration because they tend to act as barriers. So in Figure 3.60, the two tiers in the classification represent the distinction between **international migration** and **national migration** (i.e. taking place within the boundaries of a state). The fact that people are frequently **forced** to uproot and move is significant, so there is a strong case for distinguishing between these migrations and those that are **voluntary** in character (Table 3.12). Finally, and perhaps most important geographically, the classification should take into account the sorts of environments involved in any migrational move. With international migration, the LEDC and MEDC distinction is significant, whereas for national migration the difference between urban and rural environments is important.

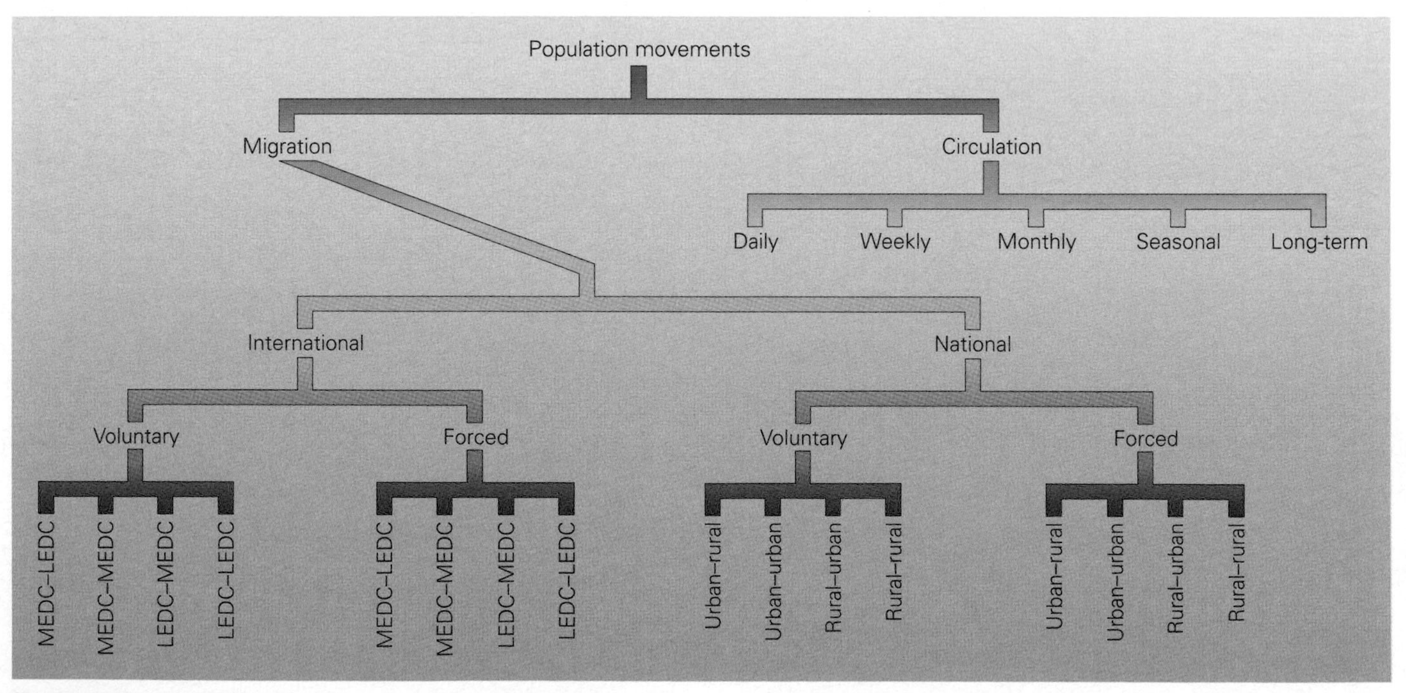

Figure 3.60 *Classification of population movements*

	Forced	Voluntary
LEDC to LEDC	• movement of Hindus and Muslims after the Partition of India • migration of Ethiopians into Sudan	• labour recruitment in Venezuela • Indian labour to Trinidad
LEDC to MEDC	• expulsion of Asians from Uganda • evacuation of Tristan da Cunha	• Turkish guest workers in Germany • West Indian immigrants to UK
MEDC to MEDC	• emigration of Jews from Germany • refugee movements in former Yugoslavia	• movement of Soviet Jews to Israel • retirement moves from UK to Spain
MEDC to LEDC	• British penal settlements in Australia • Pilgrim Fathers to USA	• white settlers to British colonies • Japanese branch plant staff in Indonesia

Table 3.12 *Examples of different types of international migration*

ACTIVITIES

1. Can you think of any difficulties with the criteria used for distinguishing migration from circulation?
2. How important do you think it is to make the distinction between migration and circulation?
3. Suggest an example of each of the five types of circulation (Figure 3.60).
4. Do you think that the rural–urban distinction is important in international migration as well as national migration?

Finally, we must consider the significance of global patterns of international migration – past and present. Throughout history, migration has had a profound effect on the spread of different cultures. The movement of people has been responsible for the spread of different languages and religions. The great migration streams out of Europe over the last four centuries have done much to spread what might be called 'European culture', i.e.:

- the English language to North America and Australasia
- Roman Catholicism to Latin American and SE Asia
- the British and French education systems to Africa.

These cultural diffusions were associated with political developments. During the seventeenth, eighteenth and nineteenth centuries, migration was encouraged by Britain, France and Spain in order to build up extensive colonial empires. The main international migrations since 1500 have not been exclusively out of Europe (Figure 3.61). There have been important movements from India towards East and South Africa, SE Asia and the Caribbean. Large numbers of people have moved from China into various

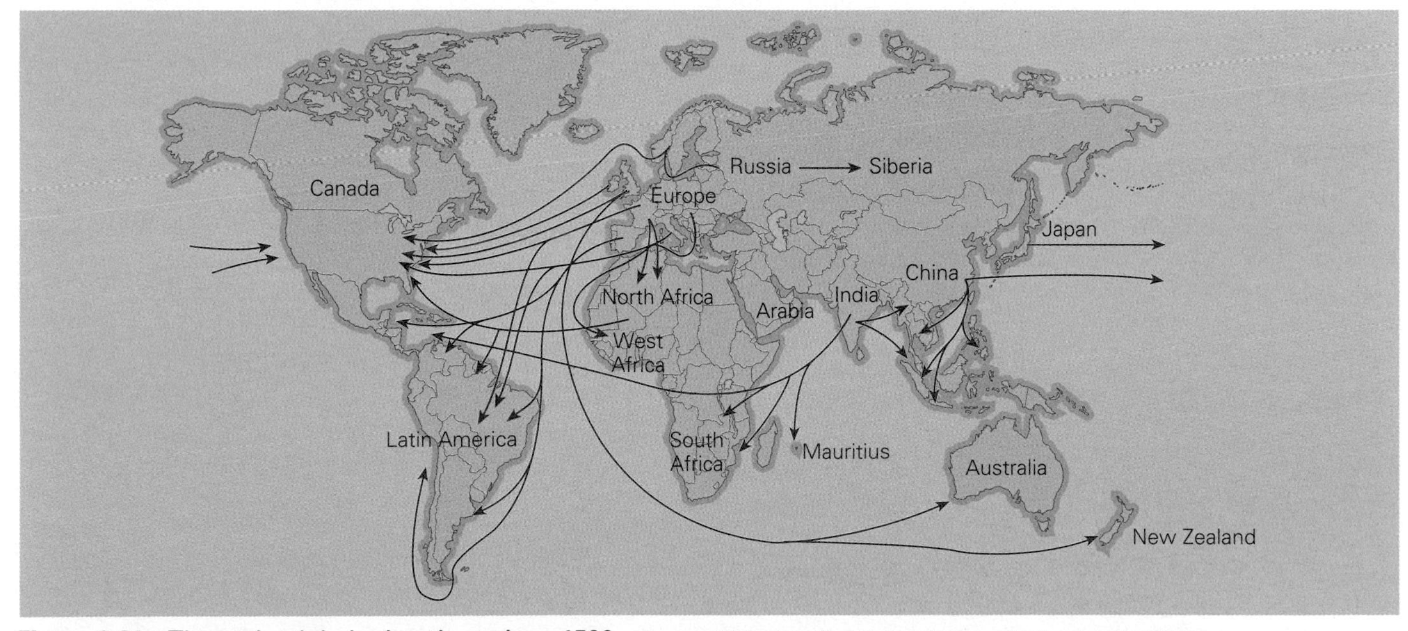

Figure 3.61 *The main global migrations since 1500* Source: Witherick, *Population Geography*, Longman, 1990.

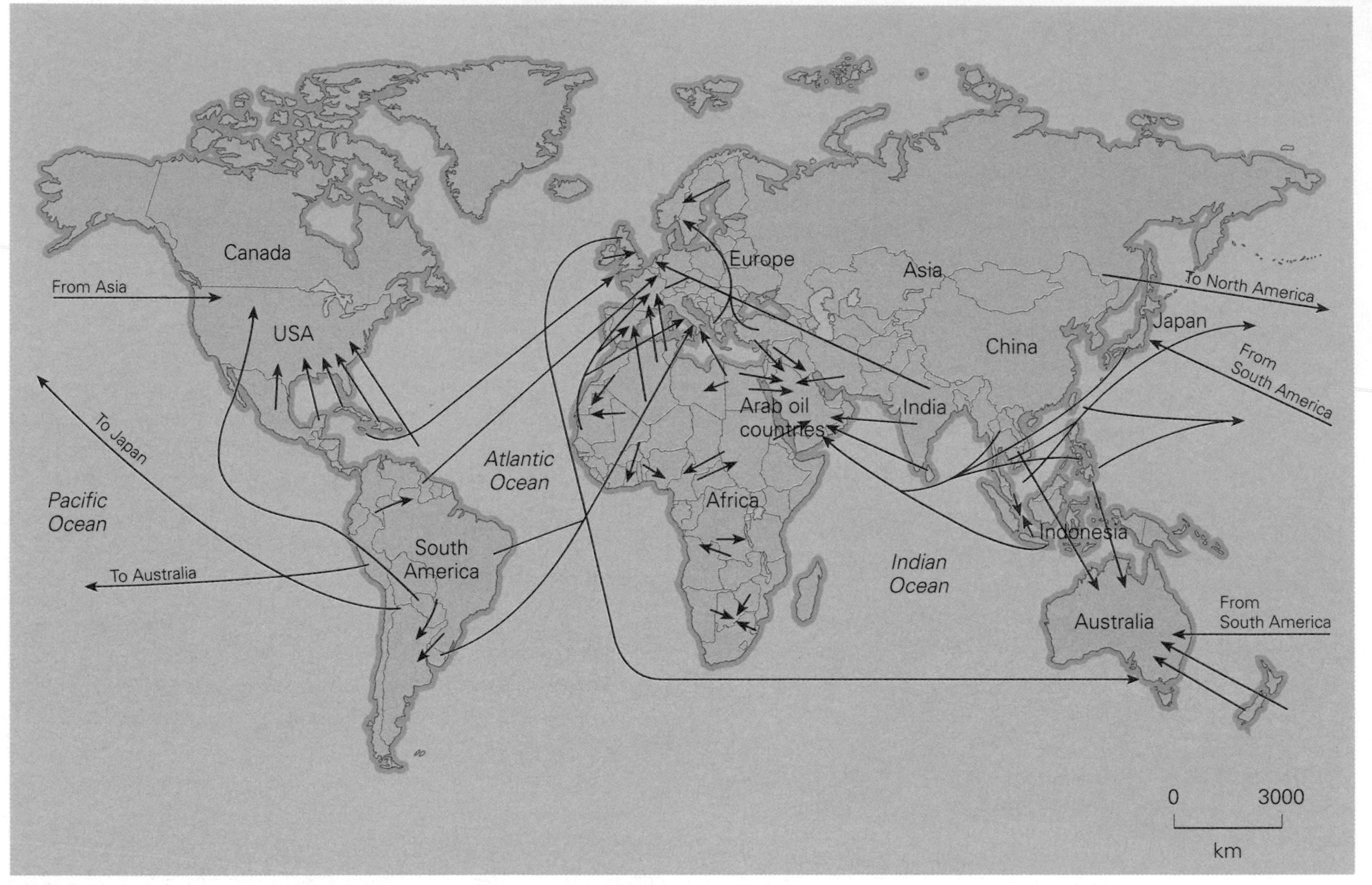

Figure 3.62 *The main global migrations of the last 25 years* Source: Boyle, *Exploring Contemporary Migration*, Longman, 1998.

parts of the Pacific region. No less significant during the eighteenth and nineteenth centuries was the movement of slaves from West Africa to the USA and the Caribbean.

If we study the global map of recent international migrations (Figure 3.62), it is possible to detect two types of area: areas of convergence and areas of divergence. The former, comprising North America, Europe and Australia, represent major destinations for migrants. People are being drawn to them from those areas of diverging migration flows. These are mainly LEDCs, and people are being lured from them by employment opportunities and the prospect of a better standard of living. The USA appears to be drawing large volumes of immigrants from Caribbean countries; Europe attracts people from Africa; while Australia appears to have a wider catchment. An interesting area is the Middle East with the oil-rich states recruiting unskilled labour from southern Europe, North Africa and the Indian subcontinent.

The map of global migration flows is testimony to the existence of global disparities. The honeypot destinations are undoubtedly the more affluent corners of the globe which are perceived to be offering a better life. We need to remember that movement between nation states is generally tightly controlled by means of visas and quotas. Were there not these barriers to movement, there is no doubt that migration flows would be much heavier.

Migration swings in the Caribbean

Nowhere in the world has there been such a marked turnaround in migration flows as in the Caribbean. During European colonisation in the seventeenth and eighteenth centuries a plantation economy developed on many of the West Indian islands. The principal crops were sugar, cotton and tobacco. The plantation system required large inputs of labour and this was gradually met by importing slave labour from West Africa. Thus there developed the so-called 'triangular trade' between Africa, the West Indies and Europe (Figure 3.63). The trade circuit also involved North America and so became quadrangular in form. With the abolition of slavery in the early nineteenth century, the labour needs of the plantations were met by labour from the Indian subcontinent and China.

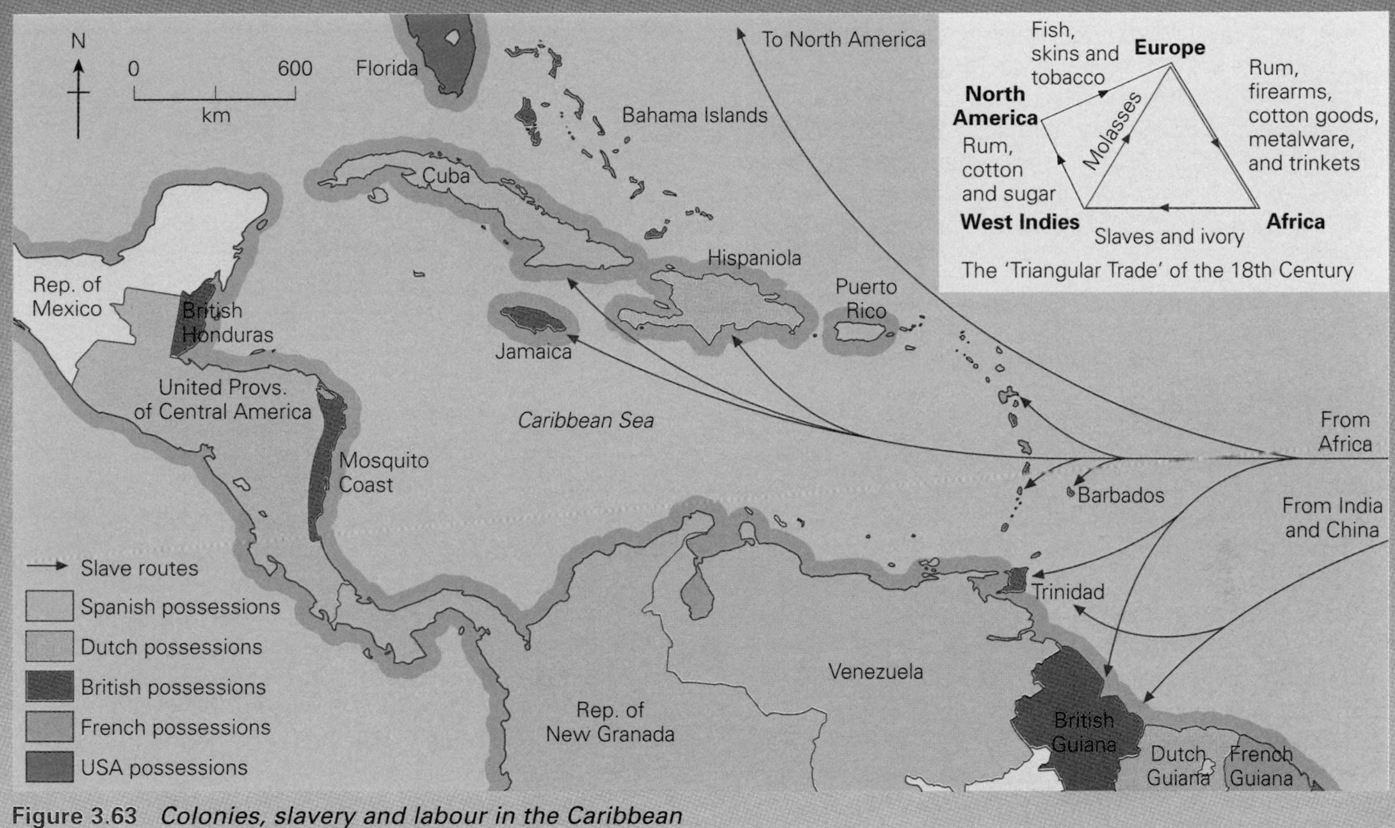

Figure 3.63 *Colonies, slavery and labour in the Caribbean*
Source: *Philip's Certificate Atlas for the Caribbean,* 3rd Edition, 1998.

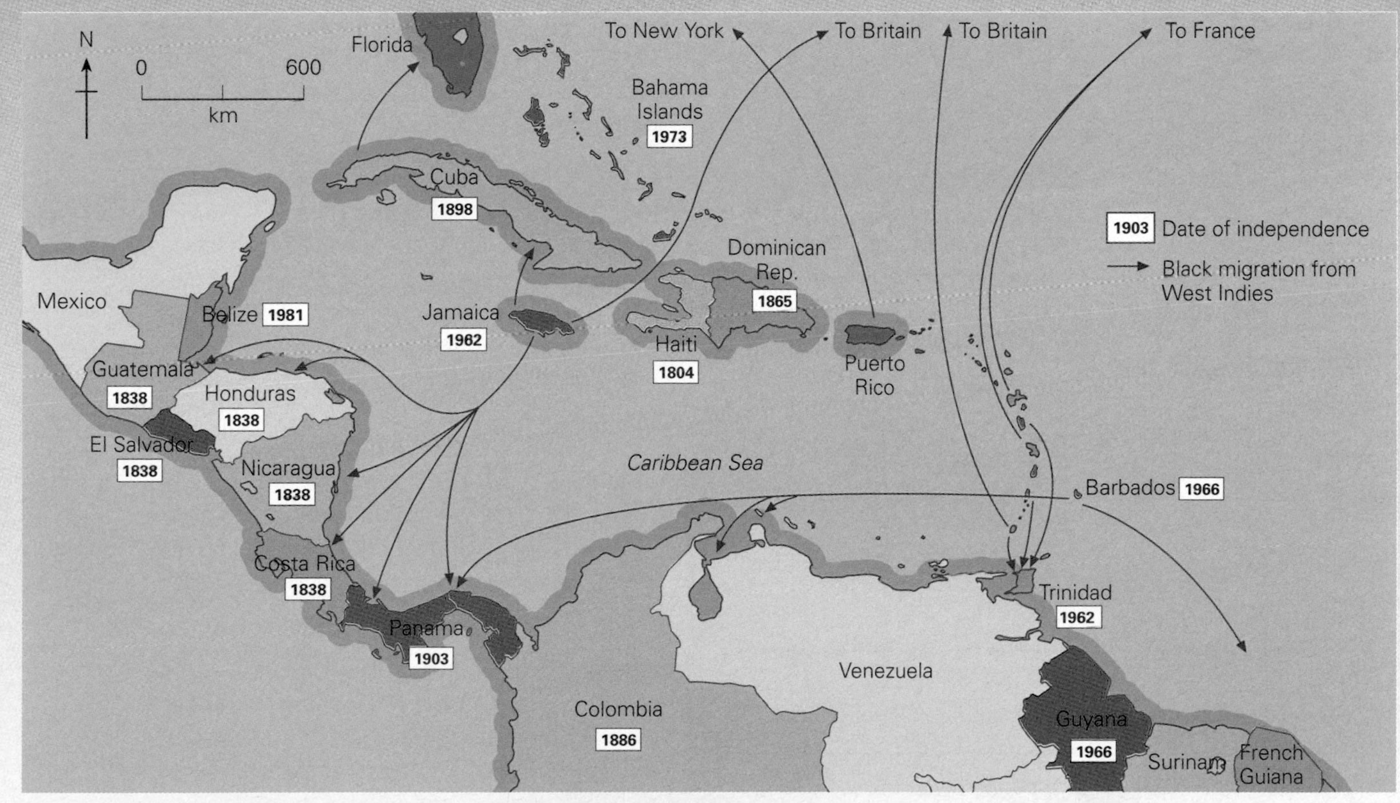

Figure 3.64 *Independence and emigration from the Caribbean*
Source: *Philip's Certificate Atlas for the Caribbean,* 3rd Edition, 1998.

After the Second World War, many of the Caribbean islands gradually obtained their independence. This provoked two waves of migration. First, many white settlers returned to their homelands in Europe and were soon followed by significant numbers of people of African and Indian descent. These latter two groups were persuaded to move by the unemployment created when the plantation economy collapsed, and by Europe's need for cheap labour (Figure 3.64).

ACTIVITY

1 Analyse the Caribbean case study in terms of:
- examples of forced and voluntary migration
- the causes of both types of migration
- the consequences.

You might adopt one of two approaches: either select and research the history of one island, or research generally about the slave trade and postwar emigration.

Migration models

A vital aspect of international migration is its causes. People migrate for a variety of reasons, and most people will migrate at least once during their lifetime. It might be to do with starting work, getting married, retiring or simply moving to a larger or smaller dwelling. Whatever the reason, most migration is the outcome of two sets of forces (Figure 3.65). **Push forces** are pressures which persuade a person to move away from an area and might include the impact of natural hazards, low wages, poor schools or persecution. **Pull forces** are those which attract the migrant to a particular destination. A scenic environment, job opportunities, good services or a democratic government are typical pull factors.

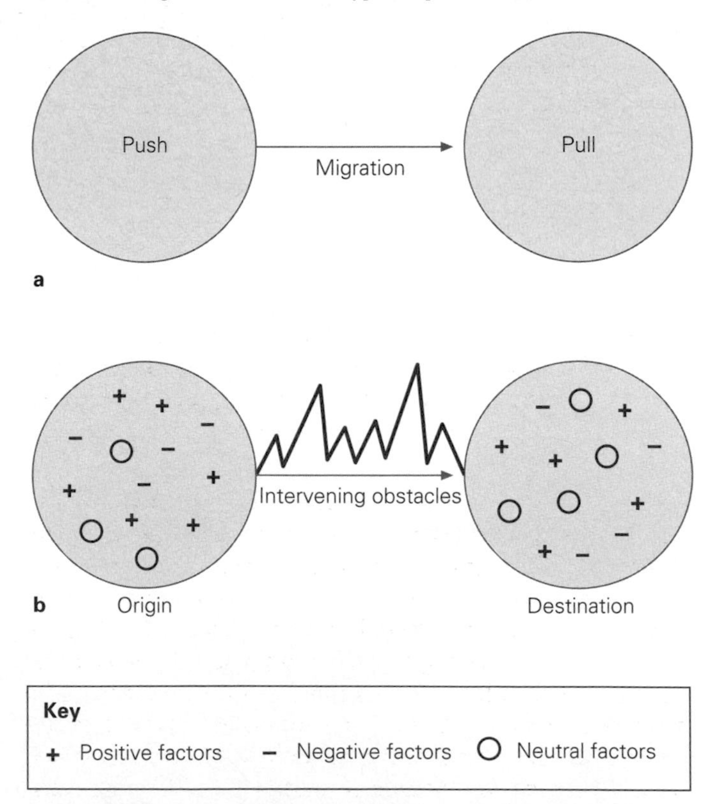

Figure 3.65 *The push-pull mechanism: a) the simple model; b) Lee's model* Source: Witherick, *Population Geography*, Longman, 1990.

Push and pull factors fall into five categories: physical, demographic, economic, social and political (Table 3.13). In some cases push and pull factors may be complementary. For example, unemployment and poor housing in the area of departure might match up with job opportunities and cheap, modern housing in the place of arrival. In other instances, migration will be motivated by a single powerful factor. It might be a push factor such as a natural disaster or ethnic cleansing, or a powerful pull factor such as a much higher salary.

	Push	Pull
Physical	• inaccessibility • harsh climate • natural disaster	• scenic quality • cheap land • hazard-free environment
Demographic	• divorce • children leaving home • ill health	• marriage • lower population densities • family or ethnic ties
Economic	• unemployment • poverty • heavy taxes	• high living standards • good wages / salary • promotion at work
Social	• declining neighbourhood • need to down-size home • shortage of suitable housing	• good welfare services • chances of upward mobility • personal safety and security
Political	• civil unrest • ethnic cleansing • planning law	• freedom of speech • political asylum • propaganda

Table 3.13 *Some reasons for migrating*

Gravity model

Newton's law of universal gravitation has been used, not too successfully, to predict the volume of migration between two places. In migration studies, the law is expressed as follows: the number of people moving between places A and B is equal to the population of A multiplied by the population of B, divided by the square of the distance between them. The logic behind this is that the potential number of migrants will be bigger where the populations of the places of departure and arrival are large. At the same time, the friction of distance acts as a brake on migration. However, it should be evident already that migration is not simply a matter of numbers of people and distance.

Lee's model

This does not attempt to isolate particular push and pull factors. Instead it sees the places of departure and arrival as possessing a range of attributes (Figure 3.65b). Each individual perceives these attributes differently, depending on personal characteristics such as age, gender, marital status, socio-economic class and education. Some of the attributes of the present location will be regarded positively and they will persuade the person to stay put. Others will be seen negatively and will encourage migration. Others will be perceived neutrally and thus have no influence on the decision-making process.

Lee's model introduces another refinement to the simple push-pull model (Figure 3.65a). This is the concept of **intervening obstacles**. These can be both real and perceived, and need to be overcome before migration takes place. Real obstacles include international boundaries and the need to obtain a visa before being allowed into another country. Perceived obstacles may take the form of anxiety about moving.

ACTIVITY

Small town	Score + (positive) – (negative) 0 (neutral)	Large city	Score + (positive) – (negative) 0 (neutral)
cheap housing		high crime rate	
countryside nearby		environmental pollution	
sense of community		traffic congestion	
limited shops		good social services	
poor schools		job opportunities	
little entertainment		wide choice of housing	

Table 3.14 *The perception and evaluation of locational attributes*

1 Study Table 3.14 which lists the attributes of two different locations: a small town and a large city. Assume you have to choose between them as a migration destination. Mark each attribute as positive, negative or neutral, and then look at the balance of your 'scores' for each location. Which location comes out on top for you? Compare your score with other people's scores.

The idea that most migration is a response to push and pull forces prompts us to question the distinction made between forced and voluntary migration. Push factors can be seen as 'forcing' people into moving, for example, redundancy could force someone to migrate if there is no alternative local employment. Where there are no credible alternatives or choices, then we are justified in assuming the migration is forced. In the case of our redundant worker, there may well be one rather stark choice: either stay put and live on unemployment benefit or move off in search of work. Refugees are often cited as the victims of forced migration, but not all would-be refugees have to move; they have the stay-or-move choice. In short, the boundary between forced and voluntary migration can sometimes be a rather grey area. Trying to distinguish between asylum seekers and opportunist refugees is an issue taxing many MEDC governments today, particularly that of the UK. It is both flattering and worrying that so many should perceive the UK to be their 'ultimate' destination. Certainly, as will be seen later (pages 147 to 151), the problem is that as the volume of such immigration grows, so increasingly tough measures have to be taken to weed out all but the most deserving cases. A country can very easily be driven to make itself highly inhospitable to anyone 'knocking at the door'.

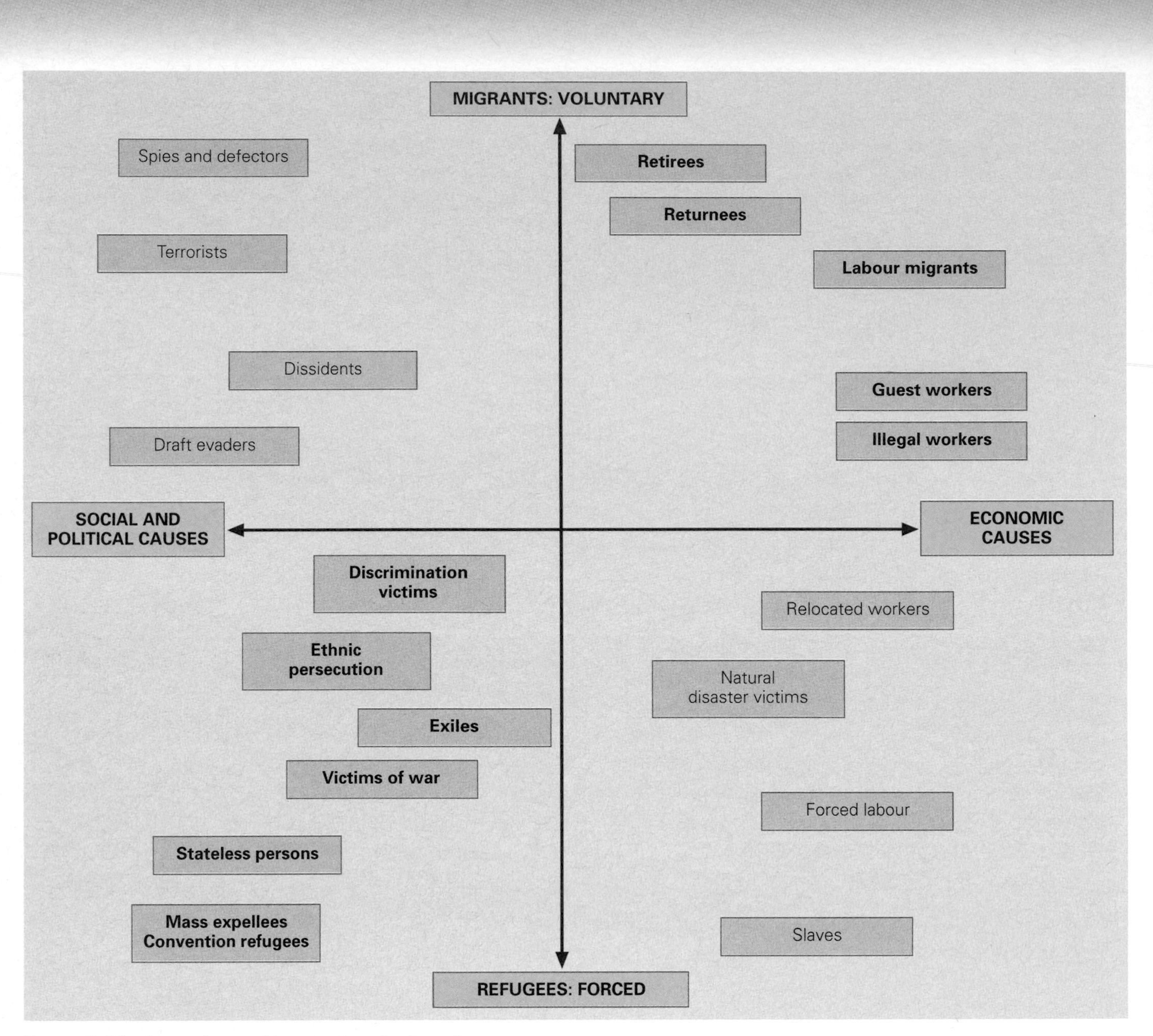

Figure 3.66 *A typology of international migration*
Source: Boyle et al, *Exploring Contemporary Migration,* Longman, 1998

Figure 3.66 is an attempt to show that there is a continuum between the two extremes of voluntary and forced international migration, and between socio-political and economic forces. Any particular migration may be located on this diagram depending on:

- the degree of coercion
- the balance between socio-political and economic factors.

The push-pull model is only one of a number of different theories to be found in studies of migration. The point has already been made that in most cases the decision to migrate rests with the individual. Frequently people tend to behave and react in a similar way in a given situation. It then becomes possible to generalise about the behaviour of migrants. One of the first people to identify such generalisations was Ravenstein in the 1880s. He identified factors such as the impact of distance, the magnetism of cities with their employment opportunities, and the selectivity of migration in terms of age and gender. Ravenstein's theory was aimed more at internal than international migration. But today's world is very different. Advances in transport have reduced the friction of distance and the emergence of a global economy has encouraged a greater mobility of labour. At the same time, international movements are now much more tightly controlled by governments than in the past.

Finally, it might to helpful to highlight some rather more theoretical statements about migration in general.

The two-way nature of migration

Often the movement of population between any two places involves two-way, but unequal flows. The stronger direction in such two-way migration is known as the **dominant migration**, while the weaker flow in the opposite direction is known as the **reverse** or **counter-migration**. In such cases, the total volume of movement is known as the **gross interchange**, whilst the difference between opposing movements is the **net interchange** or **net migration balance**. All this can be illustrated by migration between Pakistan and the UK. The dominant migration is to the UK. In 1997, nearly 6,000 Pakistanis entered the country, but in the same year there was also a reverse migration of 2,000 people.

Intervening opportunities

Stouffer put forward the view that the volume of migration between two places is related not so much to distance, but to opportunities. Specifically, he stated that the amount of migration over a given distance is directly proportional to the number of opportunities at the place of destination, and inversely proportional to the number of opportunities perceived between the place of departure and the intended destination. These opportunities can take many different forms: jobs, housing, good services and amenities, etc. They are things that persuade migrants to settle down 'en route' rather than complete the originally intended migration journey.

Differential migration

This is based on the concept that some people and some groups of people are more likely to migrate than others. Particularly significant factors in differential migration are age, gender, education and occupation. For example, in many countries, young adults appear to be most migratory. The significance of gender depends on the level of development in the country or region. In MEDCs, women are disproportionately more involved in short-distance migration and men take part in more international migration. In LEDCs, men make up the majority in all migration streams. Education has a direct bearing on occupation and possibly therefore on mobility and evidence shows professional people to be more migratory than skilled and unskilled workers.

ACTIVITY

1 Listed below are three of Ravenstein's Laws:

- 'Most migrants travel short distances and with increasing distance, the numbers of migrants decrease.'
- 'The major direction of migration is from agricultural areas to centres of industry and commerce.'
- 'Most migrants are adult, and families rarely migrate out of their country of birth.'

How well do you think these laws hold up with respect to international migration today?

Write your own notes on them and then discuss your ideas in small groups.

EXTENSION ACTIVITY

This can be undertaken as a class research topic in a school with a multi-ethnic catchment.

a Identify the ethnic groups represented in your school population.

b Assess their relative proportion in the school population.

c Compare your percentage values with those for the UK as a whole (data can be obtained from the Office of National Statistics).

d Select a sample of people from different ethnic backgrounds who would be happy to answer questions and try to find out:

- whether they are first, second or third generation immigrants
- where their families lived before coming to the UK
- when their families came to the UK
- why their families choose to live in your local area
- the extent to which they are able to retain their cultural traditions.

8 Impacts of international migration

Together with natural increase, migration has a major influence on the distribution of population. Since migration actually involves the removal and relocation of people, it would be more accurate to say that its role is one of redistribution. In some instances, migration acts as a rolling pin, evening out spatial differences by pushing people from densely to less-densely populated areas. In other instances, it acts more like a broom, sweeping people towards favoured locations. As a result, spatial differences in population density are increased.

Important though the redistribution role is, migration has other consequences at both ends of the migration route, and these can be either positive or negative (Table 3.15). One of the limitations of the push-pull model (Figure 3.65) is that it implies everything will be fine once the migration journey is completed. After all, the migrants will have escaped those negative aspects providing the 'push' in the region of departure. They are now free to enjoy those positive aspects that have pulled them to their chosen area. In reality, the situation is often much less clear-cut. Most migrants encounter problems of some sort at their destination, e.g. the pain of adjusting to an environment and a way of life that may be very different from that in the region they have just left. It could also be the stress of finding somewhere new to live or finding a job. These are costs that have an impact on the individual.

There are also costs and benefits that are felt at a national level (Table 3.15). For example, if the destination is a popular one, the sheer volume of inward movement can create problems such as shortages of food, housing and jobs, or too great a strain on social and welfare services, physical infrastructure and the environment. Migration can have negative consequences for the destination just as it does for the place of departure.

Finally, since migration flows are rarely one-way, nearly all countries are likely to perform a dual role, as both destination and place of departure. For example, in 1995 while 100,000 immigrants entered Australia, 28,000 Australians emigrated. This two-way nature of migration may possibly serve to 'neutralise' some of the impacts.

In a surprisingly large number of instances, migration simply shifts a problem from one area to another or replaces one problem with another, as the following case studies show.

ACTIVITIES

1 Can you think of any other positive or negative consequences of migration to add to Table 3.15?

2 Research the problems that confronted new migrants when they arrived in Britain in the 1950s and 1960s. You might use the headings: housing, jobs and assimilation.

Positive	Negative
Country of departure (source)	
• relief of shortages e.g. food, housing, jobs, services • reduced pressure on resources • emigrants send money back to relatives • increased influence / awareness overseas • if migrants return, they take new skills back with them • reduction of birth rate in overpopulated areas due to emigration of people of child-bearing age	• loss of human resources, e.g. labour, enterprise, skills • communities and regions drawn into vicious circle of decline • growth of emigration culture • dependence on remittances • premature ageing of population due to emigration of younger people
Country of arrival (host)	
• enrichment of human resources, i.e. enterprise, skills, capital, etc. • cultural diversification and emergence of a more multi-ethnic society • unwanted jobs filled by cheap labour • opening up of peripheral regions	• pressure on food supplies, housing, jobs, services, etc. • discrimination against immigrants, particularly if members of ethnic minorities • congestion, particularly in major cities • spread of disease • predominance of males leading to social problems

Table 3.15 *Some of the positive and negative consequences of international migration*

The movement of Russian Jews to Israel

In 1950, the parliament of the newly-established state of Israel passed a law that gave Jews anywhere in the world the right to enter and settle in the country. During the second half of the twentieth century, Jews from all over the world decided to return to what they regard as their 'spiritual home'. One of the largest flows was from the former Soviet Union. In a period of 25 years, no less than one million Russian Jews made the move.

Since Jews in the former Soviet Union were largely regarded as dissidents, permission to migrate to Israel was generally not too difficult to gain. However, whilst Russia was happy to see the departure of this ethnic minority, people in Israel complained that the country was being swamped by Russians. A recent settler from Russia summed it up:

'... I have become a poor person. And I am still a member of a minority group. This is funny. In Russia we were told: you're different, you're Jews. Here we are told: you're different, you're Russian.'

In a wider context, while the immigration of Russian Jews has helped to swell the Israeli population, it has done nothing to ease the long-standing Palestinian problem. Indeed, it has probably made it worse, for as Israel's population grows by natural increase and migration, so there is more settlement in disputed lands claimed by the Palestinians.

Figure 3.67 ***Russian Jews arriving in Tel Aviv, Israel***

Nomadism

There are migrations still going on today that pre-date international boundaries. Nomadic people might be described as the world's perpetual migrants. Within Africa and Asia, many areas are occupied by such people (from the Fulanis to the Mongols), whilst the New World also has many examples, such as the Aborigines of Australia and Eskimos of North America.

Three broad types of nomad are distinguished:

- the gatherer nomads who move in groups of between 20 and 60 persons, for example the Bushmen of the Kalahari desert
- the pastoral nomads who herd livestock and include the Masai of East Africa and the Sami of Finland
- the trader nomads, for example the Gypsies.

The impacts of these long-established migrations are largely environmental, politics and cultural. Perhaps the greatest environmental impacts are created by those pastoral nomads who traditionally roam over land too dry, too steep or too rocky for sedentary farming. Problems arise because the amount of such land is rapidly shrinking as population pressure requires extension of the cultivated area. In the circumstances, nomads now tend to remain longer in one location and to do so until serious environmental degradation sets in, for example until vegetation is over-browsed, grazing deteriorates and soil becomes exposed to wind erosion. In the past, they would have moved on long before the first of such symptoms appeared.

In today's world, there is much more sensitivity about national borders. Certainly, there is increasing resistance to the idea of people roaming freely and crossing frontiers at will. There are government pressures on the nomads to settle down. Wherever they move, nomads stand out as a people apart and this readily generates tension and distrust between them and sedentary people. This is well exemplified by the situation created in Europe by the movement of Gypsies.

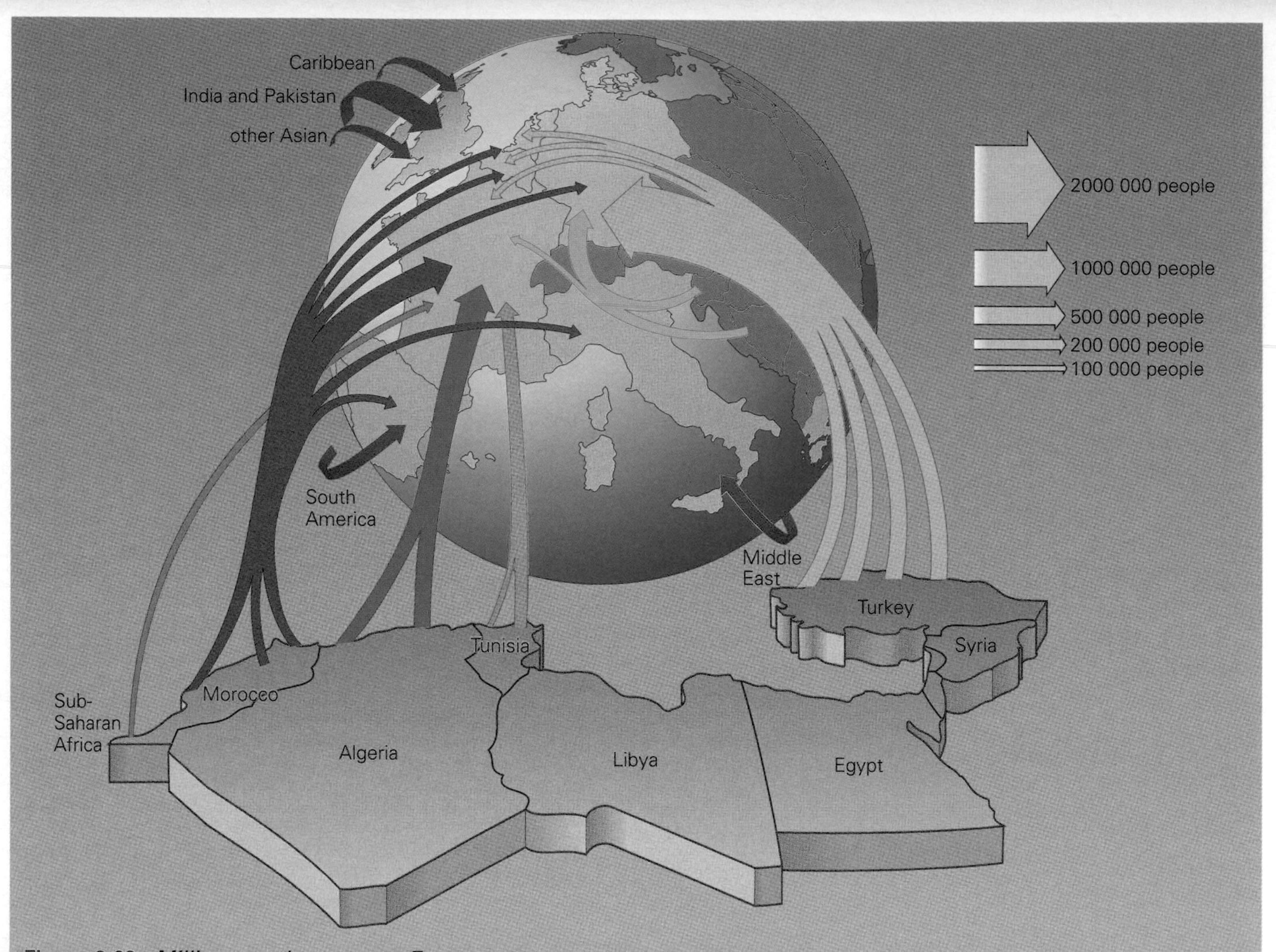

Figure 3.68 *Millions on the move to Europe* Source: *The Guardian,* 14 June 1991.

Turkish guest workers in former West Germany

Most of the positive and negative consequences of migration set out in Table 3.15 apply to the guest-worker migration between Turkey and the former West Germany. This started in the 1950s and was caused by the very successful rebuilding of the West German economy after the Second World War (1939-1945). A vast number of new jobs were created. Job vacancies quickly outstripped the national labour supply, thus the government was forced to encourage the recruitment of foreign labour. In particular, people were needed to fill poorly-paid, unskilled jobs. Turkey, along with a number of countries in southern Europe, was happy to supply the much-needed cheap labour.

For a time the arrangement worked well, with benefits being reaped by the Turkish immigrants, the West German economy and those parts of Turkey supplying the guest workers. However, with the economic recession of the 1970s the German attitude changed. It was argued that Germans should come first when it came to filling the dwindling number of jobs. A ban was placed on the recruitment of foreign workers, but Turkish immigrants continued to arrive. In the 1980s grants were offered to persuade Turks to return home. Even greater pressure was put on them in the 1990s with the reunification of Germany. The new Germany now had its own supply of relatively cheap labour from what was formerly communist East Germany.

Even today, there is still a sizeable Turkish community in Germany, and there is also considerable tension. The Turks resent being treated as 'second class' citizens; they feel discriminated against, particularly by the police. The Germans criticise the Turks for not becoming part of German society. They are seen as keeping themselves to themselves, maintaining their own culture, keeping their Turkish citizenship, occupying poor housing and straining social and welfare services.

Figure 3.68 shows us that Germany is only one of a number of European countries to have recruited foreign labour. By so doing, they have given hope to many people fleeing from natural disasters, political oppression and economic depression. This case study and the waves of migration to Western Europe raise a number of issues that are discussed in the next section.

Remittances to Pakistan

Many international migrants maintain links with their country of origin. A common link is the sending of money (known as **remittances**) 'back home' to relatives and friends left behind. In some countries, these remittances represent a notable proportion of the GNP. In Pakistan the figure is around 6 per cent.

In assessing the impact of remittance payments, it is difficult to isolate their effects from the effects of other sources of income. An analysis of remittance expenditure in Pakistan has shown that nearly 65 per cent is spent on the consumption of goods and services, just over 20 per cent is spent on buying real estate, while much of the remainder is invested in agricultural, industrial and commercial enterprises.

This analysis clearly indicates that there are benefits for Pakistan and other countries in exporting large numbers of migrants. The spending of remittance money on goods, services and property helps to support local jobs, whilst the investment money might be seen as creating work and helping production. On top of this, there is the added bonus that emigration helps to reduce pressure on scarce resources. There is, however, a possible downside. Regular and sizeable remittances can easily lead to a culture of dependence on such money.

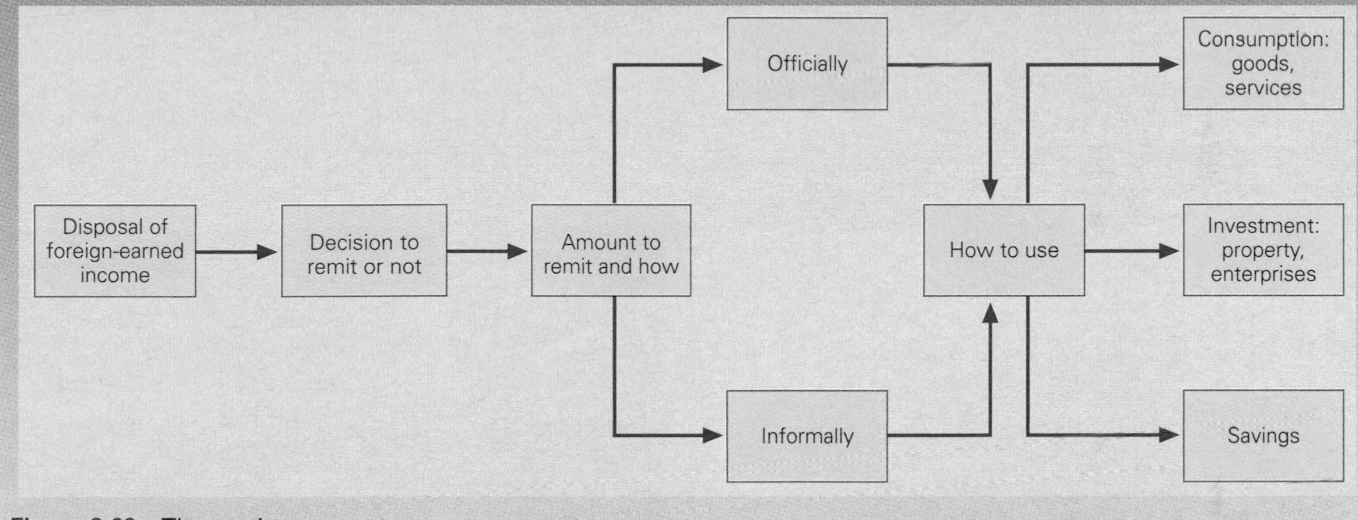

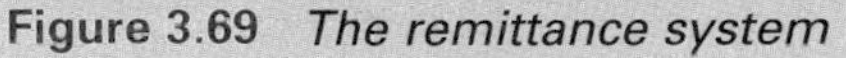

Figure 3.69 *The remittance system*

Ireland – a land with an emigration culture

Ireland has a very long history of emigration. In 1991, the population of the Republic stood at 3.5 million, yet it was estimated that 60 million people worldwide could trace an Irish descent. Emigration rates were particularly high during the nineteenth century, being boosted by famines and political oppression. The emigration trait persists today; it remains the natural thing for younger people to do. Ireland has been described as 'a peripheral country linked to a more developed set of core countries – notably Britain – through migration.' This peripheral status has become so embedded over 300 years that it is hard to break the mould. As the emigration tradition persists, so it remains difficult for Ireland to expand and diversify its economy. At the same time, there are undoubtedly parts of the world benefiting from this Irish 'export'. In the USA, in particular, the Irish have made a significant contribution to the evolution of American culture and identity.

Figure 3.70 *The St Patrick's Day Parade in New York: evidence of a long history of Irish migration*

Australia – the fate of its indigenous population

Australia is a flagship example of a multi-ethnic nation, still drawing immigrants from many parts of the world (see Table 3.18 on page 152). Cities such as Sydney, Melbourne and Brisbane are now reaping the benefits of a multi-cultural society. However, there is a dark chapter in the country's migration history. It concerns the Aborigines and the impact of European migration and colonisation on this indigenous population.

European settlement of Australia from 1788 onwards drastically interfered with Aboriginal economic, social and religious life. At that time, the indigenous population possibly numbered around 750,000. Gradually, their homelands were taken over for farming, mining and urban settlement. The process of colonisation by the Europeans was frequently violent; many Aborigines were killed. More devastating than these killings was the impact of disease. Smallpox, syphilis, TB, measles, influenza and leprosy were all introduced into Australia by migrant settlers and drastically reduced Aboriginal numbers. The remnant members of tribes dispossessed of their lands were reduced to loitering around the new settlements, relying on handouts of food and clothing. They lived in makeshift camps without basic services. Many became addicted to alcohol and tobacco.

Despite the establishment of reservations, usually on unwanted marginal land, and the introduction of protective legislation, the number of Aborigines continued to decline. In 1930 the Aboriginal population reached an all-time low of 300,000. Over the last 30 years, however, their numbers have begun to pick up, helped by the fact that people are now more willing to admit to having Aboriginal ancestry. The population is now around 450,000 and the Aborigines have gained in political strength. Perhaps their greatest achievement to date has been winning back some of their former lands. Today, over one-seventh of Australia's land area is under Aboriginal ownership. Despite this, the greatest concentrations of the indigenous population remain in the cities, in suburbs of low socio-economic status.

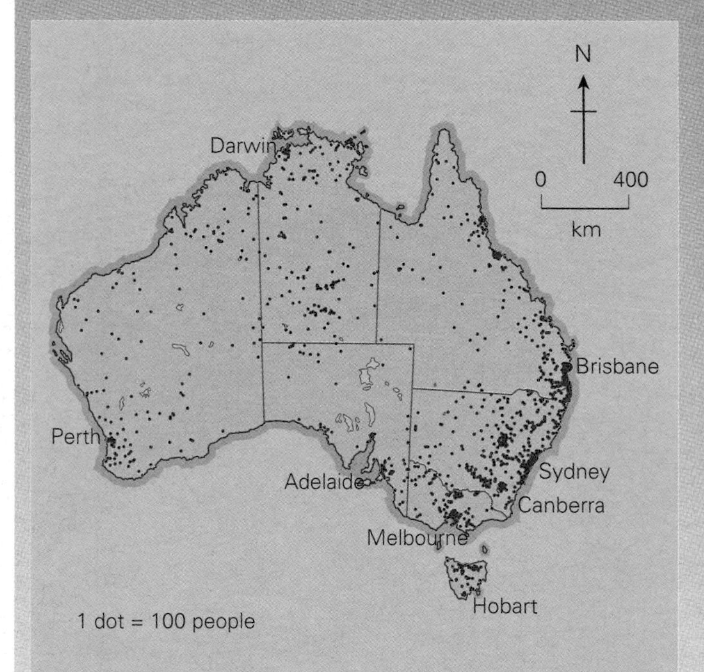

Figure 3.71 *The distribution of the indigenous population of Australia, 1996* Source: *Australian Bureau of Statistics.*

Figure 3.72 *Aboriginal urban dropouts*

Figure 3.73 *Aboriginal athlete Cathy Freeman*

ACTIVITY

1 Study the above case studies with a view to identifying the positive and negative impacts of migration for each.
- Summarise your findings in a table like Table 3.15.
- Which of the case studies do you think had the most positive impact?
- Which of the case studies do you think was most negative in its outcome?

Give reasons for your answers.

9 Key issues of international migration

Given the complex nature of international migration, it is hardly surprising that whilst it creates advantages, it can also give rise to a whole range of problems. These problems are most acute where migration is either forced or tightly controlled by governments (see case studies, pages 143–146). In nearly all such cases, concern centres on the threat to what are known as either 'civil liberties' or 'human rights'.

Freedom of movement

In an ideal world, everyone should have the right to migrate. With a few notable exceptions, this is normally guaranteed within individual countries. It is when migration crosses international boundaries that problems can occur. There is an inevitable tension between the right to migrate and government control over the movement of people across its frontiers. A government's prime duty is to protect the national good. This may involve controlling immigration so as to avoid problems caused when the speed or volume of immigration gets out of hand. The best examples are provided by emergency situations caused by natural hazards or political strife:

- the million or more people who, within only five days in 1994, fled the genocide in Rwanda to seek sanctuary in neighbouring Zaire and Tanzania
- the mass exodus of the 'boat people' from Vietnam after the communists overran the country in 1975; over 50,000 of them headed for tiny and congested Hong Kong.

Legitimate government intervention may also involve restricting emigration, particularly if it is likely to debilitate the country. In practice, it may be that there can rarely be a true freedom of international movement.

The Wall comes tumbling down

The Berlin Wall and hundreds of kilometres of security fence were built by the communists to keep the two parts of a divided Germany apart. They remain as vivid symbols of a political assault on freedom of movement. The Wall and the security fence were built to prevent East Germans from leaving for West Germany.

With the gradual collapse of communism in Eastern Europe, the Berlin Wall was opened for the first time in November 1989. During the course of one weekend, tens of thousands of East Germans rushed across the border. They did so, laden with as many belongings as they could carry. In their rush to escape (thinking that the opening of the Wall would be short-lived), they abandoned their homes and even their children. Within a week, 9.5 million of East Germany's total population of nearly 17 million had applied for and been granted an exit visa to visit West Germany.

Today, Germany is reunited and all Germans are free to move both within and outside the country

Figure 3.74 *The Berlin Wall – a symbol of a political assault on freedom of movement*

ACTIVITIES

1. With your fellow students, debate the proposition that 'governments have the right to control international migration'.
2. Find out what happened to the Vietnamese boat people who headed for Hong Kong.

The right to work

The right to work is akin to freedom of movement. Whether it is a human right is also debatable. Everyone should have an equal opportunity to find legitimate work, but can this right be guaranteed if a person looks for work in another country? Clearly, there is much to be gained, both by the individual and the host country if there are vacant jobs to be filled. As the Turkish guest worker case study (page 144) clearly shows, everything is fine as long as the demand persists. But what happens when there is an economic downturn and workers are laid off? Are the immigrant workers paid unemployment benefit? Do they volunteer to move on to some other worker-hungry location? Or are they forced to move on by the government? We live in an age of globalisation. Ideally, this means two things as far as employment and labour are concerned. Firms need to be free to move in search of labour; equally labour needs to be free to move in search of employment.

ACTIVITIES

1. Identify some of the advantages and disadvantages of allowing an unimpeded international movement of labour.
2. On an outline map of the EU, plot the data in Table 3.16 by means of proportional flow lines. Write a brief account based on your completed map.

The movement of labour within the European Union

One of the features of the European Union is its open-door policy. This means that citizens of member states are free to move between member states in pursuit of work. In the 1970s and 1980s, there were large movements of workers from southern countries such as Greece, Spain and Portugal heading mainly in the direction of West Germany.

Table 3.16 shows migration within the EU involving the UK. The figures suggest there has not been a major movement in the direction of the UK (other than from the Irish Republic). This may be due to high unemployment in the UK from 1980 to 1994. It can also be seen that the UK has not been a significant exporter of people (other than to Germany).

	UK nationals living in other EU states (000s)	EU nationals living in UK (000s)
Germany	117	62
Irish Republic	64	443
France	50	59
Netherlands	39	29
Belgium	26	5
Italy	23	82
Greece	14	21
Denmark	13	13
Portugal	12	26
Sweden	12	18
Spain	7	34
Luxembourg	4	–
Austria	3	9
Finland	2	4
TOTAL	386	845

Table 3.16 *Migration within the European Union involving the UK, 1996*
Source: *Office of National Statistics, Social Trends,* 1998.

Other human rights that need to be respected

While it may not be possible to guarantee freedom of movement and the right to work for the reasons just outlined, there are other rights that certainly need to be respected. These are the human rights of freedom of speech, freedom of worship and equal opportunities. The denial of such rights has certainly been a powerful push factor in international migration. Some of the worst abuses in recent years have been perpetrated under the name of **ethnic cleansing**, as in parts of former Yugoslavia.

The denial of civil liberties not only triggers emigration. It can also prevail in destination locations, especially where migrants form ethnic minorities within the host nation. This was the case with those immigrants from the Caribbean who entered Britain during the 1950s and 1960s. It has taken much parliamentary legislation to protect their civil liberties and those of their descendants.

Ethnic cleansing in Kosovo

In 1990 Kosovo was an autonomous province of Yugoslavia. With the collapse of communist control in 1991 and the break-up of Yugoslavia as a nation state, Kosovo reluctantly became part of an enlarged Serbia (Figure 3.75). The basic problem was that of Kosovo's two million people, 90 per cent were ethnic Albanians and only 6 per cent Serbian. The Kosovo Liberation Army (KLA), supported by the majority of ethnic Albanians, came out in open rebellion against Serbian rule. In reprisal, the Serbian Government started to victimise anyone thought to be a KLA sympathiser. The international community, while supporting the idea of greater autonomy for the Albanian community, opposed the KLA's demand for complete independence. The Serbian strategy was to rid the province of its Albanian connection by 'persuading' those of Albanian stock to emigrate to Macedonia or Albania. In short, the Serbians were in the business of ethnic cleansing (by killing and forced migration), as they had been earlier in neighbouring Bosnia-Hercegovina.

Threats of military action by NATO if Serbia did not stop this ethnic cleansing went unheeded. Eventually, in March 1999 NATO launched a series of air strikes against military targets in Kosovo and Serbia. Fears of more genocide by the Serbians, in retaliation for the air strikes, drove tens of thousands of ethnic Albanians to flee the country. There were graphic accounts of killings, atrocities and looting being carried out by the Serbian forces. Within a few days Kosovo was drained of many of its ethnic Albanians.

In 1999, the Serbian forces, under military pressure, agreed to withdraw. Albanian refugees began slowly to return to their homes under NATO protection. The Serbian population became the target of revenge attacks by the returning Albanians. Fearful for their lives, many fled from Kosovo, and so the process of ethnic cleansing continued, but now with a different target group.

There are no reliable statistics for the number of people now living in Kosovo and the ethnic composition of the population. A double dose of intense ethnic cleansing is bound to have had great effect. The sad part of this case is that both communities had lived peacefully side by side for 45 years under the communist regime.

ACTIVITIES

1 Write your own definition of ethnic cleansing.
2 Research examples of ethnic cleansing based on differences other than religion.

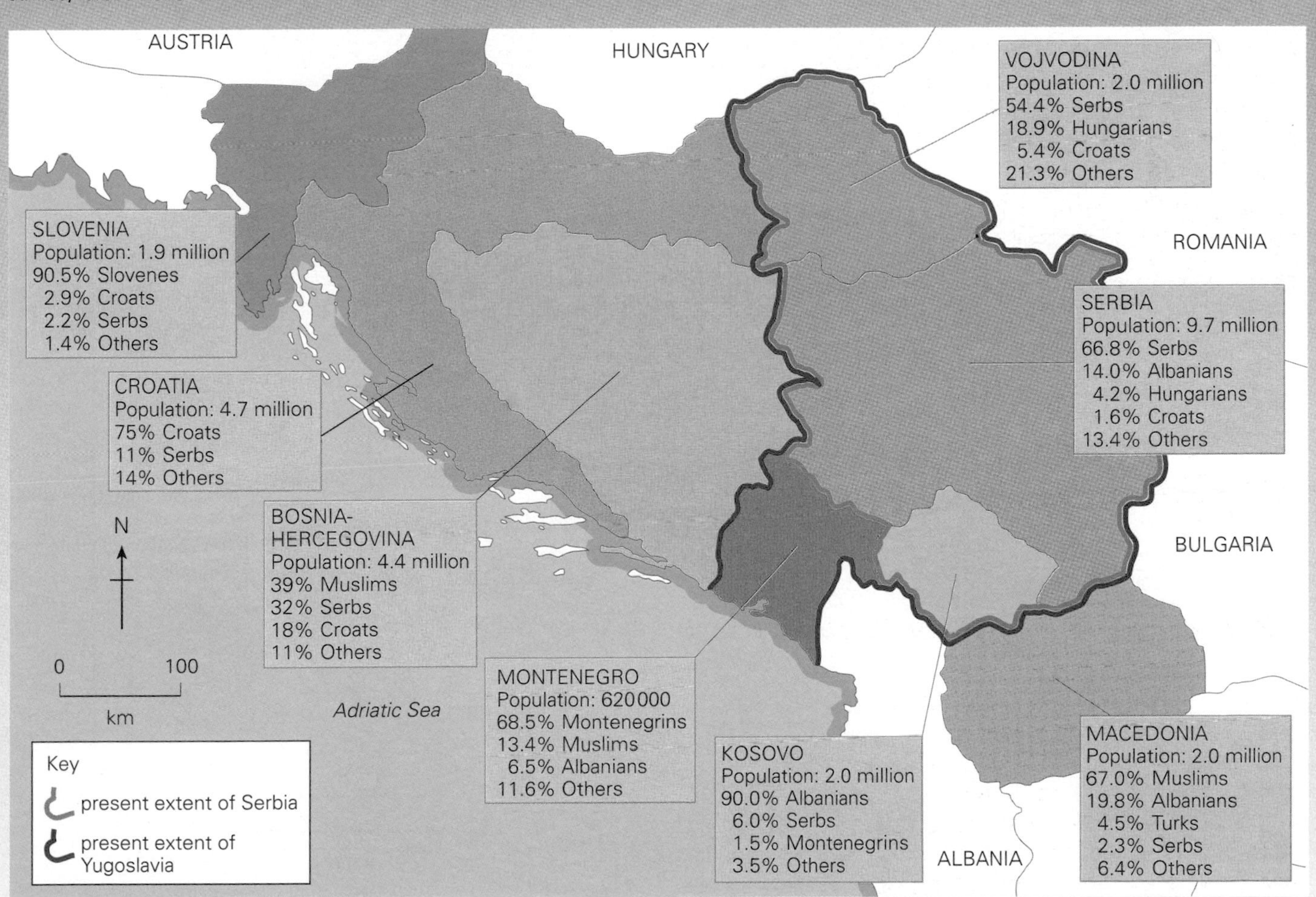

Figure 3.75 *Kosovo: its place in former and present Yugoslavia. The data are for 1990 and show the ethnic composition of Yugoslavia before its break-up.*

Refugees

Activities such as ethnic cleansing and wars create great floods of refugees. These are people who cannot return to their home country because of a fear of persecution for reasons of race, religion, nationality, political beliefs or social grouping. Figure 3.3 shows that a large proportion of the world's refugees originated in African countries. It is interesting to compare that map with Figure 3.76 showing refugee destinations.

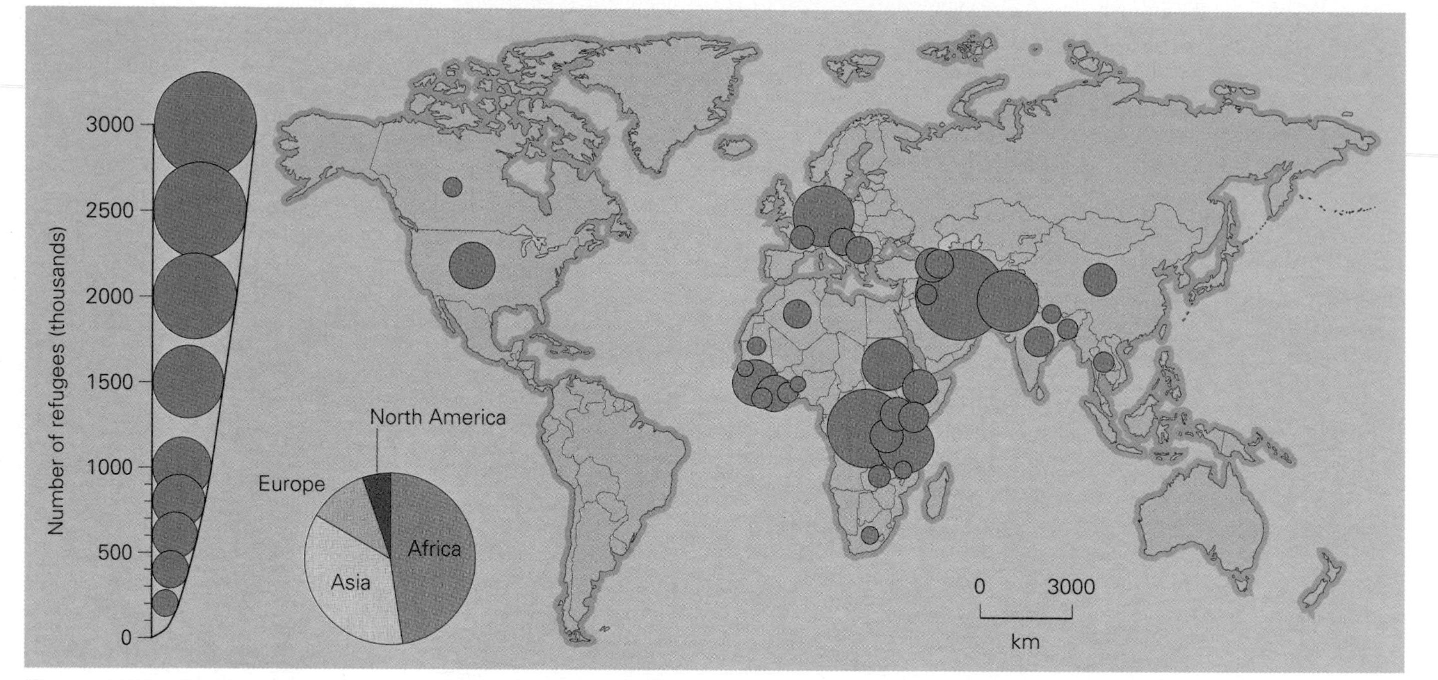

Figure 3.76 *The location of the world's refugees, 1995* Source: Boyle et al, *Exploring Contemporary Migration,* Longman, 1998.

The migration waves of the Gulf War

The Gulf War (1990–1991) illustrates how war can be a powerful migration trigger, and how people can easily become pawns in power games. The war was started when Iraq invaded Kuwait and then threatened Saudi Arabia. The situation quickly generated several huge waves of refugee movement. involving around 5 million people.

In the first wave, between August and December 1990, over 1 million foreign workers and professionals left Kuwait fearing for their safety under Iraqi rule. At the same time, Saudi Arabia harassed 850,000 Yemenis out of the country as a reprisal for the Yemen's support of the Iraqi invasion.

In the second wave, between April and May 1991, Kurds began to flee from Iraq to escape persecution and genocide. Two million tried to leave the country, with 1.3 million crossing into Iran and a further 500,000 entering Turkey.

The third wave began after the defeat and expulsion of Iraqi forces from Kuwait. Thousands of Palestinian and other workers fled from Kuwait because of persecution by the Kuwaiti militia.

Thus the territorial ambitions of one country led to the forced migration of 5 million people from 15 different nationalities, within less than one year. Much of the migration was motivated by fear (real or imagined).

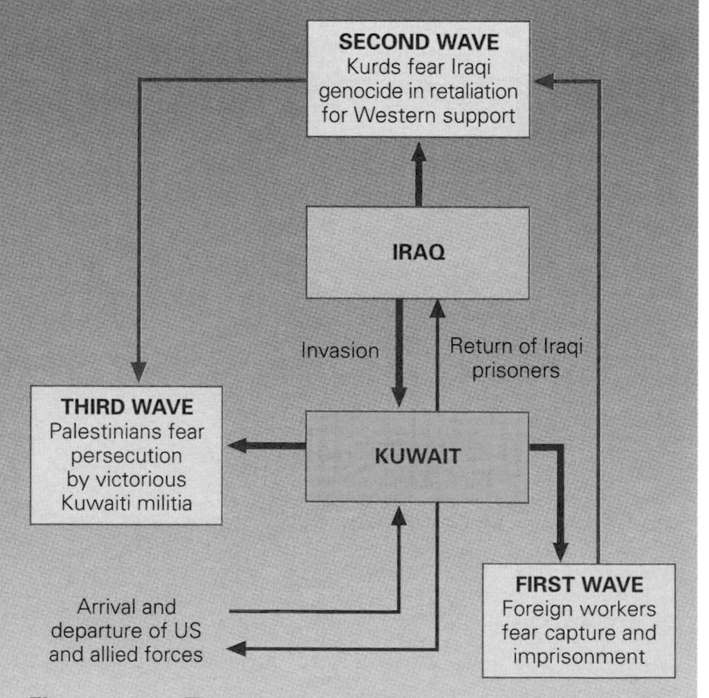

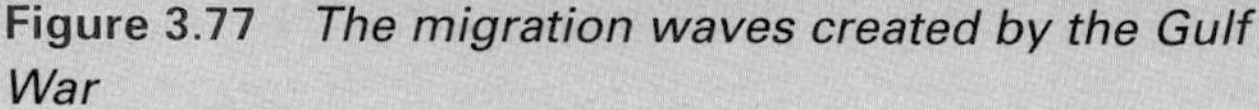

Figure 3.77 *The migration waves created by the Gulf War*

ACTIVITIES

1. Suggest reasons for the global refugee pattern shown in Figure 3.3.
2. Write a brief account comparing the patterns shown in Figures 3.3 and 3.76.
3. Represent the data in Figures 3.3 and 3.76 as a flow map.

Political asylum

Perhaps the thorniest of issues associated with international refugees is that of political asylum. Having been forced out of one country, where do refugees go? There are countries which are prepared to grant asylum to anyone whose survival or well-being is seriously threatened if they remain where they are. Equally, there are countries who regard all refugees as potential illegal immigrants. The trouble in today's world is that any country with a liberal attitude toward asylum-seekers quickly becomes a honeypot destination for refugees. The UK has recently tightened up the rules that apply to asylum-seekers. This has been caused by a marked rise in the number of refugees trying to enter the country. Many come from former Yugoslavia and Eastern Europe. The basic problem is how to distinguish between genuine asylum-seekers (people forced to migrate) and those who simply wish to move to a country perceived as offering a better life style.

Asylum-seekers in the UK

In 1998, a total of 31,600 requests for asylum in the UK were considered and 46,000 new asylum-seekers entered the country (Table 3.17). About 70 per cent of the requests were refused. Only 15 per cent were recognised as political refugees and granted asylum. The remainder were not recognised as refugees, but were granted exceptional leave to remain. There has certainly been a marked rise in the number of people seeking asylum. A recent survey revealed that immigration and asylum now ranks fourth behind health, education and employment as the most serious issue facing Britain.

Figure 3.78 *'I blame the government for letting too many immigrants in'* Source: *The Times*, 20 April 2000.

	Asylum-seekers (000s)	**Immigrants (including asylum-seekers) accepted for settlement** (000s)
Europe	17.7	7.6
Africa	12.4	16.1
Asia	11.2	30.1
Middle East	2.8	0.2
Americas	1.0	10.8
Oceania		-3.7
Others	0.9	1.8
TOTAL	**46.0**	**69.8**

Table 3.17 *Entry into the UK, 1998*
Source: *Office of National Statistics, Social Trends*, 1998.

The issues raised in this section show that migration, particularly international migration, has its challenges. However, we should not be drawn into thinking that there is a huge and unsatisfied wish to migrate being thwarted by governments. Instead, we should remember that there are strong forces that tie people to their home areas. There is personal security to be found in living in familiar surroundings along with friends and relatives. These ties are often so strong as to discourage migration, even where migration may offer many benefits. For most people, therefore, deciding to emigrate requires a very powerful combination of push and pull factors.

ACTIVITY

1 Set out the arguments for and against the UK Government tightening up on asylum seekers. You could organise this as a debate, with some people speaking for and some against the tightening up approach. Research your speeches carefully, using resources such as www.bbc.co.uk/news

This concludes the discussion of global challenges relating to population. There is little room for optimism as regards meeting the five challenges introduced in section 1. The slowing down of the global growth rate is the single most important achievement to date. The next chapter moves on to look at the economic world, but we should not forget that people play a vital role in it. People create many of the demands and provide the labour that drives the global economy. People make the decisions, be it through government or business, that shape growth and change in the global economy.

EXTENSION ACTIVITY

Australia has a rich cultural diversity. The 1996 Census recorded that 3.9 million of its 18.3 million people had been born overseas in one of over 200 countries. A further 3.8 million had one or both parents born overseas. There were 2.6 million people who spoke a language other than English at home. The census recognised 96 religious denominations as well as 282 major languages within the population (including 170 Aboriginal languages).

	1983	1988	1993	1998
Population (millions)	14.9	16.5	17.7	18.5
Birth rate Death rate Natural increase	16/1000 7/1000 9/1000			14/1000 7/1000 7/1000
Arrivals Permanent settlers	469,671	495,919	571,952	419,414
Departures Permanent settlers	112,657	103,181	137,662	144,740
Net im-migration	357,014	392,738	434,290	274,674

Table 3.18 *Components of population change in Australia, 1983–1998*

Using the data provided, write an analytical account of Australian immigration. You should include in your report what you see as the main benefits and challenges of Australian immigration. Illustrate your report with appropriate diagrams.

Country	Settlers (000s)	Percentage of all settlers
	1964–1968	
UK and Ireland	361.6	50.4
Greece	67.0	9.3
Italy	63.2	8.8
Yugoslavia	38.5	5.4
Germany	18.3	2.5
Malta	16.5	2.3
	1974–1978	
UK and Ireland	142.6	35.8
New Zealand	22.6	5.7
Lebanon	21.7	5.4
Yugoslavia	15.5	3.9
Greece	10.5	2.6
USA	10.1	2.5
	1984–1988	
UK and Ireland	91.9	18.5
New Zealand	62.6	12.6
Vietnam	37.8	7.6
Philippines	27.0	5.4
South Africa	14.7	3.0
Poland	7.7	1.5
	1994–1998	
New Zealand	58.3	13.9
UK and Ireland	53.6	12.8
China	29.8	7.1
Vietnam	19.4	4.6
Hong Kong	19.0	4.5
Philippines	17.1	4.1

Table 3.19 *The top sources of Australian immigrants*

Chapter Four: Globalisation and the global economy

1 Introduction

A look around the average family home in any economically developed country produces evidence that we live in an age of globalisation. The clues may include:

- a TV and video (made in Taiwan)
- a holiday brochure about package holidays abroad
- a PC (made in Malaysia) with its connection to the Internet
- apples (grown in South Africa)
- a Nissan car (assembled in Gateshead)
- the mother's voluntary work at the nearby OXFAM shop
- the daughter's job in a UK branch of a US investment bank
- the son's plans to take a 'gap year' travelling the world after he leaves school.

Whether we like it or not, we are increasingly plugging into an economic system that operates at a global scale. According to World Bank estimates, less than 10 per cent of the world's labour force now remains isolated from this expanding system that increasingly links together all the countries of the world. The basic business of this **global economy** is the world-wide exploitation of resources, and the world-wide production and marketing of goods and services.

No matter where we live, our primary concern is to have access to the basic necessities of life, i.e. adequate shelter, food and clothing. This is true whether we live in Banjul or Birmingham. For some people, perhaps more so in less economically developed countries (LEDCs), the key is having enough land to be self-sufficient. For the majority, however, the key requirement is work. Today, most jobs are increasingly influenced by the state of the global economy. Therefore, so too are our well-being and quality of life.

The growth of the global economy is widely referred to as **globalisation**, or more correctly, **economic globalisation**. Globalisation refers to any process of change operating at a world scale and having world-wide effects. It could be physical (e.g. sea-level change) or human (e.g. economic development) or both (e.g. global warming). Such processes are geographical because they have the potential to affect much of the Earth's environment and people. They can also lead to different outcomes in different parts of the world. For example, the climates of the world are changing, but the precise nature of that change varies from place to place. Similarly, while economic globalisation is causing the economies of the world to move closer together, it, too, is having impacts that vary from place to place.

The impact of globalisation on the working lives of three people

1. Joe lives in a small town in southern Texas. He used to work as an accounts clerk in a textile firm. The firm eventually went out of business as cheap imports from Mexico forced textile prices down. Joe went back to college to study business administration and now works for a Japanese factory recently set up in the area.
2. Pedro runs a small car upholstery business in a town in central Mexico. Sometimes, when work is short, he crosses the US border illegally and helps to harvest crops on farms in California. His wife, Maria, now works for a US-owned firm in one of Mexico's 'maquiladoras' (duty-free manufacturing centres close to the US border).
3. Xiaopei is a factory worker in Shenzen, a Special Economic Zone in China. After fleeing the poverty of nearby Sichuan Province and becoming part of China's floating population, she has eventually found work. This is with a new firm from Hong Kong that produces clothing for the US and Japanese markets.

Figure 4.1 *Three citizens of globalisation: Joe, Pedro and Xiaopei*

ACTIVITIES

1. Take a look at your own home and family, and list those things that you think show evidence of globalisation.
2. Explain why a secure job may be so important to a person's well-being and quality of life.

What are the main global economic groupings?

All countries are united by the fact that they undergo development. At the same time, they differ in terms of the degree to which they are developed. Development has been likened to an electric cable. The power which countries need to drive them from primitive to more advanced states passes through a development cable (Figure 4.2). The core of the cable is made up of economic growth, technology and enterprise. The outer casing of the cable is composed of many different strands. The strands represent different aspects of the development process as a whole. It is vital to understand that development is not only about economic progress.

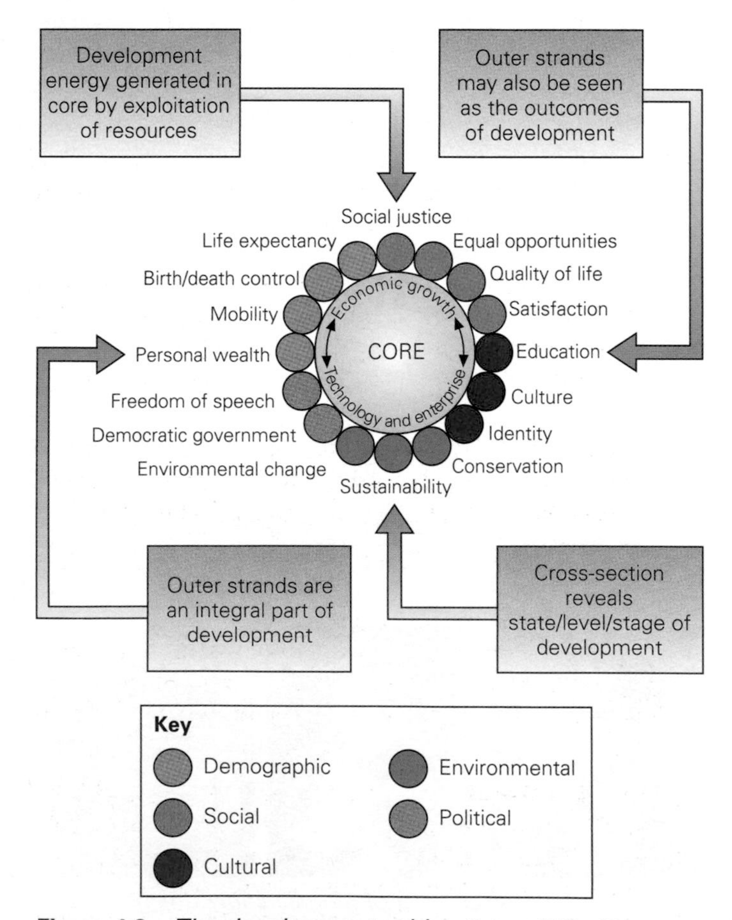

Figure 4.2 *The development cable* Source: Witherick, *Development, Disparity and Dependence*, Stanley Thornes, 1998.

Development may also be likened to a pathway leading from primitive to advanced development (Figure 4.3). Countries move along that pathway at different speeds, and as a consequence are spread out along it, although there is a tendency for them to cluster into groups.

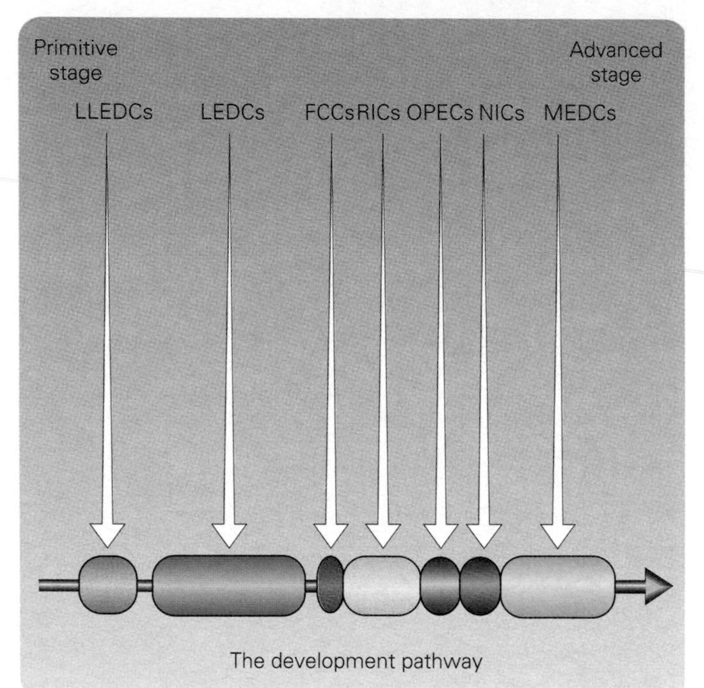

Figure 4.3 *The development pathway*

Two main groups are recognised: more economically-developed countries (MEDCs) and less economically-developed countries (LEDCs). The MEDCs are the countries furthest along the development pathway. For most of them the driving force has been industrial development and their populations enjoy the highest standards of living. In contrast, the LEDCs survive mainly on agriculture, much of it of a subsistence nature and at best supporting only a modest standard of living.

It is important to understand that the development pathway idea is a generalisation. There may be more than one path to development, especially if the development process is sensitive to the specific conditions that exist in a particular country. For example, LEDCs may follow different paths to development than MEDCs.

ACTIVITIES

1. Explain what is meant when it is said that development is not only about economic progress.
2. List other ways in which you think MEDCs differ from LEDCs. You might work under the headings of: population, economy, social conditions.

Other groupings can be recognised along the development pathway (Figure 4.3). Countries lagging behind the main LEDC cluster are the least economically-developed countries (LLEDCs). Here the development process can be so slow as to be almost negligible (Table 4.1). These are the poorest countries in the world and most are found in Africa.

Countries breaking away from the LEDC group, where the pace of development is speeding up, are closing the gap between themselves and the MEDCs. They are sometimes referred to as 'middle-income' countries, but this single term seems to embrace three small groups: the newly-industrialising countries (NICs), the recently-industrialised countries (RICs) and the oil and petroleum exporting countries (OPECs) (Figure 4.3). The NICs and RICs are similar in that development is based on manufacturing, but there is a difference in the timing of development and therefore position along the development pathway. The NICs started their modern industrialisation in the 1960s, whereas in the RICs the process began in the late 1980s and 1990s.

	GNP per capita (1995)	**Mean annual growth of real GNP** (1985–1995)	**Human develop-ment index** (1995)	**Food intake** (1995) (calories per day)
LLEDCs				
Ethiopia	$100	–0.5%	0.244	1,610
Nepal	$200	2.4%	0.347	1,957
LEDCs				
Bangladesh	$1,380	2.1%	0.368	2,019
Morocco	$1,110	0.8%	0.566	2,984
FCCs				
Russia	$2,240	–5.1%	0.792	no data
Hungary	$4,120	–1.0%	0.857	3,503
RICs				
Thailand	$2,740	8.4%	0.833	2,432
Chile	$4,160	6.1%	0.891	2,582
OPECs				
Saudi Arabia	$7,040	–1.9%	0.774	2,735
Venezuela	$3,020	0.5%	0.861	2,618
NICs				
South Korea	$9,700	7.6%	0.890	3,285
Portugal	$9,740	3.7%	0.890	3,634
MEDCs				
UK	$18,700	1.4%	0.931	3,317
USA	$26,980	1.4%	0.942	3,732

Table 4.1 *Profiles of countries representing the main economic groupings*

The final group shown in Figure 4.3 comprises those former communist countries (FCCs) that are now struggling to convert their economies along capitalist lines.

When it comes to investigating the global pattern of development, two measures are widely used:

- **Gross National Product (GNP) per capita** This is the total value of economic production achieved by a country in one year divided by the total population (Figure 4.4).
- **Human Development Index (HDI)** This index was devised by the UN in 1990. It takes into account three variables which are given equal weight: income per capita, adult literacy and life expectancy. It takes the highest and lowest values recorded for each variable by the countries of the world. The interval between those values is in its turn given a value of 1, and then the actual value for each country is scored on a scale of 0 to 1 (from worst to best). The most wealthy MEDCs have an index approaching 0.999 whilst the poorest LLEDCs score around 0.300 (Figure 4.5).

GNP is a good indicator of economic development and wealth. The HDI recognises that there is more to development than just economic progress.

ACTIVITIES

1. Which of the four measures shown in Table 4.1 do you think best distinguishes the economic groupings? Explain why.
2. The table provides an important reminder that economic development can be a faltering process. Suggest possible reasons for the negative values recorded by the mean annual growth of real GNP.

For much of the twentieth century, three major divisions of the world were recognised. The divisions, based mainly on political and economic criteria, may be less valid today, but their titles remain widely used in the media.

- The **First World** comprises those countries, largely MEDCs, where a capitalist system prevails, as in Western Europe, North America and Australasia. Although described generally as **free market economies**, in virtually all countries there is a varying degree of government intervention.

- The **Second World** consists of those socialist and communist countries where government economic control is paramount. These include a mix of MEDCs and LEDCs. The break-up of the Soviet Union in the early 1990s and the communist bloc of Eastern European states in 1985 to 1995 started a process of economic restructuring. The collapse of communism allowed former communist countries to move towards capitalism and the First World, thus the extent of the Second World has declined. Only a small number of countries such as China, North Korea, Vietnam and Cuba remain as Second World countries.
- The **Third World** embraces those relatively poor and under-developed countries (LLEDCs and LEDCs) located mainly in Asia, Africa and South America. Many have recently achieved political independence from colonial powers and are being drawn into the global economy.

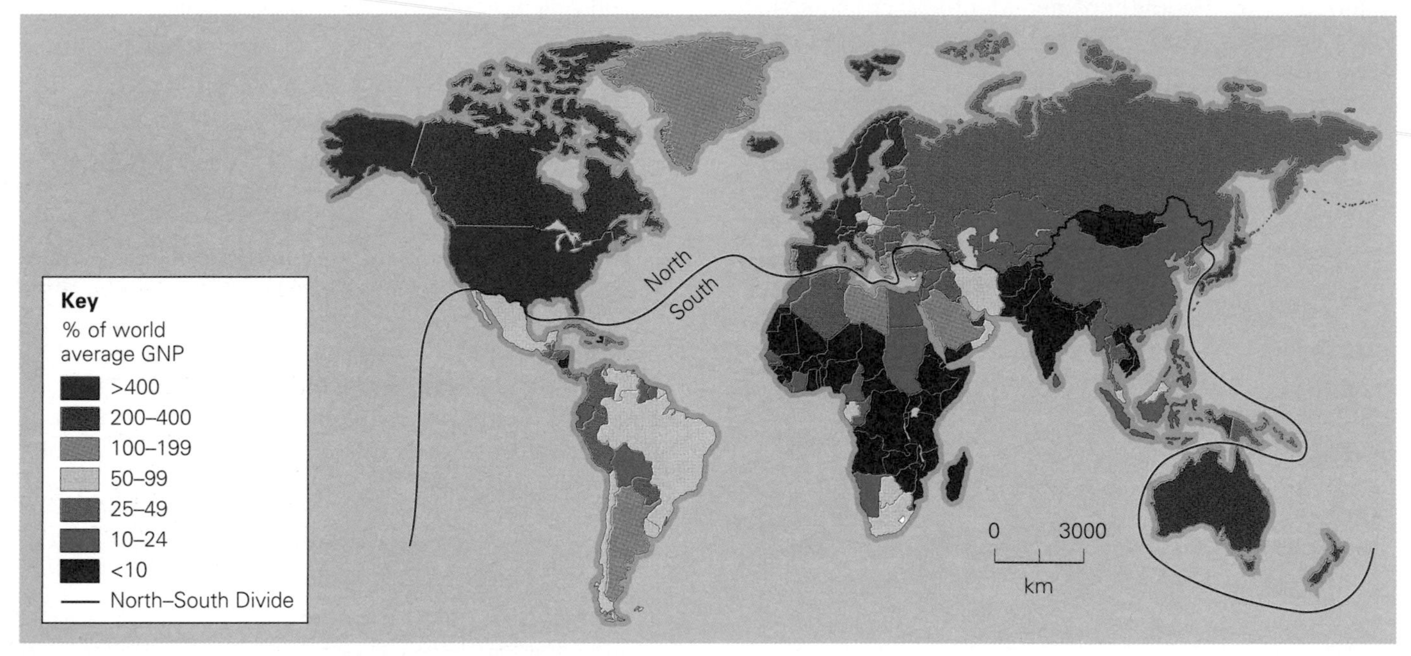

Figure 4.4 *The global distribution of economic wealth (GNP)*
Source: *Philip's Modern School Atlas, 92nd Edition*, 1998.

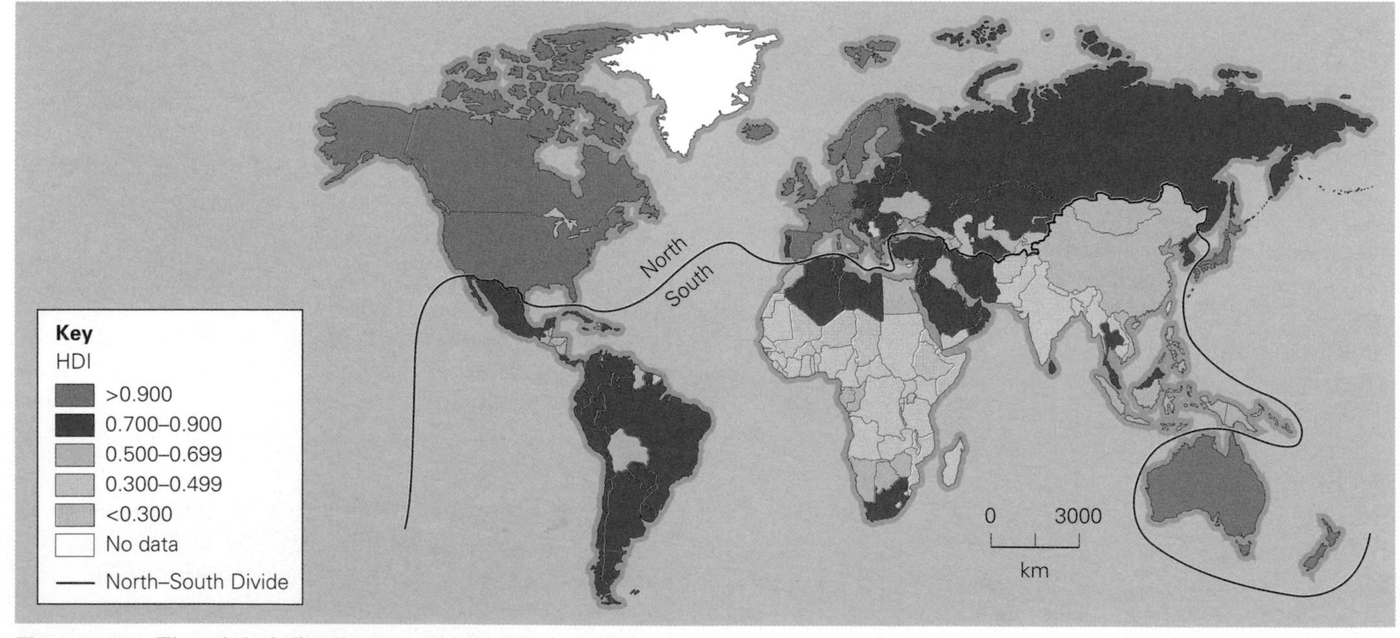

Figure 4.5 *The global distribution of HDI (Human Development Index) values*
Source: *Philip's Modern School Atlas, 92nd Edition*, 1998.

A line has been drawn on Figures 4.4 and 4.5 to show another subdivision of the world that is widely recognised. The line (known as the **North–South Divide**) separates the rich North (the MEDCs of temperate latitudes) from the poor South (the LEDCs of the tropics and sub-tropics). Between them lies the **development gap** which we might imagine as the space separating them on the development pathway. During the second half of the twentieth century, the gap between the LEDCs and MEDCs gradually became occupied and filled in by other groups, such as the OPECs, NICs, RICs and FCCs (Figure 4.3).

ACTIVITIES

Compare Figures 4.4 and 4.5.

1 To what extent do they reveal similar patterns?
2 To what extent do they convince you that the North–South Divide is a valid global distinction?

A vital question now needs to be asked. Why are there these differences in development between MEDC and LEDC, between First World and Third World, and between North and South? Why are some countries further along the development pathway than others? The answer lies in the factors identified in Figure 4.6.

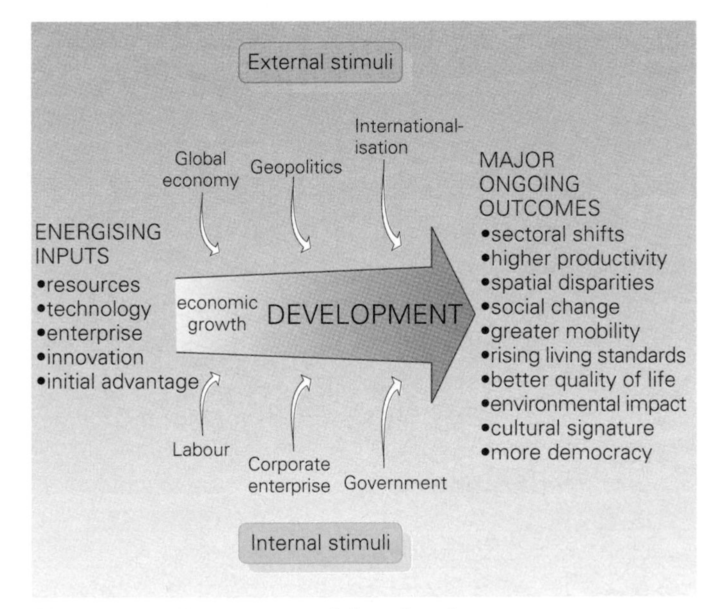

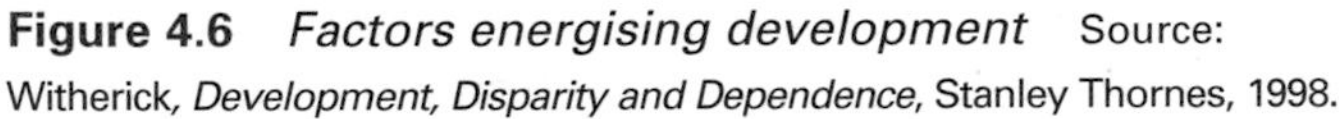

Figure 4.6 *Factors energising development* Source: Witherick, *Development, Disparity and Dependence*, Stanley Thornes, 1998.

The **initial advantage** shown in Figure 4.6 refers to the benefits of being the 'first in the field'. The countries that were the first to industrialise inevitably gained considerable momentum. This momentum has tended to persist and even today helps to keep many of the 'early leader' countries amongst the leading pack of MEDCs. The process of **cumulative causation** also helps maintain momentum. For example, early economic success during the sixteenth to nineteenth centuries gave leading countries political and military strength. This strength allowed these countries to develop their resources and colonise new lands. During the twentieth century, with the gradual decline of colonialism, these same countries have maintained their momentum by becoming influential leaders of trading blocs such as the European Union (EU) or the North American Free Trade Agreement (NAFTA), and of global organisations such as the World Trade Organisation (WTO) or the United Nations (UN).

ACTIVITIES

1 What do you understand by the terms **initial advantage** and **cumulative causation**?
2 Explain and give examples of the 'inputs' and 'stimuli' shown in Figure 4.6.

What links exist between the groupings?

Although the North and South may be separated by the development gap, it would be wrong to think that they are isolated from each other. Links exist between European nations, like the UK, France, Portugal and Spain and their current and former overseas colonies. These links arose for the following reasons (Figure 4.7):

- Trade – importing primary products; exporting goods and services.
- Labour – sending out settlers, civil servants and executives; later bringing in cheap labour.
- Foreign investment – investing particularly in agricultural and mining projects.
- Aid – assisting less-developed parts of the world for motives ranging from 'doing good' to 'being greedy'. The former might be illustrated by the work of missionaries and the latter by the granting of high-interest or 'tied' loans.

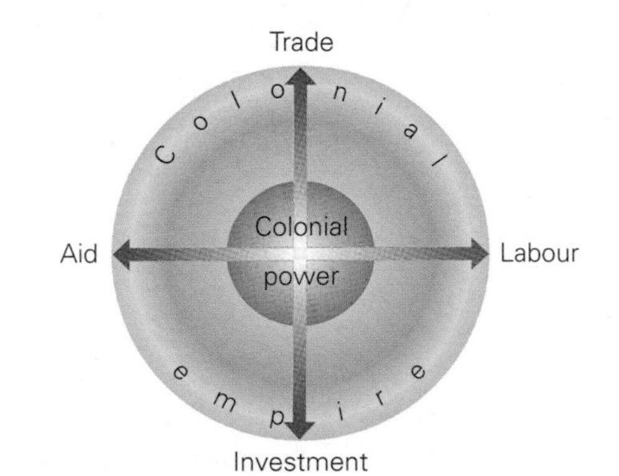

Figure 4.7 *The four traditional links of internationalisation*

In most respects, the outcomes of these traditional links were rather one-sided. The situation was one in which the North (the colonial powers) exploited the South (the colonies). That bias has shifted very little, if at all, in today's world. Nonetheless, there have been other significant changes.

Perhaps most important has been **decolonisation** since the middle of the twentieth century. As the European powers withdrew from their colonies, so ended the North's political domination of the South, but this was soon replaced by an economic domination. Key players in gradually bringing about economic domination have been the huge **transnational corporations** (TNCs). These are multi-business companies that operate in more than one country. With their headquarters firmly in the capitals of the North, the TNCs have developed an increasingly diverse range of business interests spread over an ever-widening area. The TNCs have become the prime movers and shapers of economic globalisation. As major players in the global economy, they can sometimes exercise more power and influence than many national governments.

Decolonisation and the emergence of the TNCs have altered the character of the four traditional links of **internationalisation** (Figure 4.7). But despite these alterations, the benefits of trade, labour movements, investment and aid remain tipped in favour of the North and its MEDCs. The economic playing-field is not a level one. It is the uneven distribution of wealth in the world that not only drives these links, but also determines their flow patterns and balances.

ACTIVITIES

1. Draw a map showing the extent of the British Empire at the end of the nineteenth century. Identify the ways in which the UK benefited from its colonies. What did the colonies gain?
2. Define the following terms: the North-South Divide, decolonisation, transnational corporation. Can you think of some examples of the last term?

In the remainder of this section, the character of these four links binding MEDCs with the rest of the world: trade, labour, foreign investment and aid are briefly examined (Figure 4.8).

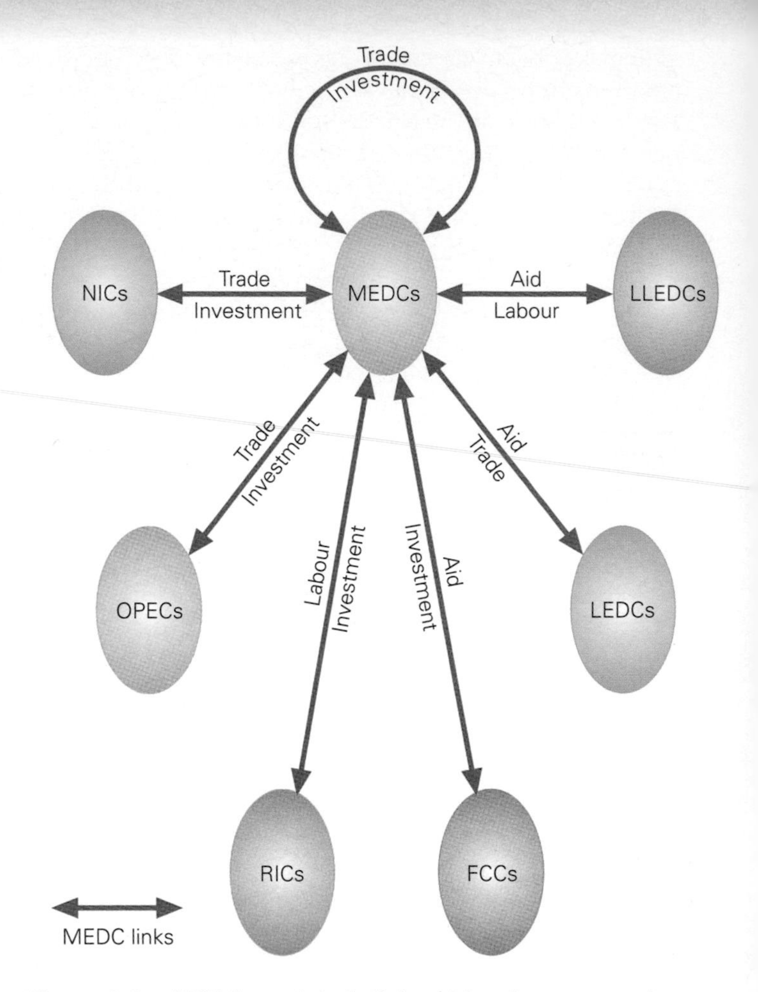

Figure 4.8 *MEDCs and their links with other economic groupings*

Trade

The key features of the global distribution of trade are:

- The volume of global trading is expanding enormously. More and more places are exploiting their resources and selling them on the world market or producing goods that are in global demand.
- Global **visible trading** (trading in resources and products) is dominated by the North (Figure 4.9), but favourable trade balances (exports exceeding imports) are not exclusive to it (Figure 4.10).
- The pattern of world trade is increasingly influenced by three **trading blocs** (groups of countries with formalised trading agreements)(see case study 'The global triad', page 160).
- A rise in **invisible trading** (trading in services) makes this a significant component of global trade (see case study 'The trade in invisibles', page 160)
- Although trade is made up largely of two-way flows of goods and services, the flows between any two countries are rarely evenly balanced (Table 4.2)

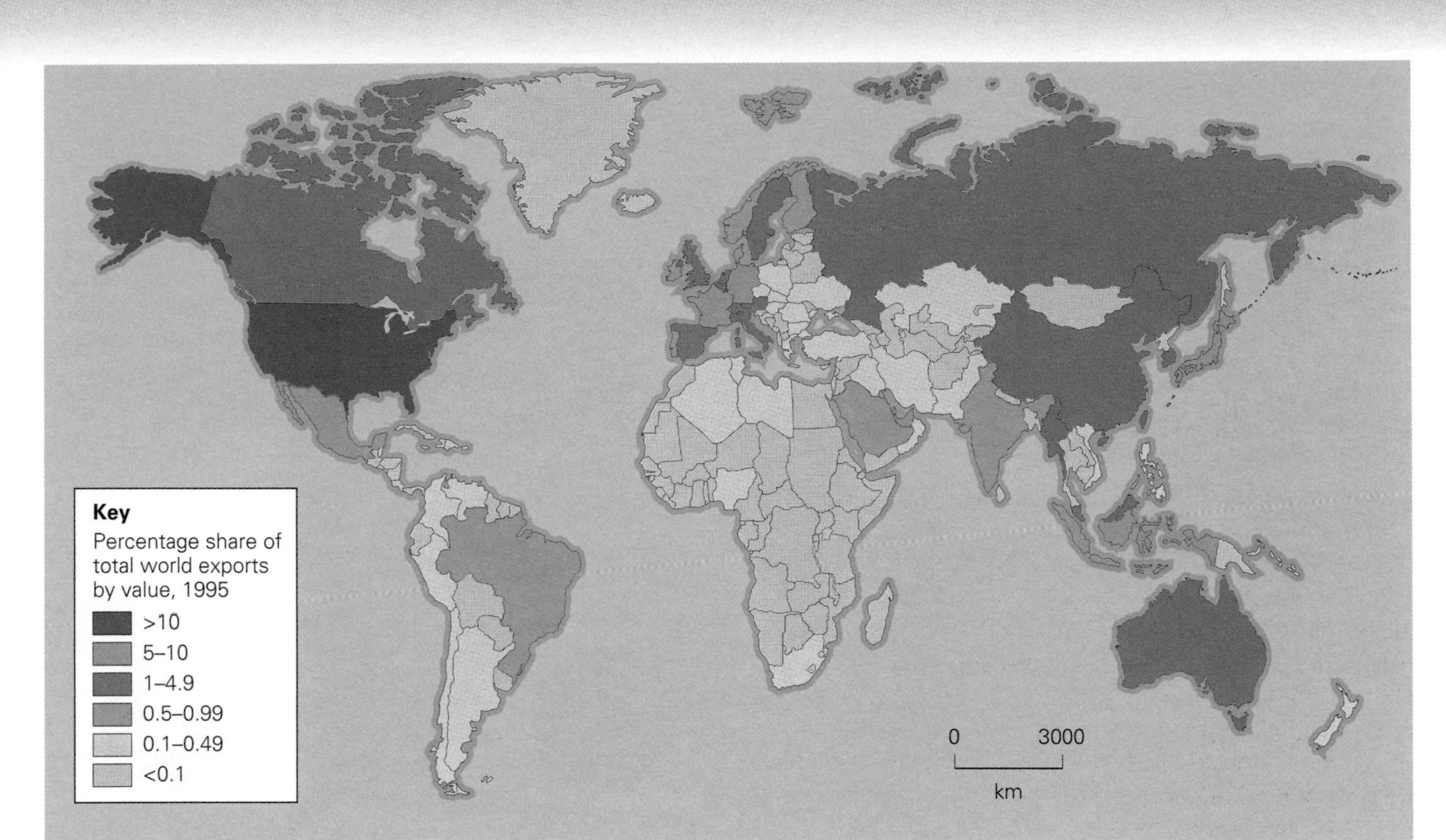

Figure 4.9 *The global distribution of visible trade shares, 1995*
Source: *Philip's Modern School Atlas, 92nd Edition*, 1998.

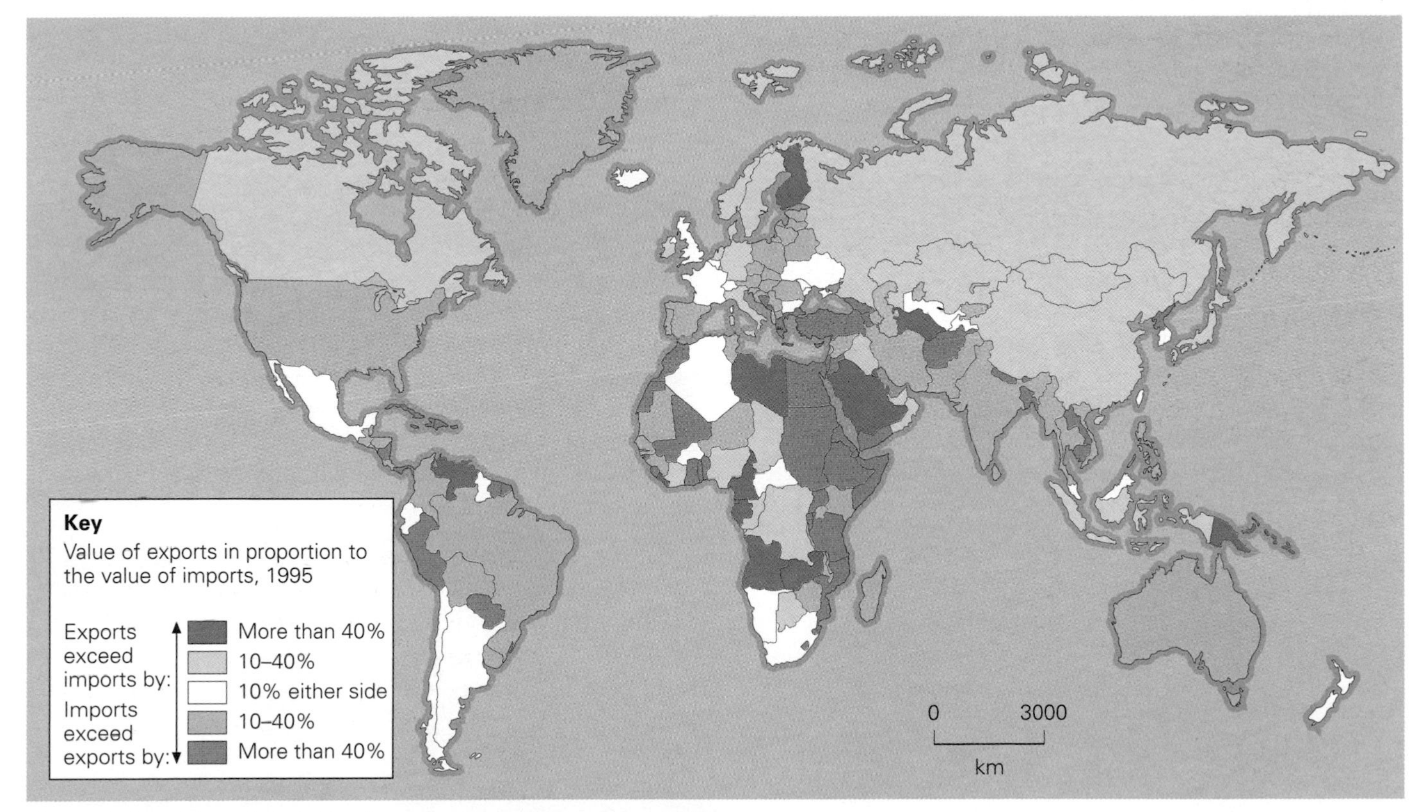

Figure 4.10 *The global distribution of trade balances, 1995*
Source: *Philip's Modern School Atlas, 92nd Edition*, 1998.

The global triad: EU, NAFTA and Asia Pacific

A large proportion of global production, trade and investment is concentrated in three regions: Europe, North America and East Asia. Economic integration within each of these regions has an increasing influence on global trade patterns (Figure 4.11).

The **European Union** (EU) is the most highly developed and complex of the three trading blocs. There are now 15 member states operating a single market (but not yet using a single currency). In theory, there are no trade barriers between these countries, and each country is protected to some degree by the barriers with which the EU has surrounded itself. The EU is constantly enlarging by admitting new members.

The **North American Free Trade Agreement** (NAFTA) was set up in 1994. It aims to eliminate trade and investment restrictions between the USA, Canada and Mexico. NAFTA seeks to bring about an integration of US capital, Canadian resources and Mexican oil and cheap labour.

The **Asia Pacific Economic Cooperation Forum** (APEC) was set up in 1989. There are now 18 member countries which include Japan, the Asian Tigers (South Korea, Taiwan, Singapore and Hong Kong) and the three members of NAFTA. The USA is keen to strengthen its economic and political links with Asia, particularly given the growth of the EU.

While trade within these trading blocs and with independent areas outside them is increasing, trade between the trading blocs decreases. There is now increasing trade tension or friction between the blocs, with talk of trade wars and threats of **protectionism** (erecting trade barriers in order to protect production and employment from foreign competition).

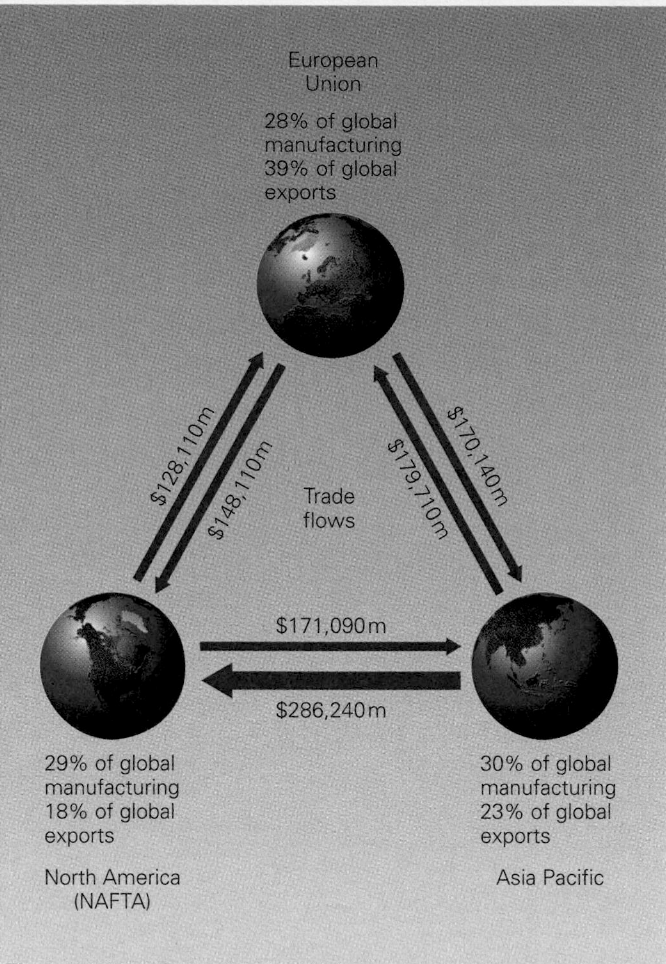

Figure 4.11 *The global triad*

Trade friction goes bananas

Bananas are a source of trade friction between the EU and the banana producers of the USA and Central America. The USA claims that when it comes to buying bananas, member countries of the EU favour producers in their former colonies rather than buying from the cheapest sources. The World Trade Organisation has upheld the American complaint and ordered that sanctions be placed on certain EU exports. This means that certain goods may be subject to 100 per cent duties on entering the USA from the EU. This doubles the price and clearly makes those goods uncompetitive in US shops.

The trade in invisibles

Trade in invisibles involves the export and import of services, including financial services, such as banking and insurance, as well as tourism and international transport. Invisibles account for about a quarter of the total value of world trade. Traditionally, the UK has had a surplus in its invisible trading which has helped to pay for the long-standing deficit in its visible trading. It is interesting to compare Japan, the UK and the USA in terms of their balance of payments, i.e. the difference between visible and invisible trade (Table 4.2).

	Visible trade balance (US$bn)	Invisible trade balance (US$bn)	Balance of payments (US$bn)
Japan	131.02	–15.92	115.10
UK	–19.52	7.28	–12.24
USA	–121.09	53.38	–67.71

Table 4.2 *Mean annual trade balances of Japan, the UK and the USA (1990s)*

ACTIVITIES

1 Explain why:
- USA, Germany, Japan and France have the largest shares of world exports (Figure 4.9)
- invisibles trading is so valuable
- the creation of trading blocs alters the pattern of world trade
- the UK does better in invisible trading than Japan
- the South is characterised by invisible trading deficits.

2 Find out which countries are the main producers and consumers of (a) bananas and (b) tin.

3 Represent the data in Table 4.2 by means of an appropriate diagrammatic technique.

Labour

The key features of the global labour force are:

- more job opportunities are created as the global economy expands
- greater mobility of labour
- wage differentials widening between the North and South, and between the most highly and lowly paid workers in a particular country
- more women in the workforce.

The following case studies illustrate these points.

Shop floor attracts workers of the world

Today, shop floors all over the UK are drawing labour from across the globe. According to the Office of National Statistics, about 400,000 job-seekers, most of them EU citizens, migrated to Britain in 1998. This was more than at any other time on record. Many appear to have been attracted by the relatively high wages and plentiful job opportunities in the UK, particularly in the booming service industry. Shops, restaurants and bars have employed many of these migrant workers.

Of the 29 members of staff at a sandwich bar in London, 2 were British and 16 other nationalities were represented. Four were from Spain; 3 from each of South Korea, Italy and France; 2 from each of Algeria, Denmark and Sweden, and one from each of Portugal, Hungary, Turkey, the USA, Thailand, Jamaica, Nigeria and Pakistan.

Figure 4.12 *The staff of a sandwich bar in London*

Growing use of foreign doctors is 'exploitation'

Out of just over 110,000 doctors currently working in the National Health Service (NHS), about 85,000 are from the UK and the rest come from overseas. Currently, there is a shortfall of GPs, hospital consultants and nurses. Increasingly, doctors and nurses who have been trained abroad are being hired to fill the vacancies. They come mainly from LEDCs, particularly India and Pakistan. The recruitment has been described as 'an abysmal exploitation of the resources of other countries, especially Third World countries.' Certainly, populations badly in need of medical services are losing out.

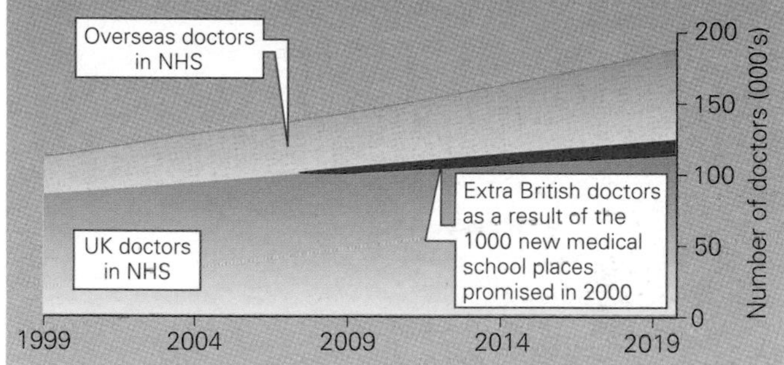

Figure 4.13 *How the NHS relies on overseas doctors*
Source: *The Times*, 8 November 1999.

It is estimated that by 2019 the UK demand for doctors will have risen to 180,000, with one third from overseas (Figure 4.13).

This case study makes the important point that professional people, like manual and service workers, are responsive to spatial differences in wage and salary levels, as well as to opportunities to advance their careers.

Women in the global work force

The growth of the global economy has drawn a huge number of women into employment. Women represent an ever-increasing percentage of the global labour force.

In the South, as men have become more involved in commercial agriculture (much of it producing commodities for the North) and non-farm occupations (often located in towns and cities), women have become increasingly responsible for the production of staple foods. In the North, many of the jobs in the expanding service sector and in the factories that offer flexi-time or part-time working have been taken up by women.

ACTIVITIES

1. Outline the factors that have increased the mobility of labour.
2. Explain the likely effects of widening wage differentials.
3. Suggest reasons why there are more women at work in the UK today than there were 25 years ago.

Foreign investment

Foreign investment describes the various ways in which businesses from one country gain entry to, and become involved in, the business life and markets of another. Since the investment is being made mainly by private-sector companies, ranging in size from small family businesses to giant TNCs, the dominant driving force is profit taking. The more specific motives range from the chance to gain direct access to lucrative foreign markets, to seeking out new sources of energy and raw materials, as well as exploiting cheap labour. The patterns of investment flows can be influenced by government which may either encourage or discourage inward investment (see page 186).

The key features of global foreign investment today are

- a change in capital sources, i.e. a shift from governments to TNCs
- support for the **branch economy** involving the setting up of factories and offices in cheaper (more competitive) locations
- shifts in capital destinations, including the former communist countries (see Romania case study)
- competitive bidding.

Competitive bidding

The demand for foreign investment is high and there is often competition between states (and between communities within the same state) to gain such investment. This competition has intensified over the last 30 years. The greater the competition between potential host countries, the weaker is their position with regard to the potential investor, usually a TNC. Cut-throat bidding allows TNCs to play one state off against another to gain the highest return on their investment. This is good news for the TNC shareholders, but bad news for the host government. In many cases, the latter will be forced to offer various sorts of financial and tax incentives to win the investment.

Romania moves towards a market economy

Romania has lagged behind other Eastern European nations in switching its economy from a centralised communist system to a market capitalist one. The privatisation of state-owned enterprises, many of them in debt or in need of modernisation, only began in the 1990s. Overseas investors have not been keen to invest in the country. This situation is beginning to change as there are signs that Romania has started to make the economic transition.

Figure 4.14 *A steel plant in Romania*

Since 1990, foreign investment has totalled $4 billion. Investors from the Netherlands have put up 15 per cent of that money, followed by investors from Germany (11 per cent), Italy (10 per cent) and France (8 per cent). The French firm Renault has recently acquired a stake in the Romanian car manufacturer Dacia (Figure 4.14). Renault's plans include upgrading technology to improve quality and launching a new model. The output target is 200,000 cars by 2010. This Renault deal is a sign that Romania's privatisation programme is beginning to accelerate. More than 440 companies, including 68 large enterprises, are up for sale. The list includes Romania's largest steel plant, located near the Danube port of Galati, which in 1998 produced more steel than any other plant in Europe. About 20 bids have already been received from foreign investors.

There are clear risks associated with investment in the former communist countries, but the potential returns can be substantial.

ACTIVITIES

1. Suggest reasons why much of the investment behind globalisation is provided by TNCs rather than national governments.
2. Write a definition for the term **branch economy**.
3. What do you think are the particular risks associated with foreign investment in Romania?

Aid

The key features concerned with global aid are:

- an increase in Third World debt
- NGOs and UNO coming to the fore
- a decrease in national giving
- more strings attached.

Factfile on Third World debt

- The debt problem for many Third World countries dates from the 1970s and 1980s. Many LLEDCs and LEDCs borrowed too much and invested it badly. The money was often loaned on a long-term basis by MEDC governments as part of aid programmes, and by global financial institutions like the International Monetary Fund and the World Bank. The economies of these borrowing nations have failed to grow and so have not produced the revenue necessary to pay back the loans or even the interest.
- In 1997 the total debt owed by the South to the North was £1.5 trillion, up from £1 trillion in 1990.
- Each day the South pays the North £475 million in debt service.
- Every baby born in the South owes over £300.
- In many poorer countries, aid grants are dwarfed by the debt burden (Figure 4.15).

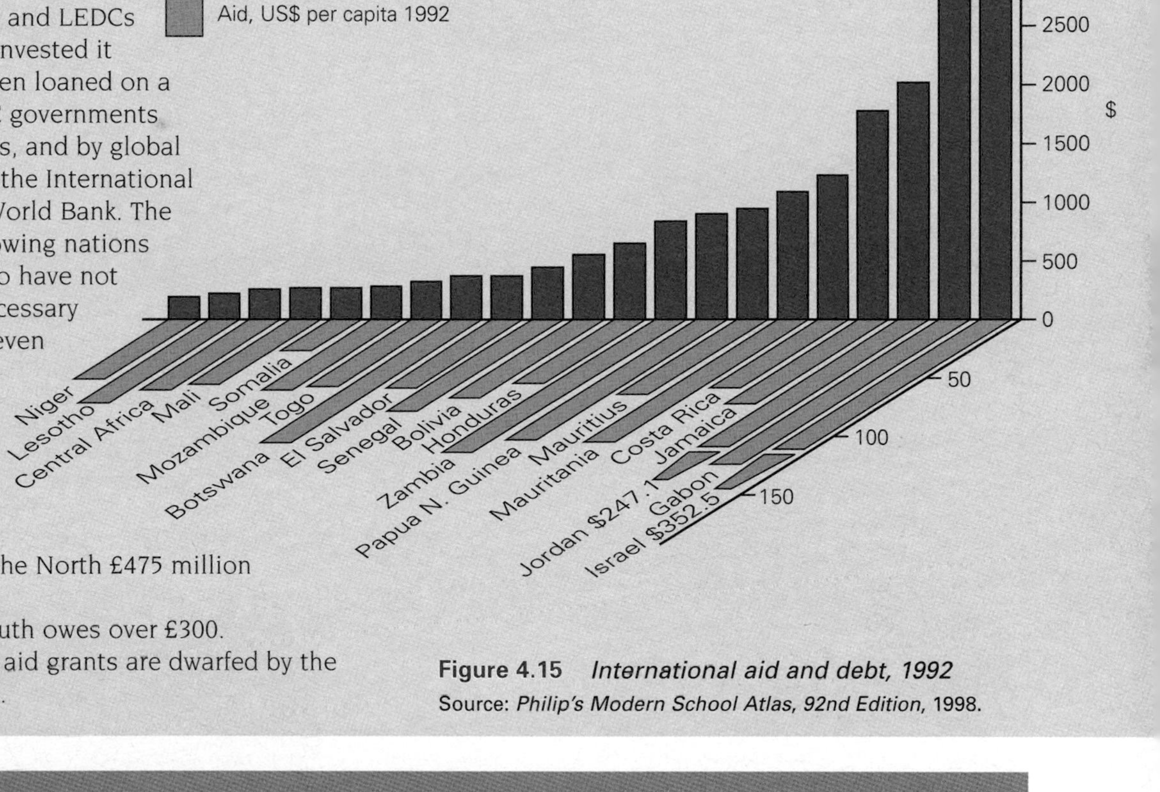

Figure 4.15 *International aid and debt, 1992*
Source: *Philip's Modern School Atlas, 92nd Edition*, 1998.

International aid and GNP

Figure 4.16 shows the top ten aid donors. The Organisation for Economic Cooperation and Development (OECD) has recommended that MEDCs should give aid to the value of 0.7 per cent of GNP. Only four of the top ten donors actually meet that figure. The UK is well down the donor league-table and since 1965 the amount given has fallen from 0.47 to 0.31 per cent of GNP. Over the same period, US aid has dropped from 0.5 to 0.15 per cent. Japan's aid has never exceeded 0.3 per cent of GNP.

The trend is for MEDCs to give less aid (in real terms) and for this shortfall to be met by the UNO and by NGOs like Oxfam, CAFOD and the Red Cross.

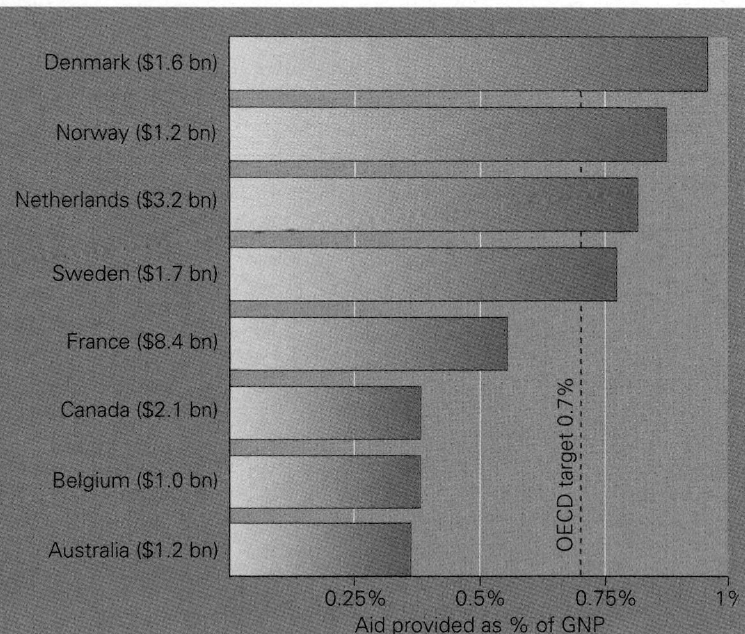

Figure 4.16 *International aid and GNP, 1995*
Source: *Philip's Modern School Atlas, 92nd Edition*, 1998.

Aid with ulterior motives

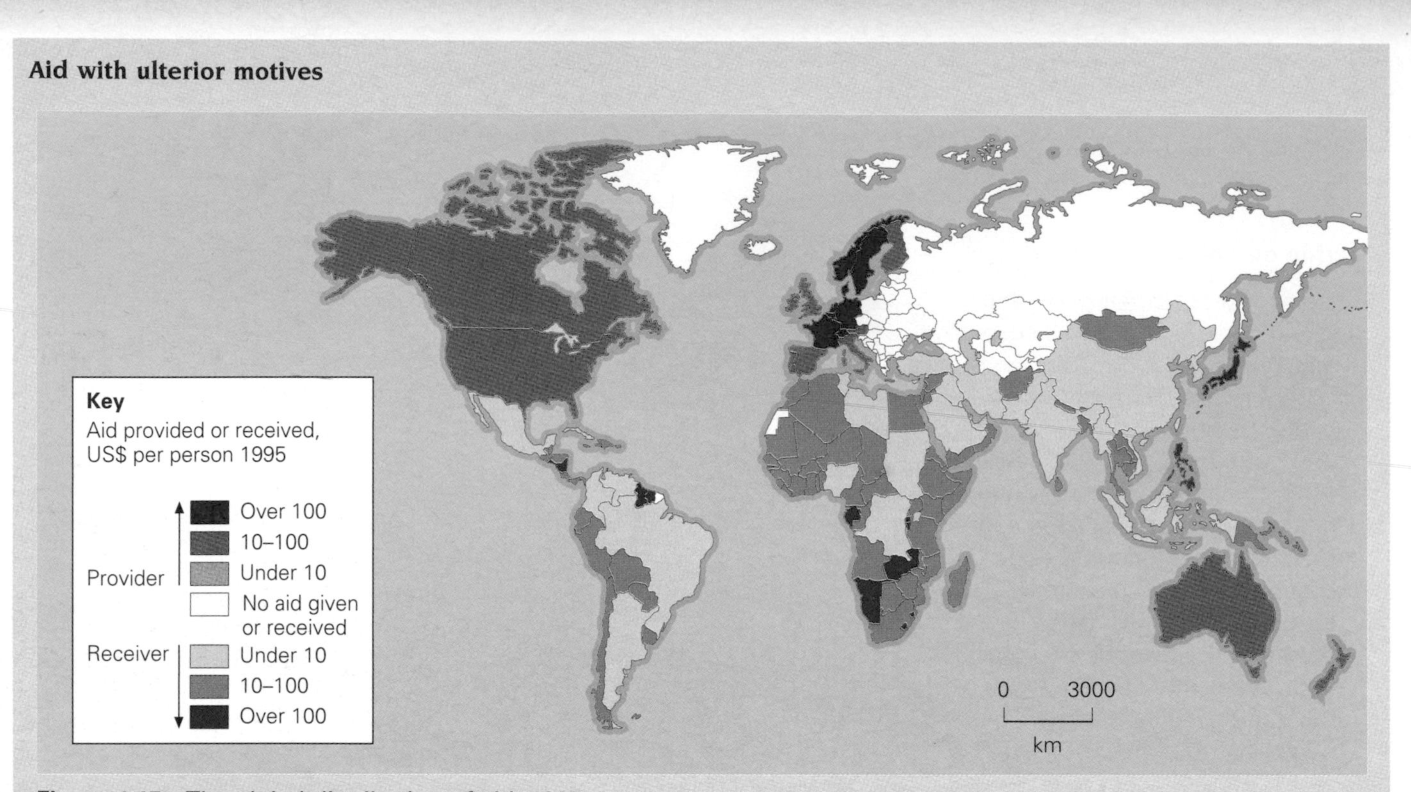

Figure 4.17 *The global distribution of aid, 1995* Source: *Philip's Modern School Atlas, 92nd Edition*, 1998.

The global map of aid distribution has a strong political flavour (Figure 4.17). Although the humanitarian need has not been great, in the past South Korea and South Vietnam (the former capitalist half of Vietnam) have received above-average aid from MEDCs. The reason for this was the desire of Western powers, particularly the USA and UK, to limit the spread of communism.

Bilateral aid (direct aid between two countries) from several countries can also be seen as reflecting particular political hopes and former colonial ties. For example, much British and French aid has been directed towards former African colonies, Japanese aid is distributed mainly within Asia, and aid from OPECs has been directed mainly to Arab countries.

Over the years, scandals have been revealed showing that the giving of aid has often had strings attached. A recent example was the UK's grant of aid to help the Pergau Dam project (Figure 4.18). In return, the Malaysian Government was persuaded to buy British military equipment. Sadly, this is only one of an increasing number of instances of 'tied' aid.

Figure 4.18 *The Pergau Dam, Malaysia: a symbol of aid with strings attached*

The most obvious outcome of all these four links; trade, labour, foreign investment and aid, is a rising tide of **global interdependence**. Countries and the economic groupings to which they belong are not only being drawn closer together in an economic sense, they are also becoming increasingly dependent on each other.

ACTIVITIES

1. Discuss the view that donor countries should have a say in how the aid they give is used.
2. Find out the difference between bilateral aid and multilateral aid.

2 Factors encouraging a global economy

The gradual breaking down of national frontiers lies at the heart of economic globalisation. **Production** or **commodity chains** (linked sequences of functions or stages) are spreading across more and more countries, as businesses exploit the comparative advantages of different locations. What this means is that areas can specialise in those activities for which they are best equipped and most competitive. The parts of a motor car assembled in the UK are likely to be drawn from many countries, including LEDCs which offer the advantage of cheap labour. Among the high-tech industries, the manufacture of microchips, with its distinct production stages, also lends itself to the geographical separation of these stages (Figure 4.19). Linking these spatially separated stages together in an efficient way is vital to the success of the new international production or commodity chains.

Production chain	Locational requirements	Location
1 Circuit designed and photographed	High-level scientific, technical and engineering personnel	Capital intensive
2 Circuits etched onto wafers	An extremely pure production environment and suitable utilities (pure water, waste disposal)	MEDC
3 Wafers sliced into chips	Clean production environment	Labour intensive
4 Chips bonded to circuit boards	Low-skill labour	LEDC
5 Chips baked and coated		
6 Chips tested	Low-skill labour	Either labour or capital intensive
7 Chips assembled into products	Proximity to consumer market	LEDC more likely
	The low weight : high value characteristic of the product at all stages of the production chain, except possibly the last, permits transportation over virtually any geographical distance. As a consequence, proximity to modern transport networks is critical	

Figure 4.19 *Stages in the microchip production chain*

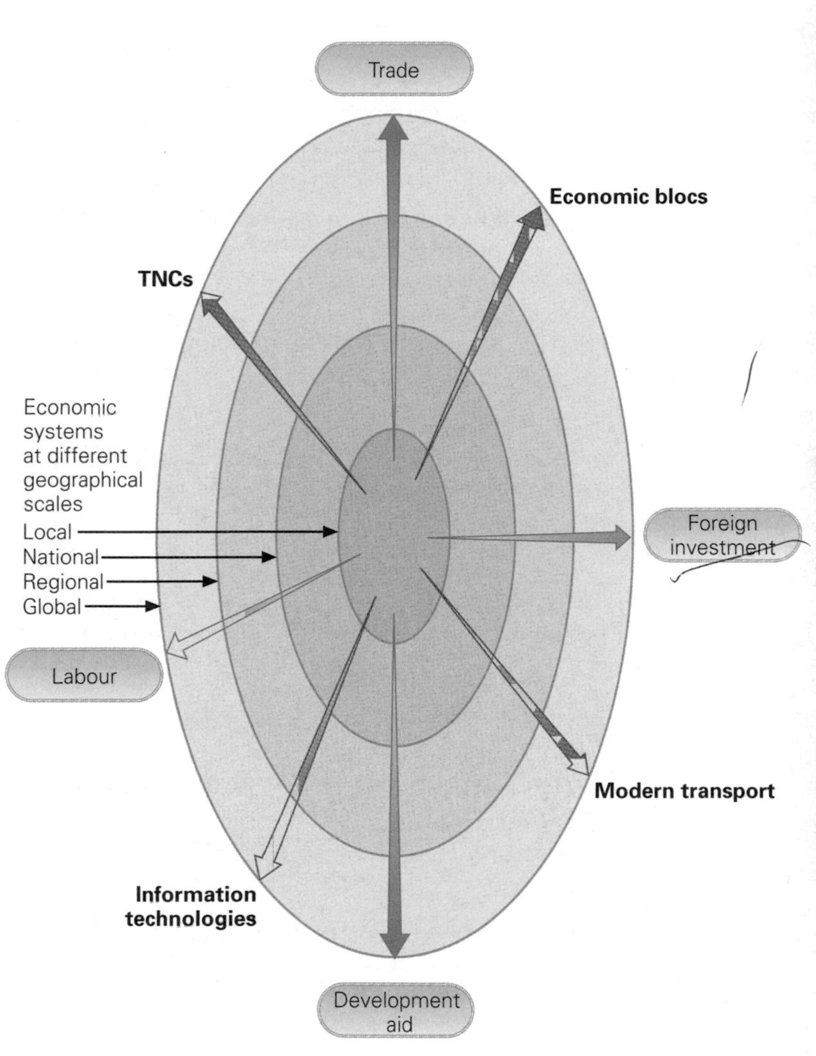

Figure 4.20 *Moving towards a globalised economy*

Globalisation is being promoted through the four traditional links of internationalisation examined in the previous section (Figure 4.7). However, the scaling up of that process has been driven by four significant developments (Figure 4.20):

- the emergence of large transnational corporations (TNCs) with increasingly diverse business interests spread over an ever-widening area
- the growth of regional economic or trading blocs, such as the EU, NAFTA and APEC. The encouragement of free trade between member countries is another way of breaking down the economic barrier effects of national boundaries
- the development of modern transport networks capable of moving commodities quickly and relatively cheaply (Figure 4.21)

- advances in information and communication technologies. These are crucial to decision-making, management and generally overcoming the friction of time and distance that inevitably exists between locations scattered around the globe. In an age of volatile markets, the need to be constantly in touch and informed is paramount.

The last of these four developments, the communications revolution, has given rise to what is called the **global informational economy**. It is a new mode of economic production and management. Productivity and competitiveness rely heavily on the generation of new knowledge and on access to, and the processing of, appropriate information. The most important sectors of this informational economy are:

- high-tech manufacturing
- design-intensive consumer goods, ranging from high-fashion clothing to entertainment products (video games, etc.)
- business and financial services.

The communications revolution

During the last 25 years, a number of new technologies have done much to bring about the shrinking of time and space:

- satellites
- computers
- optical fibres

The linking of these technologies has been particularly important, and has led, amongst other things, to the Internet and to a spectacular gearing up of electrical and electronic mass media.

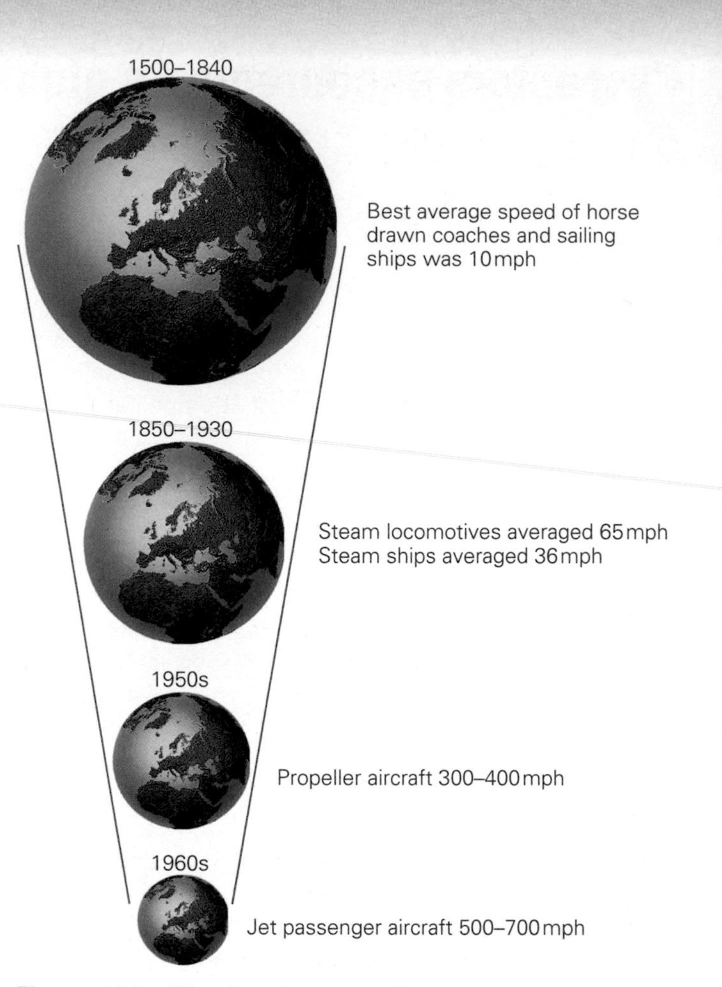

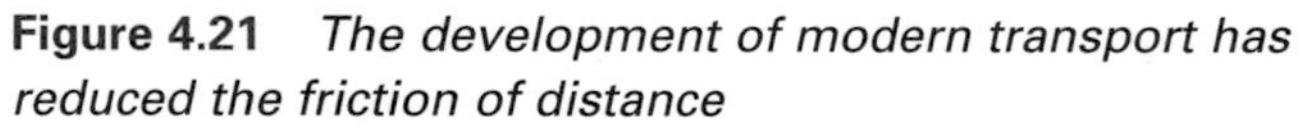

Figure 4.21 *The development of modern transport has reduced the friction of distance*

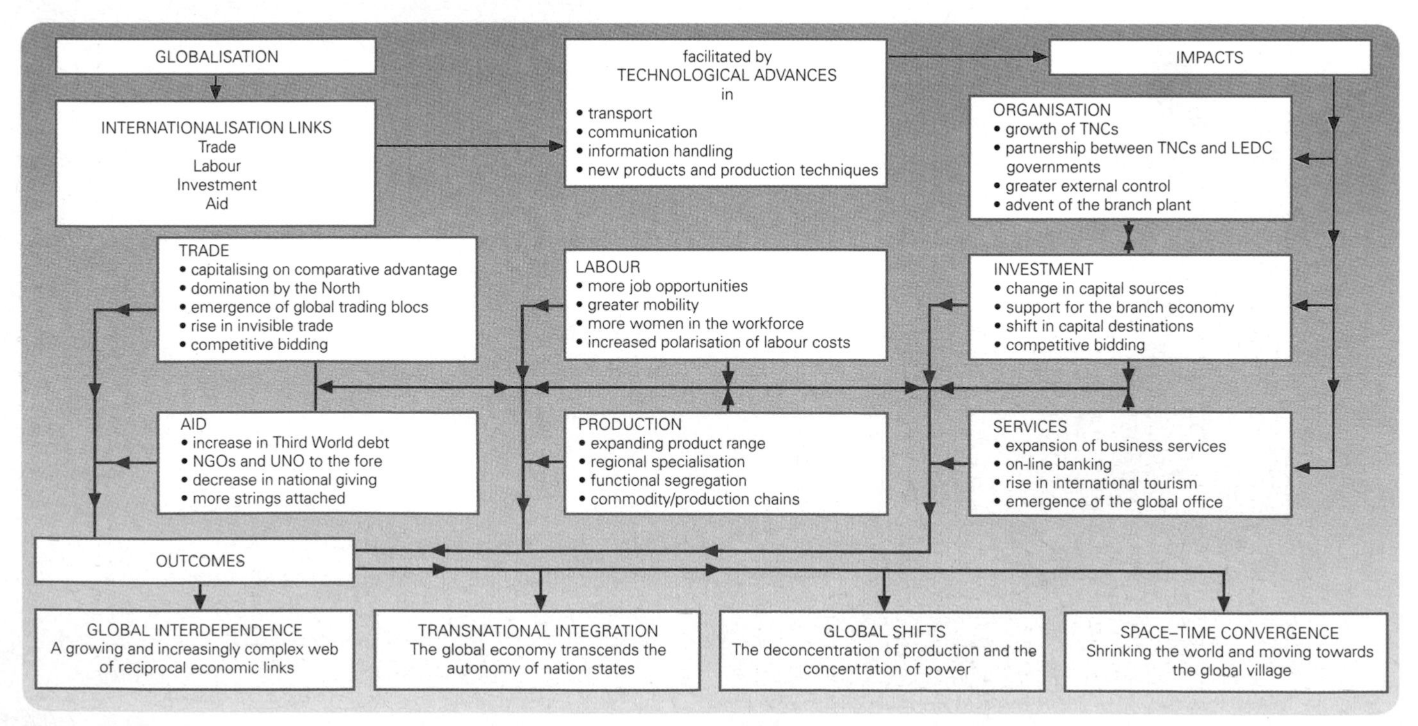

Figure 4.22 *Globalisation: processes, components and outcomes*

Components of the global economy

Globalisation is a complex set of processes and players. Figure 4.22 attempts to unravel and simplify it. It tries to draw together points made in this and the previous section. This diagram provides a useful reference framework for the ground covered in the remainder of this chapter.

Figure 4.22 shows that three new components have joined the four traditional links of internationalisation. These are **organisation**, **production** and **services**, and are briefly described below.

Organisation

Of immense importance here is the emergence of TNCs. The TNCs, above all else, have been the main organisers of economic globalisation. A TNC can exercise more power and influence than many national governments. Indeed, their net economic wealth exceeds that of many LEDCs (Figure 4.23). They are able to organise production and distribution over huge distances across international frontiers.

Production

Production through agriculture and manufacturing has always been in the economic equation, but their position has changed. Both are now characterised by a widening of product range and increasing regional specialisation. Regions play more and more to their strengths. Modern technology allows areas to cash in on their **comparative advantages**. At the same time, a spatial sorting of different functions leads to the segregation of:

- management and research, mainly located in important cities in the North
- skilled labour in advanced production regions
- unskilled labour in peripheral regions, mainly in the South.

Such commodity or production chains are networks of labour and production that criss-cross global space (Figure 4.19).

Services

Banking, finance and **business services** (e.g. personnel recruitment and training, advertising and marketing) have boomed during globalisation. They are vital to production and to the functioning of the TNCs. Developments like on-line banking mean that money involved in business transactions can be moved around the globe in a matter of seconds. The new **global office**, as it is called, is a major employer, particularly in the North where it creates far more jobs than manufacturing.

Also in the service sector, but different in character, is tourism. International tourism is now a major global activity, making a substantial contribution to the economic wealth of many countries (Figure 4.24).

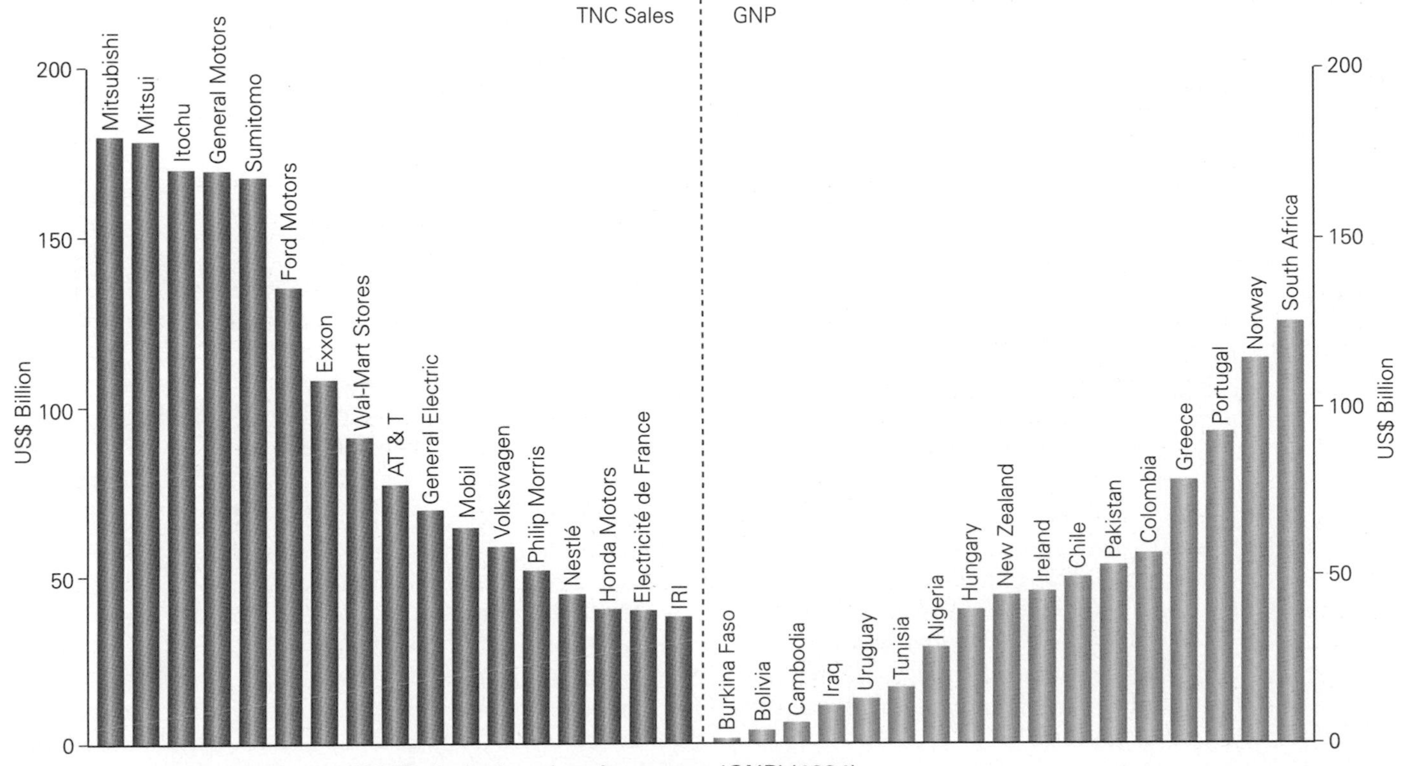

Figure 4.23 *A comparison of TNCs (sales) and nation states (GNP)* (1994)

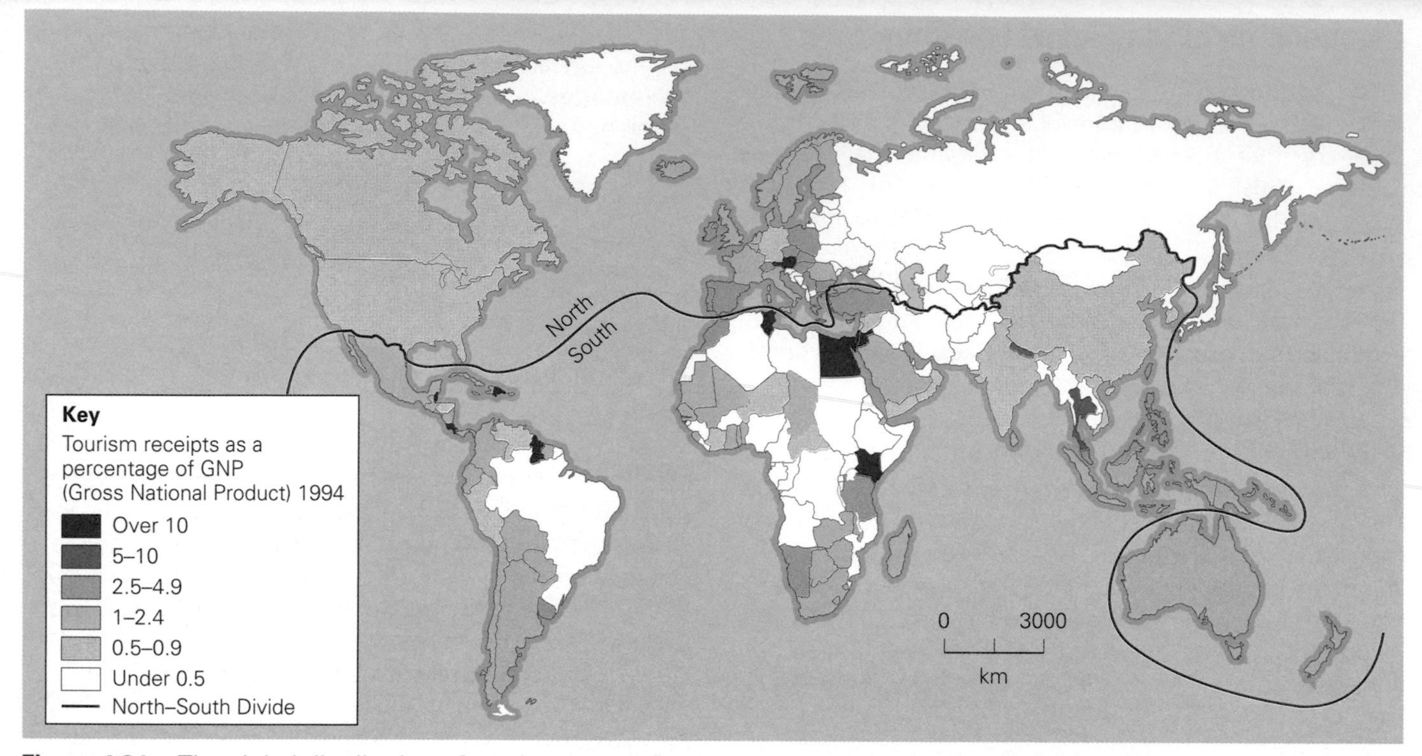

Figure 4.24 *The global distribution of tourism, 1994* Source: *Philip's Modern School Atlas, 92nd Edition*, 1998.

Tourism – a global overview

Global tourism grew by nearly 50 per cent during the 1990s. The number of international tourists leapt from 25 million in 1950 to around 650 million at the turn of the millennium. The earnings of the global tourist industry will soon exceed those from the sale of oil. Tourism is already the largest industry in the world in terms of employment, with 1 in every 15 workers owing their job to it.

All but one (China) of today's top ten tourist destination countries are north of the North-South Divide. LEDCs, particularly in Asia, are slowly increasing their share of the international tourist trade which currently stands at around 20 per cent. Although the benefits of tourism are real and substantial in terms of employment and earning foreign currency, there is a downside, particularly for LEDCs. This includes adverse impacts on traditional culture and society, as well as on the environment. The physical and human systems of many LEDCs have only a limited carrying capacity and one that is easily exceeded. Much international tourism, particularly the package holiday business, is in the hands of a relatively small number of companies based in the North. This means that the profits of the industry tend to 'leak' out of the country where they are earned rather than being retained to drive the development process forward.

ACTIVITY

1. Explain the link between economic power and political influence.
2. Think of some of the ways in which new technology has helped agriculture and manufacturing.
3. Identify some factors that have encouraged the globalisation of tourism.

Outcomes of globalisation

The outcomes of globalisation are shown by Figure 4.22 to be fourfold and all are of a geographical nature. **Global interdependence** refers to the web of intricate economic links that bind countries together. **Transnational integration** is a more political phenomenon concerning the gradual loss of political independence by nation states as a result of the superior political influence of the global economy and its lead players such as the TNCs.

While the fate of the global economy and the future of globalisation rest on international cooperation and goodwill, it would be wrong to think that there is any sort of equal partnership among participating nations. Far from it: exploitation and greed are to be found everywhere. Countries differ immensely in terms of wealth, power and influence, and may be grouped accordingly. Due to **global shifts**, some countries gain whilst others lose.

The all important shifts are:

- the movement of production away from the global cores to parts of the South
- the concentration of power in the political capitals of the North and the HQs of TNCs.

Countries also differ in terms of the way their economies are run. In some countries the government provides firm direction, whilst in others TNCs and private organisations have more influence.

Space-time convergence is a little different from the other three outcomes in that it is both a facilitator and an outcome of globalisation. The term means a 'shrinking' of the world (Figure 4.21). The advances in transport that help drive globalisation increase our ability to reduce the friction of distance; we can now travel further in a given unit of time and for less cost. Modern communications allow us to ignore distance altogether; they have reduced the friction of time. The space-time convergence is leading to a state referred to as the **global village**. The term conjures up a cosy image of everyone being drawn ever closer together into a tight-knit community.

ACTIVITIES

1 Explain how technological advances in transport and communication bring about space-time convergence.
2 Why might space-time convergence be vital to the success of a TNC?
3 Describe the link between space-time convergence and the global village.

Finally, it should be pointed out that not everyone agrees that we have a fully globalised economy. Globalisation is by no means complete. It is an on-going process and no doubt will continue to evolve. It is clear that there is a growing network of global interdependence involving three categories of global citizenship: core, periphery and semi-periphery (Figure 4.25). The next section investigates this network in more detail and will focus on one vital question: Why has globalisation done so little to bring about an equality among those nations that find themselves drawn ever closer together? Indeed, the signs are of an increasing inequality, with the strong exploiting the weak.

EXTENSION ACTIVITY

Choose two of the LLEDCs listed below, one from Group A and one from Group B.
Group A: Burundi, Ethiopia, Mozambique, Sierra Leone, Tanzania, Uganda, Zaire.
Group B: Afghanistan, Bangladesh, Cambodia, Haiti, Nepal, Togo, Vietnam.
Research:

- the main characteristics of poverty in your selected countries
- possible reasons for their poverty
- ways, if any, in which they are currently involved in the global economy
- what they might have to offer future globalisation.

Write a short report comparing your two sets of findings. Illustrate it with relevant maps and diagrams.

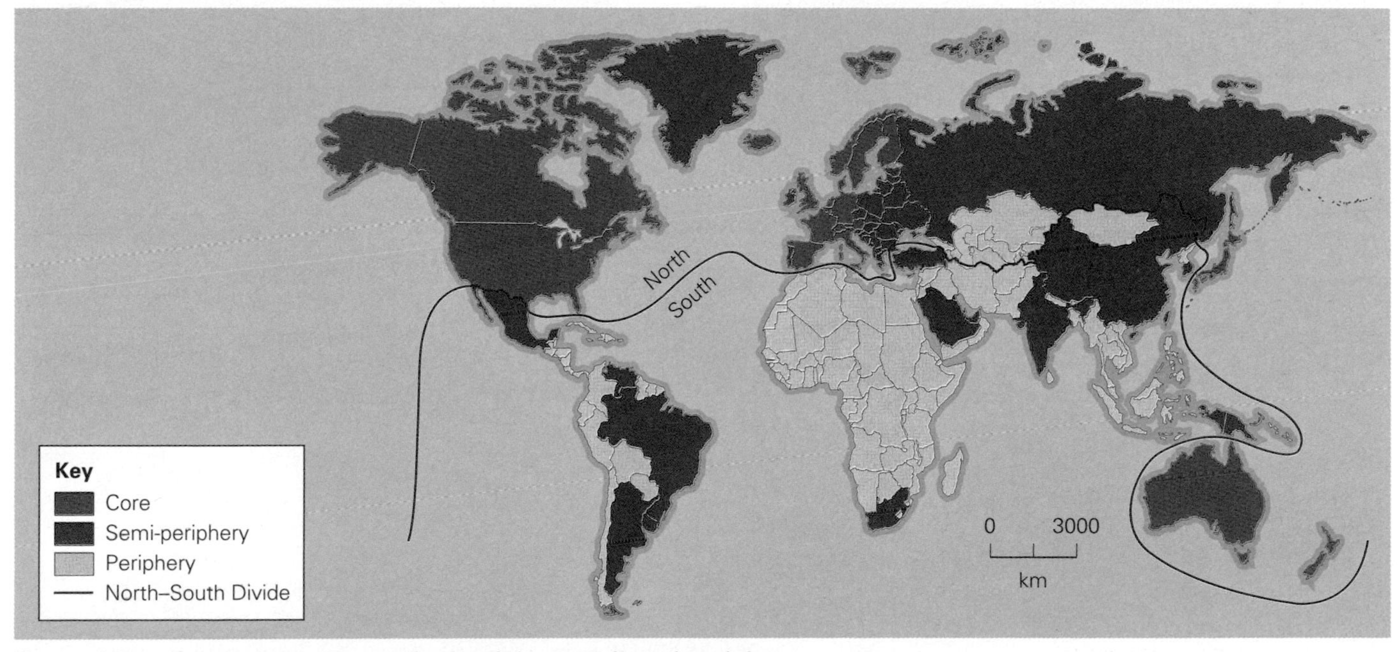

Figure 4.25 *The global system: core, periphery and semi-periphery*
Source: Knox and Agnew, *The Geography of the World Economy*, Arnold, 1998.

3 Changes in the character and location of the global economy

In this section we investigate the production and service components of globalisation (Figure 4.22). Production concerns both agriculture and manufacturing and the service sector is very diverse. Both are important in the global economy.

Production

The globalisation of agriculture

Over the last 25 years, the global food industry has been one of the world's fastest growing industries. TNCs have greatly increased their investment in this sector of the economy. Figure 4.26 summarises the factors that have encouraged this interest in agriculture. The interest has centred on:

- export-oriented agriculture, that is producing goods (mainly foods) in the South for sale in the markets of the North
- the production and global distribution of seeds, pesticides and fertilisers.

The impact of export-oriented agriculture has been particularly spectacular in some countries. For example, in 1970 Thailand exported no pineapples, but 10 years later it had become the main exporter after Hawaii (Figure 4.27). The Philippines experienced a similar rise in the production and export of bananas during the 1960s and early 1970s.

Figure 4.27 *Pineapple production in Thailand*

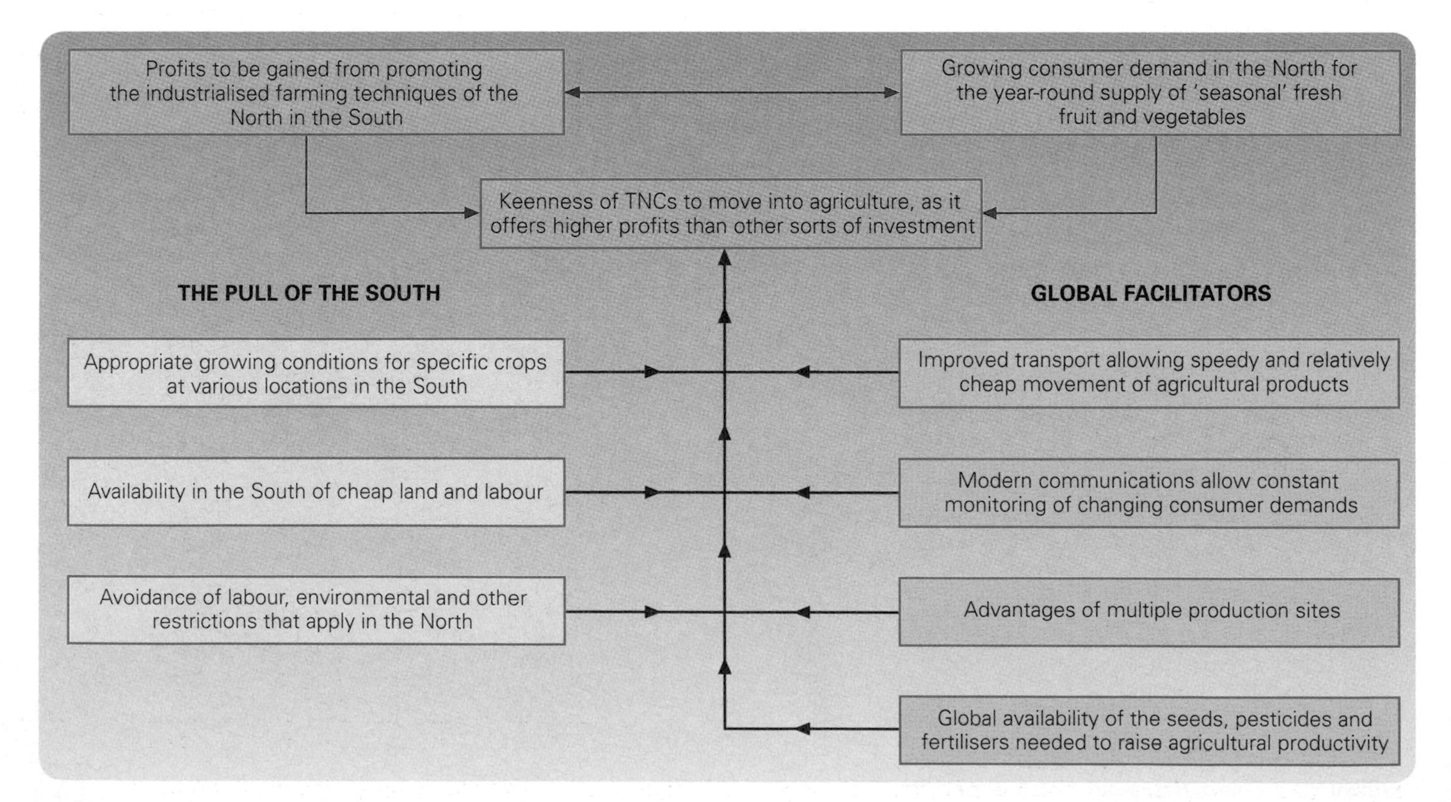

Figure 4.26 *Factors encouraging the globalisation of agriculture*

The process giving rise to these shifts in global agriculture (and in manufacturing) is referred to as **global sourcing**. It involves using industrialised farming techniques and multiple sites, particularly in the South, in the production of a single commodity in order to:

- reduce labour costs
- ensure year-round supplies of seasonal crops (such as strawberries grown in Chile for sale in Europe during January)
- avoid labour regulations about hours of work and rates of pay
- escape environmental regulations about the use of herbicides and pesticides (Figure 4.26).

ACTIVITIES

1. Check that you understand the significance of the factors shown in Figure 4.26.
2. Explain what is meant by **global sourcing**.
3. Think of the possible advantages and disadvantages for an LEDC of becoming involved in export-oriented agriculture.
4. Look at the fresh fruit and vegetables section of your local supermarket and list the countries of production. How strong is the evidence of globalisation? Show your findings in diagrammatic form.

Global shifts in manufacturing

The global distribution of manufacturing is very uneven (Figure 4.28). The great majority of the world's manufacturing production is concentrated in a small number of countries. In fact, over 50 per cent is accounted for by three countries (Table 4.3) and over 80 per cent by North America, Western Europe and Japan. Only two of the countries listed in Table 4.3 might be regarded as LEDCs: South Korea and Brazil.

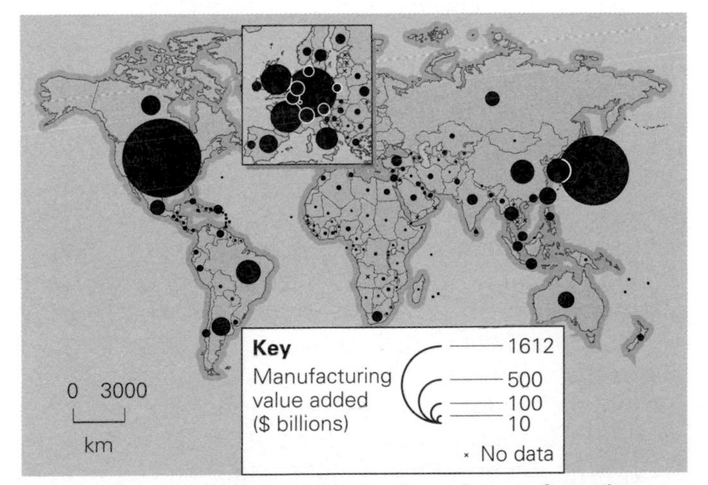

Figure 4.28 *The global distribution of manufacturing, 1994* Source: Dicken, *Global Shift*, Paul Chapman Publishing, 1999.

Rank	Country	Value added by manufacturing (US$ million)	Percentage of world total
1	USA	1,611,763	26.9
2	Japan	1,257,761	21.0
3	Germany	692,191	11.6
4	France	268,611	4.5
5	UK	243,653	4.1
6	South Korea	159,172	2.7
7	Brazil	154,425	2.6
8	China	139,031	2.3
9	Italy	128,486	2.2
10	Canada	100,322	1.7

Table 4.3 *The world's ten leading manufacturing nations, 1995*

Despite the fact that manufacturing today is highly concentrated globally, the pattern is a changing one. If we were to compare the current situation with that of 50 years ago, significant global shifts would be apparent. Figure 4.29 shows that during the second half of the twentieth century, the industrialised North's share of world manufacturing declined from 95 to below 80 per cent. Today, more than 20 per cent of manufacturing production occurs in the South compared with 5 per cent half a century ago.

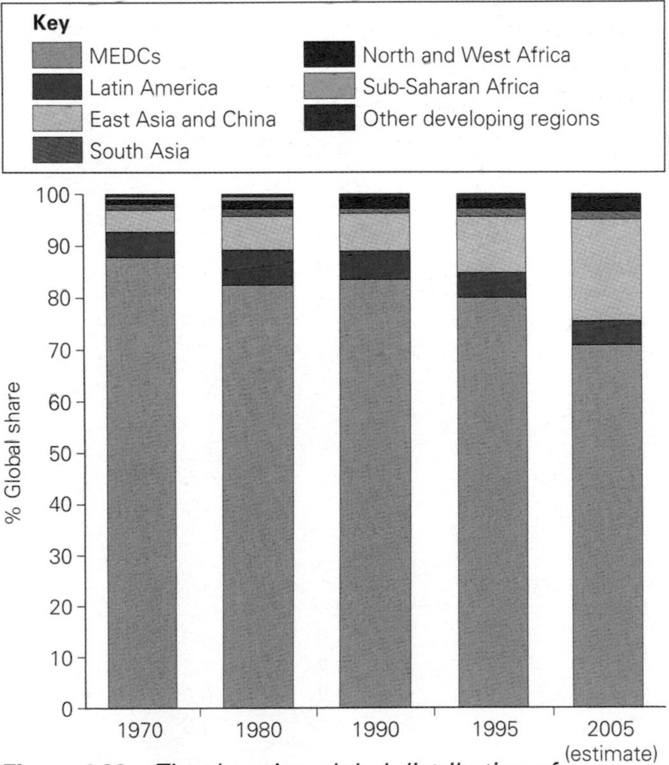

Figure 4.29 *The changing global distribution of manufacturing, 1970–2005*

While there has been this broad global shift, it is important to understand that there have been wide variations in the fortunes of manufacturing both within the North and the South.

The changes in the North may be summarised as:

- a substantial decline in the USA's share of global manufacturing (from 40 to 25 per cent)
- lower rates of manufacturing growth in the leading producers of Western Europe (France, Germany and the UK), indeed, negative rates have occurred (Table 4.4)
- shifts within Western Europe from the coalfields and other old industrial strongholds to more 'peripheral' locations (such as Portugal and Spain) offering various incentives to lure new factories
- the spectacular rise of Japan from defeat and destruction at the end of the Second World War to being ranked second in the global manufacturing league table since the 1980s
- the collapse of manufacturing in the transitional (FCC) economies, i.e. the former Soviet Union and the former communist countries of Eastern Europe. During the 1990s, their share of global manufacturing output fell from 15 to 3 per cent.

Country	Average annual rates of change in manufacturing production % 1960s	1970s	1980s	1990s
MEDCs				
USA	5.3	2.9	3.9	3.2
Japan	13.6	6.5	6.7	0.1
Germany	5.4	2.1	1.0	–1.1
France	7.8	3.2	–0.5	–0.3
UK	3.3	–0.5	1.3	0.5
NICs				
South Korea	17.6	15.6	10.6	8.2
Taiwan	16.3	13.5	7.5	4.7
Singapore	13.0	9.7	3.3	8.5
RICs				
Malaysia	–	11.1	6.3	15.8
Thailand	–	–	–	13.1
Indonesia	–	–	–	10.7
China	–	–	–	20.6
LEDCs				
India	4.7	5.0	8.3	3.0
Brazil	–	8.7	1.2	2.7
Argentina	5.6	0.7	0.0	10.0
Mexico	10.1	7.1	0.0	2.4

Table 4.4 *The changing manufacturing fortunes of selected countries*

During the same period, the situation in the South was characterised by:

- the concentration of much of the growth in manufacturing up to the 1980s in the NICs of the Asia Pacific area (the 'Tiger' economies of South Korea, Taiwan, Singapore and Hong Kong)
- the occurrence during the 1990s of faster rates of growth in other parts of SE Asia, notably in the RICs of Malaysia, Thailand, Indonesia and China
- the remoteness of much of the rest of the South from modern manufacturing, particularly Africa and the Caribbean, but less so parts of Latin America.

Thus, within the core countries of the North (Figure 4.25) there has been a pronounced shift in the centre of gravity of manufacturing production. At the same time, there has been considerable acceleration of manufacturing growth in the global periphery of the South. It is equally clear that this recent growth has been very unevenly distributed.

The global motor vehicle industry

The motor vehicle industry was to the twentieth century what the Lancashire cotton mills were to the nineteenth century. The significance of the industry today lies in its vast scale, and immense and diverse spin-off effects:

- the growth of linked industries making materials and components
- the creation of jobs in the service sector
- the ability of people to move around and transport goods
- our everyday life and our patterns of settlement.

Some three to four million workers are estimated to be employed directly in the manufacture of motor vehicles. Another nine to ten million workers are engaged in the making of materials and components, whilst probably more than five million people are employed in the selling and servicing of vehicles.

In terms of organisation, the motor vehicle industry is one of the most globalised of all manufacturing industries. It is an industry of TNCs, many of which are increasingly organising their activities on international, integrated lines.

Between 1960 and 2000, global production of motor vehicles increased by 200 per cent, from 13 million to around 40 million vehicles. During those 40 years, major changes occurred in the global distribution of the industry. Figure 4.30 shows the distribution in 1995, while Table 4.5 shows the major shifts which occurred at a national level. Most of the production of motor vehicles now takes place in the global triad of Western Europe, North America and Asia Pacific. Similarly, much of the trade in motor vehicles occurs between and within these three major producing regions (Figure 4.31).

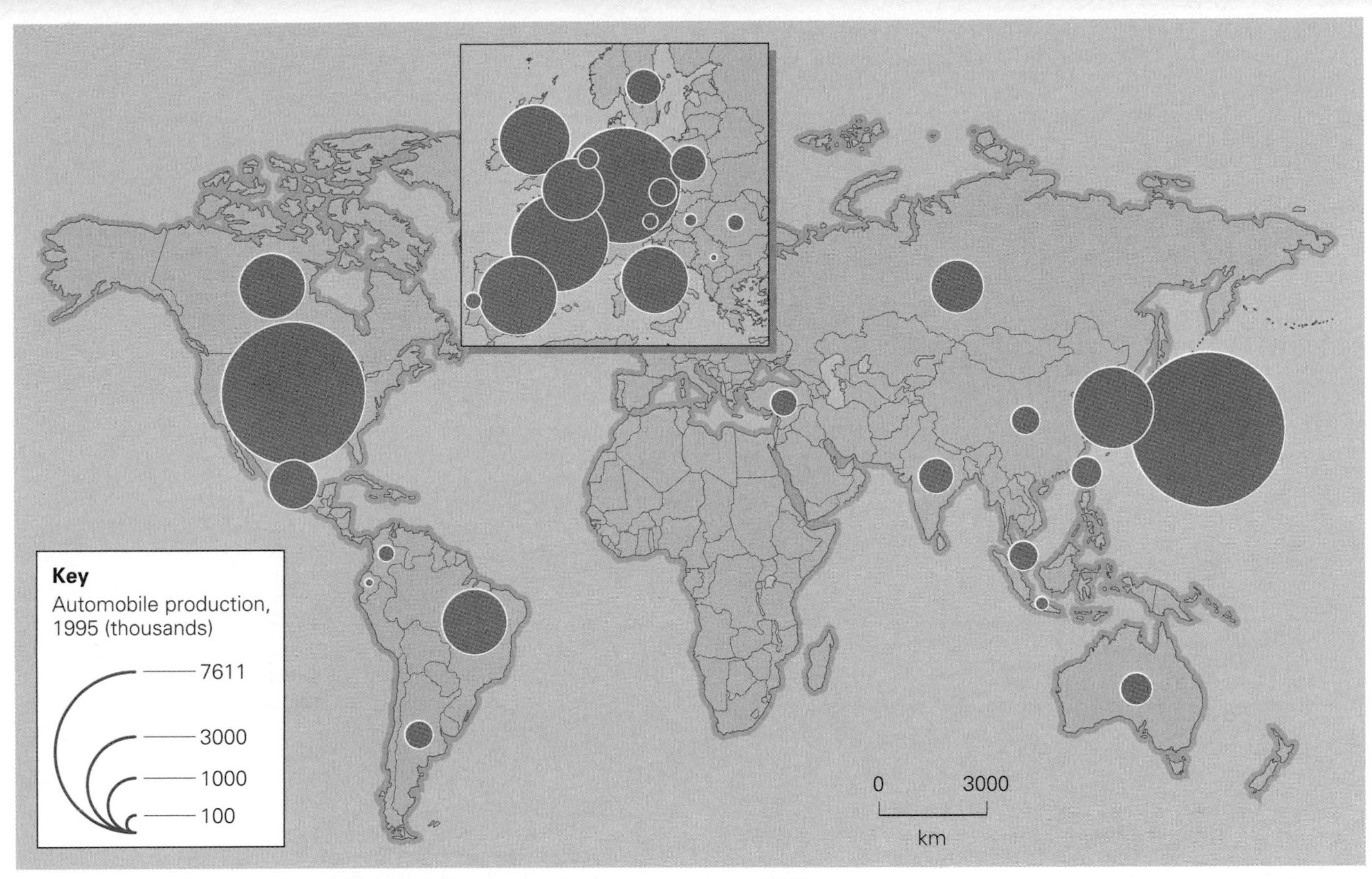

Figure 4.30 *The global distribution of motor vehicle production, 1995*
Source: Dicken, *Global Shift*, Paul Chapman Publishing, 1999.

Country	% share of global output 1960	% share of global output 1995	Output (1995) (000 units)
France	9.0	8.2	3,050
Germany	14.0	11.8	4,360
Italy	4.6	3.8	1,423
Spain	0.8	5.3	1,959
Sweden	0.8	1.1	388
UK	10.4	4.1	1,532
Canada	2.5	3.6	1,339
USA	51.4	17.1	6,350
Japan	1.3	20.6	7,611
Malaysia	–	0.5	195
South Korea		5.4	2,003
Taiwan	–	0.8	282
Argentina	0.2	0.6	227
Brazil	0.3	3.5	1,303
Mexico	0.2	1.9	699
Czech Republic	–	0.6	228
Poland	–	1.1	392
Australia	–	0.8	292
WORLD	100.0	100.0	37,045

Table 4.5 *Changes in the distribution of motor vehicle production, 1960–1995*

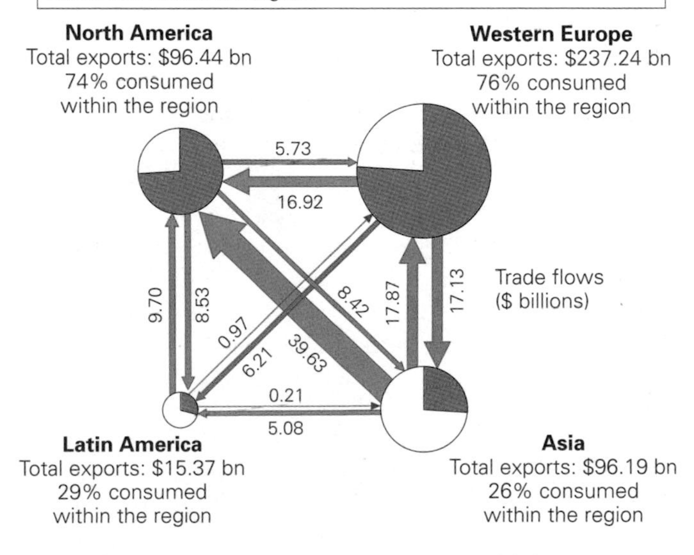

Figure 4.31 *The global trade in motor vehicles*

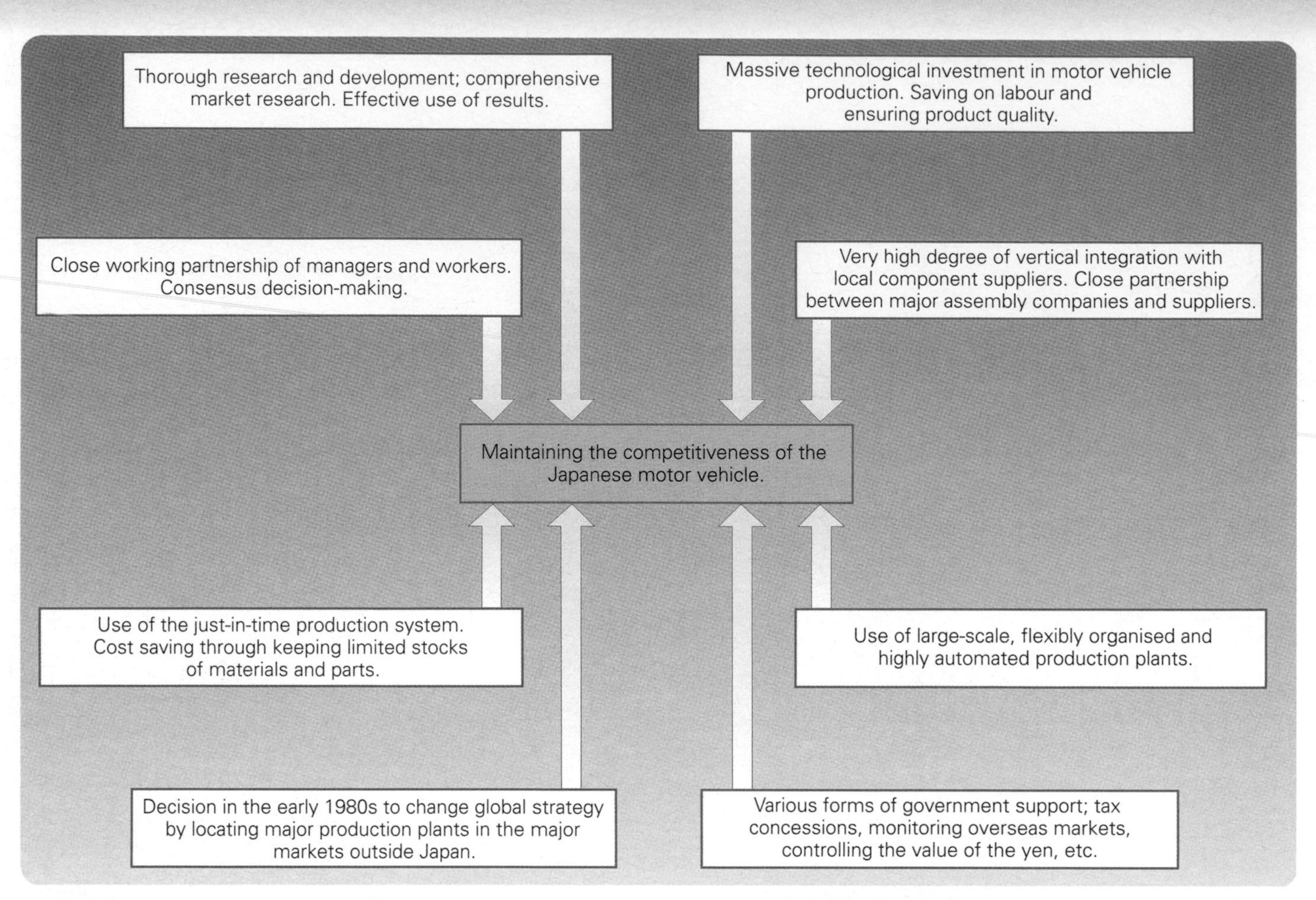

Figure 4.32 *Factors contributing to the competitiveness of Japanese motor vehicle production*

The rise of Japan as a producer was the single most important development in the motor vehicle industry during the second half of the twentieth century. This was achieved initially during the 1950s and 1960s by the price competitiveness of Japanese exports (Figure 4.32). From the early 1980s onwards, Japanese companies began to change their global strategy by locating major production plants in their major overseas markets (**offshore production**) (Table 4.6).

The move to offshore production was encouraged by two factors. First, the economics of production have become such that it is now more economic to assemble motor vehicles close to major markets than to ship finished vehicles around the world. Secondly, offshore production is a form of **import substitution** used by most motor manufacturers to help penetrate those markets where governments are concerned about levels of foreign vehicle imports. For example, a Nissan vehicle made in the north east of England does not count as an import, particularly if it contains a high percentage of 'local content', i.e. materials and parts made in the UK. Such offshore production by this Japanese company also offers the advantage of creating local jobs.

Rank	Company	Country of origin	% share of global production	% produced offshore
1	GM	USA	14.5	49.7
2	Ford	USA	10.8	56.9
3	Toyota	Japan	9.4	17.5
4	VAG	Germany	7.5	43.7
5	PSA	France	6.3	21.1
6	Nissan	Japan	5.7	33.5
7	Renault	France	5.2	24.6
8	Fiat	Italy	4.6	25.7
9	Honda	Japan	4.1	41.7
10	Mitsubishi	Japan	3.1	20.1
11	Mazda	Japan	3.0	23.1
12	Chrysler	USA	2.7	43.3
13	Hyundai	South Korea	2.5	–

Table 4.6 *The leading motor vehicle companies: market shares and offshore production, 1995*

There have been other important developments that might also be seen as outcomes of globalisation. These include:

- the growing demand for motor vehicles in the South
- the emergence of lesser production centres in Latin America, SE Asia and Eastern Europe (Table 4.5).

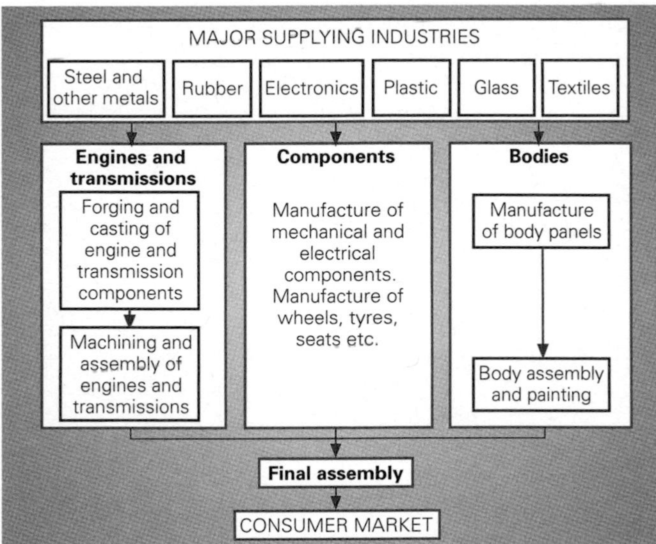

Figure 4.33 *The motor vehicle production chain*

Both of these, as well as the other developments previously discussed, have been facilitated by:

- the way the motor vehicle industry is organised. This allows different stages in the production chain to be spatially separated (Figure 4.33)
- the involvement of TNCs capable of organising production and distribution on a global scale
- development take-off in favoured areas of the South and improvements in physical infrastructure (e.g. improved transport and communications)
- government intervention in order to gain a slice of this profitable industry for individual countries. Intervention also involves controlling the access that foreign vehicle manufacturers have to domestic markets, as well as subsidising domestic production.

The resulting complexities are illustrated by the global assembly line of one motor vehicle manufacturer, Volkswagen (Figure 4.34).

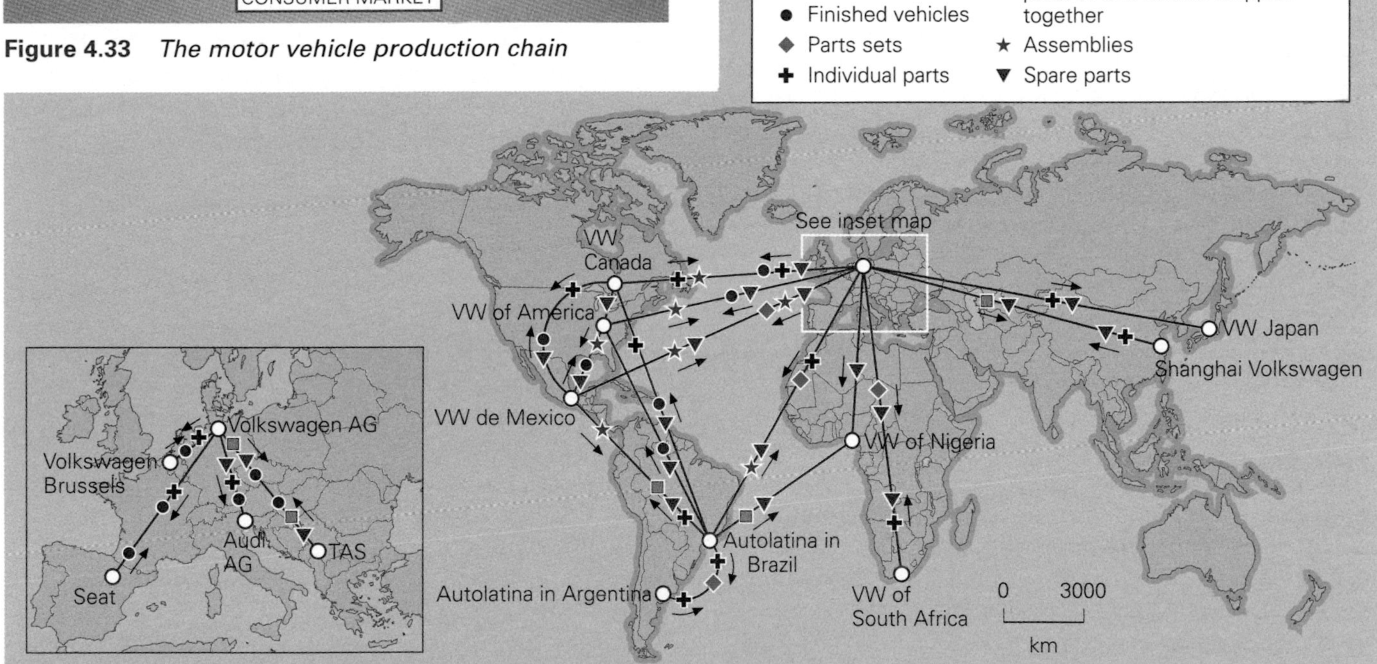

Figure 4.34 *Volkswagen's global assembly line*

Source: Knox and Agnew, *The Geography of the World Economy*, Arnold, 1998.

ACTIVITIES

1. Construct a diagram to show the major impacts of the motor vehicle on:
   - the location of economic activity
   - everyday life
   - the environment.
2. Modify a copy of Figure 4.26 to show the factors that you think are encouraging the globalisation of the motor vehicle industry.
3. Write a short account summarising the main features of Figure 4.34.

Measuring spatial distributions

Unevenness in geographical distributions has been an important theme running through this and the previous chapter. Diagrams such as Figures 4.28 and 4.30 can give a good visual impression of spatial unevenness. However, there are other techniques that actually measure and analyse it. The **location quotient** and the **Lorenz curve** are two such techniques.

The location quotient (LQ) is a statistical measure of concentration in a particular area (region or country) compared with the average for a larger area (country or the world). In the present context, it may be used to show how much a particular activity is concentrated in a given country compared with the global average. This is done by using the simple formula:

$$LQ = \frac{\text{\% of total workforce in country A working in activity X}}{\text{\% of global labour force working in activity X}}$$

An LQ of 1 indicates that an activity is represented in a given country in exactly the same proportion as it is globally. An LQ of less than 1 suggests that the activity is under-represented, while an LQ greater than 1 indicates that the activity is over-represented, i.e. there is a geographical concentration of that particular activity in the chosen country.

The Lorenz curve is drawn on graph paper and makes use of cumulative percentage data. The vertical axis shows the cumulative percentage, and points are plotted in rank order from the highest to the lowest value (Figure 4.35). The highest percentage value is plotted first; the second highest value is then added to this value; the third highest value is then added to this cumulative value and so on. A straight line drawn from the origin to the final cumulative value represents an even distribution. The greater the deviation of the plotted cumulative percentage line from the line of evenness, the higher the degree of concentration.

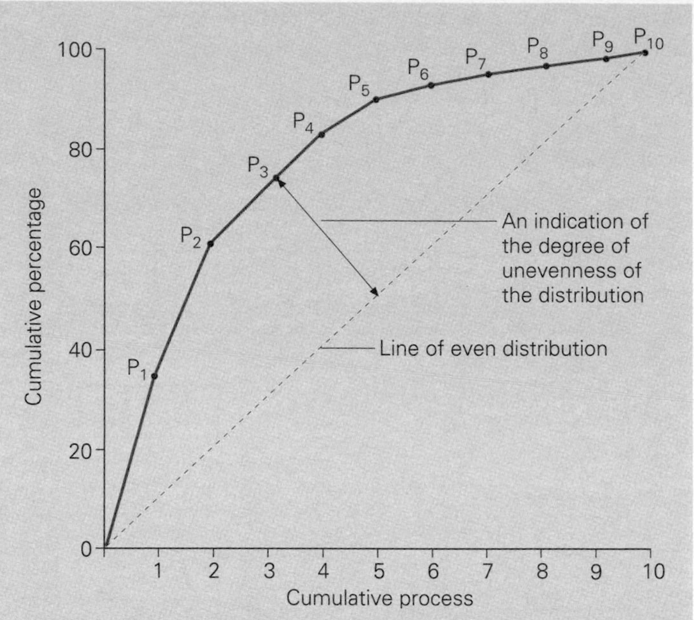

Figure 4.35 *A Lorenz curve showing an uneven distribution*

ACTIVITIES

1 Using the percentage share of global output data in Table 4.5:
   a plot Lorenz curves for 1960 and 1995
   b write a short account explaining your findings.
2 Obtain the following data about employment in the motor vehicle industry (or any other industry of your choice):
   - percentage of total employed in England and Wales
   - percentage of total employed in each county of England and Wales.

   Data of this kind can be obtained from the Office of National Statistics.
   a Calculate the location quotients for each county.
   b Map your results.
   c Write a short account describing the key features of the distribution of the industry you have chosen.

Services

One of the most significant developments in the global economy over the last few decades has been the rapid growth of service industries. Table 4.7 shows that in 1995 services accounted for the largest share of GDP in all but the low-income countries. International trade in services has also grown immensely and is now an important driving force in the global trading system. The service sector has been attracting an increasing share of foreign direct investment and in many of the leading MEDCs this investment is now more than in manufacturing. As a consequence, services are becoming increasingly globalised. What this means is that service firms are establishing a presence in foreign markets and providing services to local customers.

	% of GDP		
Country group	**1965**	**1985**	**1995**
Low income	30	32	38
Middle income	46	48	52
High income	54	61	64

Table 4.7 *The contribution of the service sector to GDP, 1965–1995*

The service sector is very diverse, far more so than manufacturing (Figure 4.36). Services range from the very basic, e.g. cleaning and maintenance, to sophisticated activities that are knowledge and information-intensive (e.g. insurance and banking). The service sector includes retailing and wholesaling, entertainment and social services (education and health care). Construction, transport and communication are also part of the sector, as well as recreation and tourism.

There is a tendency to see services as something quite distinct from goods. We need to recognise, however, that services play an vital part in manufacturing production chains. This is most obvious where globalisation has created production chains that reach across international frontiers (as in the motor vehicle industry). Figure 4.37 shows four service groupings related to the production of goods. The **upstream** sector represents the start of the production chain and the **downstream** sector is at the end of the production chain. Of these, the latter is particularly significant for it has a direct bearing on the competitive strength of the product in the market place. The other two are more integral to the production process itself. **Onstream production services** are normally **internalised** (carried out by the producing firm itself). In contrast, the **onstream parallel services** are **externalised** and put out to independent, specialist service firms. This link with production has been important in stimulating the globalisation of services. As manufacturing industries have globalised, so too have those services that are an integral part of their production chains.

Financial services

Banking services (commercial and retail)
Other credit services (including credit cards)
Services related to administration of financial markets
Services related to securities markets (including brokerage, portfolio management)

Business services

Rental/leasing of equipment
Real estate services
Installation and assembly work
Professional services (including legal services, accountancy, management services, advertising, market research, design services, computer services)

Transportation services

Freight services
Passenger transport services
Charter services
Services auxiliary to transport (including cargo handling, storage)
Travel agency and tour operator services
Vehicle rental

Communication services

Postal services
Courier services
Telecommunications services (including telephone, telegraph, data transmission, telemetrics, radio, TV)
Film distribution and related services

Health-related services

Human health services (including hospital services, medical and dental services)
Veterinary services

Trade, hotel and restaurant services

Wholesale trade services
Retail trade
Agents' fees/commissions related to distribution
Hotel and similar accommodation services
Food and beverage serving services

Figure 4.36 *A selection of service activities*

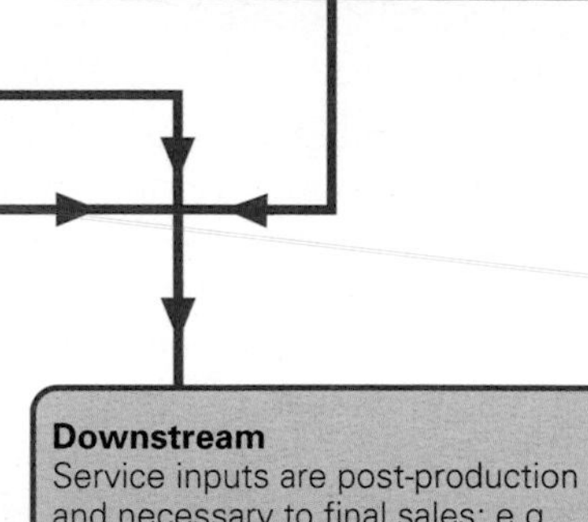

Figure 4.37 *The links between services and production in a production chain*

Type	Primary functions
Commercial bank	Administers financial transactions for clients (e.g. making payments, clearing cheques) Takes in deposits and makes commercial loans, acting as intermediary between lender and borrower
Investment bank/ securities house	Buys and sells securities (i.e. stocks, bonds) on behalf of corporate or individual investors Arranges flotation of new securities issues
Credit card company	Operates international network of credit card facilities in conjunction with banks and other financial institutions
Insurance company	Indemnifies a whole range of risks, on payment of a premium, in association with other insurers/reinsurers
Accountancy firm	Certifies the accuracy of financial accounts, particularly via the corporate audit

Table 4.8 *The main types of financial service*

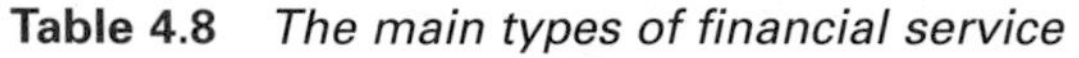

Most international service companies are single-service providers. They specialise in a particular service function and supply it to different countries through a network of branch offices. Some of the services offered are strongly complementary, for example between airlines and international hotel chains. From this complementarity there has emerged a new player on the global stage – the **transnational service conglomerate** (TSC). These are firms that operate internationally in a number of related service industries and aim to provide what has been termed a **global package deal**.

Besides the increased integration of services and production, and the emergence of TSCs, there have been two other major developments within the service sector of the global economy. They are:

- the growth and globalisation of financial services
- the growth and **outsourcing** of information services.

The main types of financial service are shown in Table 4.8. They have expanded enormously during the last 25 years and are playing a vital part in globalisation. Today international financial flows and foreign currency exchanges dwarf the value of the global trade in goods. These services have benefited particularly from advances in information technology. The benefits include:

- increased productivity
- a faster turnover of investment capital
- the instant electronic transfer of funds
- a quicker response to exchange-rate changes.

Technological advances in communication and data handling are not only playing a vital part in globalisation, they are also generating a diversity of information services. These include the collection and collation of information on market conditions throughout the world, the handling of data on crime and credit-rating, the connection of businesses and people to the Internet and the development of customised software.

An increasingly common characteristic of the information service industries is the **outsourcing** of some parts of their activities. For example, UK insurance companies process claim forms in cheaper, offshore locations such as Ireland. US software firms have well-developed outsourcing links with India. The processing of American Airline tickets is undertaken not at the company's HQ in Dallas, but in Barbados; similarly, Swissair has a newly-established ticketing centre in Delhi. The search for cheap labour locations is something which these service industries share with some branches of manufacturing.

ACTIVITIES

1 List the key developments in the service sector that have been discussed above. Suggest reasons for each of those developments.

2 Interview a local manufacturer and find out what services are used by the firm. Produce a brief report.

The Clark-Fisher model

The Clark-Fisher model shows how, as an economy grows, the relative importance of different sectors changes (Figure 4.38). In its pre-industrial state, the economy is dominated by the primary sector. Over time, and with development, manufacturing gradually becomes the powerhouse of economic growth. To support this industrial base and the demands of an increasingly affluent population, a demand is created for a wide range of services including transport, utilities (water and electricity supplies), consumer and financial services. Gradually, this tertiary service sector becomes the most important component of the economy. This sequence of events has been evident in the development of most MEDCs. In the most developed nations a quaternary sector has emerged, involving services such as information processing and research and development.

The model works well for the countries of the North. It remains to be seen whether it will prove equally valid for the countries of the South. There is a suspicion that globalisation may speed up the sequence of events, and also possibly change the sequential pattern. For example, in some countries, involvement in export-oriented production might prolong the relative importance of the primary sector. Equally, breaking into international tourism might prompt a by-passing of the industrial phase. At present, it seems unlikely that, outside tourism, the service or tertiary sector will dominate to quite the same degree as it does in the North. The prospect of an emerging quaternary sector seems particularly remote at the moment. Globalisation may never reach all parts of the South. Some countries may well remain in a pre-industrial state and develop very slowly.

Current thinking favours the idea that there is more than one path towards development. It is now argued that the process must be sensitive to the particular conditions prevailing in a country. However, in recognising that countries will differ in their development pathways, it is assumed that the end-game of all those pathways is to achieve standards of living and qualities of life that prevail in MEDCs.

ACTIVITY

1 Make a matrix of two colums (North or MEDCs; South or LEDCs) and four rows (primary sector; secondary or manufacturing sector; tertiary or service sector; quaternary sector). In each of the eight slots, insert comments summarising the impacts of globalisation and the major changes of the last 25 years.

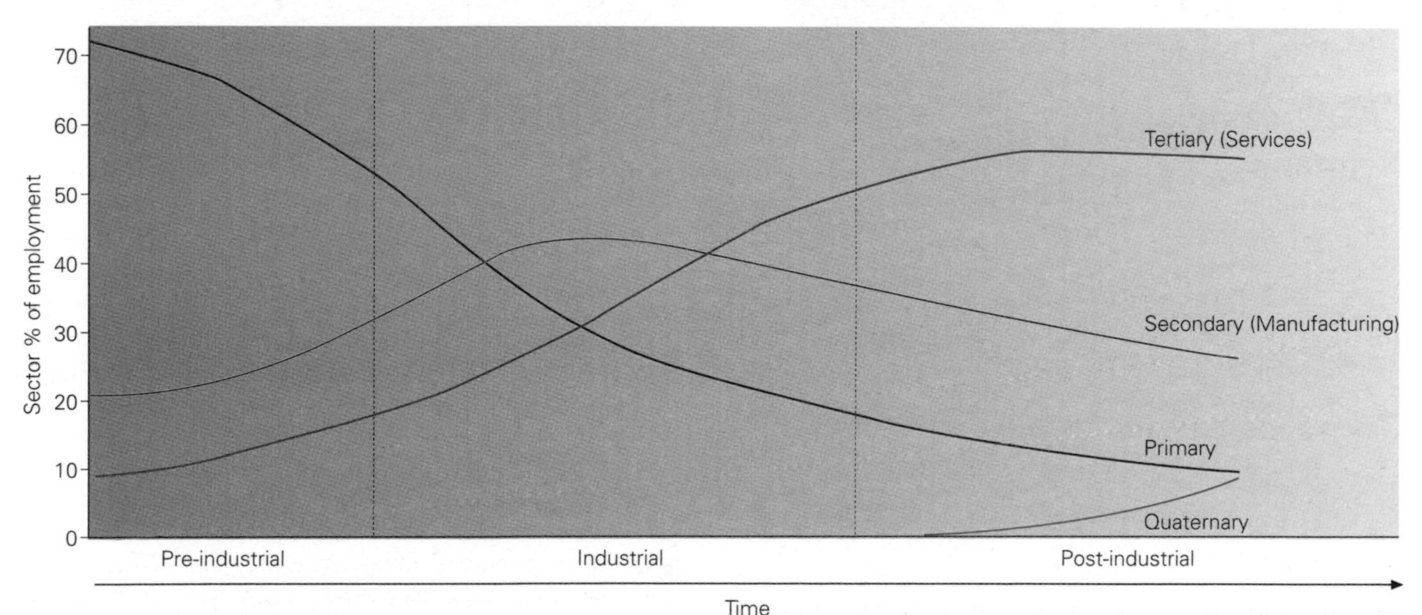

Figure 4.38 *The Clark-Fisher sector model*

4 Key players in changing the location of economic activity

The changes to the global economy discussed in the previous section are largely controlled by three key players (Figure 4.39):

- transnational corporations (TNCs)
- national governments
- international organisations.

The last of these covers a variety of organisations, but most are inter-governmental, for example the United Nations (UN) and its various agencies, the International Monetary Fund (IMF), the World Bank and the World Trade Organisation (WTO). Alongside these, there are regional economic blocs like the European Union (EU) and the North American Free Trade Agreement (NAFTA). Strictly speaking, the heading also includes non-governmental organisations (NGOs), but few of these play a significant pro-active role in global economic affairs.

Figure 4.39 *The major players in the global economy*

Transnational corporations (TNCs)

A transnational corporation is defined as a firm which has the power to co-ordinate and control operations in more than one country, even if it does not own them. Few would challenge the claim that the TNC has become the prime shaper of the global economy. Its potential power is so great that it even threatens the autonomy of nation states. That power flows from three basic characteristics of the TNC:

- its ability to co-ordinate and control the stages in a production chain, no matter whether those stages are within a single country or scattered across several
- its ability to take advantage of national differences in production factor costs (natural resources, labour, capital) as well as state incentives
- its ability to switch its resources and operations between locations at a global scale.

TNCs have largely been responsible for the creation of production chains that now spread across the globe. In this way, they have helped to fashion the changing geography of the global economy. But all this would not have been possible without technological advances in transport and communication.

TNCs are essentially capitalist enterprises: only a small number are state-owned. As such they behave according to the rules of capitalism, and the number one rule is the drive for profit. This is followed by other motives such as increasing market share and becoming the industry leader. TNCs operate in an increasingly competitive world, so it is often the case that one firm's profit is another's loss. Because of this, and the strong corporate survival instincts, the behaviour and decision making of TNCs can often appear ruthless.

Ri	Ra	Index	Company	Country	Industry
1	60	92.3	Thomson Corp.	Canada	Publishing and printing
2	71	92.2	Solvay	Belgium	Chemicals
3	50	91.4	RTZ	UK	Mining
4	17	90.5	Roche Holdings	Switzerland	Pharma-ceuticals
5	42	88.8	Sandoz	Switzerland	Pharma-ceuticals
6	15	88.4	ABB	Switzerland	Electrical equipment
7	52	87.3	Electrolux	Sweden	Electronics
8	13	86.5	Nestlé	Switzerland	Food
9	24	85.0	Philips	The Netherlands	Electronics
10	23	84.5	Unilever	UK/The Netherlands	Food

Key Ri = rank by index of transnationality
Ra = rank by total foreign assets

Table 4.9 *The top ten 'global' TNCs*

TNCs can be ranked according to a number of different criteria. Table 4.9 indicates two of them:

- the index of transnationality
- the total value of foreign assets.

The index of transnationality is the ratio of foreign assets to total assets, foreign sales to total sales and foreign employment to total employment, i.e. the percentage of a TNC's business conducted overseas from its HQ location.

It is generally agreed that a firm will become transnational and engage in international production when all of three conditions are present:

- a firm possesses ownership-specific advantages (e.g. a patent, some proprietary right of use, specific knowledge)
- it is more profitable for the firm to exploit these advantages itself than to lease or sell them to other firms
- location-specific factors (resources, markets, production costs, political conditions) make it more profitable for the firm to exploit those advantages in overseas rather than domestic locations.

Once those conditions apply, the firm might be expected to go through a sequence of transition from domestic to overseas production (Figure 4.40).

TNCs are highly diverse and vary according to :

- size
- spheres of activity
- geographical spread
- mode of operation.

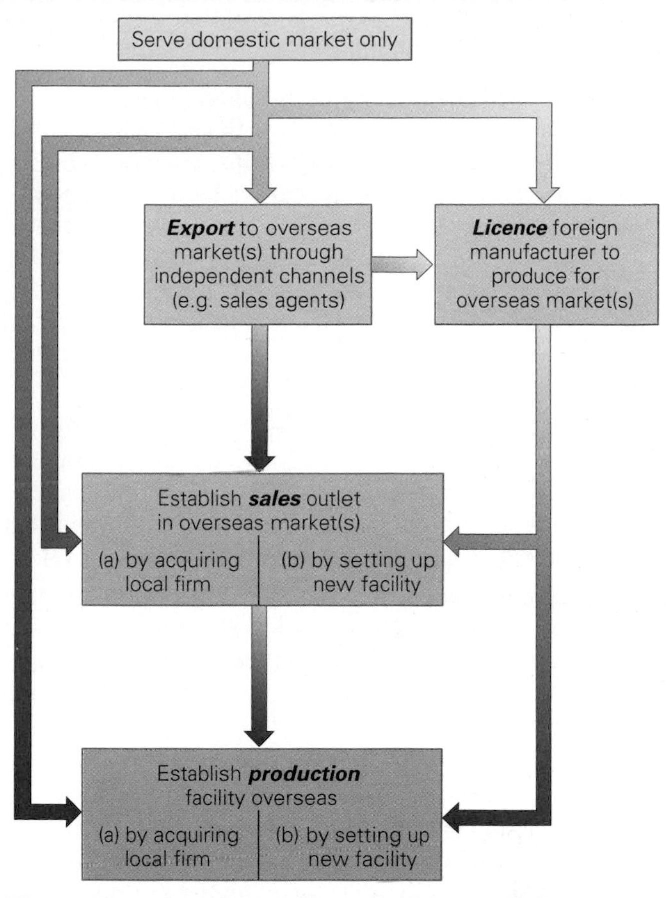

Figure 4.40 *Sequential development of a TNC*
Source: Dicken, *Global Shift*, Paul Chapman Publishing, 1999.

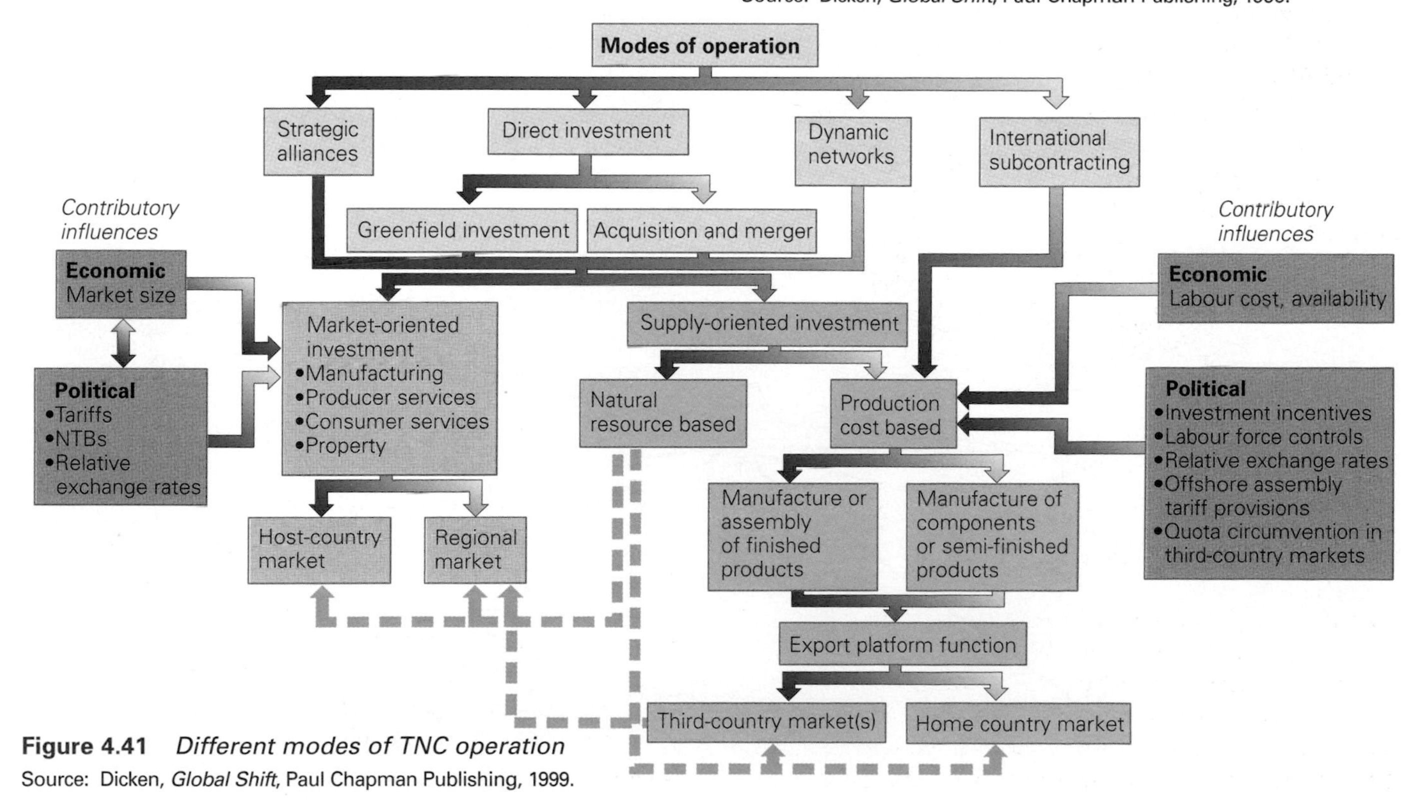

Figure 4.41 *Different modes of TNC operation*
Source: Dicken, *Global Shift*, Paul Chapman Publishing, 1999.

The mode of operation is particularly important. Figure 4.41 recognises four different modes:

- **Direct investment** is the established mode of operation, and typically involves the setting up of branch plants in overseas locations. Such branch plants may be acquired by merger, by purchasing an existing plant or by greenfield development. All the activities acquired by direct investment are an internal or integral part of the TNC.

More recently, TNCs have become locked into external networks with many other firms by the three following modes of operation:

- **Dynamic networks** are created when almost all the stages in the production chain, except central co-ordination and control, are contracted out to independent firms. The final product is still marketed under the lead company's brand name (Figure 4.42).
- **Strategic alliances** are a relatively recent development and involve various forms of collaboration between firms on an international scale. The collaboration might relate to such fields as research, production and marketing.
- **International subcontracting** Developments in transport and communication now allow TNCs to establish subcontracting networks over vast distances. The main motivation is cost minimisation, particularly locking into areas of very cheap labour. Subcontracting offers a number of benefits. The firm avoids having to invest in new plant, there is flexibility to meet sudden shifts in demand, and costs are reduced.

All TNCs have corporate headquarters which function as central control units. Here strategic decisions are made about investments that shape and direct the whole enterprise. Many TNCs also operate regional offices which constitute an intermediate tier in the corporate hierarchy. These co-ordinate and control activities of branch plants, affiliated firms and subcontractors across groupings of countries. At a global scale only a relatively small number of cities contain a large proportion of TNC corporate and regional headquarters (Figure 4.43). Such global cities have been described as the 'control points of the global economy.' Three global cities – London, New York and Tokyo – stand head and shoulders above the rest. Below them is a tier of lesser global cities serving each of the three leading economic regions (Asia, Europe and North America) along with others serving Australia and Latin America.

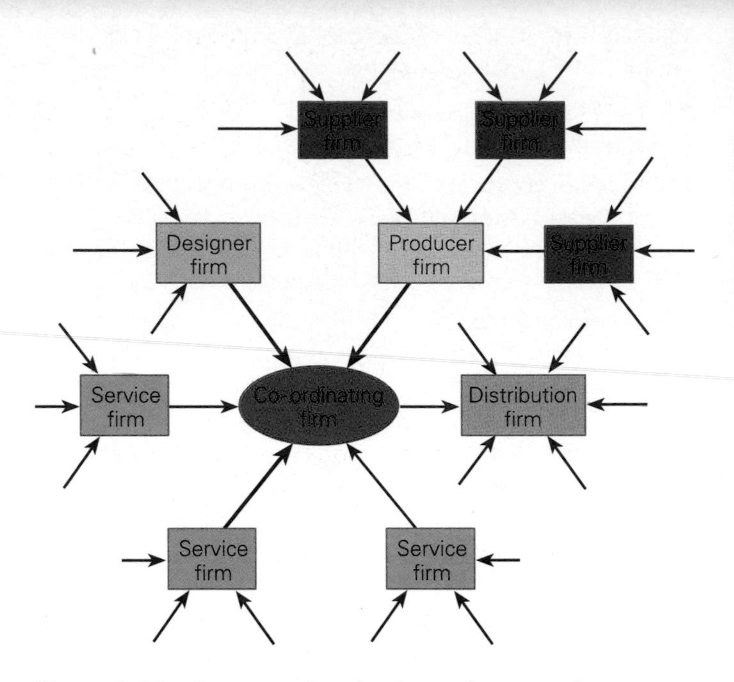

Figure 4.42 *An example of a dynamic network*

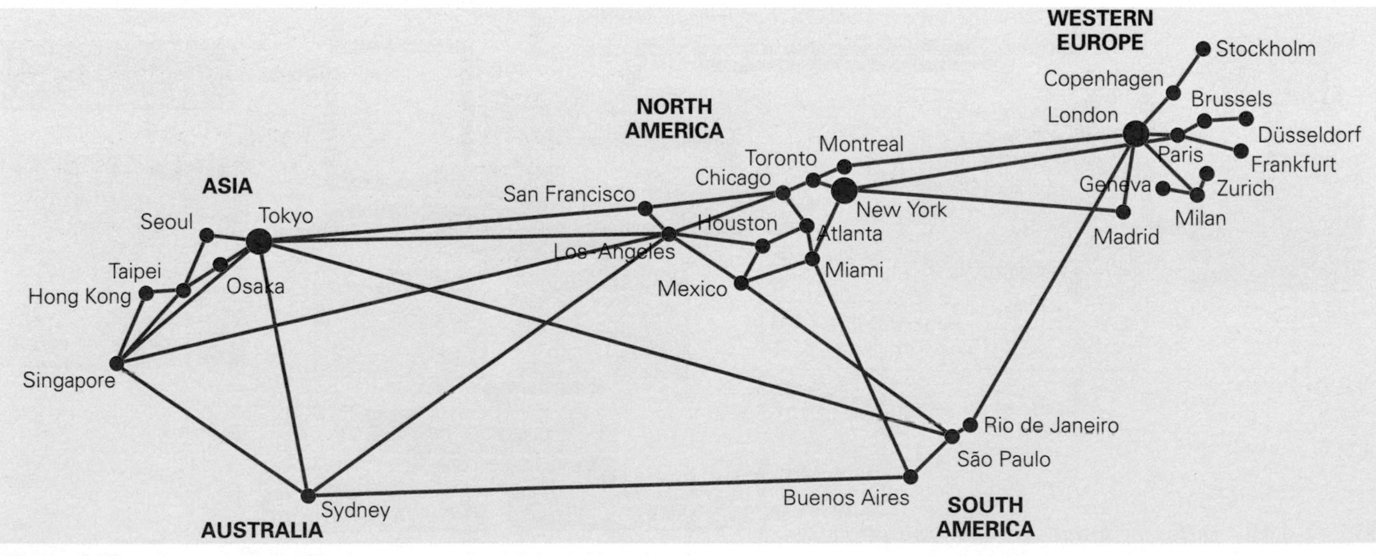

Figure 4.43 *The global cities*

Monsanto – providing agricultural solutions

The US based firm Monsanto might be described as a more traditional TNC in that its mode of operation is that of direct investment. Much of the firm's growth has been by merger and acquisition. It may be a traditional company in terms of its organisation and its long history, but its general field of operation – biotechnology – is highly topical. Monsanto is active in the contentious business of genetic modification.

Table 4.10 outlines the history of the company. It shows both the geographical spread of Monsanto and its frequent repositioning with regard to production. The mission statement of the company today describes it as a leading provider of agricultural solutions to growers worldwide. Its employees are claimed to provide top-quality, cost-effective and integrated approaches to help farmers improve their productivity and produce better quality foods. But the long history of Monsanto has a twist in its tail. In 2000 this TNC became a wholly-owned subsidiary of another TNC, Pharmacia.

Date	Milestones
1901	Monsanto chemical works opens in St Louis. Saccharin is one of its first products.
1913	A branch office opens in New York. At this time the company employs about 100 staff.
1918	The first acquisition is made – a chemical company in Illinois.
1919	Monsanto goes international when it acquires a 50 per cent stake in a Welsh chemical company. A sales office is opened in Chicago.
1927	The company goes public; shares are sold as a way of clearing debts.
1929	Two more US companies are acquired: one concerned with rubber chemicals; the other with chemicals for textiles, paper and leather production.
1930	A chemical company in Melbourne is purchased.
1932	Becomes involved in a joint venture in Canada.
1935	Monsanto makes another acquisition and moves into the soap and detergent industry.
1936	Research laboratories in Ohio are acquired, thus moving the company into research and development. Monsanto starts to mine its own phosphate rock.
1940	New offices opened and activities expanded in Australia.
1943	Plant built in Texas at the request of the US Government to produce a key raw material in the making of synthetic rubber needed by the Allied Forces in Second World War.
1947	Opens an office in India.
1951	Operations established in Brazil and Japan.
1955	Lion Oil acquired, primarily to provide petrochemical raw materials.
1957	A 50 per cent stake in a US company moves Monsanto into plastic bottle technology.
1960	Monsanto's Agricultural Division is created, being particularly concerned with the production of herbicides, insecticides and fertilisers.
1962	HQ of Monsanto Europe established in Brussels.
1969	Lasso herbicide is launched. Its success turns around the struggling Agricultural Division.
1976	One-third of Monsanto's sales are outside the USA. Roundup herbicide is commercialised to become the world's largest selling herbicide.
1981	Moves away from commodity chemicals towards high-value proprietary products and toward new technologies. Biotechnology is firmly established as the strategic research focus.
1982	Monsanto scientists genetically modify a plant cell for the first time in history.
1983	Company scientists succeed in growing plants with genetically-engineered traits.
1984	Acquisition takes Monsanto into pharmaceuticals and sweeteners.
1985	Strategic restructuring puts the emphasis on agriculture, pharmaceuticals and food.
1991	Unit formed to sell genetically-engineered, insect-protected potatoes.
1993	Acquisition leads company into lawn and garden products.
1995	Several genetically-modified products (soya, potatoes, cotton and tomatoes) approved for commercialisation.
1995–1997	Major acquisitions made that put the company in the forefront of life-sciences areas.

Table 4.10 *Milestones in the evolution of Monsanto*

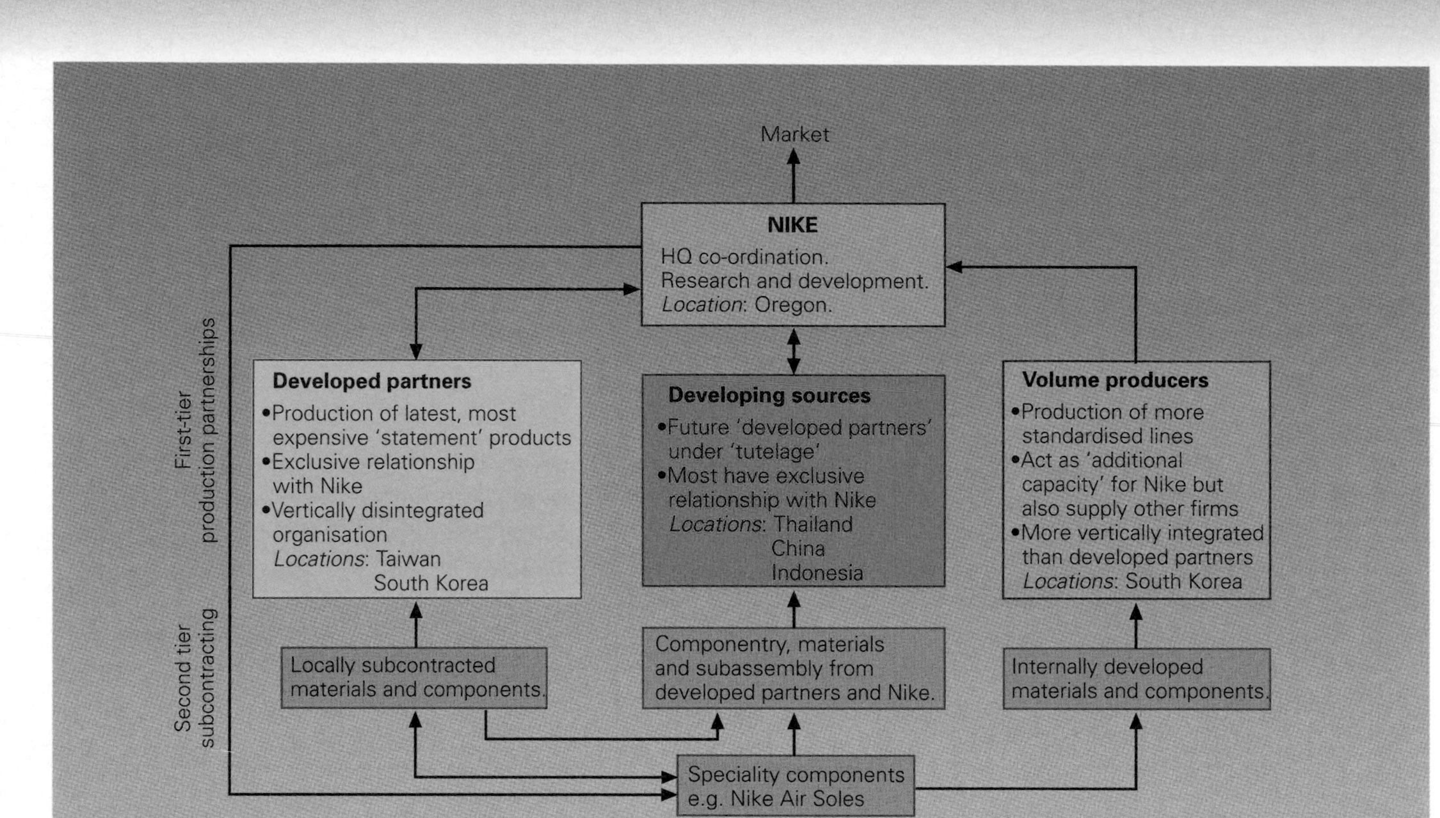

Figure 4.44 *The Nike network* Source: Dicken, *Global Shift*, Paul Chapman Publishing, 1999.

Nike – a manufacturer of statement products

The Nike logo is recognised throughout the world. It is associated with a range of clothing products that are largely linked to sport. In terms of its mode of operation, Nike belongs to the international subcontracting category (Figure 4.41). Nike does not wholly own any production facilities. Instead, it acts as a production co-ordinator from its headquarters in Oregon (Figure 4.44). Three categories of primary production form the first tier of subcontractors. A second tier of material and component subcontractors supports production in the first tier. All production takes place in SE Asia, taking advantage of low production costs.

One distinctive aspect of Nike is that marketing, advertising and consumption trends dictate what will be manufactured. Since production is so driven by fashion, opting for a subcontracting mode of operation has given Nike the flexibility to cope with the vagaries of changing fashion.

WWP – a transnational service conglomerate

WWP is one of a growing number of transnational service conglomerates. They are a relatively recent outcome of globalisation and operate internationally in a number of related service industries. The general mode of operation of WWP puts it in the dynamic network category (Figure 4.41).

The WWP Group has its headquarters in London and is one of the largest service conglomerates in the world. It employs 20,000 people in 780 offices in 83 countries. It grew very rapidly during the 1980s through a series of mergers and acquisitions. It owns two of the world's largest advertising agencies and provides clients worldwide with an unparalleled range of specialised skills.

ACTIVITIES

1 Make a series of notes summarising the key features of TNCs.

2 Research a TNC of your choice by visiting its website and prepare a brief report under the headings of
- activities
- global distribution.

Compare your findings with those of your fellow students.

National governments

Market economy	Planned economy
The market is paramount. The government regulates the economy in a general way (e.g. by controlling interest rates) to make the most of market opportunities. Decisions about investment, production and distribution are left to private companies. The government does not concern itself with what activities should or should not exist.	The government directs the economy by setting national economic and social targets. It strongly guides the market and makes decisions about investment and the allocation of resources. State ownership means that there is a large public sector, but privately-owned companies do exist. The private sector is equally bound by the same national targets. Policy choices are based on ideological dogma.
The main responsibilities of government: • to maintain economic stability • to provide physical infrastructure, especially those with high fixed costs • to supply public goods such as education and defence • to improve the markets for labour, finance and technology.	The main responsibilities of government: • to give top priority to development • to maintain national economic competitiveness • to sustain the autonomy of the state, often through a single-party system • to control the market.
Examples: Japan, UK and USA	Examples: China and Cuba

Table 4.11 *The two dominant types of economy*

There are 170 nation states in the world today. They differ enormously in terms of the extent to which their governments are active and influential in economic affairs, both nationally and globally. Broadly speaking, most fall into one of the two types outlined in Table 4.11.

In general, national governments intervene in order to protect or promote their position in global affairs. Intervention may therefore be negative or positive. It is mainly felt in three areas of economic activity:

- trade
- foreign investment
- industry.

Trade

Government intervention in trade has a long history. The world economy of the seventeenth and eighteenth centuries was mainly shaped by the policies of the great nations of Europe (the UK, France, Portugal and Spain). The UK's reign as the world's leading industrial nation was brought to an end in the late nineteenth century when the USA and Germany put up barriers to the import of British goods. The great world recession of the 1930s was aggravated by the fact that many nations 'retreated' behind trade barriers. In the last quarter of the twentieth century, the world was swept by a new wave of trade protectionism (**neomercantilism**) as many governments tried to manage trade in a variety of ways. The main types of intervention are listed in Table 4.12.

Influencing imports	Influencing exports
• Tariffs – taxes are levied on imports, so increasing their price and making them less competitive.	• Incentives – financial help and tax concessions to export producers.
• Import quotas and licensing, i.e. rationing the volume of imports.	• Export credits and guarantees.
• Tightening regulations concerned with labelling, packaging, health and customs to make importing more difficult.	• Establishing export processing zones and free trade zones.
• Exchange rates – deliberate raising of rates to make imports more expensive.	• Exchange rates – deliberate lowering of rates to increase competitiveness of exports.
• Local content – requiring that all imports should involve a specified proportion of local materials or parts.	• Embargo on strategic exports and voluntary export restraint – these are designed to reduce exports.

Table 4.12 *Major types of trade intervention*

Two important points need to made here. The first is that nearly all the devices in Table 4.12 are designed to either suppress imports or encourage exports. Only rarely is the situation reversed, e.g. where a particular imported material or product may be strategically needed or where a government feels that it should discourage certain types of export (i.e. armaments). Second, few if any nations are completely free agents. Most are required to abide by the rules of international trade laid down by the World Trade Organisation. Many are also obliged to observe the particular rules of any regional trading bloc to which they might belong.

Foreign investment

In the world of TNCs and complex international investment flows, it is in the interests of most governments to monitor and control foreign investment. As with trade, foreign investment operates in two directions – inward and outward. In general, most national policies are concerned with inward investment (Table 4.13). Governments may also place restrictions on the export of capital for investment, if it is felt that it is being used for something that is not in the national interest, or is destined for a country with whom political relations are difficult.

Controlling inward investment	Controlling outward investment
• government screening of investment proposals • excluding foreign firms from specified sectors of the economy • restricting the degree of foreign ownership of domestic enterprises • insisting that local people occupy managerial positions • requiring a certain level of local content • restricting the export of profits • controlling the location of foreign investment	• requiring government approval of overseas investment proposals • restricting the export of capital (by amount or by destination) • introducing exchange control regulations

Table 4.13 *Some ways of controlling foreign investment*

LEDCs are keen to attract foreign investment in order to help the development process. Equally, there are MEDCs that are anxious to encourage inward investment in order to bolster stagnant or declining economies. This is particularly true of the peripheral regions of the EU. Indeed, so keenly felt is the need for investment here, that all manner of positive incentives are offered. For example, inward investment in remote parts of the UK may receive benefits offered by both the EU (through the European Regional Development Fund) and the British Government (through its Assisted Areas schemes), as well as by county and local authorities. The large number of Japanese companies that have set up branch plants in parts of the UK over the last three decades testifies to the power of these incentives.

Foreign investment in Japan

Japanese companies are widely recognised as one of the major contributors to foreign investment at a global scale. Success stories like Telford, on the opposite page, emphasise that investment. It would be wholly wrong, however, to think of Japan as only a source of investment flows. It is a target too.

Of the investment into Japan in 1997 nearly one-half came from the EU (with the UK contributing around one-third of that) and one-sixth from the USA. Overall, just over half of the investment was in manufacturing. An analysis of factories owned by foreign companies shows the top five industrial activities to be chemicals, electronics and electricals, general machinery, pharmaceuticals and metals. Unfortunately, the conventional categories used in the collection of industrial data in Japan conceal what is the real focus of interest for foreign investment, namely high-tech activities such as the manufacture of micro-chips, new materials and advanced communications equipment.

In recent years, the amount of foreign investment in the service sector has been increasing. Commerce, business services, banking and insurance have been the main targets.

Despite the growth of inward investment, it is still greatly overshadowed by outward flows. Ten years ago, the outward investment was 20 times greater than inward investment; today the difference is 8 times.

It might seem strange that the Japanese government is keen to encourage inward investment by companies rivalling its own. But the Japanese economy is still in the doldrums and anything that might kick-start a recovery is to be welcomed.

Inward investment and the revival of Telford

Within Telford, one of the UK's post-war New Towns (located in Shropshire), lies Coalbrookdale, widely recognised as the birthplace of the Industrial Revolution. Critical to the birth of modern industry were the local resources of fuel (wood for charcoal and later coal), iron ore, fireclay and water power, together with the human resources of innovation and enterprise.

Coalbrookdale boomed industrially from the mid-eighteenth century to the turn of the nineteenth century. The main reasons for its subsequent decline were:

- the exhaustion of local raw materials
- competition from other industrial areas
- the cramped nature of the area
- changes in technology (with respect to transport and industrial processes).

By the 1950s, deindustrialisation had resulted in high levels of unemployment and out-migration. In 1963, the area was chosen as the site for a New Town, the main aim being to rejuvenate the area by housing the overspill population from the nearby West Midland conurbation. In 1968 the Telford Development Corporation set about trying the revive the industrial fortunes of the area. Initially, it was not too successful as continuing job losses in the traditional metal and engineering industries were greater than the number of new jobs brought into the area. Fortunes began to change in the 1980s. Significant developments included:

- the opening of the M54 motorway linking Telford to the national road network
- the creation of an Enterprise Zone which meant that financial incentives were available to persuade industrialists to move into the area
- the creation of two up-market campus sites to attract foreign investment
- the availability of money from the EU Regional Development Fund
- the granting of Intermediate Area status which made even more financial support available
- a successful record in persuading foreign companies to set up branch plants (Table 4.14).

Employees	Company	Activity
2000+	*Epson (Telford) Ltd	Computer printer manufacturer
	*EDS	Information technology
1000–1999	*Denso Manufacturing (UK) Ltd	Air conditioning
	GKN Sankey	Automotive engineering
500–999	Aga-Rayburn	Cookers and fabrication
	Alvis Vehicles Ltd	Military vehicle manufacturer
	Bandy Telford Ltd	Steel tubing manufacturer
	Hutchinson UK	Rubber manufacturer
	Johnson Control Automotive	Automotive components
	*Makita Europe Manufacturing	Power tool manufacturer
	Poly-lina PLC	Polythene bag manufacturer
	*Ricoh Products (UK) Ltd	Photocopier manufacturer
	* = *Foreign parent company*	

Table 4.14 *The top private sector employers in Telford, 1998*

By 2000, Telford had become a growth area enjoying a wider mix of industries than before, and recognised as an important centre for high-tech industry. Thanks to local enterprise, various forms of government support and foreign investment, Telford remains a manufacturing centre with 40 per cent of its workforce in that sector.

The number of people working in foreign-owned companies has grown considerably. In 1998, Telford had the highest concentration of Japanese and Taiwanese manufacturing companies in the UK. Inward investment has involved the arrival of 152 foreign companies and the creation of 16,800 jobs (almost one quarter of total employment) in the area (Figure 4.45).

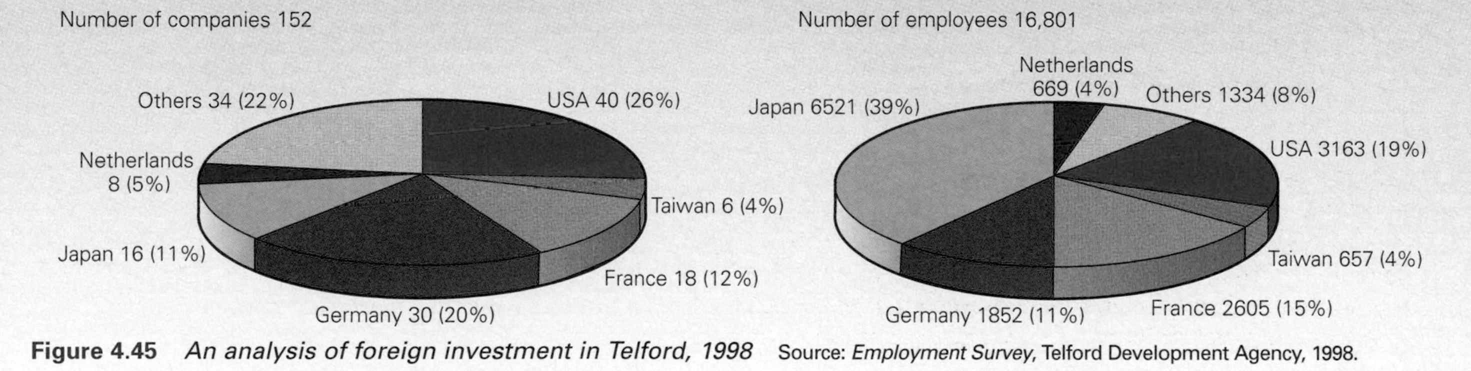

Figure 4.45 *An analysis of foreign investment in Telford, 1998* Source: *Employment Survey*, Telford Development Agency, 1998.

Industry

Industry is the third area in which governments are able to exercise control. The top two boxes in Table 4.15 indicate that intervention can be both stimulating and restraining. The bottom box shows that such devices may be applied generally across the whole of a nation's industries (primary, secondary and tertiary). Equally, they may be applied selectively to particular industries or to particular geographical locations. The boundaries between government intervention in trade, in foreign investment and in industry are becoming increasingly blurred. This is illustrated by regional aid programmes where foreign investment is directed towards particular industries in particular areas, with the aim of not only reducing unemployment, but also of altering the balance of trade, i.e. reducing imports and boosting exports.

Stimulating	Restraining
• investment incentives – tax, interest rates • labour – subsidised cost, training • small firm policies • industrial restructuring policies	• state ownership • merger and competition restrictions • labour regulation – unions, immigration • environmental, health and safety regulations
These interventions may be applied to: • particular industrial sectors (to bolster declining industries or stimulate new ones) • particular types of firm (to attract foreign firms with import substitution in mind or encourage new ones) • particular geographical areas (to revive depressed areas or create areas of growth potential)	

Table 4.15 *Main types of industrial intervention by governments*

Finally in this section, it is necessary to look briefly at the relationship between TNCs and national governments in the global economy. On the one hand, the relationship can be cooperative, but equally, it can be one of rivalry and conflict. National governments need TNCs to generate wealth and provide jobs. Government preference would be that such firms operate only in their country, but that is not an option so far as the TNC is concerned. TNCs not only span national boundaries; they also embrace within their corporate boundaries parts of national economies (Figure 4.46). Conversely, TNCs need national governments to provide the physical infrastructure (transport and services) and the social infrastructure (educated workers, the legal protection of property, etc.) that are vital to the production process.

ACTIVITIES

1 Summarise the ways in which national governments can influence:

a trade
b foreign investment
c industry.

In which of these three fields do you think the influence is strongest? Answer this by investigating the experiences of two MEDCs (e.g. the UK and France, or Japan and Australia).

The likely outcome for any country hosting part of a TNC will be a loss of sovereignty and autonomy, an external dependence on technology and capital, and **truncation**. Truncation occurs because in many cases a particular country will accommodate only one function in a TNC's long production chain. The specialisation that is implicit in that one function tends to work against a balanced development of the host economy as a whole.

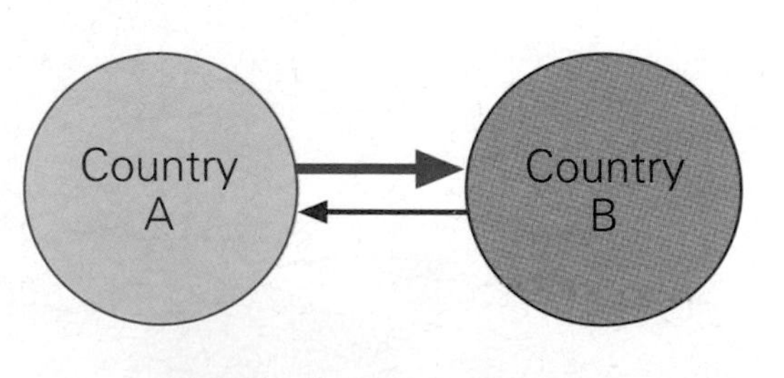

Countries linked through trade.

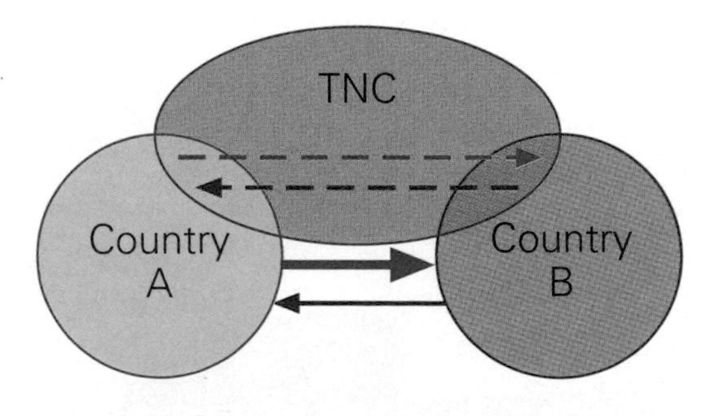

Countries linked through the internal markets of transnational companies

Figure 4.46 *International and TNC-government relationships*
Source: Dicken, *Global Shift*, Paul Chapman Publishing, 1999.

EXTENSION ACTIVITY

1 Medico is a TNC based in London specialising in pharmaceuticals. Its Research and Development department has come up with a new anti-malaria drug taken in pill form on a monthly basis. Trials have been conducted and the drug is about to be approved for sale to the public. The company has decided to concentrate global production of the drug in one new plant, and that this plant should be located in or near to a major city and close to an international airport. The plant will have a labour requirement of 2,400 workers. Two-thirds of the jobs will require minimal training and are classified as 'unskilled', but technical, marketing and managerial staff will also be needed.

Medico have drawn up a shortlist of nine possible locations (Figure 4.47): London, Lisbon, Prague, Mexico City, Brasilia, Delhi, Hong Kong, Jakarta and Nairobi. Imagine that you have been asked to recommend which of these would offer the best location in terms of minimising production and distribution costs. In making your recommendations, you should remember:

- Anti-malaria drugs are needed by tourists and business people from non-malaria areas when visiting any of the malaria areas shown in Figure 4.47.
- Medico is keen to take advantage of government incentives to encourage inward investment.
- Your report should show the reasoning behind your recommendations. It might be useful to prepare a table which clearly shows the relative merits of the nine locations.

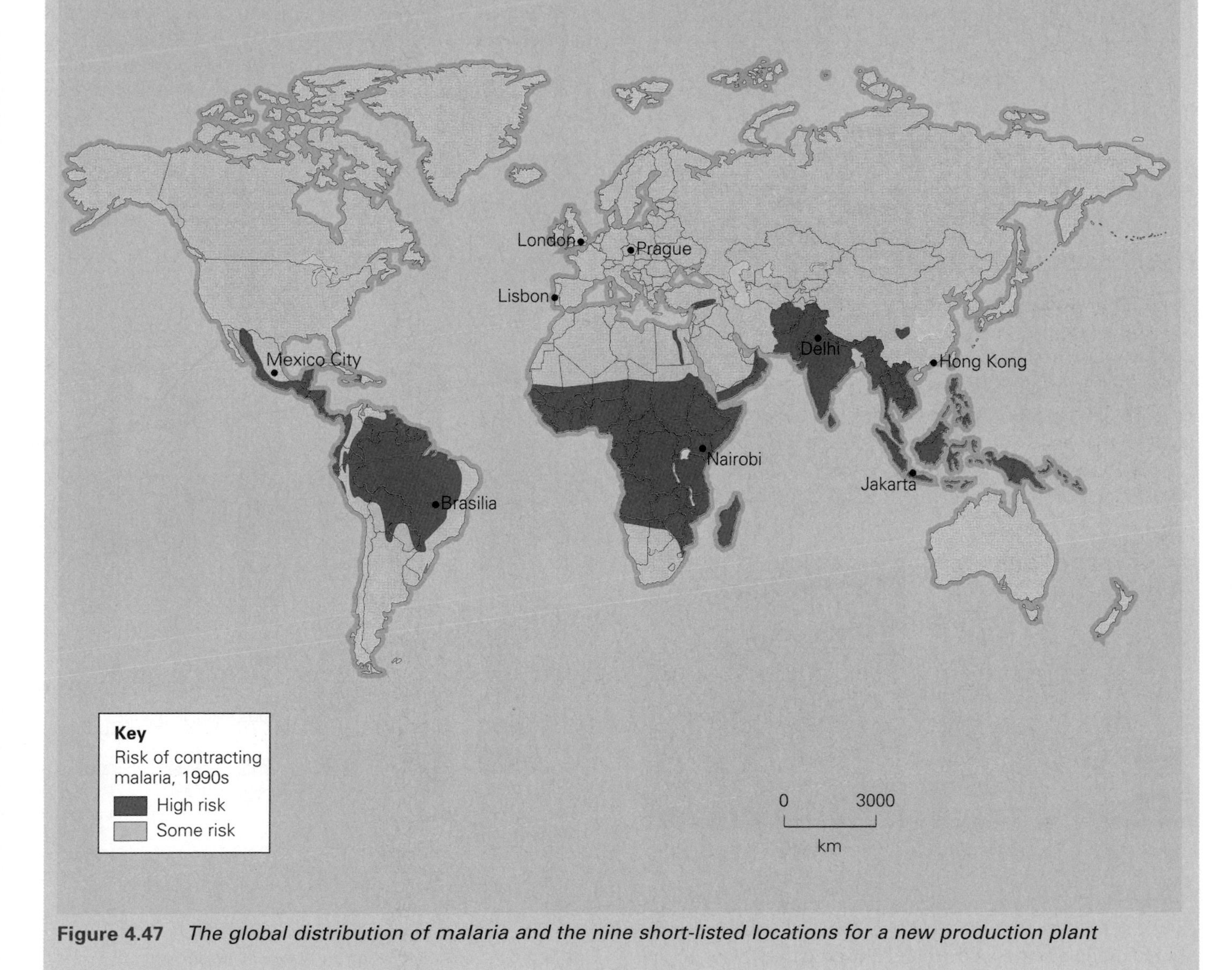

Figure 4.47 *The global distribution of malaria and the nine short-listed locations for a new production plant*

5 Implications of changes in economic activity

Globalisation and its associated shifts in the location of economic activity have generated four major geographical outcomes (Figure 4.48).

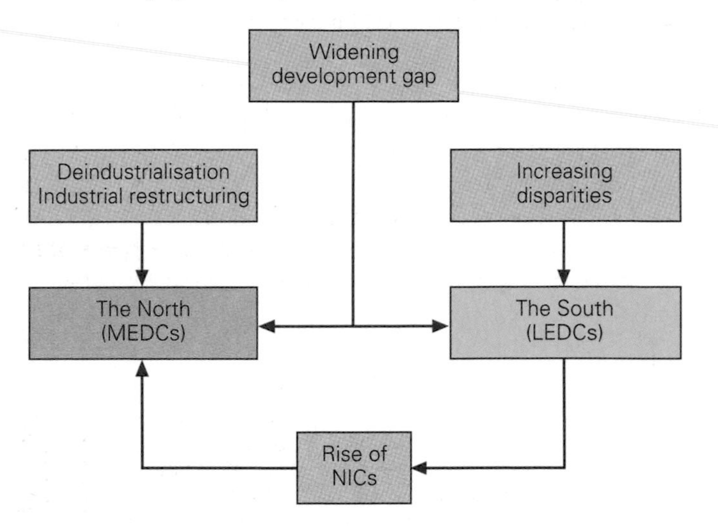

Figure 4.48 *Four geographical outcomes of globalisation*

A widening of the development gap

During the 1990s, growth in the global economy averaged 2 per cent per year compared with 3 per cent per year during the 1980s, and 5 per cent per year during the 1950s and 1960s. As the global growth rate has fallen, so the development gap between countries has widened. In 1965, income per head for the top 20 per cent of the world's population was 25 times that of the poorest 20 per cent. By 1999, this gap had more than doubled to 64 times (Figure 4.49).

Figure 4.49 *The widening development gap*

The world's poorest countries have shown no sign of catching up with the MEDCs. Only a handful of Asia Pacific countries have managed to sustain growth rapid enough to catch up with the group of rich nations (Figure 4.3).

Deindustrialisation in the North

The term **deindustrialisation** is used to signal the relative decline of manufacturing in most of the MEDCs. The percentage of the national labour force engaged in manufacturing has declined, and so too has the percentage contribution to GDP. The major cause of the relative decline has been the strong growth in services. Despite the fact that foreign competition has caused some manufacturing industries to decline to the point of extinction, and that others have moved offshore to cheaper and less regulated locations, manufacturing remains an important sector of an MEDC economy (Figure 4.50). In many cases, its character has changed. **Industrial restructuring** has seen the traditional industries, such as iron and steel, chemicals, ship-building and textiles replaced by consumer and high-tech industries. This restructuring has led to a redrawing of the industrial map.

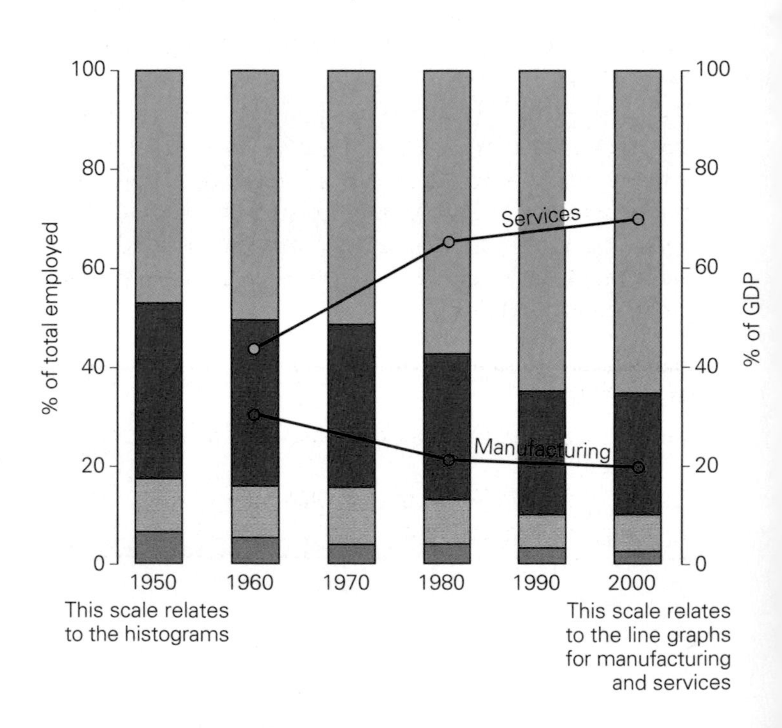

Figure 4.50 *Sectoral shifts in the UK economy, 1950–2000*

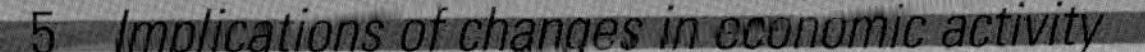

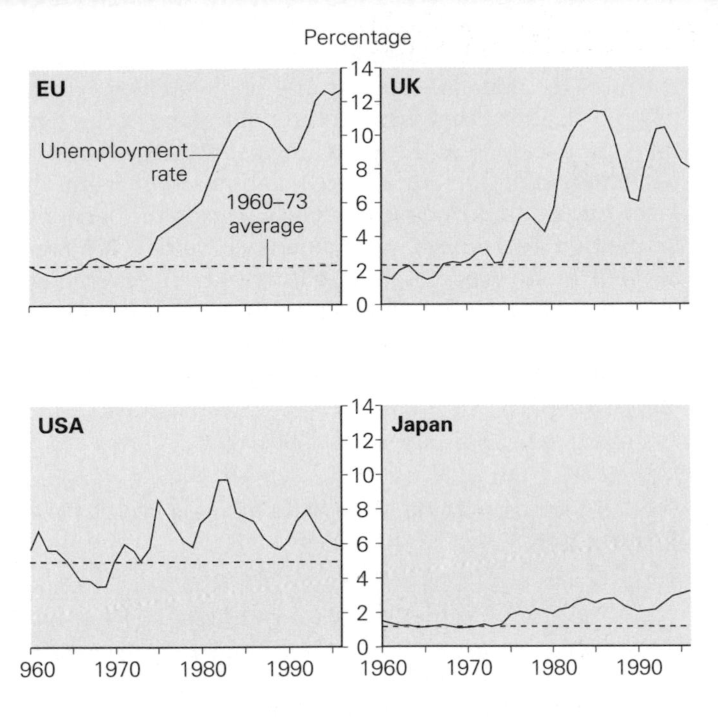

Figure 4.51 *Unemployment rates in the EU, UK, USA and Japan, 1960–1996* Source: Dicken, *Global Shift*, Paul Chapman Publishing, 1999.

Deindustrialisation and industrial restructuring caused high rates of unemployment in MEDCs during the last quarter of the twentieth century. Figure 4.51 shows that Japan was the only country to keep unemployment down to an acceptable level.

The case study of Telford (page 187) may be used to illustrate the changing fortunes of an area that slipped from being the birthplace of the Industrial Revolution to becoming one of the corpses of deindustrialisation. It also illustrates how industrial restructuring and inward foreign investment have helped restore the area to a reasonably prosperous condition.

ACTIVITIES

1. Distinguish between deindustrialisation and industrial restructuring.
2. Why do you think that unemployment levels have remained relatively low in Japan?

Rise of the NICs

The spectacular industrial growth of a small number of developing countries is possibly one of the most obvious outcomes of globalisation. Four of these NICs – the Asian Tigers (South Korea, Taiwan, Singapore and Hong Kong) – have experienced so much economic growth that it is no longer appropriate to regard them as developing countries. Behind them on the development scale come a group of countries including Brazil, India, Mexico and Thailand, which are located in the South, but are sometimes grouped as RICs due to their high rate of economic development (Figure 4.3). Growth in all these countries has centred on the manufacturing sector and has been driven by **import substitution** (manufacturing what was previously imported) and **export promotion** (producing goods with high levels of demand globally).

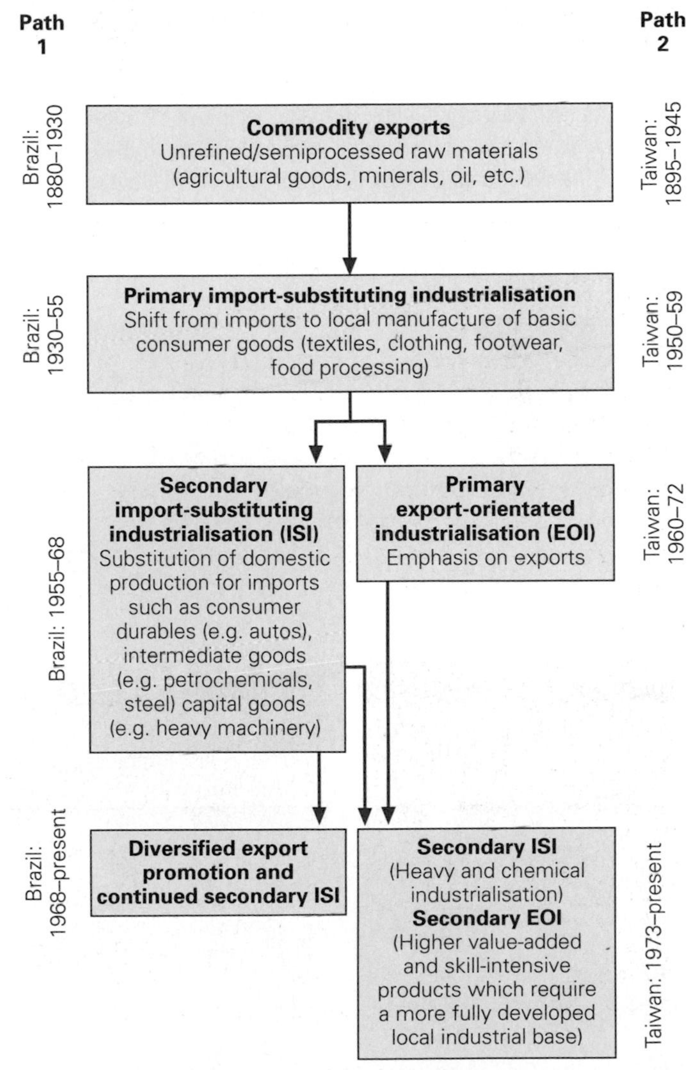

Figure 4.52 *A model of industrialisation paths; 1 = Latin America, – 2 = East Asia*

Figure 4.52 shows some examples of NICs and RICs that have progressed through a series of industrialisation stages. The nature of the pathways has not been the same for all countries. Indeed, the model shows a fundamental difference between the Latin American sequence and what has happened in East Asia. The first two stages of 1) exporting unrefined or semi-processed raw materials and 2) primary import-substitution are common to both regions (but not Singapore – see case study below). In stage 3, Asian industrialisation was mainly export-oriented (primary and secondary), while in Latin America the focus was mainly on import-substitution. It is only in stage 4 that both regions show an inclination to diversify and mix both types of industrial development.

The Asian Tigers, perhaps because of their decision to go for export-oriented industrialisation, have certainly been the ones to capitalise most on the opportunities created by globalisation. They were in the right place at the right time, producing what the global market wanted. They also benefited from the experiences and lessons learnt by Japan during its 'economic miracle'. For example, Japanese production techniques were emulated and TNCs were allowed more freedom. Also, the nature of government intervention was rather different in East Asia from that in Latin American states: it was less dictatorial, more flexible and more encouraging to grass roots enterprise and initiative.

Singapore: one of the Asian Tigers

The Republic of Singapore came into being in 1959, when it ceased to be a British colony. Its newly-won independence was given up in 1963 when Singapore joined the Malaysian Federation. As it turned out, this was only to be for two years, and since 1965 Singapore has gone its own way. A situation of high unemployment, poverty and political unrest was soon transformed, and Singapore has become one of the world's wealthiest nations (Figure 4.53). This rise is all the more remarkable considering Singapore's small size (622 km²) and the fact that it has to import all of its water, energy and industrial raw materials, and most of its food.

Since 1965 the development of Singapore has gone through three distinct phases:

- Up to the mid-1970s, the government encouraged export-oriented industry, as well as inward investment by TNCs. The mix was particularly successful and it is in these two respects that Singapore departs from the industrialisation model (Figure 4.52). It also never experienced stage 1.
- During the late 1970s industrial restructuring led to a shift from labour-intensive to capital-intensive industries. The result was considerable automation and a significant broadening of the product base.
- Since the mid-1980s the emphasis in the economy has gradually shifted towards the service sector. Services now account for 64 per cent of GDP compared with 27 per cent for manufacturing.

Singapore's remarkable economic success would seem to be explained largely by three factors:

- Its natural harbour and related port functions. Of all the Asian Tigers, Singapore is the most dependent on trade.
- The quality of its human resources (75 per cent Chinese, 15 per cent Malay and 5 per cent Indian). They are well educated, hardworking and ambitious. The only problem on the labour front is the lack of unskilled labour and professional people.
- The firm leadership provided by the government, and the consistency of that government in terms of politics. This firmness also involves a tight control on behaviour, restricted press freedom and a largely one-party democracy.

In terms of facing the three challenges previously outlined, Singapore seems to be the best placed of the Asian Tigers and is now officially an MEDC.

Figure 4.53 *Singapore skyline*

The success of the NICs has not been without its problems. These include high levels of environmental pollution, poor working conditions and poor pay, dubious financial practices and widespread political corruption. The outbreak of 'Asian flu' in the late 1990s drew particular attention to the last two factors. Three issues present a particular challenge:

- sustaining future economic growth at an acceptable rate in a less favourable global climate
- ensuring that the benefits of economic success are shared fairly by all the population
- reducing the financial debt that most NICs have incurred since the late 1970s as a result of overseas borrowing.

ACTIVITIES

1 'The fact that the four leading NICs are located in Asia is just coincidence.' Discuss.
2 Find out about the development path of Mexico and produce a short case-study report modelled on that for Singapore.

Brazil moves into the global arena

At long last, South America's fitful economic giant is showing signs of stirring and making a global impact commensurate with its size, population and resources. After decades of boom-bust cycles, the world's fifth largest country has begun to look to external markets rather than being pre-occupied with its enormous internal one. It is gradually positioning itself to become a notable global player.

One of the most significant moves has been by the Brazilian government which has dismantled the country's protectionist walls against international trade. Tariff barriers on imports were reduced from 40 to 7.5 per cent. Exports increased by 17 per cent in 1999 and were expected to grow by 20 per cent in 2000. The value of trade doubled in the 1990s with imports tripling.

Industries and services which were almost totally state-owned in 1994 are being privatised in what has been called the world's biggest privatisation exercise. Foreign investments are flowing in at an unprecedented rate. International business people are actively sizing up new opportunities for profitable enterprise. The best opportunities are perceived as being in information technology, banking, electronic equipment, semiconductors, biotechnology and power generation. The international confidence in the new Brazil is such that foreign investments are estimated to exceed $30 billion this year, making the country the third most popular recipient of foreign investment after the USA and China.

Although blessed with extensive natural resources and a population of 165 million, Brazil has suffered over its 500 year history from dictatorial leadership, chronic political instability and economic protectionism. As a consequence, it remains a land of strong contrasts between wealth and poverty, between developed and undeveloped areas. Brazilians worry whether the current enthusiasm for globalisation will deliver greater and fairer prosperity.

(based on a feature article by Michael Knipe in *The Times*, 19 December, 2000)

Increasing disparity among the LEDCs

While the gap between MEDCs and LEDCs continues to increase, so too do the disparities that exist between the nations of the South. Tables 4.16 and 4.17 provide some illustration of this within what the World Bank calls the 'low-income countries' such as Mozambique, Laos and Bangladesh. Look at the range of values given for the three development indicators (Table 4.16) and the ranges shown for the sectoral shifts in employment (Table 4.17). This increasing disparity may be explained in terms of a differential exposure to globalisation. While some LEDCs have been reached by globalisation, others remain untouched. The reason why some countries have been affected may be due to such factors as better resources, better accessibility, more progressive government and the perceptions and enterprise of particular TNCs.

	Per capita income ($)	**Life expectancy** (years)	**Infant mortality** (per 1000 live births)
Mean	380	56	58
Range	80–720	38–73	25–163

Table 4.16 *Development indicators for low-income countries, 1995*

	Percentage of the labour force					
	Agriculture		**Industry**		**Services**	
	1960	1990	1960	1990	1960	1990
Mean	77	69	9	15	14	16
Range	54–95	18–94	1–18	2–31	3–37	–

Table 4.17 *Sectoral labour shifts in low-income countries*

The backmarkers of the Asia Pacific region

The Asia Pacific region is widely recognised as the world's leading **sunrise region** (new economically booming region). Whilst the region undoubtedly contains a significant number of the world's most successful and dynamic economies, it also comprises at least four countries with economies that seriously lag behind the rest. They are Cambodia, Laos, North Korea and Vietnam.

	GNP per capita ($)	Human development index	Food intake (calories per day)	Population per doctor	Adult Literacy M (%)	Adult Literacy F (%)
Cambodia	270	0.348	2,021	9,374	47	20
Laos	350	0.459	2,259	4,446	56	31
North Korea	1000	0.765	2,833	nd	5	5
Vietnam	240	0.557	2,203	4,498	74	47

Table 4.18 *Comparative development indicators, 1995*

These countries have certain features in common that have a bearing on development (Table 4.18).

- They are all small countries, and only one of them (North Korea) is endowed with natural resources. However, the example of the four Asian Tigers suggests that these features need not be disadvantages.
- In terms of economic sectors, agriculture and other primary activities account for the largest share of GDP. Manufacturing is already export-oriented rather than geared to import substitution.
- Inward foreign investment is being encouraged in two of the countries (Vietnam and Laos), but only in a lukewarm manner.
- All four countries were battlefields during the second half of the twentieth century. War and its associated destruction of infrastructure has undoubtedly had a debilitating effect on development.
- All four countries have been ruled by communist or socialist governments. It may well be that communism, with its planned economies, is unable to deliver development at the pace and scale achieved by market economies.
- Internal tensions continue to simmer in all four countries. The longer they do so, the longer they are likely to hinder development.

In an age of globalisation, it seems that these countries have to make a choice. Either they confine their overseas contacts to the diminishing number of Second World economies, or they forget their political ideologies and seek out those overseas contacts which promise the best returns. Only the latter offers any real promise of closing the development gap that separates them from the other Asia Pacific economies.

Spatial differences and disparities do not end at a national level. They also exist between different parts of an individual LEDC. Perhaps the greatest of these internal differences occur between urban and rural areas as development usually occurs with urbanisation. This is illustrated by the fact that in Africa, 29 per cent of the urban population lives in absolute poverty compared with 58 per cent of the rural population. Economic growth becomes polarised in the leading cities and is accompanied by rising volumes of rural-urban migration that gradually debilitate rural areas.

The immediate prospect is that the four spatial outcomes of globalisation (Figure 4.48) will persist and disparities seem set to intensify before they diminish.

EXTENSION ACTIVITY

Find out more about each of the four backmarker countries – Cambodia, Laos, North Korea and Vietnam, and attempt the following:

1. Rank the countries in terms of their development potential and give the evidence that supports your ranking.
2. For your top ranking country, identify what you see as the main obstacles to development and suggest how these might be overcome.
3. For the same country, outline and justify the directions and forms of development that you would recommend as being more appropriate

You may choose to undertake this exercise with respect to four of the least developed countries in Africa (Ethiopia, Malawi, Sierra Leone and Tanzania) rather than those prescribed above).

6 Future changes in the global economy

How might the global economy change in the future?

Further expansion of the global economy

Globalisation looks set to continue as the global economy moves ever closer to becoming a single market for labour, production and capital. Gradually all the nations of the world will be drawn into one huge web of interdependence.

It is now widely accepted that, although the global economy may continue to grow in the first half of the twenty-first century, it will not do so consistently, nor at the same rates experienced during the second half of the twentieth century. If one had to identify one single reason for this, it would be the resource situation (Figure 4.54). It is this that will put the brake on expansion.

Not only does it seem likely that the rate of growth will slow down, but coincidentally the competition to share in that growth will intensify between nations. The outcome of this scenario is not difficult to predict: the strong will become stronger, the weak will become weaker. The TNCs will become even more influential as 'architects' of evolving spatial patterns of wealth and success, poverty and exploitation. Taking a long-term view, the key question is: can economic growth be sustained for ever?

ACTIVITIES

1 Investigate the likely global resource situation by the year 2050. You might visit the WWF website: www.panda.org
2 Discuss the view that global economic growth will continue forever.

New markets, products and services

While the global demand for producers and services will Increase, it is possible to identify what are called **emerging markets**, i.e. parts of the world that are likely to significantly increase their buying power for such goods and services (Figure 4.55). Certainly, the growth of these markets and satisfying their demands will help fuel growth in the global economy.

It is difficult to envisage the appearance of any truly new products in the immediate future. Rather more certain is that the product base of manufacturing will continue to shift. Some of the traditional heavy industries will continue to decline, perhaps to the point of extinction, but this may well be compensated by increased production of:

- consumer and household goods as levels of personal affluence rise
- the range of equipment related to the information and communications age, from fibre optics and microchips to personal computers and mobile telephones
- new materials developed as substitutes for non-renewable resources that are fast becoming exhausted.

Figure 4.54 *Resources – a brake on economic growth*

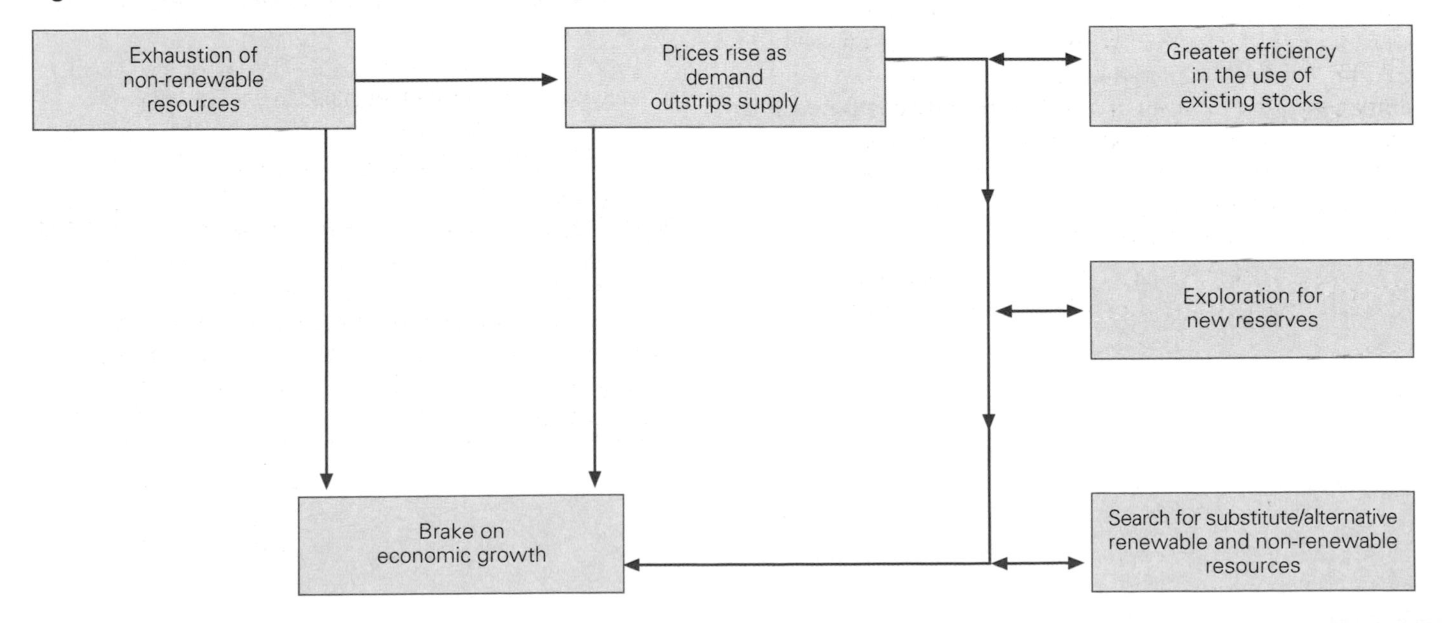

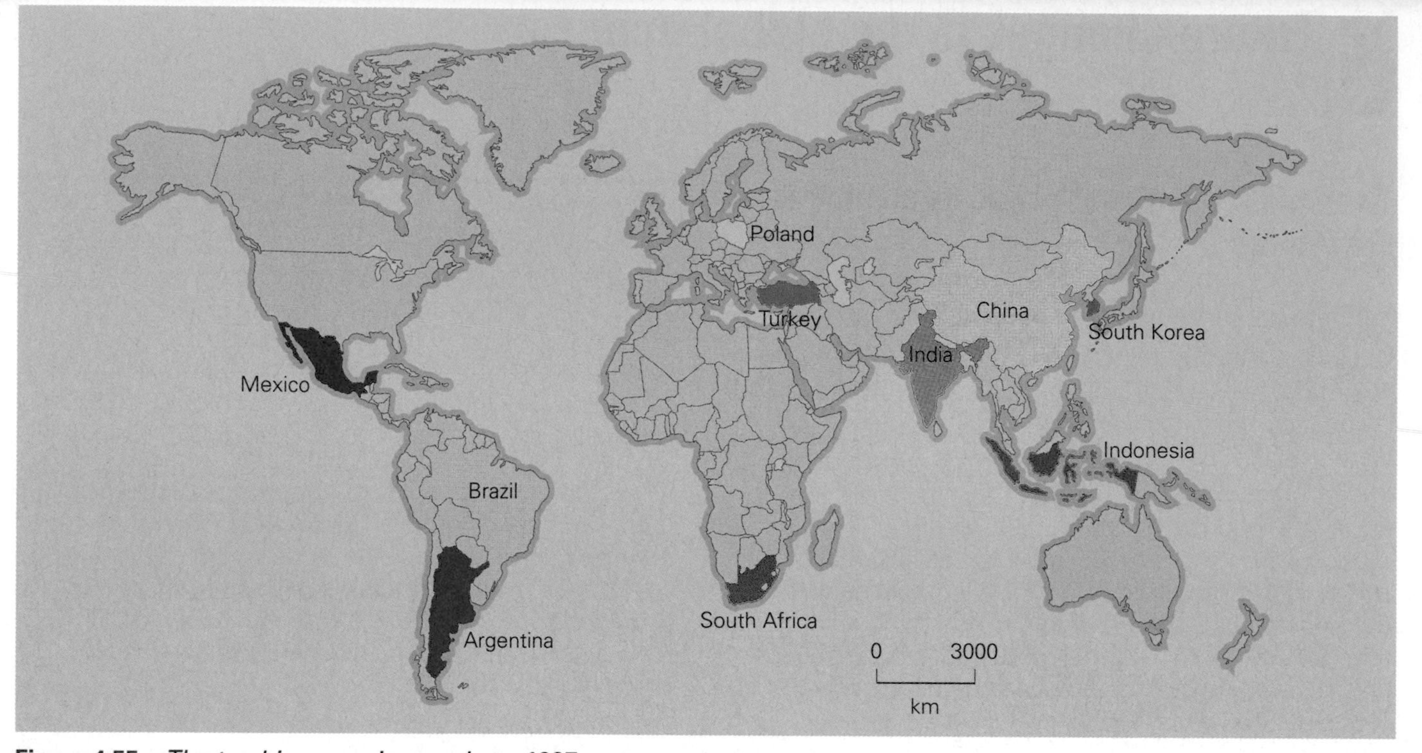

Figure 4.55 *The ten big emerging markets, 1997* Source: US Department of Commerce, 1997.

The decline in the percentage of people engaged in manufacturing looks set to continue as industrial robots replace human operatives and production processes become more automated (Figure 4.56). The service sector has been employing the labour shed by manufacturing. This trend may continue, but as new technology increases productivity, so it may also be possible for services to be provided by a smaller proportion of the potential working population.

Information services will undoubtedly be one growth area of the tertiary and quaternary sectors, but many of these services can be provided from anywhere in the world. More countries will become **outsourcing centres** for jobs in information. Continuing globalisation of the labour market will mean more companies moving jobs to locations offering skilled, cheap labour.

Another service growth area is tourism, resulting from:

- increased personal wealth and leisure, particularly in the North
- advances in air transport, for example, the development of huge 'super-jumbo' aircraft capable of carrying 1000 passengers. Between 1995 and 2020 the number of air travellers is expected to treble
- the opening up of new tourist destinations, particularly in China and SE Asia
- the globalisation of business.

One other development that might be noted is the further internationalisation of currency and equity markets. The former will play an important part in the growth of global tourism, whilst the latter may be particularly significant for the TNCs.

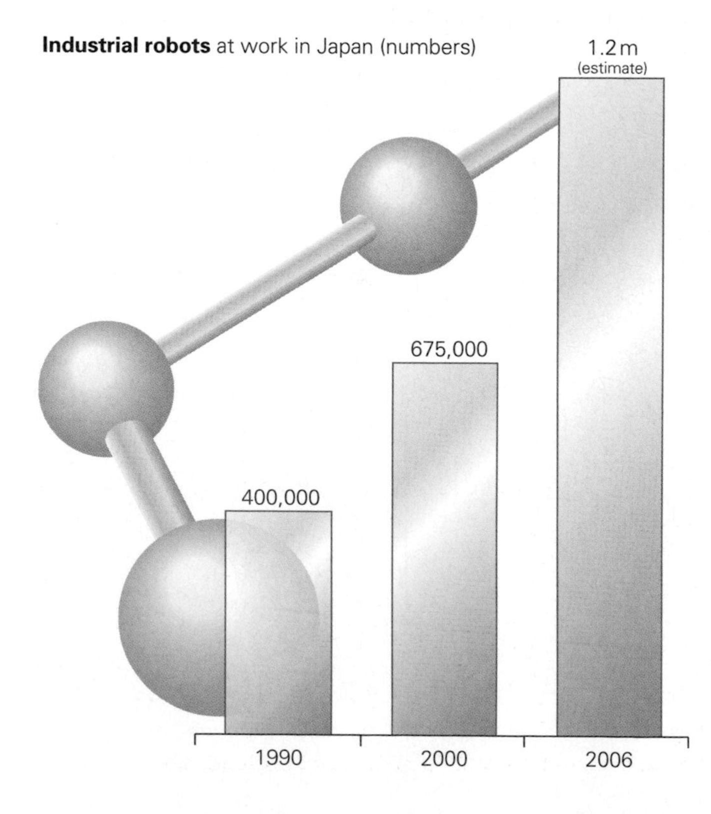

Figure 4.56 *The number of industrial robots at work in Japan* Source: *Atlas of the Future*, 1998.

Toyota drives on

Toyota is the third largest car-maker in the world, producing 5.2 million vehicles in 1998. It is a global company, operating 55 branch plants in 25 countries, and selling vehicles in another 135 countries. The company has recently entered another dimension of globalisation. It has joined a handful of Japanese companies (including Toshiba, Mitsubishi, Honda and Sony) that are listed on overseas stock markets. What this means in effect is that instead of being almost exclusively Japanese, its shareholder base has become more international.

What is it that encouraged Toyota to take this next step in globalisation and become less Japan-centric? If a company is to survive and prosper in the global super league, it must maintain, or better still expand, its market share. Expansion requires new investment. Given the recent depressed state of the Japanese economy, Toyota, like other companies, found it increasingly difficult to raise the necessary capital on the Tokyo Stock Exchange. Listing automatically opens the doors to investors throughout the world. However, in order to be listed, Japanese companies must make important changes in matters concerning accountancy and disclosure in order to bring them into line with their Western competitors. How companies are run is vital to investor confidence.

This reform could well fuel merger and acquisition activity, for example the merger of Daimler and Chrysler, and Renault's investment in Nissan. It may not be too long before Toyota looks for expansion and a larger share of the global market, not just through foreign shareholders, but perhaps in some sort of merger with another motor manufacturer. Being listed makes this more of a possibility and has moved Toyota to a higher level of globalisation.

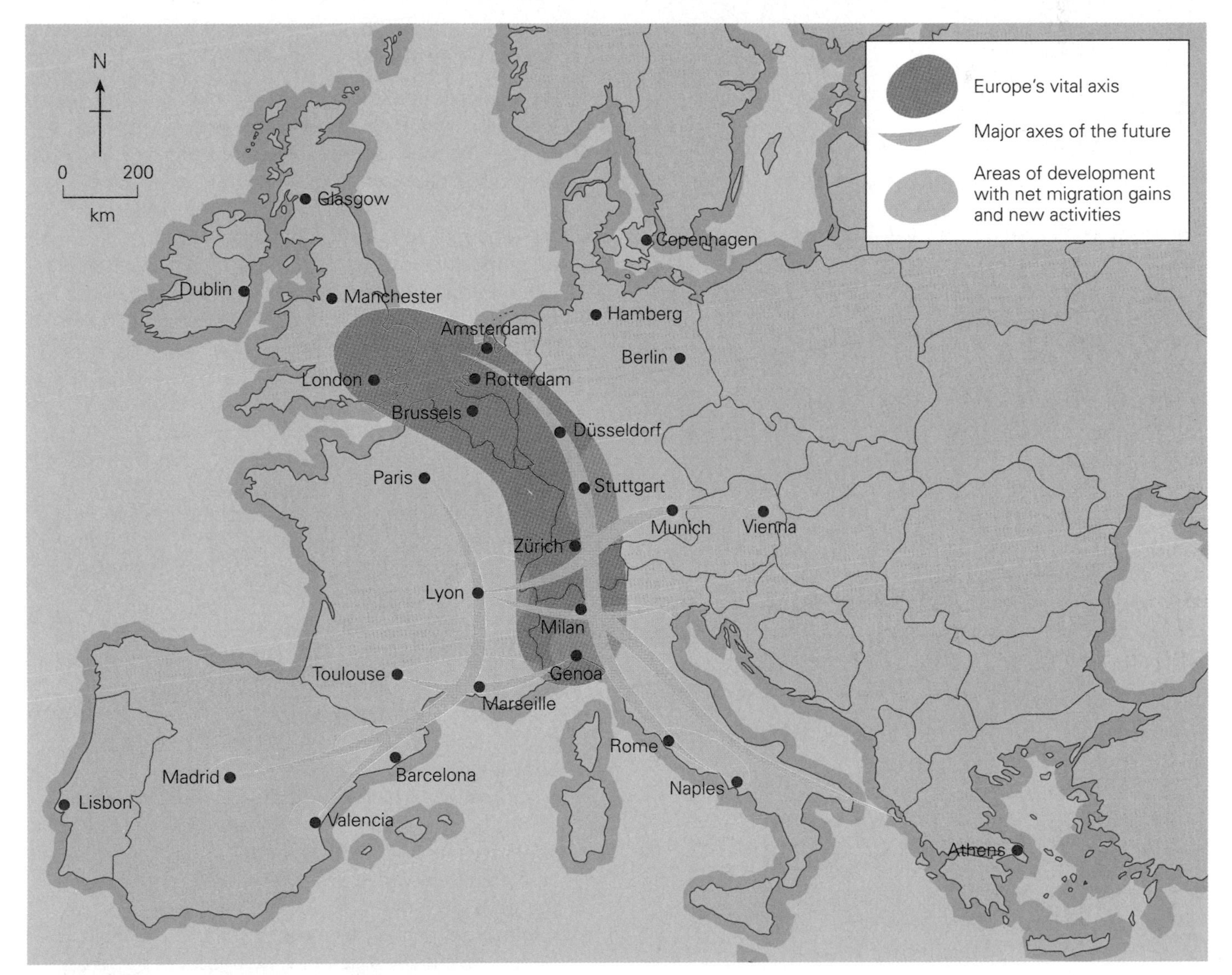

Figure 4.57 *Europe's major growth axis*

Source: Dicken, *Global Shift*, Paul Chapman Publishing, 1999.

Globalisation will continue to affect the geographical patterns of economic activity at three spatial scales:

- At the macro-scale, there will be further concentration of activity and power within the global triad (Figure 4.11).
- At the meso-scale, established growth axes will be extended and new ones emerge. An example of the former is to be found in Western Europe (Figure 4.57), while the urban corridors emerging in Asia Pacific (Figure 4.58) exemplify the latter.
- At the micro-scale, there are highly localised agglomerations (mainly long-established cities and their regions) which to varying degrees will share some of the global growth.

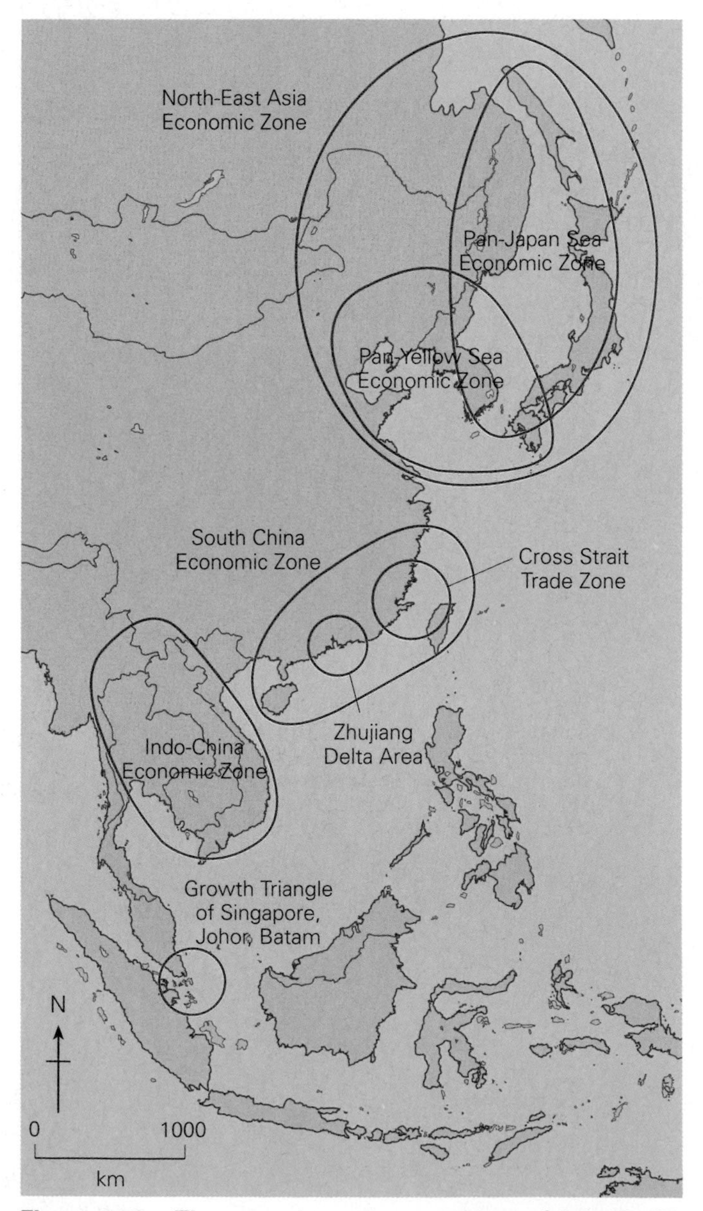

Figure 4.58 *The emerging urban corridors of Asia Pacific*
Source: Dicken, *Global Shift*, Paul Chapman Publishing, 1999.

ACTIVITIES

1. Explain how the globalisation of business is likely to contribute to the rise in tourism.
2. With reference to Figure 4.57, describe and explain the anticipated pattern of future growth axes.
3. A new growth axis is emerging along the USA–Mexico border. Why do you think that this is proving to be a boom region?

The impact of new technologies on lifestyles

The advances in transport and communications technology that have played such an important part in promoting globalisation will continue to have profound effects. This will affect our lifestyles in the North, in particular the way we live and work.

In the world of work, the following trends are expected to become more apparent:

- the percentage of people in paid work will continue to increase globally, but in some countries (notably in Western Europe and Africa) the percentage will fall
- the overall demand for labour will be reduced by higher levels of automation and productivity
- more people will live in a state of semi-unemployment, due to the impacts of automation, deindustrialisation, economic restructuring and underdevelopment
- more people will cross national frontiers and travel globally in search of work
- more people will work part-time, be self-employed or move into the informal economy
- there will be less job security and a greater need for flexible working
- working from home will become the norm for an increasing number of people
- women will account for an increasing percentage of the labour force (40 per cent by 2010).

These changes in the world of work, as well as the new technologies themselves, will have the following impacts on society and everyday life:

- the inequality between people with jobs and those without will intensify, so therefore will the gap between rich and poor
- advances in medicine and the associated increase in life expectancy mean that society will have to support an increasing number of people of pensionable age
- with an increasing number of women in paid work, traditional gender roles will change
- the Internet is likely to have the single greatest impact on the lifestyles of a vast number of people (Figure 4.59).

The Internet

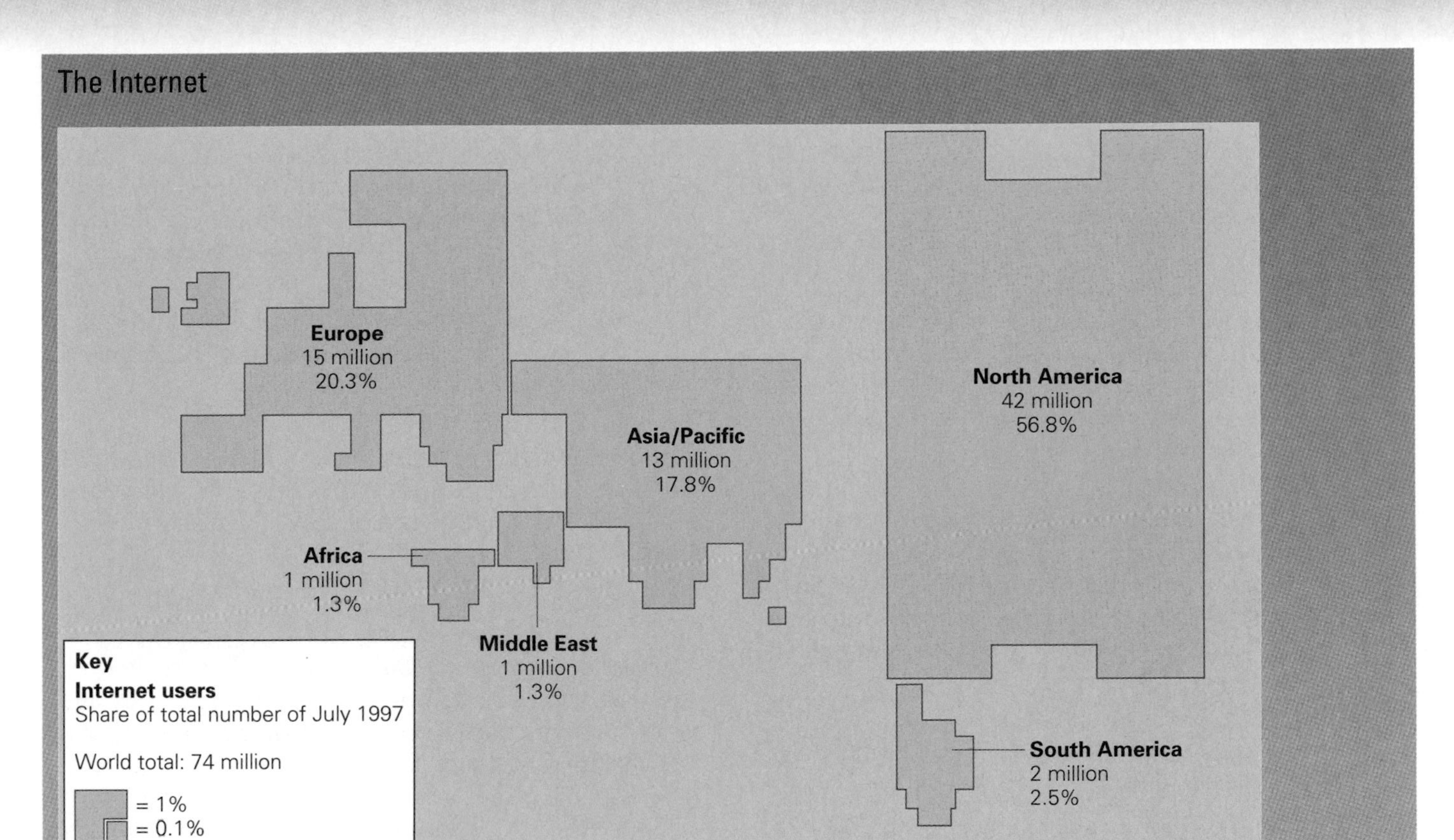

Figure 4.59 *The global distribution of Internet users, 1997* Source: *Atlas of the Future*, 1998.

The Internet has been, and will continue to be, the great facilitator of globalisation. It has significantly reduced the 'friction of distance', allowing almost instantaneous transfer of information, decisions and capital. While globalisation is increasingly drawing all of us into this global network, each year at least one million more of us are also making use of the Internet in our everyday lives (Figure 4.59). The Internet will provide a rich source as you complete some of the activities set out in this book: it is there to data-enrich your studies. Education and medical care are just two examples of the Internet's conquest of space. Through the Internet it is now possible for teachers and doctors to be 'present' anywhere on the planet.

Online banking, travel and shopping services will grow rapidly and be accessed directly from home. People will meet new and old friends and interact with them in virtual spaces, eventually with language translation built in. News, radio and television, and many forms of information and entertainment will increasingly be delivered in channels and broadcast by technology on the Internet. In the year 2000 only a small proportion of the world's population had a personal computer (Figure 4.60). Over the next 20 years, new technologies will change this. For an increasing number of us in the 'information-rich' regions of the world, the prospect is of a more home-based lifestyle.

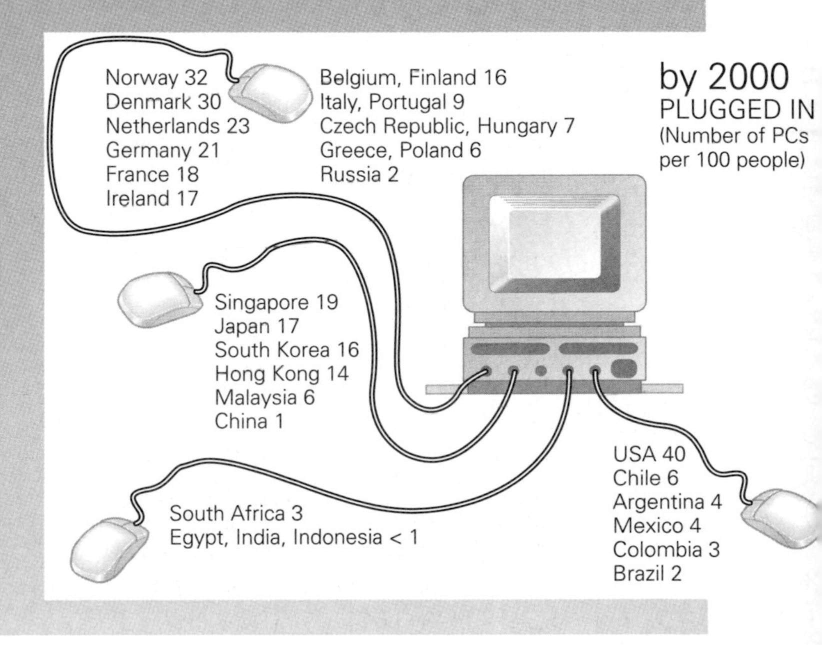

Figure 4.60 *PC-ownership in selected countries, 2000*
Source: *Atlas of the Future*, 1998.

The brave new world of work and its jargon

Advances in communications have already begun to affect the way business are run and therefore how people work. Gradually, there is emerging in MEDCs a whole new working culture that brings with it a growing vocabulary of jargon.

Soho

Acronym for small office, home office. A small office is classified as a business with less than 10 people, while a home office is dedicated space within the home where a resident works permanently or occasionally. Ideally, it should contain at least a phone, computer, modem and a fax/copier/scanner to keep in touch with head office or clients.

Teleworker

Someone who works permanently from home, either for themselves or for a company. The term derives from the expectation that they will spend much of their time communcating down a phone line via a modem. Two million Britons already belong to this category, the majority of them telehubbies whose first job is to settle the children in front of the television!

Telecottager

A person who works away from a main office building but shares a rented room with other workers.

Flexible worker

Someone with the enthusiasm and technology to work from a variety of locations including head office, home and on the move. British Telecom has been encouraging this sector with its Option 2000 programme and currently has 3,500 flexible workers.

Hot desking

This describes working for a company without having a permanent desk of your own. When you need to be in the office, you turn up and plug your laptop into the first available desk.

Hotelling

Now adopted by high-powered, high-tech workers who spend most of their lives either on the move or working at home. If they need to attend head office, they book a desk or conference room in advance.

These new styles of working may have many profound consequences. For example, they may well reduce the degree to which societies are centralised on towns and cities. They offer hope for the revival of rural and peripheral areas. They promise to ease traffic congestion and rush hour nightmares.

ACTIVITIES

1 Investigate the causes of the eight trends (identified on page 198) taking place in the world of work.
2 Explain what is required to 'support' an ageing population. Identify some possible solutions to the problem.
3 Identify:
a the various ways we currently use the Internet.
b possible future uses.
4 Discuss the possible geographical outcomes of the lifestyle changes outlined above.
5 What lifestyle changes, if any, might be anticipated in the South?

7 Addressing the development gap

In 1965, the poorest 20 per cent of the world's population earned 2.0 per cent of global income. By 1990, it had fallen to 1.4 per cent; today it stands at 1.3 per cent. In 1965, the income of the top 20 per cent of the world's population was 25 times that of the poorest 20 per cent. Today, the difference is 64 times.

The challenge here is a two-stage one. The first is to halt the growing difference between rich and poor nations. The second is to narrow the development gap and to achieve a more equitable world. The widening gap between rich and poor will only be halted and then closed by a concerted effort on a number of different fronts, some of which are discussed below (Figure 4.61).

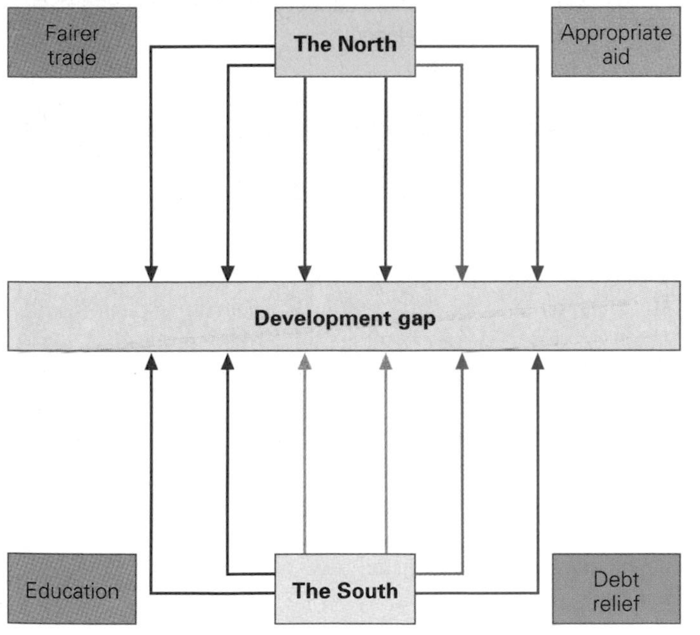

Figure 4.61 *Closing the gap*

Closing the development gap

Fairer trade

There is no doubt that trade can do much to stop the development gap widening, perhaps even reduce it (Figure 4.62). Rich and poor countries both have needs, particularly in terms of goods. A significant number of these needs are reciprocal. For example, the rich nations have need of primary products, many of which are produced in poor countries. At the same time, poor countries need manufactured goods, many of them produced by the richer nations. There is considerable potential for a growing interdependence between rich and poor. Trade is the medium for developing this potential, but it needs to be fair trade. Fair trade involves an equal partnership rather than exploitation of the weak by the strong; trade which is unimpeded by trading blocs, tariffs and subsidies.

Figure 4.62 *Two ways of closing the gap: a) trade and b) education*

Education

Education is neither a luxury nor a privilege (Figure 4.62), it is a fundamental human right. More than 50 years after the signing of the Declaration of Human Rights, millions of children are still being denied basic primary education. Why is education regarded as the key to bridging the widening gap between rich and poor? The answer lies in the link between education and development. Education helps to propel the development process in two main ways. It makes people more aware of the benefits that development can bring, such as raised living standards, better well-being and improved quality of life. It also provides people with the basic skills that are needed to move development forward. Much development is as dependent on human resources as on natural ones and education enriches human resources.

People who are denied education can never realise their human potential, and they and their children will be open to the worst forms of exploitation. In Afghanistan, Angola,

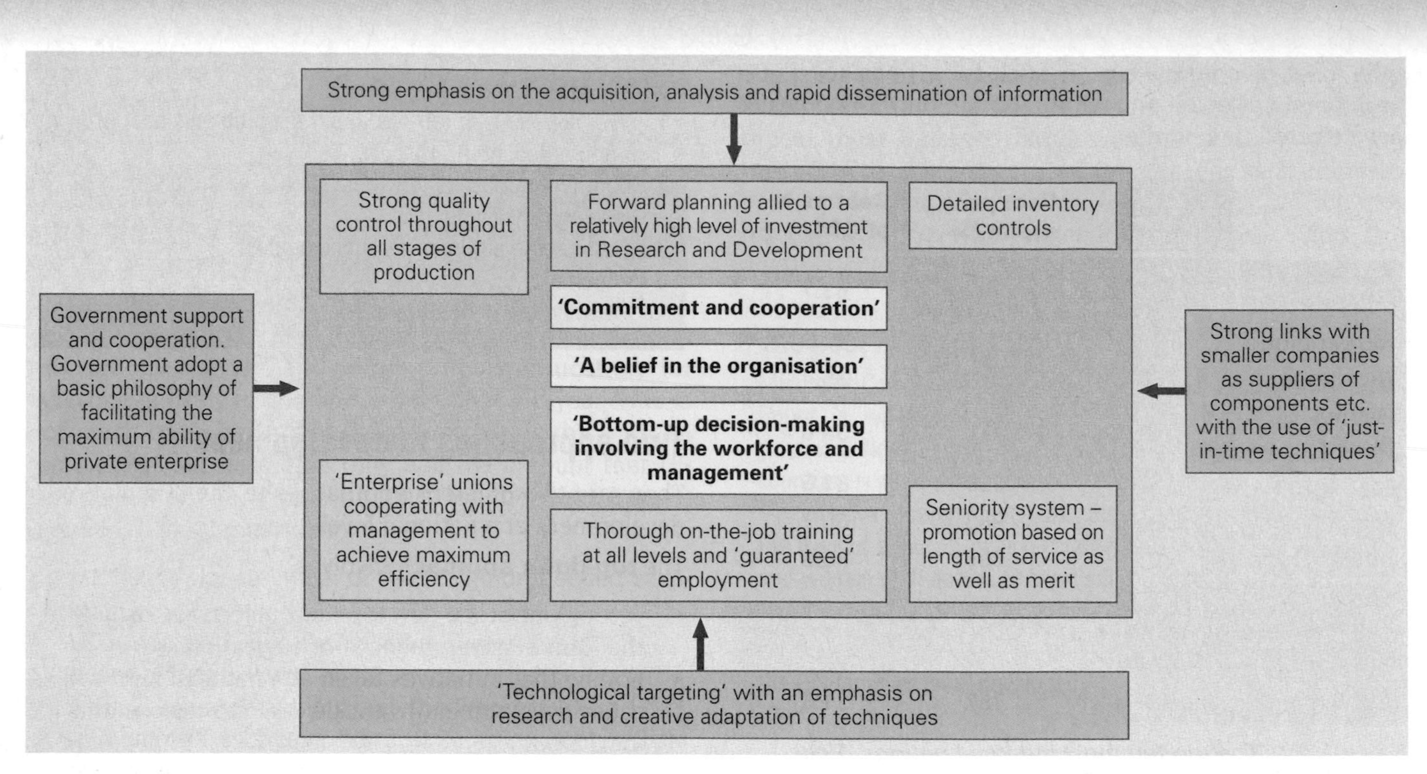

Figure 4.64 *The key components in Japan's development*

EXTENSION ACTIVITY

1 Investigate the ways in which the development of Mexico and Singapore have been government-led (i.e. top-down). Have there been any national plans? What aspects have been included in such plans; do they cover all sectors of the economy? Has the social dimension of development received any government direction?

The role of non-government organisations

While it is the responsibility of all governments to bring about a narrowing of the development gap, it is clear that non-government or voluntary organisations (NGOs) have an important part to play (Table 4.20).

In some respects, NGOs have already shown the way by extending practical rather than financial aid. They can often be involved where global politics prevent governments from doing so. For example, while Western governments (including the UK) cut off aid to Ethiopia because of the war against neighbouring Eritrea, Oxfam and other voluntary organisations remained active. Ethiopia's ranking as 170th out of 175 countries in the Human Development Index league table clearly signals the potential human disaster if all aid were to be cut off. In such cases, the role of NGOs is to 'hold the fort' until normality returns and donor governments feel they can resume their aid programmes.

1	Humanitarian responsibility comes first.
2	Aid is given regardless of race, creed or nationality on the basis of need alone.
3	Aid will not be used to further a particular political or religious endeavour.
4	NGOs shall endeavour not to act as instruments of government policy.
5	Culture and custom are to be respected.
6	Disaster response should where possible be built on local capacities.
7	Ways shall be found to involve programme beneficiaries in the management of relief aid.
8	Relief aid must strive to reduce future vulnerabilities as well as meeting basic needs.
9	NGOs should hold themselves accountable to those they seek to assist and those from whom they accept resources.
10	Disaster victims shall be recognised as dignified humans, not hopeless objects.

Table 4.20 *The Red Cross code for NGOs*

EXTENSION ACTIVITY

1 Investigate the types of aid provided by one of the following NGOs: Oxfam, FarmAfrica, CAFOD or the Red Cross.

8 Can sustainable development be achieved?

What is sustainability?

Sustainability describes the relatively recent and hazardous situation that faces the world. It means 'the ability of something to maintain itself indefinitely.' It matters to us all today because the Earth cannot maintain, or sustain itself at the current rate of resource use. People have always tended to assume that the Earth will provide resources forever, and that it will always be able to cope with endless pollution. Today it is clear that this is not the case. The human population is now degrading the Earth at such a rate that it is unable to cope or recuperate. The time has come to take drastic recovery measures.

Conservation organisations use the term 'sustainability' in several contexts. They refer to:

- **sustainable use of resources** – using natural resources, such as forests, rivers, fisheries and minerals for food, medicine, fuel, building and so on, but remaining within the limits of the environmental carrying capacity
- **sustainable development** – improving the quality of life of the global population within the carrying capacity of the Earth's finite resources. Meeting the needs of the present generation, particularly the needs of the poor, without compromising the ability of future generations to meet their own needs
- **sustainable economy** – the product of sustainable development. It maintains the overall stock and productivity of human capital (man-made capital and natural capital).

In all three contexts, sustainability can be likened to having a bank account or an investment which produces interest. If we live off the interest, not the capital, then the future will be secure. If we live off the capital, however, it will disappear altogether in the fullness of time. Table 4.21 shows the key principles of sustainable living.

1	Respect and care for others
2	Improve the quality of human life
3	Conserve the Earth's vitality and diversity
4	Minimise the use of non-renewable resources
5	Keep within the Earth's carrying capacity
6	Change personal values and behaviour
7	Enable communities to care for their own environment
8	Integrate development and conservation nationally
9	Create a global alliance to help nations to develop sustainably

Table 4.21 *The nine principles of a sustainable society*

ACTIVITIES

1 With reference to the sustainable use of resources, explain what is meant by 'remaining within the limits of environmental carrying capacity'.

2 Which of the nine principles set out in Table 4.21 do you think is the most important? Justify your choice.

3 Find out the nature of the major decisions taken at the Earth Summit held in Rio de Janeiro in 1992. To what extent have those decisions been implemented?

Reconciling the conflict between resource availability and demand

Friends of the Earth claim that consumerism is 'a deadly virus sweeping the globe'. There is clearly a tension between the high and rising levels of consumption and waste in MEDCs and the over-exploitation of resources in LEDCs. In the North, consumption and waste are the outcomes of personal affluence. For example, the average person in the UK consumes 35 times as much aluminium and 35 times as much energy as the average person in India. In the South, over-exploitation of resources is the outcome of poverty. Poverty drives people to farm on fragile soils, and degrade ecosystems in an endless search for firewood. Poverty drives governments to overuse resources in their keenness to sell to the North, and so gain much-needed capital. Over-exploitation therefore drives environmental destruction.

The consumption patterns of people are rooted in habits and cultural traditions. The Japanese taste for whalemeat and the American liking for beef are two cases in point. Personal preference, quality, durability and value for money are among the things that influence what we buy. What few realise is that cost-cutting to bring down the market price often involves taking short-cuts with the environment, i.e. the market price is often well below the true cost of production. This situation will only be rectified when consumers show a willingness to pay the higher price which is associated with producing things in a more environmentally friendly manner. This is known as **green consumerism**. It also includes a commitment to recycling waste products (Figure 4.65).

Consumer organisations were originally set up in the North to point consumers towards the best and safest products to buy, and to protect them against abuses and fraud. Today, those same organisations are slowly introducing an environmental dimension to their work. For example, some are beginning to test the environmental

Figure 4.65 *Recycling household waste*

impact of a number of products. The results are published in magazines (Figure 4.66). The Dutch consumer organisation, Consumentenbond, assesses, amongst other things, the environmental soundness of energy and water use, emissions, noise and odour, radiation and packaging. The findings are summarised on product labels. This pioneering venture is expensive and its methods need refining. A German consumer organisation, Stiftung Waretest, checks the accuracy of 'green' labels on products.

Figure 4.66 *A 'green' consumer magazine*

In a survey within the EU, 80 per cent of consumers said that they were willing to buy green products and 50 per cent said that they were willing to pay more for them. However, green consumerism has yet to show that it can make a measurable difference. As the International Organisation of Consumers Unions has pointed out: 'while many 'green' consumers shop religiously for phosphate-free cleaning products and for toilet rolls made from recycled paper, they are not ready to get rid of the second car, move into a smaller and non air-conditioned home, eat a lot less meat, or make other life-style changes that would significantly reduce their environmental impact.'

Can green consumerism ever really help the South? It is only likely to do so if it actively involves the North paying a fair price for the resources it consumes. The onus rests with the North, both to cut consumption and to trade fairly.

Economic sustainability versus environmental sustainability

Economic sustainability is the creation of an economy that can be sustained well into the future on the basis of present and possible future resource stocks. Environmental sustainability is the sustainable use of non-renewable and renewable resources. There is inherent conflict between these two forms of sustainability as illustrated by the case of Norway.

Which country does the most environmental damage?

The Norwegians enjoy one of the highest standards of living in the world. This well-being has been based largely on the exploitation of resources: fish, timber and more recently oil. Certainly, the Norwegians have a thriving economy which is sustainable well into the future. At the same time, they generally pride themselves on their 'green' credentials and their environmental awareness. However, a recent report produced by the World Wide Fund for Nature (WWF) shows that they are the world's most environmentally destructive people (Figure 4.67).

The WWF report looked at the pressure that nations put on global ecosystems through their exploitation of four key natural resources: cereals, marine fish, wood and freshwater. It also investigated the contribution each nation makes to global warming through carbon dioxide emissions.

Per head of the population, a Norwegian puts four times as much pressure on the environment as the average global citizen (Figure 4.67). Norway's consumption of marine fish is particularly high. Per person, Norway catches 450 kg of fish each year, more than 10 times the global average. Much of this fish is not eaten directly, but fed to salmon on fish farms around the coast.

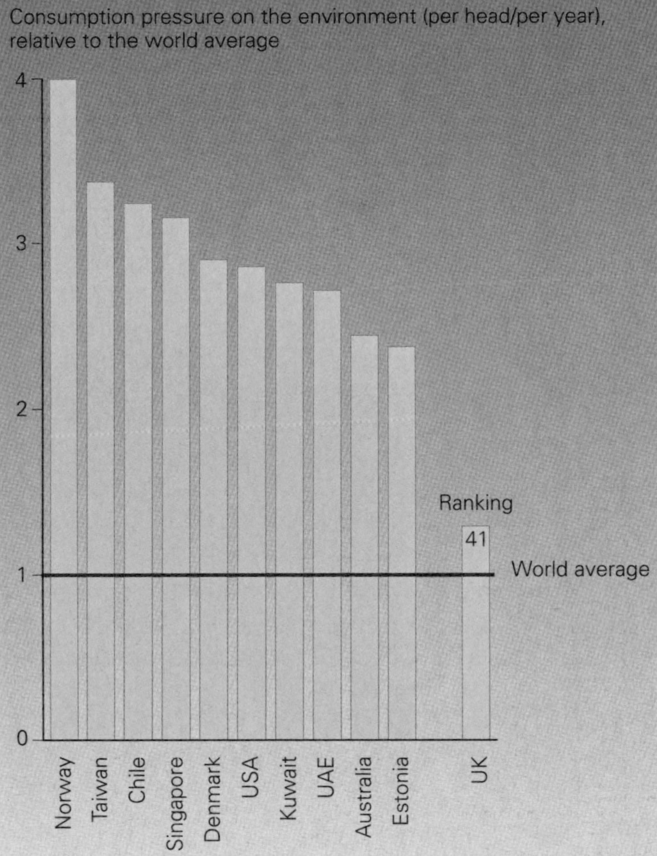

Consumption pressure on the environment (per head/per year), relative to the world average
4
3
2
1
0
Ranking
41
World average
Norway
Taiwan
Chile
Singapore
Denmark
USA
Kuwait
UAE
Australia
Estonia
UK

Figure 4.67 ***Consumption pressure on the environment: the global leaders***
Source: *WWF Living Planet Report*, 1998.

ACTIVITIES

1. Suggest ways in which Norway might reduce its pressure on the environment.
2. Select two countries (one MEDC and one LEDC) and compare them in terms of the ways in which the economy and the environment are in conflict.

The viability of green growth

The concept of green growth has arisen from the search for some sort of compromise between economic and environmental sustainability. **Green growth** is defined as development that can be sustained without adversely affecting the environment. Criteria for monitoring the general health of the environment during the development process include:

- biodiversity
- the rate at which any renewable resource taken from the environment is replenished
- pollution levels.

No national government has in place a comprehensive programme of green growth. Indeed, it has to be questioned whether such a programme would be attainable or viable. However, examples of green growth are to be found in specific sectors of economic activity, such as water supply, farming and tourism.

Food security

Food security is perhaps the South's greatest concern: how to ensure an adequate food supply for its ever-increasing populations. It is already clear that the globalisation of agriculture encourages the growth of export crops, and does so at the expense of local food production. It is not in the best interests of an LEDC to think that these exports can buy in necessary food. Perhaps perversely, when it comes to food supply, it is better for an LEDC to forget about globalisation and to strive instead for self-sufficiency. The challenge is how to do this in a sustainable way. For a while, the South looked to the Green Revolution. It certainly raised food output, but it failed to deliver sustainability. Today, there is increasing interest in **permaculture** as possibly providing the solution. This method of farming uses no outside inputs such as chemical fertilisers and pesticides, yet its yields can be several times higher than with chemical farming.

Ecotourism – an example of green growth

Tourism is an activity which has the potential to provide much hope for the South in terms of generating jobs and revenue. However, much tourism development to date has caused serious environmental damage, and potential economic and social benefits to an LEDC have been lost because development has been in the hands of foreign investors.

Ecotourism is an environmentally friendly form of tourism that exploits the environment in a non-damaging way. The emphasis of any ecotourist development is that it should be on the same scale and in keeping with its immediate environment. This means that development should be the outcome of local enterprise and investment, and that the benefits (jobs, profits, etc.) are retained within the local community (Figure 4.68). There are many projects that claim to be examples of ecotourism projects, but all too often these claims are spurious. There are, however, some genuine and successful ventures, such as the Asa Wright Nature Centre in Trinidad and the Manu Wildlife Centre in Peru.

Today, ecotourism is an expanding niche market for environmentally aware tourists. While ecotourism may be more beneficial to the environment than mass tourism, it does have its problems. For example, low-impact schemes are likely to become more damaging as they become more successful. Also it is difficult for such small tour operators to compete with the much cheaper package holidays put together by the major tour operators. For these reasons, ecotourism remains an alternative form of tourism for the wealthy who are interested in natural history and local culture.

Figure 4.68 *The ecotourist questionnaire*

Source: *The A-Z of World Development*, New Internationalist, 1998.

Finally, back to people

We need to conclude this exploration of globalisation by returning to ideas outlined in Chapter 3 on the population dimension. Whether globalisation will deliver more benefits than costs and do so for the great majority of the world's population is a hotly debated issue. Globalisation certainly has the potential to deliver what most people desire – an improved quality of life. Sustainability does not reject this as a legitimate desire, but it does demand a balanced relationship between people and nature. The frugal use of resources and care for the environment can easily be undone by high rates of natural population increase. Equally, with population in check, it becomes that much easier for globalisation to deliver sustainable growth.

With global rates of population growth beginning to decline, the world has a chance to correct the resource-population balance. We all have a responsibility to ensure that the rise in population is kept under control. Birth rates should be held at or close to replacement level. A widely held view is that couples should limit their families to no more than two children, and in those societies where partnerships come and go, the number of offspring per union needs to be less. That may sound brutal, but the alternative may be a world with no future. Curbing population growth is perhaps the greatest global challenge of them all!

ACTIVITIES

1 To what extent do you agree with the view that:
   - population control is the key to achieving sustainable development?
   - population control should be mandatory rather than voluntary?
   - globalisation will have little impact on rates of population growth?
2 Find out more about the Green Revolution and permaculture.

Reference materials

Chapter 1 Weather and climate

Websites

Images - weather systems
satpix.nottingham.ac.uk – Nottingham University archive of Meteosat images
www.bbc.co.uk/weather – current weather from BBC
ows.public.sembach.af.mil/GifImages/metsatanal.gif – satellite image analysis of European weather
www.meto.gov.uk/weather/charts/animation.html – animated weather charts for current forecast from Met Office
www.wetterzentrale.de – German weather centre – very good for imagery

Images - global and climatic
www.ghcc.msfc.nasa.gov/GOES/globalir.html – customise global meteorological imagery
www.ghcc.msfc.nasa.gov/temperature – global temperature anomalies for any recent date and place
www.meto.gov.uk/sec2/sec2cyclone/tcim.html – tropical cyclone images and movies from Met Office
www.pbs.org/wgbh/nova/elnino/anatomy/origins.html – El Nino animations and explanation
www.ssec.wisc.edu/data/sst/latest_sst.gif – global sea surface temperatures (updated weekly)

Articles and information
www.usatoday.com/weather/tg/wamsorce/wamsorce.htm – air masses (US based)
www.usatoday.com/weather/nino/wnino0.htm - El Nino
www.usgcrp.gov - US Global Change Research Program
www.meto.gov.uk/weather/index.html – world weather

Books

Geography Intranet Project - Weather and Climate; Hodder and Stoughton – an AS/A2 level Intranet for running on school/college networks
Regional Climates of the British Isles, D. Wheeler and J. Mayes, Routledge 1997 – regional case studies of UK weather, excellent for extension work

Articles/Periodicals

El Nino - La Nina, Nature's vicious cycle, *National Geographic*, March 1999 – detailed case studies
Global climate change, *China Review*, Autumn/Winter 1998 – Eastern perspective on the climate change issues
Scientific American, April 2000 – wide range of articles on weather and climate issues
Storms, *Tephra* (New Zealand Ministry of Civil Defence publication), June 1997 – very focussed edition looking at the hazards caused and how to manage them
Taken by storm, BBC *Wildlife*, May 2000 – impact of storms on forest ecology

Chapter 2 Ecosystems and conservation

Websites

www.eco-portal.com – excellent general links site
www.unep-wcmc.org – world conservation monitoring centre
www.unesco.org/whc/nwhc/pages/sites/main.htm – UNESCO World Heritage Committee
www.wri.org – excellent general ecosystem/conservation site

Forest biomes
forests.org/forsite.html – forest, rainforest, biodiversity and climate change internet resources
forests.org/world.htm – rainforest conservation archives
www.wri.org/forests/temperat.html – temperate forests
www.wri.org/facts/forests.html – forest facts
www.wri.org/wr2000/forests_page.html – world resources institute summary

Grassland biomes
www.wri.org/wr2000/grasslands_page.html – world resources institute summary

Marine biomes
www.botany.hawaii.edu/seagrass/ – sea grass information
www.greenpeace.org/~oceans - Report on the World's Oceans, May 1998
www.ncl.ac.uk/tcmweb/tcm/crlinks.htm – coral reef links
www.wri.org/wr2000/coast_page.html – world resources institute summary

Articles

The Rainforest Paradox, *Geography Review*, September 1998 – succinct introduction to the rainforest system.
Reefs at Risk – A joint publication by World Resources Institute (WRI), International Center for Living Aquatic Resources Management (ICLARM), World Conservation Monitoring Centre (WCMC), United Nations Environment Programme (UNEP) 1998 – very detailed publication with maps and graphs available from www.wri.org

Chapter 3 Global Population and Migration

Websites

www.census.gov/main/www/popclock.html – world population
migration.ucdavis.edu – migration news
www.peopleandplanet.net
www.popnet.org – general population site
www.prb.org – Population Reference Bureau
www.statistics.gov.uk – Office for National Statistics
www.wwf-uk.org
www.unfpa.org – Printed Nations Fund for Population Activities (UNFFA)
www.undp.org/popin/wdtrends/6billion – UN Population Information Network

Periodicals

Human Development Report, UNDP (annual)
People and the Planet (quarterly)
World Bank Atlas (annual)

Books

The Age of Migration, S. Castles, Macmillan 1998
Coping with Population Challenges, L. Lassonde, Earthscan 1999
Population and Development Database CD-ROM – available from Population Concern, Studio 325, 53-79 Highgate Road, London NW5 1TL
Population Geography, M. Witherick, Longman 1990
Exploring Contemporary Migration, D. Boyle, K. Halfacree and V. Robinson, Longman 1998

Chapter 4 Globalisation and the Global Economy

Websites

www.bized.ac.uk – information of business worldwide
www.fao.org – Food and Agriculture Organization
www.iied.org – Institute of Environment and Development IEED
www.sustainabledevelopment.org/blp/unchs/
www.worldbank.org World Bank Development Projects

NGOs

www.actionaid.org.uk
www.cafod.org.uk
www.charitynet.org
www.christian-aid.org.uk
www.oneworld.org
www.oxfam.org.uk

Periodicals

New Internationalist (monthly)
UNDP *World Development Reports*, World Bank (annual)
UNDP *Human Development Reports*, Oxford University Press (annual)

Books

The A to Z of World Development, *New Internationalist* 1998
Development Geography, R. Hodder, Routledge 2001
Development and Underdevelopment, G. Nagle, Nelson 1998
EPICS – *Development, Disparity and Dependence*, M. Witherick, Stanley Thornes 1998
The Geography of the World Economy, P. Knox and J. Agnew, Arnold 1998
Global Shift: Transforming the Global Economy, P. Dicken, Paul Chapman Publishing 1998
Globalisation: what's it all about, Birmingham Development Education Centre 2001
India: Globalisation and Change, P. Shuman Smith, Arnold 2000
Manufacturing Industry: The Impact of Change, M. Raw, Collins 2nd edition 2000
Population Resources and Development, J. Chrispin, Collins 2nd edition 2000
The World Bank Atlas of Development, World Bank 1999
World Development Indicators, World Bank 1998

Index